SOCIAL ISSUES IN DEVELOPMENTAL PSYCHOLOGY
SECOND EDITION
HELEN BEE

DISCARD

D1109285

HARPER & ROW, PUBLISHERS
NEW YORK, HAGERSTOWN, SAN FRANCISCO, LONDON

Sponsoring Editor: George A. Middendorf
Project Editor: Cynthia Hausdorff
Designer: Michel Craig
Production Supervisor: Kewal K. Sharma
Compositor: Bi-Comp Incorporated
Printer and Binder: The Murray Printing Company
Art Studio: J & R Technical Services Incorporated

SOCIAL ISSUES IN DEVELOPMENTAL PSYCHOLOGY, Second Edition

Copyright © 1978 by Helen Bee
All rights reserved. Printed in the United States of America. No part of
this book may be used or reproduced in any manner whatsoever without written
permission except in the case of brief quotations embodied in critical articles
and reviews. For information address Harper & Row, Publishers, Inc., 10 East
53rd Street, New York, N.Y. 10022.

REF
BF
723
.P25
B4
1978

Cop.1
Soc

Library of Congress Cataloging in Publication Data

Bee, Helen L   Date-   comp.
  Social issues in developmental psychology.

  Includes bibliographies and index.
    1. Parent and child.   2. Sex differences
(Psychology)   3. Poverty—Psychological aspects.
4. Education, Preschool.   I. Title.
BF723.P25B4   1978   155.4   77-9592
ISBN 0-06-040584-8

CONTENTS

DISCARD

Section 2. Day Care

PART III. THE EFFECTS OF POVERTY

PART IV. COMPENSATORY EDUCATION

DISCARD

v

PREFACE TO THE SECOND EDITION

DISCARD

The intent of this edition, like the intent of the first, is to acquaint students with some of the major social issues that touch on the area of developmental psychology, to focus attention on some of the theoretical and practical problems, and to demonstrate that it is possible to address such sticky, complex problems with scientific strategy. I am not attempting merely to be "relevant," but to show that relevance can be rigorous.

I have made two sorts of changes in revising the book. First, all the overview chapters have been completely rewritten so that research and commentary published in the past three to four years could be included. There has been a great deal of recent research in many of the areas covered in the book, so there are major changes in some of the overviews. Second, I have changed about half of the selections so that students may be exposed to more recent, or better designed, studies in these areas. In doing this, I have had to give up some of the pro-and-con format of the first edition; but I think the selections included here reflect the state of the art in each of the six areas better than was the case in the earlier edition.

My thanks again to all the authors who allowed their work to be reprinted in this book, and a special thanks to Arlene Ragozin, who prepared a special version of her dissertation for use here.

HELEN BEE

PART I

DISCARD

SEX
DIFFERENCES
IN
DEVELOPMENT

OVERVIEW

Sex Differences

Since the previous version of this chapter was written, several things have happened that have both simplified and complicated the job of writing such an overview. First, a lot of the conclusions that were quite generally accepted five years ago about the existence of sex differences in several areas of behavior have now been disputed with new data. As you will see from the following summaries, there are now far fewer areas in which clear sex differences are found, so in a sense there is now less to explain. But at the same time there has been a marked surge of interest in the whole set of issues, so there is a great deal more information to be discussed as well as more notions about how the findings might be explained. So, although the job is in some ways easier because there are fewer differences to account for, the complexities and subtleties of the task have also increased.

In preparing this overview, I have drawn heavily on the recent (but already classic) review and analysis of the data on sex differences by Maccoby and Jacklin (1974).[1] Any serious student of the problems and issues posed by the study of sex differences will want to read their book firsthand because it is both extremely thoughtful and interesting and virtually encyclopedic in coverage.

OBSERVED SEX DIFFERENCES
To simplify the mountains of material available now on sex differences in each of several areas, I have prepared a series of

[1] Since Maccoby and Jacklin have provided such thorough and up-to-date reviews of the literature in so many areas relating to sex differences, I have not duplicated their efforts here by listing all the earlier references. In the pages that follow, I have given references to recent research not reviewed by Maccoby and Jacklin, classic papers and other studies you should know about.

summary tables (Tables 1 through 5). This condensed look at the data is inevitably going to be oversimplified, so you should be careful about sweeping conclusions drawn from entries in these tables. And you should also bear in mind that the quality and quantity of data involved in each entry vary enormously; I have tried to indicate where the data are especially bad, but you should be watchful.

Sex Differences in Cognition
One of the general conclusions quite common in earlier reviews of this literature was that girls are more verbal and boys are better at mathematical tasks. But it was primarily the more routine verbal tasks girls were supposed to be better at; boys were thought to be better at any kind of reasoning, whether verbal or mathematical. These generalizations have not stood well the test of additional data. As you will see in Table 1, there is only a weak difference, if any, found consistently between boys and girls in verbal skills up to at least adolescence. Among older girls and women, greater verbal skills are frequently in evidence. A similar conclusion holds about mathematical ability; there is little or no sex difference in this area until at least adolescence. Even among adults, the usual difference favoring males is often quite small.

There is *no* good evidence that girls are consistently less skilled at reasoning tasks (see Keating and Schaefer, 1975, for a recent study), nor are they regularly found to be less good at "set-breaking" or "analytic" tasks. For example, on measures of anagram ability, in which the subject must make new words out of a given set of letters or out of the letters contained in a key word, the subject must break out of the "set" of looking at the letters in particular configurations. On this sort of analytic task, when a sex difference is found, girls do better. But for problems like the Luchins water jar tasks, which may involve some mathematical or perhaps spatial visualization ability, boys are frequently found to excel. In this task the subject is asked to figure out how to get X amount of water using two or more jars of different sizes. In the early problems a rather lengthy and cumbersome procedure is needed, but partway through the series of problems the task shifts so that it is possible to solve the problem in a much simpler and more direct way. Boys seem more likely to notice and shift to the simpler way sooner, thus "breaking the set" of the early problems. So while there appear to be some differences in the type of task performed well by males and females, there is no overall superiority of one sex or the other across reasoning, logic, and analytic tasks.

The most consistent difference in this domain is in the area of spatial skills—for example, the ability to visualize the back of things or to do manipulations in the head with objects in space—in which males are consistently superior. But this superiority is not regularly found in children younger than 10 to 12 years of age, and there is even some evidence that on a spatial test involving disembedding, preschool *girls* may be better than boys (Coates, 1974).

In general, sex differences in skill on various types of intellectual tasks are comparatively scarce before adolescence; the major differences emerge clearly only in late adolescence and in adults. Girls do get better grades from the beginning of school, and boys are *much* more likely to have learning problems, such as reading difficulties, but tests of achievement or capability on basic skills do not generally show differences in the early years.

The other point worth underlining in these findings is the fact that even when differences do emerge quite consistently, such as in verbal skills and spatial skills, the distributions *always* overlap. Thus, there are many girls and women with excellent spatial ability, and many boys and men with poor spatial skills. The consistency of the difference does require explanation, but the size of the difference is ordinarily fairly small.

As further evidence that the basic cognitive processes are the same in the two sexes, look at the findings summarized in Table 2. There is *no* evidence of sex differences in performance on any type of learning task. Whatever processes and behaviors enter into the several types of learning listed, girls and boys appear to have them in equal degree. The same seems generally true for memory, although there is some indication that girls have somewhat better verbal memory. This difference is not found in every study; but when there is a sex difference, it is the girls who are better. However, nonverbal memory does not show this sex difference.

Sex Differences in Personality and Motivation

It is in the area of sex differences in personality and motivation that many of the persistent myths and stereotypes have been shattered, or at least bent, by recent studies and analyses of the data. You will see in Tables 3 and 4 that virtually the only large and consistent finding is that males are more aggressive than females. This finding is consistent across ages, across tasks, and across types of aggression (see Moyer, 1974, for an additional review of this evidence).

Beyond that, so many of the earlier notions (including some I stated myself in the first edition of this book) seem to be plainly

TABLE 1   SUMMARY TABLE OF SEX DIFFERENCES IN COGNITIVE SKILLS"

Characteristic or skill	Age of subjects			
	0–1 year	1–6 years	6–12 years	12 plus years
Verbal abilities	*Girls maybe;* some studies show greater vocalization for girls	*Slight edge to girls* to age 3 if any difference; boys catch up by age 3	*No difference* except among poor children, where girls higher	*Girls and women* better at a variety of verbal tasks in late adolescence and adulthood, including verbal reasoning
Mathematic skills	—	*No difference* except among low social class groups, where girls better at counting and equivalent	*No difference;* no consistent results	*Boys and men* generally higher on math skills in late adolescence and adulthood, although the size of difference varies a lot
Spatial ability, including tests of field independence	—	*No difference,* although girls may be better at field independence tasks at this age	*Probably no difference,* although some studies show boys slightly ahead	*Boys and men;* advantage in this area gets larger through adolescence and adulthood

Breaking set	—	No difference	Not enough data	Mixed; on verbal breaking-set tasks, girls do as well or better (e.g., anagrams); on more heavily spatial problems, boys often higher
Reasoning and logic	No difference on object concept	No difference on Piagetian tasks	No difference	No difference on formal operations tasks generally
Verbal creativity	—	No difference	Girls higher	Girls and women
Nonverbal creativity	—	No difference	No difference	No difference
Total IQ or equivalent	—	Girls may have slight advantage	No difference	No difference consistently
School grades	—	Girls better	Girls better	Girls better
School problems (e.g., reading problems)	—	Boys more	Boys more	Boys more

a The primary source for this information is Maccoby and Jacklin (1974), with updating from more recent studies.

TABLE 2 SUMMARY TABLE OF SEX DIFFERENCES IN LEARNING AND MEMORY[a]

Characteristic or skill	Age of subjects			
	0–1 year	1–6 years	6–12 years	12 plus years
Learning tasks, including conditioning, paired associate learning, oddity learning, discrimination learning, partial reinforcement, delay of reinforcement, incidental learning reversal/nonreversal shift learning, probability tasks, learning through imitation	*No difference*	*No difference*	*No difference*	*No difference except that adult women are somewhat faster in eyelid conditioning, which may be the result of greater anxiety; when anxiety reduced, the sex difference in conditioning disappears*
Memory:				
Verbal memory	—	*Maybe girls*	*Girls somewhat better*	*Girls somewhat better*
Memory for objects or digits	—	—	*No difference*	*No difference*
Memory for social stimuli (e.g., faces, names)	—	*None, scarce data*	*None, scarce data*	*None, poor data*

[a] The primary source for this information is Maccoby and Jacklin (1974), with updating from more recent studies.

TABLE 3 SUMMARY TABLE OF SEX DIFFEENCES IN PERSONALITY"

Characteristic or skill	Age of subjects			
	0–1 year	1–6 years	6–12 years	12 plus years
Dependency:				
(1) proximity seeking toward adults	*No difference*	*Generally no difference*	*Probably no difference*	—
(2) proximity seeking toward peers	—	Boys may "tag along" more	*No good data*	—
(3) friendly interest in age mates	—	Boys somewhat more "sociable," especially at ages 2–4 or so; this category is *not* higher for boys just because of rough and tumble play, because that is not included here	*Maybe boys:* some indication girls have a few close chums, whereas boys are in larger groups	*Not clear:* women more often talk about liking others and about the importance of liking, but it is not obvious that this means greater friendly interest
Nurturance toward others	—	*No difference* consistently in help-giving; nurturance rare at this age anyway	*Not clear:* across cultures, girls more often responsible for younger siblings; lab studies show no difference in help-giving	*Very little data:* some new evidence that males as nurturant toward newborn, but this not true for other mammals
Empathy	—	*No difference*	*No difference:* mixed results	*No clear difference*

TABLE 3 *(Continued)*

Characteristic or skill	0–1 year	1–6 years	6–12 years	12 plus years
Compliance and conformity	—	*Girls more compliant to adults' requests or commands*	*No clear difference*	*No clear difference*
Fear, timidity and anxiety	*No difference*	*No difference in timidity or fear; girls may report themselves as more fearful*	*Girls often report more fears, or are rated as more fearful by teachers, but observational records do not show sex differences at these ages in fearful or timid behavior*	
General text anxiety		*No good data*	*Girls report more anxiety, but some good evidence that boys are more reluctant to report fears or anxiety*	
Frustration tolerance and reaction	—	*Boys may have more outbursts of anger or upset than girls; not clear that boys respond to frustration by attacking barriers; conflicting data*	*No good data*	*No good data*
Crying	*No consistent difference*	*Boys in some settings: some studies show boys cry more at separation from mother; others show preschool-age boys cry*	—	—

		more from frustra-tion; girls more from injury		
Activity level	*No difference*	Mixed: boys often found more active, but seem to be so largely when with groups of other boys; no difference when alone; boys may spend more time outdoors in large muscle activity	*Maybe boys: mixed results; when differences are found, they show boys more active, more energetic*	*Poor data: no clear difference*
Aggression	—	*Boys more* This difference is highly consistent across situations and types of aggression, including verbal aggression; girls are less often aggressed *against* as well, so boys are both the victims and the aggressors more often	*Boys more*	*Boys and men more*
Competition versus cooperation	—	Boy-Boy pairs more competitive than girl-girl pairs	*Maybe boys*	*Mixed: probably none, but this question has not been well addressed among adults*
Dominance	—	Boys seen as "tougher" by peers from nursery-school age on; dominance hierarchies present for both boys' and girls' groups	*Boys seen as "tougher"*	*Probably men, but dominance among adults is less generalized across situations; in marriages no clear tendency for males to dominate*

[a] The primary source for this information is Maccoby and Jacklin (1974), with updating from more recent studies.

wrong. Girls are *not* more oriented toward social stimuli and cues and are not more attentive to people. The lack of difference in responsiveness to social cues shows up in a number of ways: Girls are not more compliant to the wishes of others (except for a period in the preschool years when they are more influenced by adults' requests) (Cantor, 1975); they are not more empathetic (see Deutsch, 1975, for recent data); they are not more likely to seek to be near adults and are, if anything, *less* likely to seek to be near peers. And girls are *not* more nurturant toward others, younger children, or helpless creatures (although the amount and quality of the data here is fairly poor). These pieces of evidence taken together seem to show that males are at least as interested in and attentive to social cues and are at least as good at interpreting them.

Another myth that appears to be broken by the Maccoby and Jacklin analysis is that girls are less achievement oriented. The data do *not* show this to be the case in any consistent manner. Both in performance on achievement-oriented tasks and in projective tests of achievement motivation, girls are usually found to be as achievement oriented as boys. There seems to be no consistent tendency for girls to strive more than boys to achieve in order to reach social goals, such as approval. And recent studies of "fear of success" do *not* show that young girls or teen-age girls are more fearful in this way (Jackaway, 1974; Romer, 1975).

Finally, there is no indication that girls and women have lower self-esteem than boys and men. In self-report measures, girls list as many things they like about themselves as do boys. There are, however, a few studies of adult women that hint at the possibility that over the adult years there may be a decline in self-esteem; although whether this is true for most women, or only for those whose early career aspirations are not fulfilled, or for some other group, is simply not knowable from the available information.

I do not want to suggest by this summary that there are no differences in these domains. Of course there are differences, as Tables 3 and 4 show. But except for the difference in aggression and related behaviors, the sex differences are far more subtle or more situation- or age-specific than had been thought. For example, between the ages of about 2 and 5, there is a set of behaviors on which the sexes differ: boys may show more angry or frustrated outbursts; they may cry more; they are more active physically when with other boys; and they show more exploration of their environment and more curiosity about new things.

The picture that emerges from this collection of findings is of a boy who is motorically active with a lot of movement from place to place and a lot of shifting from task to task; who encounters more new things as a result of his explorations, but also experiences more frustration. A recent study of preschool-age children's use of space confirms this overall picture. Harper and Sanders (1975) observed children in preschool over a two-year period, noting whether the children played indoors or outdoors and the number of different play areas they used. In both years boys used the outdoor space significantly more of the time, whereas girls spent more time indoors. The boys also covered more territory, used about half again as much space in their movement, and entered more of the different play areas than did the girls. Harper and Sanders also noted that the girls who wore blue jeans were not more likely to spend time outdoors than were the girls who wore dresses, and encouragement from the staff for outdoor play by girls did not significantly reduce the sex difference. So at this age there is a consistent sex difference in the style and scope of children's play. Boys use more space and more large-muscle activity. These differences in style of play, or in general activity level, seem to be far less marked among older children than among the preschoolers. And among adults there is no obvious or consistent difference in activity level and no difference in skill at large-muscle tasks (see Table 5).

Another cluster of more subtle sex differences is in the area of self-concept. I said earlier that girls and women do not have generally poorer images of themselves, and that is true. But it is also true that girls and women are less *confident* about their ability to perform well on new tasks, particularly on intellectual tasks, and are less likely to feel as if they are in control of their own fate.

These two pieces of information seem, on the face of it, to be totally contradictory. But there may be some sense in the mixture of results. Women report just as many positive things about themselves, but the positive things they report are *different* from those reported by males. Women are more likely to see their positive qualities in skills of relating to others, such as leadership, cooperativeness, or attractiveness; whereas males are more likely to select "personal" characteristics, such as ambition, energy, fair-mindedness, or practicality, to describe themselves (see Maccoby and Jacklin, pages 158–180, for a review of this literature). Maccoby and Jacklin suggest that these findings may be understood in terms of greater ego investment by the two sexes in somewhat different "arenas," the males hav-

TABLE 4   SUMMARY TABLE OF SEX DIFFERENCES IN MOTIVATION AND SELF-CONCEPT[a]

Characteristic or skills	Age of subjects			
	0–1 year	1–6 years	6–12 years	12 plus years
Self-concept:				
(1) General self-esteem from self or teacher ratings	—	*None*	*None consistently:* girls often rated higher	*Mixed,* although there is some evidence of a *decline* in self-esteem among adult women
(2) Confidence in task performance	—	—	*Probably boys:* not much data	*Boys and men:* by college age, men clearly more confident that they will do well on tasks
(3) Locus of control	—	*No difference*	*No consistent difference*	*Boys and men:* difference seems to be clearer for adults, where men more *internal,* women more *external*
(4) Sense of dominance and power	—	—	*Boys more*	*Boys and men more*
(5) Defining self in terms of social characteristics, e.g., cooperativeness, leadership	—	—	*Girls more*	*Girls more*

Motivation and task orientation

(1) Achievement motivation, projective tests	—	*Probably none*	Probably none	*Mixed*: on some measures women are higher in achievement motivation; males respond more to achievement-arousing conditions
(2) Achievement striving as shown in behavior	—	Girls: not much data	No clear difference	*Probably no difference*
(3) Avoidance of success	—	—	No difference	*Mixed results*: maybe women
(4) Risk taking	—	—	Probably none	*Maybe boys*
(5) Task persistence	—	None	None	*None*
(6) Curiosity & exploration	—	Boys aged 3–6; not for younger children	Mixed	*Mixed*
(7) Person orientation: sensitivity to social reinforcement	—	—	No difference	*No difference*
(8) Peer influence	—	Boys more peer oriented	Boys more peer oriented	*Boys and men*: performance on a task is more influenced by the presence of a peer than is true for women

[a] The primary source for this information is Maccoby and Jacklin (1974), with updating from more recent studies.

TABLE 5 SUMMARY TABLE OF SEX DIFFERENCES IN PERCEPTUAL-MOTOR DEVELOPMENT[a]

Characteristic or skill	Age of subjects			
	0–1 year	1–6 years	6–12 years	12 plus years
Dexterity and Coordination:				
(1) Gross body coordination	—	*Probably boys*	*Probably boys*	*Probably boys*
(2) Finger dexterity: (small muscles)	—	*Maybe girls*	*Girls, particularly on speed tasks*	*Girls and women, particularly on speed tasks*
(3) Manual dexterity (large muscles)	—	*None*	*None*	*None*
Skeletal maturity	*Girls more mature at birth*	*Probably girls[b]*	*Probably girls*	*Probably girls*
Motor maturation (e.g., age of walking)	*No difference*	*No difference*	—	—

Perception:				
(1) Visual	Boys may habituate faster to visual stimuli; mixed findings	Probably no difference	No difference	No difference
(2) Auditory	No difference	No consistent difference	No difference	No difference
(3) Preference for auditory versus visual information	No difference	No good data, but no evidence that girls are more "auditory" and boys more "visual"		
(4) Taste and smell	Maybe girls more responsive to taste	Maybe girls	Girls: poor data	Girls and women: poor data
(5) Touch	No difference in sootheability	Mixed	Poor data: girls may have somewhat finer touch discrimination	Girls
(6) Pain	—	Girls	Girls	Girls
		Not much information, but girls and women seem to have a lower tolerance for pain; no good data on whether they also have a lower threshold for recognizing or experiencing pain		

a The primary source for this information is Maccoby and Jacklin (1974) with updating from more recent studies.
b Tanner, 1970.

ing focused on personal achievement and women on skillful social interactions. Each sex, then, has a higher self-esteem in its
own arena and overall feelings of self-worth are about equal.

This synthesis of the data makes quite good sense except
that it is difficult to coordinate this set of findings with the evidence that in childhood girls are not more oriented toward other
people or toward social encounters. Thus one of the puzzles to
be explained is how girls who, up to adolescence at least, are not
more person oriented than boys emerge as adults investing a
greater amount of their attention and sense of self-worth in social encounters.

I should emphasize that not all authors agree with the
summary conclusions drawn from the Maccoby and Jacklin review. As you will see when you read her selection in this part,
Hoffman makes some assumptions about sex differences in
independence and achievement motivation that are not entirely
consistent with Maccoby and Jacklin's conclusions. Bardwick
also disagrees and goes to some length to explain the possible
origins of a presumed greater dependence among girls and
women. She concludes that "girls are characteristically more
dependent, in either direct or indirect forms, than boys. Girls are
also inter-personally oriented" (Bardwick, 1971, p. 121). She
further suggests that "girls may be motivated by their high
needs for affiliation and not by needs for achievement" (p. 120).

Obviously the data are open to several interpretations and
different authors have placed greater or lesser weight on specific
studies that may show differences of a particular kind. But I am
impressed by the lack of clear-cut sex differences in such areas
as dependency, passivity, and achievement motivation when the
full range of studies is examined at once, as Maccoby and
Jacklin have done. It seems to me that before we expend a great
deal of energy trying to explain or understand sex differences in
a behavior or skill, we need to be as sure as possible that there is a
difference, and that it is a stable and replicable phenomenon.
Many of the differences Bardwick emphasizes do not stand up
well to such criteria.

Sex Differences in Perceptual-Motor Skills

Table 5 summarizes the findings in sex differences in
perceptual-motor skills. Again the differences are far out-
weighed by the similarities between the sexes. Girls are quite
commonly described as being on a "faster maturational timetable," but the evidence is more mixed than one might think. Girls
are apparently ahead in skeletal maturity from birth through puberty. Tanner (1970) estimates that boys are about four weeks

behind girls at birth, and remain at about 80 percent of the girls' maturity level through puberty. (Maccoby and Jacklin reach a different conclusion, apparently based on a different set of data. See page 18 of Maccoby and Jacklin for their discussion.)

It is far less clear that girls are ahead in general neurological development. On measuring infant perceptual-motor skills, girls are *not* found to be developing at an accelerated rate (Bayley, 1965), as one would assume if the development of their nervous system were more rapid.

In the area of physical coordination the results are similarly mixed. Girls are better from quite young ages at tasks involving fine motor coordination, such as finger dexterity; whereas boys seem to have better gross body coordination—although this is *not* reflected in earlier ages for walking or other motor milestones.

In the perceptual sphere the data base is fairly weak, particularly for such senses as taste, smell, and pain; but the findings do seem to show that there is no preference for auditory stimuli on the part of girls versus a preference for visual stimuli on the part of boys. However, such a distinction has been suggested by several authors based on fragments of data on infants (e.g., Garai and Scheinfeld, 1968). Some authors suggest that it is the greater "auditory stimulus hunger" of girls that accounts for their more rapid language development because they listen more attentively to voices. The systematic review of this evidence by Maccoby and Jacklin reveals no evidence for greater auditory attentiveness in girls. There is, however, some evidence that girls may be slightly more sensitive to (have lower thresholds for) taste differentials, and additional findings suggest that girls and women may be less tolerant of pain. These differences need to be explored further to see how widely they are found and under what conditions.

Sex Differences as a Function of Age

I have organized the summary tables by age so that you could get some sense of the areas in which sex differences emerge and of the ages at which they are first regularly found. With the exception of aggression, skeletal maturity, some perceptual differences, and perhaps verbal abilities, most differences are not regularly observed until at least school age, and many not until adolescence. This is particularly true of sex differences in cognitive skills, most of which emerge in adolescence. Young boys and girls are far more alike than different in skills and behavior. Only at adolescence can we begin to see differences or attitudes that appear consistent with the sex-difference stereotypes of our culture. The relative lack of early sex differences has implications for any explanations of sex differences.

SEX-ROLE STEREOTYPES

Having written lengthy pages and tables describing observed sex differences (and non-differences), it seems reasonable to write a few pages about what people *think* sex differences are or ought to be. What are our cultural stereotypes for males and females? Do they match the sex differences charted in the preceding pages?

The literature on sex-role stereotypes is well reviewed in a recent paper by Broverman, Vogel, Broverman, Clarkson, and Rosenkrantz (1972). Several conclusions emerge. First, sex-role standards and stereotypes are very consistent across sex, age, religion, and education. Characteristics perceived by adults of both sexes as being "male" traits make a kind of "competency" cluster including independence, objectivity, activity, competitiveness, logical thought processes, business skill, worldliness, adventurousness, ability to make decisions easily, self-confidence, acting like a leader, and ambitiousness. Women are consistently rated or perceived as being *low* in these characteristics, but they are viewed as being high in a "warmth and expressiveness" cluster including gentleness, tactfulness, awareness of the feelings of others, neatness, talkativeness, and ability to express tender feelings. Agreement on the sex-stereotyping of these traits is extremely widespread and has apparently not changed significantly despite the reevaluation of sex roles now going on in some segments of our society.

Second, most of the "masculine" traits are seen as highly socially desirable, whereas "feminine" behavior is more often seen as being less desirable. Thus, males and females perceive independence, assertiveness, and competence to be valuable. The absence of these traits (seen as characteristic of women) is regarded as undesirable. The warmth and expressiveness qualities are also seen as desirable, but comparatively there are fewer stereotypic "female" qualities perceived as good or desirable.

Broverman and her associates have also demonstrated that this lopsided view of the desirability of the male and female stereotypes is held by mental-health professionals (Broverman, Broverman, Clarkson, Rosenkrantz, and Vogel, 1970). Psychologists, social workers, and other health professionals rate the healthy adult and the healthy male in similar ways, but the healthy female is *not* seen as having the same qualities as the healthy adult. Thus generally desirable characteristics for *any* adult are likely to be stereotypically *male* qualities. In some sense, the more a woman conforms to the female stereotype, the less likely she is thought of as "healthy" by mental-health professionals.

In sum, not only are there persistent and consistent sex-role stereotypes in our culture, but these stereotypes are also systematically biased in favor of males; more male qualities are highly valued than are female qualities.

These stereotypes begin very early. To cite only some recent evidence, Urberg and Labouvie-Vief (1976) have found consistent sex-role stereotyping in seventh-graders. Etaugh and Rose (1975) found that seventh-graders (especially boys) rated stories ostensibly written by male authors as better written and more interesting than the same stories with a female author's name attached. Williams, Bennett, and Best (1975) have attempted to see how far down in the age range such sex-role stereotypes can be detected. They found clear stereotyping as early as second grade along the lines found by Broverman and associates. Kindergartners showed weaker stereotyping. There was also some evidence in this study that the masculine stereotype is formed earlier and more firmly than is the feminine one because traits such as aggression, strength, independence, and loudness were all clearly seen as male qualities by the children, whereas many of the female qualities tested were more weakly stereotyped, even at fourth-grade level.

To what extent do these widespread stereotypes correspond with the "reality" of sex differences I have already outlined? There is *some* correlation, but it is by no means perfect. The stereotyped female is less independent, less logical, less active, and less competitive than the male, none of which appears as a consistent "real" difference when the data are analyzed. Aggressiveness and self-confidence are part of the male stereotype, and there are some kinds of "real" differences on these dimensions. Similarly, awareness of the feelings of others is part of the female stereotype, although there is no adequate evidence suggesting that men are actually less aware of others' feelings. Talkativeness and interest in appearance are also part of the female stereotype, and there are data to show that such differences frequently exist. Women are in actuality far more competent than the stereotype suggests, and men are far more warm and expressive than their stereotype would have us believe.

Do these stereotypes affect behavior in any important ways? The limited evidence about the impact of sex-role stereotypes on behavior suggests that although children and adults are *aware* of the existence of the stereotype and can provide information about it if asked about the "ideal" or typical man or woman, most distinguish themselves from this stereotyped picture. Rosenkrantz and his colleagues (Rosenkrantz, Vogel, Bee, Broverman, and Broverman, 1968) found that college student subjects rated *themselves* as less extreme than they had rated the typical woman or man. A link between stereotypes and behavior is also shown by the fact that women who perceive themselves as higher on the competence dimensions included in the masculine stereotype are likely to have fewer children than women low on the competence items. College women whose self-image includes higher scores on the competence items plan to have fewer children than do women who have more stereotypically feminine self-images (see Boverman et al., 1972, for a review).

The more interesting and probably more important question is where the stereotypes come from. Since the stereotype and "reality" do not correspond well, how does the stereotype continue to exist? Equally, where do the observed sex differences come from?

POSSIBLE ORIGINS OF SEX DIFFERENCES
Biological Evidence

There are two classes of arguments offered that can be grouped roughly under the heading of "biological evidence." First, there is evidence suggesting that at least some of the observed sex differences are genetic in origin; second, there is evidence suggesting that hormone differences lie behind observed behavioral differences.

The best case for a genetic origin of any of the observed sex differences can be made for spatial ability. The basic research finding is that parent-child resemblance in spatial ability is cross-sex: Boys' scores on spatial-abilities tests are predicted best by their mothers' scores, and girls' scores are predicted best by their fathers' (Stafford, 1961; Corah, 1965; Hartlage, 1970; Bock and Kolakowski, 1973). This finding runs counter to what would be intuitively sensible for an environmental explanation and raises the possibility of a sex-linked heritability for spatial ability. Stafford has suggested that the findings make sense if at least one important genetic component for spatial skill is carried on the X chromosome and is recessive. If this were the case, a girl, with two X chromosomes, would have to receive the recessive gene from both parents in order to have high spatial ability, which is comparatively unlikely. Boys, on the other hand, with one X chromosome, would have to receive a recessive gene from their mothers only. Therefore, boys would not only resemble their mothers more closely in spatial ability, but also would be more likely to inherit the high spatial-ability gene, hence having higher spatial ability as a group. Making such assumptions, geneticists have been able to make some quite precise predictions about what the correlations on spatial-ability tests between parent and child ought to be. The actual correlations turn out to be very close to those predicted by this genetic model. So at least a partial genetic determination of spatial ability seems possible.

What this line of argument does not explain is the fact that sex differences in spatial ability emerge strongly only at adolescence. One possibility, of course, is that the tests we use to measure this skill in young children are not tapping the skill in the same way or as fully as tests used with older children and adults. Another possibility is that the skill is "triggered" in some way by hormonal changes in adolescence, although that is speculation only.

I want to underline strongly the fact that even with this type of sex-linked genetic component, there are many women with excellent spatial skills and many men without it. The difference is merely that it is more *likely* for a male to inherit the gene (or genes) that increases the potential for good spatial ability.

Other cognitive abilities do not appear to have this type of sex-linked genetic contribution, although they *may* have a moderate to high degree of heritability. In his review of this evidence, Vandenberg (1968) shows that both verbal and spatial abilities have high levels of heritability, whereas numerical ability seems to be less influenced by inheritance. For example, in the case of both verbal and spatial abilities (but less so for number skills), identical twins are more like one another than are fraternal twins. But in the case of *verbal* ability, the genes involved are apparently *not* sex-linked because children are about as like their mothers as their fathers in verbal skill. So for explanations of adult differences in verbal skill, we will have to look elsewhere.

A much more common kind of biological argument is that differences in hormones produce some or all of the observed behavioral sex differences. The greatest research interest has been in the effect of prenatal hormone differences and their possible effects. During the prenatal period, there is a point at which the normally developing male embryo receives a sharp jolt of androgen (the male hormone). This increase in androgen is what apparently produces the development of male physical characteristics. If androgen is not added at this time, the fetus develops as a female, even though it may be genetically XY. Similarly, a genetically female embryo (XX) can develop into a physical male if androgen is introduced into the system at the critical point (Money, 1971). Obviously this early hormonal event is critical for the development of physical sex differences. But can prenatal hormone differences account for any part of behavioral or cognitive differences?

In the case of sex differences in aggression, the answer seems to be Yes. Maccoby and Jacklin summarize the factors that lead them to conclude a biological basis for aggression:

> Let us outline the reasons why biological sex differences appear to be involved in aggression: (1) Males are more aggressive than females in all human societies for which evidence is available. (2) The sex differences are found early in life, at a time when there is no evidence that differential socialization pressures have been brought to bear by adults to ''shape'' aggression differently in the two sexes. (3) Similar sex differences are found in man and subhuman primates. (4) Aggression is related to levels of sex hormones, and can be changed by experimental administration of these hormones. (Maccoby and Jacklin, 1974, pp. 242–243)

Evidence supporting the fourth point is now quite extensive. The paper by Phoenix, Goy, and Resko, included the selections, is an example of research supporting such a conclusion. The repeated finding is that male hormones administered prenatally to genetically female monkeys or other primates lead to greater rough-and-tumble play and greater levels of aggression. Several studies suggest that the same phenomenon is found in humans as well.

Ehrhardt and Money (1967) and Ehrhardt and Baker (1974) have studied groups of girls who because of various accidents experienced heightened levels of androgen prenatally. In the Ehrhardt and Money study, some were girls whose mothers had been given progestin (a drug occasionally given to inhibit spontaneous abortion and chemically similar to androgen) during the pregnancy. In the Ehrhardt and Baker study, all the subjects had inherited a tendency for the adrenal glands to secrete excessive amounts of hormones similar to androgen (called AGS or adrenogenital syndrome). These girls are typically born with somewhat masculinized external genitalia, which is corrected surgically. In addition, girls with AGS have to have continued hormone therapy after birth.

In the more recent and better controlled Ehrhardt and Baker study, the AGS girls were compared with their normal sisters through interviews with mothers, fathers, and other family members. Results show the AGS girls were considered by others and themselves to be much more interested and involved in vigorous outdoor play, similar to the rough-and-tumble play seen in the androgenized female monkeys. (There was also a tendency for these girls to be more aggressive in comparison with their normal sisters, but the difference was not statistically significant.) The AGS girls were also less interested in playing with dolls than were their sisters and more often preferred to play with boys rather than girls. They perceived themselves and were perceived by others in most cases as being "tomboys." I should emphasize that these girls did not experience conflict about their female role and were not considered deviant by their family or peers. However, their behavior does differ in systematic ways from that of their hormonally normal sisters, and is entirely consistent with the research on subhuman primates.

Another type of behavior that seems to show hormonal effects is that of "maternal" behavior toward infants. In rats the maternal behaviors involved in the care of the newborn pups are clearly hormonally influenced. Rosenblatt, in a number of papers (1969, 1975), has shown that administration of hormones to virgin females decreases the latency of their maternal behavior toward the newborn. Reducing the hormones during pregnancy (by ovariectomy) decreases the responsiveness of the mother rat to her young. Virgin females and males will eventually respond to the young with "mothering" behavior, but lacking the appropriate hormones, the latency for this nurturant behavior is longer than it is for the mother. There is further evidence that the hormones are not enough by themselves to guarantee nurturant behavior. Contact with the infant(s) immediately after birth is also critical in establishing the caregiving relationship.

Recent work by Kennel and his associates with human mothers provides support for these hypotheses. (Kennel, Jerauld, Wolfe, Chesler, Kreger, McAlpine, Steffa, and Klaus, 1974.) They have found that mothers who are allowed to spend a great deal of time with their infants immediately after birth are more strongly attached to their infants than are mothers who have experienced a normal hospital routine. One possibility is that the mother, immediately after birth, has heightened hormone levels that increase in some way her "readiness" to become attached to her infant. Research with premature infants also shows a weakened attachment between mother and child if the mother has been separated from the child or not permitted to handle the baby (Leifer, Leiderman, Barnett, and Williams, 1972).

Before you conclude that *all* maternal or nurturant behavior is hormonally determined, let me reemphasize that non-mothers may (and do) show nurturant behavior toward the young, and mothers who had little contact with the infant immediately after birth also showed nurturing behavior. So hormones are not the *only* factor involved in nurturant behavior. As further counter-evidence there is one recent study by Parke and O'Leary (1974, cited by Maccoby and Jacklin) in which the behavior of fathers and mothers with their newborn infant was observed. In this study, fathers showed as many or more nurturant behaviors to-ward their child as did the mothers.

Thus, while it seems clear that there are hormonal bases for some aspects of "maternal" behavior, some greater "readiness" on the part of mothers to become attached to their infants im-mediately after birth, these hormonal patterns do not inevitably mean that women are more nurturant than men.

The possible role of hormone differences in accounting for observed sex differences in cognitive skills is much more dif-ficult to pin down. Baker and Ehrhardt (1974) analyzed the test scores of their fetally androgenized girls and found *no* evidence that the AGS girls were less verbal or better at mathematical skills or at spatial tasks than their normal sisters. On the other hand, there are studies that seem to show that among males, at least, those who are most "masculine" in appearance and in hormone levels are likely to be *less* good at spatial-abilities tasks than are the less masculine males (Peterson, 1973, cited in Mac-coby and Jacklin, 1974; Klaiber, Broverman, and Kobayashi, 1967). This is a very confusing finding since it would lead one to suppose that girls, being least masculine in hormone pattern, should be best at spatial skills, and we know this not to be the case. Equally confusing is the fact that boys seem to show a relative rise in spatial abilities just at adolescence when their levels of androgen are rising. Broverman and his associates (Broverman, Klaiber, Kobayashi, and Vogel, 1968) have at-tempted to explain these confusions by suggesting that while androgen has a suppressing effect on spatial abilities, estrogen (the female hormone) has a *more* suppressing effect, but since the research has been done entirely with males, there is no way to know if this is true.

What these several confusions point to, however, is the need to keep an open mind about the possibility that there may be hormonal effects on cognitive functioning, beginning perhaps at adolescence when sharp increases in sex hormones occur. But the nature of such a possible effect is not obvious at the moment

One final point on biological evidence: Korner's brief review of sex differences among newborns (in the selections) highlights the possible *initial* (presumably biological) differences to which parents respond. Korner emphasizes that in many areas no sex differences in neonatal behavior have been observed consistently, but there are a few differences that may be significant for the parents. Precisely where those differences come from, whether hormonal or genetic, or some other source, is unknown. But the fact that there are a few differences at birth means that all later differences *cannot* be attributed to differential experiences after birth.

Environmental Evidence

Some of the biological evidence I have just reviewed is fairly persuasive; there certainly are some biological influences on observed sex differences. But it is equally obvious that not all of the observed differences are biological in origin. Many of the differences are no doubt entirely, or partially, governed by experiences after birth.

Even in the case of children with ambiguous genital appearance (who have thus had some kind of deviant hormonal experience prenatally) experience is vital. Money (1971) describes a series of cases of individuals with such ambiguous genitalia. Some such children are reared as boys and some as girls, even though their physical appearance is similar. After examining matched pairs of such children (pairs in which the external genital appearance and diagnosis was similar, but in which one was raised as a boy and the other as a girl), Money reports that the children raised as boys consider themselves boys and behave like boys, while those raised as girls consider themselves and behave like girls. Money does not report any data on the cognitive skill characteristics of this group of anomalous children, but in other behaviors the sex of *rearing* seems to be the critical factor in determining behavior. Money suggests that:

> Despite whatever sexual dimorphism may already have differentiated in the central nervous system, the human organism at birth is still largely bipotential for dimorphism of gender-identity differentiation. More simply said, the individual's gender-identity and role . . . will differentiate in response to and in interaction with stimuli encountered after birth. (Money, 1971, p. 209)

Money is taking an extreme environmental position, and perhaps there are some limits on environmental effects; we do not know what would happen to a fully biological male raised as a female, or vice versa, but Money's general point is important. Biological patterns do not *fix* behavior immutably. Environmental influences are also critical.

But how do we discover the nature and extent of environmental influences on sex differences? There are at least two related but separable questions. First, how does a child come to know her or his gender, and how does the related sense of sex roles and sex-role stereotypes emerge? Second, how do the specific sex differences charted earlier come about? Because I think it will help to make sense of the information, let me begin by talking about gender identity and how the child comes to understand her or his own sex.

It is not until about age 2½ or perhaps 3 that most children have any consistent ability to identify themselves correctly as a boy or a girl. In an excellent recent study of children 2 to 3, Thompson (1975) found that 2-year-olds could identify the sex of other people fairly well, and could label them boy or girl (but not he or she; pronouns are harder at this age), but did not apply gender labels correctly to *themselves* and had no preference for same-sex behaviors. These 2-year-olds did, however, have some rudimentary notions of sex-stereotyped activities and toys. By 30 months, children could recognize different sexes accurately and label them with their pronouns or nouns. They could label their own picture correctly some of the time, but mastery of the gender labels, particularly for the self, is not complete at this age. There was still no preference for same-sex choices, but there was recognition of sex-stereotyped activities.

By 3 years of age, in Thompson's study, the children were quite accurate about others' and their own gender, could label correctly, and had very clear stereotypes about tools and toys. They showed some preference for same-sex objects for themselves, but did not selectively listen to a voice saying "good girl" versus "good boy." Progress through this sequence was related not only to chronological age but also to cognitive development. Children who were more advanced in their understanding of concepts of various sorts were also more advanced in the development of a gender concept.

Slaby and Frey, in the paper in the selections, explore the development of gender *constancy*. They find that the child first develops gender identity (knowing others' and own gender), then gender stability (knowing that you will be the same sex when you grow up), and then gender consistency (knowing that you do not change gender by changing tasks or clothing). The full concept of gender was not developed until about 4½ to 5, and in some children not until 5½. Kohlberg and Ullian (1974) report that gender constancy has no clear logical basis, and is not linked to genital differences, until perhaps age 6 or 7, so the process is a gradual one, and seems linked to other cognitive processes.

Evidence on the play preferences of children suggests that this developmental pattern runs parallel to the development of gender identity concepts. It is not until about age 2 that children show consistent preferences for sex-typed toys. Maccoby and Jacklin review a series of studies that show some stereotypic toy choice by age 2, which gets stronger over the preschool years. (For a representative recent study, see Fein, Johnson, Kosson, Stork, and Wasserman, 1975.) Boys seem to show preferences for large-muscle activity and girls for smaller manipulations, but this trend is not consistent. Many studies show no sex preference for such games or tasks as Tinker toys, puzzles, playhouses or block play, so it is difficult to discern the basis for the preferences. It is equally difficult to discern the relationship between the toy preferences and the child's developing gender identity because the toy preferences emerge before the child has any consistent notion of her or his own gender. It seems clear that toy preferences in the early years do not occur because the child recognizes that a given toy is "appropriate" for her or his own sex, although that undoubtedly is a factor among 5- to 6-year-old children. Nor is it obvious that early toy preferences come about because of some differential reinforcement for individual toys or types of toys on the part of parents. Although the data are scant, there is no good support for the expectation that parents systematically provide "masculine" toys for boys and "feminine" toys for girls as young as age 2. Maccoby and Jacklin suggest that the early toy preferences may be based on other factors entirely, and note that society has come to label as "masculine" the toys that boys prefer and as "feminine" the toys that girls prefer. In later years, as the child's gender constancy becomes more complete, the toy preferences appear to be influenced the other way around: the toy preference becomes dependent on the label.

Several theorists have attempted to account for the whole process of sex-role development, most notably Mischel (1970), who has emphasized the roles of imitation and direct reinforcement, and Kohlberg (1966; Kohlberg and Ullian, 1974), who has

taken a "cognitive-developmental" approach. The two approaches are contrasted concisely and well in the introduction
to the Slaby and Frey paper, so I will be very brief here.

Mischel emphasizes primarily the role of observational
learning. The child learns appropriate sex-typed behaviors
through modeling. Mischel and others who have emphasized the
role of modeling point out that simple reinforcement of sex-
appropriate behaviors will not account for the range and complexity of the sex-role concept the child acquires. But Mischel
sees the role of imitation as paramount and suggests that the
child imitates those individuals he considers similar to himself.
In addition, he assumes that children are reinforced directly for
imitating same-sex models.

Kohlberg, on the other hand, takes the position that knowledge of gender is a cognitive development that must be ac-
complished before any kind of significant sex-typing takes
place. He suggests that the child first acquires the gender concept and then imitates the models of the same sex. Mischel is
saying that the child is rewarded for imitating same-sex models
and that the gender and sex-role concepts develop as a result of
this modeling.

The evidence seems to point to Kohlberg's concept as the
more accurate, although there is still a great deal to be understood about the process. Slaby and Frey show, for example, that
children with a full gender concept are more likely to watch a
same-sex figure in a film than are children who are less advanced
in the gender concept. This supports Kohlberg's contention that
imitation of same-sex models comes *after* the development of
gender constancy. This finding is consistent with Maccoby and
Jacklin's review of studies of imitation, which shows no preference for imitating same-sex models among children below
about age 6. Bear in mind that the situation is much more
complex than this sounds. Children younger than this age do
show "sex-appropriate" toy preferences and show same-sex
peer groupings, so some kind of sex-typing is already going on.
What these data show is that the early sex-typing is probably not
occurring because of greater imitation of same-sex models (see
Maccoby and Jacklin, pages 275–302, for a detailed discussion
of these issues).

So where do the early differences in behavior come from?
Perhaps the answer for the early differences is simple: perhaps
boys and girls are simply reared differently in systematic ways,
and this is the origin of the differences at preschool age. This is a
logical notion and seems entirely reasonable to many people. It
is obvious that the sex of a newborn child is a highly salient

characteristic. When you hear that a friend has a newborn, what is the first question you usually ask? "Is it a boy or a girl?" And there are some differences in early treatment of boys and girls in such things as the color of clothing worn. It seems reasonable to go from these commonplace observations to the assumption that there are systematic differences in treatment for the two sexes during the early years.

Unfortunately this reasonable expectation has less empirical support than one would expect. Hoffman cites several studies in her paper that show differential treatment in the early years, and other researchers have found evidence for such differences. For example, Minton, Kagan, and Levine (1971) found that mothers were more likely to intrude on the child's activities, or prohibit activities, for boys than for girls, and that boys were more often punished than were girls. But Maccoby and Jacklin, in their extensive review of the evidence for differential early socialization, conclude that the similarities in treatment far outweigh the differences. They find no evidence that aggression is more commonly rewarded or encouraged in boys than in girls, and no evidence that dependence or independence is differentially rewarded (see Marcus, 1975, for recent confirmation). Girls are not talked to more than boys (although here the findings are mixed), and the two sexes do not consistently receive differential amounts of pressure for achievement.

Some consistent differences in treatment are found. Boys are handled more roughly than girls; parents engage in more roughhousing and physical play with boys than girls. Girls are perceived by parents as being more fragile and parents seem to worry more about physical injury for girls. A second consistent difference is that boys are physically punished more than are girls, and this appears to be true from infancy through adolescence. Finally, there is some evidence that parents press for behavior that is consistent with sex-role stereotypes. Particularly in the case of boys, parents of preschoolers or older children seem to be very distressed at the possibility that their son may choose "feminine" toys or activities. Fathers are especially likely to feel strongly about the importance of appropriate sex-role behavior from their sons. Daughters experience some of this pressure, but apparently to a lesser extent. So parents *say* that appropriate sex-role behaviors in their children are important to them, and one can only presume that this sense of importance is in some way(s) reflected in the parents' behavior toward the children. The problem is that the observations of parental behavior are not entirely consistent with this expectation. Aggression, for example, is a clearly sex-typed behavior, and parents worry about their son being a "sissy," but there is no evidence for systematic differential reinforcement of aggression in boys compared to girls. Perhaps we will find that as observations of socialization of boys and girls become more detailed and more subtle, some clear differences will be found. For the moment, it is obvious that we cannot explain all the differences in the children's behavior by assuming differential socialization on the part of parents.

Given what we know about the timing of the emergence of many sex differences in behavior (late childhood or early adolescence) and what I have just discussed, it begins to look as if the school years may be more critical for the development of behavioral differences and sex-role stereotypes than are the very early years. Maccoby and Jacklin's summary conclusion about the origin of sex-typed behaviors is consistent with this view:

> We believe that the processes of direct reinforcement and simple imitation are clearly involved in the acquisition of sex-typed behavior, but that they are not sufficient to account for the developmental changes that occur in sex-typing. The third kind of psychological process—the one stressed by cognitive-developmental theorists such as Kohlberg—must also be involved. This third process is not easy to define, but in simplest terms it means that a child gradually develops concepts of "masculinity" and "femininity," and when he has understood what his own sex is, he attempts to match his behavior to his conception. His ideas may be drawn only very minimally from observing his own parents. The generalizations he constructs do not represent acts of imitation, but are organizations of information distilled from a wide variety of sources. A child's sex-role concepts are limited in the same way the rest of his concepts are, by the level of cognitive skills he has developed. Therefore the child undergoes reasonably orderly age-related changes in the subtlety of his thought about sex-typing, just as he does with respect to other topics. Consequently, his *actions* in adopting sex-typed behavior, and in treating others according to sex-role stereotypes, also change in ways that parallel his conceptual growth. (Maccoby and Jacklin, 1974, pp. 365–366)

Slaby and Frey's study, and others, appears to show that a reasonably full and subtle concept of gender is not developed until school age, so we might reasonably assume that encounters at that age with sex roles and stereotypes in school and elsewhere may be critical in the formation of differential sex roles and behaviors.

What are the sources of information about sex roles for children of school age? Obviously parents continue to play some role, but since the amount of time children spend with parents after the age of 6 or so declines sharply, other influences are probably paramount. Teachers undoubtedly play a major role, as do books and TV and other media. What do we know about sex-typing in these sources?

Several recent reviews of textbooks—particularly reading books—in elementary schools (Saario, Jacklin, and Tittle, 1973; Lee and Gropper, 1974) report that there are clear sex-role stereotypes portrayed in such books. There are relatively few female characters in children's readers, and those there are tend to be shown as less aggressive, less physically exertive, less constructive or productive, less good at problem solving, more conforming. The women are most often shown at home rather than either outdoors or at work. When female characters are involved in the action of stories, most often things happen *to* the woman as a result of chance or factors outside her control; for males in children's stories, good things happen because of the male's own actions. (Note here the consistency of this finding with the increasing external locus of control noted for girls and women in the summary earlier.) These portrayals of women were clearer in third-grade readers than in first-grade readers, suggesting that the sex-role stereotyping may become stronger through the school years.

Teachers' direct sex-stereotyping in their interactions with children is more complex. Lee and Gropper, reviewing this evidence, conclude that teachers want both girls and boys to be orderly, conforming, and dependent. Perhaps because boys are less compliant, or because teachers' perceptions of boys are different, teachers direct more of their socialization efforts toward boys, giving both more attention and more criticism to the boys. There is also evidence that children perceive teachers as favoring girls over boys. Lee and Gropper summarize:

> Findings such as these indicate boys and girls do not have equal access to the typical teacher's expectations about pupil role. Pressure is placed upon boys to accommodate to a pupil role which conflicts with their own sex role and, perhaps more perniciously, on girls not to deviate from their female sex role. (Lee and Gropper, 1974, p. 389)

It does seem clear that teachers are emphasizing quite traditional female roles in their behavior toward girls. The messages to boys are more mixed because they are directly reinforced for the same kinds of conforming and docile behavior as are valued in girls, but they also receive more criticism. To complicate things still further, I should remind you that both boys and girls in school see many women (teachers) performing in a role that is competent and achievement oriented. So the sex-role stereotyping in teacher's behavior, unlike the textbooks, is more full of mixed messages about appropriate behavior for the sexes.

Sex-role information from television, however, is much more like textbooks in that the portrayals of males and females are highly stereotypic. Stein and Friedrich (1975) have reviewed this evidence and conclude that females are underrepresented in *any* kind of role on television (as is true for textbooks), and that their roles tend not to be "effective" or competent ones. Most women are shown in the home, or in outside jobs that are subservient in some way to the male roles. In children's programs the males are shown as more aggressive and more constructive, whereas females are shown as deferent and passive.

What these analyses suggest is that the information children receive about "appropriate" sex roles are moderately consistent and quite highly stereotyped from school age onward. If Maccoby and Jacklin are correct, then children should begin to incorporate gradually these various features of the stereotypes into their own concepts of sex role and gender over the early years of childhood. By adolescence some differences in behavior are noticeable in the direction of these stereotypes, although the actual differences in real-life behavior are far smaller than the stereotypes would suggest. The study by Rosenkrantz and associates (1968), cited earlier, also shows that sex stereotypes are more extreme than are people's own images of themselves. It would appear, therefore, that the several sources of social pressure move children toward, but not all the way to, the stereotypic view of sex roles.

Summary

I am sure that you realize, after reading even this comparatively brief overview of the literature, that the explanations for most of the observed differences are far more complex than this analysis suggests. Some of the observed sex differences have biological origins and are then accentuated by social pressures of various kinds. Some of the stereotypes about sex difference in behavior are simply not matched by behavior of real people in the real world, so despite the social pressures inherent in the stereotyping in films, television, and books, not all stereotypes are self-fulfilling prophecies. We are a long way from understanding how all of these processes work; but we are further in our understanding of the nature of the differences themselves, and the theoretical approaches now being taken by researchers such as Slaby and Frey seem extremely promising.

QUESTIONS FOR DEBATE OR DISCUSSION

1. If a woman you know were denied a top-level executive job on the grounds that because of her sex she was not capable of holding such a job, what would your comment be? What evidence pro or con could you muster?
2. If you were a member of a local school board interested in reducing the sex-role stereotyping in your school, what steps might you take? What evidence would you want to have first?

ADDITIONAL REFERENCES USEFUL
IN PREPARATION FOR DEBATE OR DISCUSSION

Bardwick, J. M. *Psychology of women.* New York: Harper & Row, 1971.

This book is slightly out of date now because this is a very fast-moving field. Bardwick concludes there are more sex differences in biology and behavior than do Maccoby and Jacklin, so the book may serve as a good counterweight.

Friedman, R. C., Richart, R. M., and Vande Wiele, R. L. *Sex differences in behavior.* New York: Wiley, 1974.

This edited volume contains a series of good papers, some of which are referred to in the following list of references. It is particularly good in the area of hormonal effects.

Maccoby, E. E., and Jacklin, C. N. *The psychology of sex differences.* Stanford, Calif.: Stanford University Press, 1974.

There is no better or more general reference on the subject. It is comprehensive, interesting, and insightful. An absolute *must* if you are interested in this topic.

REFERENCES

Baker, S. W., and Ehrhardt, A. A. Prenatal androgen, intelligence, and cognitive sex differences. In R. C. Friedman, R. M. Richart, and R. L. Vande Wiele (Eds.), *Sex differences in behavior.* New York: Wiley, 1974, 53–76.

Bardwick, J. M. *Psychology of women.* New York: Harper & Row, 1971.

Bayley, N. Comparisons of mental and motor test scores for ages 1–15 months by sex, birth order, race, and geographical location, and education of parents. *Child Development,* 1965, **36,** 379–411.

Bock, D. R., and Kolakowski, D. Further evidence of sex-linked major-gene influence on human spatial visualizing ability. *American Journal of Human Genetics,* 1973, **25,** 1–14.

Broverman, D. M., Klaiber, E. L., Kobayashi, Y., and Vogel, W. Roles of activation and inhibition in sex differences in cognitive abilities. *Psychological Review,* 1968, **75,** 23–50.

Broverman, I. K., Boverman, D. M., Clarkson, F. E., Rosenkrantz, P. S., and Vogel, S. R. Sex-role stereotypes and clinical judgments of mental health. *Journal of Consulting and Clinical Psychology,* 1970, **34,** 1–7.

Broverman, I. K., Vogel, S. R., Broverman, D. M., Clarkson, F. E., and Rosenkrantz, P. S. Sex-role stereotypes: A current appraisal. *Journal of Social Issues,* 1972, **28,** 59–78.

Cantor, G. N. Sex and race effects in the conformity behavior of upper-elementary school aged children. *Developmental Psychology,* 1975, **11,** 661–662.

Coates, S. Sex differences in field independence among preschool children. In R. C. Friedman, R. M. Richart, and R. L. Vande Wiele (Eds.), *Sex differences in behavior.* New York: Wiley, 1974, pp. 259–274.

Corah, N. L. Differentiation in children and their parents. *Journal of Personality,* 1965, **33,** 301–308.

Deutsch, F. Effects of sex of subject and story character on preschoolers' perceptions of affective responses and interpersonal behavior in story sequences. *Developmental Pscyhology,* 1975, **11,** 112–113.

Ehrhardt, A. A., and Baker, S. W. Fetal androgens, human central nervous system differentiation, and behavior sex differences. In R. C. Friedman, R. M. Richart, and R. L. Vande Wiele (Eds.), *Sex differences in behavior.* New York: Wiley, 1974, 33–51.

Ehrhardt, A. A., and Money, J. Progestin induced hermaphroditism: I. Q. and psychosexual identity in a study of ten girls. *The Journal of Sex Research,* 1967, **3,** 83–100.

Etaugh, C., and Rose, S. Adolescents' sex bias in the evaluation of performance. *Developmental Psychology,* 1975, **11,** 663–664.

Fein, G., Johnson, D., Kosson, N., Stork, L., and Wasserman, L. Sex stereotypes and preferences in the toy choices of 20-month-old boys and girls. *Developmental, Psychology,* 1975, **11,** 527–528.

Garai, J. E., and Scheinfeld, A. Sex differences in mental and behavioral traits. *Genetic Psychology Monographs,* 1968, **77,** 169–299.

Harper, L. V., and Sanders, K. M. Preschool children's use of space: sex differences in outdoor play. *Developmental Psychology,* 1975, **11,** 119.

Hartlage, L. C. Sex-linked inheritance of spatial ability. *Perceptual and Motor Skills,* 1970, **31,** 610.

Jackaway, R. Sex differences in the development of fear of success. *Child Study Journal,* 1974, **4,** 71–79.

Keating, D. P., and Schaefer, R. A. Ability and sex differences in the acquisiton of formal operations. *Developmental Psychology,* 1975, **11,** 531–532.

Kennel, J. M., Jerauld, R., Wolfe, H., Chesler, D., Kreger, N. C., McAlpine, W., Steffa, M., and Klaus, M. H. Maternal behavior one year after early and extended post-partum contact. *Developmental Medicine and Child Neurology,* 1974, **16,** 172–179.

Klaiber, E. L., Broverman, D. M., and Kobayashi, Y. The automatization cognitive style, androgens, and monoamine exidase. *Psychopharmacologia,* 1967, **11,** 320–336.

Kohlberg, L. A. A cognitive-developmental analysis of children's sex-role concepts and attitudes. In E. E. Maccoby (Ed.), *The develop-*

ment of sex differences. Stanford, Calif.: Stanford University Press, 1966, pp. 82–173.

Kohlberg, L. A., and Ullian, D. Z. Stages in the development of psychosexual concepts and attitudes. In R. C. Friedman, R. M. Richart, and R. L. Vande Wiele (Eds.), *Sex differences in behavior.* New York: Wiley, 1974, pp. 209–222.

Lee, P. C., and Gropper, N. B. Sex-role culture and educational practice. *Harvard Educational Review,* 1974, **44,** 369–410.

Leifer, A., Leiderman, P. H., Barnett, C. R., and Williams, J. A. Effects of mother-infant separation on maternal attachment behavior. *Child Development,* 1972, **43,** 1203–1218.

Maccoby, E. E., and Jacklin, C. N. *The psychology of sex differences.* Stanford: Stanford University Press, 1974.

Marcus, R. F. The child as elicitor of parental sanctions for independent and dependent behavior: a simulation of parent-child interaction. *Developmental Psychology,* 1975, **11,** 443–452.

Minton, C., Kagan, J., and Levine, J. A. Maternal control and obedience in the two-year-old. *Child Development,* 1971, **42,** 1873–1894.

Mischel, W. Sex-typing and socialization. In P. H. Mussen (Ed.), *Carmichael's manual of child psychology.* (3rd Ed.) Vol. 2. New York: Wiley, 1970, pp. 3–72.

Money, J. Sexually dimorphic behavior, normal and abnormal. In N. Kretchmer and D. N. Walcher (Eds.), *Environmental influences on genetic expression: biological and behavioral aspects of sexual differentiation.* (Fogarty International Center Proceedings No. 2) Washington, D.C.: United States Goverment Printing Office, 1971, pp. 201–212.

Moyer, K. E. Sex differences in aggression. In R. C. Friedman, R. M. Richart, and R. L. Vande Wiele (Eds.), *Sex differences in behavior.* New York: Wiley, 1974, pp. 335–372.

Romer, N. The motive to avoid success and its effects on performance in school-age males and females. *Developmental Psychology,* 1975, **11,** 689–699.

Rosenblatt, J. S. The development of maternal responsiveness in the rat. *American Journal of Orthopsychiatry,* 1969, **30,** 36–56.

Rosenblatt, J. S. The pre- and post-partum regulation of maternal behavior in the rat. In M. H. Klaus, T. Leger, and M. A. Trause (Eds.), *Maternal attachment and mothering disorders: A roundtable.* 1975, Johnson & Johnson Baby Products Company.

Rosenkrantz, P. S., Vogel, S. R., Bee, H., Broverman, I. K., and Broverman, D. M. Sex-role stereotypes and self-concepts in college students. *Journal of Consulting and Clinical Psychology,* 1968, **32,** 287–295.

Saario, T. N., Jacklin, C. N., and Tittle, C. K. Sex role stereotyping in the public schools. *Harvard Educational Review,* 1973, **43,** 386–416.

Stafford, R. E. Sex differences in spatial visualization as evidence of sex-linked inheritance. *Perceptual and Motor Skills,* 1961, **13,** 428.

Stein, A. H., and Friedrich, L. K. Impact of television on children and youth. In E. M. Hetherington (Ed.), *Review of child development reserach,* Vol. 5. Chicago: University of Chicago Press, 1975, pp. 183–256.

Tanner, J. M. Physical Growth. In P. H. Mussen (Ed.), *Carmichael's manual of child psychology.* (3rd Ed.) Vol. 1. New York: Wiley, 1970, pp. 77–155.

Thompson, S. K. Gender labels and early sex role development. *Child Development,* 1975, **46,** 339–347.

Urberg, K. A., and Labouvie-Vief, G. Conceptualizations of sex roles: a life span developmental study. *Developmental Psychology,* 1976, **12,** 15–23.

Vandenberg, S. G. The nature and nurture of intelligence. In D. C. Glass (Ed.), *Genetics.* New York: The Rockefeller University Press and Russell Sage Foundation, 1968, 3–58.

Williams, J. E., Bennett, S. M., and Best, D. L. Awareness and expression of sex stereotypes in young children. *Developmental Psychology,* 1975, **11,** 635–642.

Psychosexual differentiation as a function of androgenic stimulation

CHARLES H. PHOENIX
ROBERT W. GOY
JOHN A. RESKO

Among mammals, the sex of an individual is generally said to be dependent upon contribution of either an X or Y chromosome by the male. However, the mechanism whereby these chromosomes determine the sex of the individual has until recently received little attention. In practice, the sex of an individual is commonly decided upon by the appearance of the external genitalia without reference to the chromosomal status.

To each sex is ascribed a characteristic pattern of reproductive behavior which varies from one species to another. In addition, other behavioral characteristics are commonly attributed to members of a given sex. For example, the bitch is commonly thought to be more gentle than the dog, and the bull to be dangerously aggressive when compared to the cow. These behavioral characteristics, or in many cases what amounts only to expectations, are assumed to follow from the appearance of the external genitalia. In man, an elaborate set of behaviors and attitudes are labeled as masculine and another constellation of behaviors are considered feminine. The behavior expected of an individual within a given society is determined by assignment to the class male or female.

Charles H. Phoenix, Robert W. Goy, John A. Resko, "Psychosexual differentiation as a function of androgenic stimulation." In M. Diamond (Ed.) *Reproduction and Sexual Behavior*. Copyright © 1969, Indiana University Press. Reprinted by permission.

Publication No. 320 of the Oregon Regional Primate Research Center supported in part by Grant MH-08634 of the National Institutes of Health, and in part by Grant FR-00163.

Very little is known about what determines masculinity or femininity. Because research on problems of sexuality in the human is virtually impossible, researchers have looked to mammals lower on the phylogenetic scale for answers to some of the basic questions. For example, what are the biological mechanisms by which sexual and sex-related behaviors are determined?

From research on adult laboratory animals and from clinical observations, it has long been believed that hormones do not establish patterns of behavior but only serve to bring to expression previously established behavior patterns. The consensus of opinion is that gonadal hormones themselves are not masculine or feminine; they only permit the masculine or feminine pattern of behavior that exists within the individual to be brought to expression. The question arises as to whether or not the hormones, especially the gonadal hormones, play any role at all in establishing the basic sexuality of the individual.

We approached this question by first studying sexual behavior, that is, behavior instrumental to reproduction of the species, and initially directed our attention to the guinea pig. Much was known about the reproductive behavior of this species (Young, 1961), and it seemed to be a model eminently suited to the investigation.

Our first series of studies on the guinea pig led us to conclude that the gonadal hormones did indeed play a role in establishing basic patterns of reproductive behavior. We learned that when pregnant female guinea pigs are injected with testosterone propionate, the genetic female offspring from such pregnancies are masculinized (Phoenix et al., 1959). The masculinization included not only morphological characteristics which had previously been demonstrated (Dantchakoff, 1938) but, more significantly, physiological and psychosexual masculinization as well. Such experimentally produced pseudohermaphrodites possess ovaries, although there is evidence of ovarian dysfunction (Tedford and Young, 1960). The external vaginal orifice is completely obliterated, and a well-developed penis is formed. The genital tract shows variable abnormalities. The O_2 consumption rate resembles that of the male rather than that of the female (Goy et al., 1962). The spayed, adult pseudohermaphrodite when injected with estrogen and progesterone fails to display estrous behavior characteristic of the normal spayed female similarly injected with estrogen and progesterone. Not only is responsiveness to the female hormones suppressed but there is heightened sensitivity to testosterone propionate as evidenced by the increase in mounting frequency. Furthermore, the effect of the prenatal treatment is permanent. Thus, although it is possible to increase the frequency of mounting behavior in a normal female by treating the animals with testosterone propionate in adulthood, the effect is transient and mounting frequency returns to pretreatment levels when treatment is discontinued (Phoenix et al., 1959). Informal observation of the behavior of the female pseudohermaphrodite reveals a level of aggression not unlike that observed in male guinea pigs.

In producing masculinization of the genetic female both the stage of fetal development and the hormonal dosage are critical. Treatments confined to very early or late stages in fetal development are ineffective with the dosages that have been used (Goy et al., 1964). Maximum masculinization in the guinea pig was obtained when treatment with 5 mg of testosterone propionate was started at day 30 of gestation and continued daily for 6 days, followed by 1 mg per day to day 55. Other times and dosages produced variable degrees of modification. In general, the animals displaying the highest degree of psychosexual modification were also the most modified morphologically. These findings from our early research on the guinea pig led us to conclude that the gonadal hormones, especially testosterone, had a dual function. During the period of differentiation the gonadal hormones, we hypothesized, had an organizing action on the central neural tissues that controlled the display of sexual behavior. This function we contrasted to the action of the same hormones in the adult, where the hormones functioned to bring to expression patterns of behavior that had been previously established during development (Young, 1961). We viewed the action of the gonadal hormones on the central neural tissues in the developing fetus as analogous to their action on genital tract tissue, including those tissues constituting the external genitalia.

In further study of the role that testosterone plays in organizing the neural tissues that underlie reproductive behavior, genetic male rats were castrated on the day of birth and at various times to maturity (Grady et al., 1965). When rats were castrated on the day of birth and injected as adults with estrogen and progesterone, they responded much as did genetic females. Males that were castrated after the first 10 days of life failed to give typical female responses when injected in adulthood with the ovarian hormones. The results supported our hypothesis that it is the presence of the testicular hormone during the period of differentiation that masculinizes the individual whether that individual is genetically male or female.

From our work with the rat it became obvious that it was not prenatal treatment per se that was critical but treatment during the period of psychosexual differentiation. Generally one might expect that in long-gestation animals such as the guinea pig, monkey, and man, the critical stage of development would occur during the prenatal period, whereas, in short-gestation animals such as the mouse, rat, and hamster, the critical period for psychosexual differentiation might occur during the late fetal and early postnatal period. If one compares the ages at which psychosexual differentiation is found to occur in the rat, guinea pig, and monkey on the basis of postfertilization age, the differences among these species become relatively small. More work is needed, especially in the monkey, to establish the critical time limits of psychosexual differentiation, and virtually nothing is known about man.

· · ·

Largely as a result of aggressive behavior observed among pseudohermaphroditic guinea pigs we suggested in our first definitive paper on the organizing action of testosterone (Phoenix et al., 1959) that the ". . . masculinity or femininity of an animal's behavior beyond that which is purely sexual has developed in response to certain hormonal substances within the embryo and fetus." Considerable evidence gathered on the rodent has confirmed our suggestion. Cyclic running activity (Harris, 1964; Kennedy, 1964) and open-field behavior (Gray et al., 1965; Swanson, 1966, 1967) have been shown to be dependent upon the presence or absence of androgen during the period of psychosexual differentiation.

· · ·

The success achieved with work on the rodent led us to pursue the work on a species which in a number of respects was more similar to man (Young et al., 1964). We chose to work with the rhesus monkey in which sexually dimorphic social behavior in the infant had been demonstrated (Rosenblum, 1961; Harlow, 1965). If, as we had postulated, behaviors other than those instrumental to reproduction were determined by the action of testosterone during differentiation, the rhesus, because of its rich behavioral repertoire, would prove an ideal model for study.

We set about producing female pseudohermaphroditic rhesus monkeys by injecting pregnant females with testosterone propionate.[1] The procedure followed essentially that reported by Wells and van Wagenen (1954) in which they produced animals

---

[1] Testosterone propionate (Perandren) was supplied by courtesy of Ciba, Inc., Summit, N.J.

described as showing marked morphological masculinization. Pregnant rhesus were given daily intramuscular injections of 20 mg of testosterone propionate beginning on day 40 and extending through day 69 of pregnancy. The average gestation period in the monkey is approximately 168 days. Using this treatment we obtained two female pseudohermaphrodites. Both animals possessed well-developed scrota and well-formed but small penes. The external urethral orifice was located at the tip of the penis as in the normal male. Testes could not be palpated as they can be in the genetic male, buccal smears were 34 to 37 percent sexchromatin positive, and it was assumed that the animals possessed ovaries and Müllerian derivatives such as described by Wells and van Wagenen for the pseudohermaphroditic monkey and as we had observed in the pseudohermaphroditic guinea pig. We have had the opportunity to study the internal genital morphology of several treated fetuses that were aborted and in a few female pseudohermaphrodites that died shortly after birth. We confirmed the presence of an ovary in these pseudohermaphroditic animals but have not studied the internal morphology on any of the living pseudohermaphrodites whose behavior is reported here.

All the evidence from work on the guinea pig and rat in which we varied dosage and time of treatment suggested that for each species there is an optimal regimen for maximum behavioral and morphological modification. The opportunity to explore various treatments on the monkey has been sorely limited because of the few animals available coupled with the relatively high abortion rates we have encountered. It should be recalled that approximately half of the offspring from treated mothers are genetic males, thus further reducing the pseudohermaphroditic females available for study. Evidence thus far assembled suggests that the original treatment was less than optimal both for morphological and behavioral modification. We also know from our limited experience that the animal with greatest penis development is not necessarily the animal showing the greatest behavioral modification. We assume that as the number of animals we study increases, there then will be a correlation between the extent of morphological and behavioral modification. This was the situation that prevailed in our research on the guinea pig and there is no evidence for believing that the relationship will not hold for the rhesus.

The various treatment parameters employed for each surviving treated animal are indicated in Table 1. It is obvious from the table that few dosages and time periods are represented among the pseudohermaphrodites. It may be noted in the table

TABLE 1 AMOUNT AND TEMPORAL DISTRIBUTION OF PRENATAL INJECTIONS OF TESTOSTERONE PROPIONATE IN RHESUS MONKEYS

No. of off-spring	Ge-netic sex	Gesta-tional age Rx started	Gesta-tional age Rx ended	Amount and number of injections of TP into mother			
				Mg × days	Mg × days	Mg × days	Total mg
828	♀	40	69	20 × 30			600
829	♀	40	69	20 × 30			600
1239	♀	38	66	25 × 25"			625
1656	♀	40	111	10 × 50 →	5 × 22		610
836	♀	40	89	25 × 10 →	15 × 20 →	10 × 20	750
1616	♀	39	88	25 × 10 →	15 × 20 →	10 × 20	750
1619	♀	39	88	25 × 10 →	15 × 20 →	10 × 20	750
1640	♀	39	88	25 × 10 →	15 × 20 →	10 × 20	750
1558	♂	42	92	25 × 10 →	15 × 20 →	10 × 20	750
1561	♂	39	45	25 × 7			175
1618	♂	43	92	25 × 10 →	15 × 20 →	10 × 20	750
1644	♂	44	113	10 × 50 →	5 × 20		600
1645	♂	39	129	25 × 10 →	10 × 19ᵇ →	5 × 22ᵇ	550
1648	♂	39	119	25 × 3 →	5 × 78		465
1653	♂	43	134	25 × 10 →	10 × 17 →	5 × 24	540
1966	♂	40	109	15 × 10 →	10 × 40 →	5 × 20	650

" Injected 6 days per week.
ᵇ Injected on alternate days.

that the mother of pseudohermaphrodite 1239 was treated with testosterone 6 days per week. This procedure followed exactly one of the treatments described by Wells and van Wagenen (1954). The abortion rate in animals so treated was as high as in animals treated 7 days per week and thus the 7-day-per-week treatment schedule was followed in all other animals. Animal 1656, who received hormone through day 111 of fetal life, possesses the most extensively modified external genitalia. However, its initial dosage level was low and the total amount received was also relatively low. We are now preparing a series of treatment schedules which will extend later into pregnancy. The rationale for adopting the more protracted treatment procedure is based upon evidence obtained in our laboratory. Using the gas chromatographic technique, testosterone has been shown to be present in the plasma of the male rhesus fetus late in gestation and even on the day of birth. In small samples of plasma that have been analyzed at intervals during the first 30 days of life no detectable amounts of testosterone were found, whereas comparable-sized samples of plasma from adult male rhesus did reveal the presence of testosterone. By continuing testosterone treatment during late pregnancy we hope to produce conditions which resemble more closely the hormonal environment of the genetic male, thus maximizing degree of modification of the genetic female. In a proportionate sense, the situation for the rhesus may not be greatly different from that which exists for the guinea pig. In that species, the best psychological modifications of the genetic female were obtained with treatments extending to day 55 or 65 of the 68-day gestational period. The organizing action of testosterone is therefore very likely completed at or shortly after birth in the rhesus.

The first two pseudohermaphrodites studied by us and the two untreated females with whom they were studied were taken from their mothers at birth and fed at appropriate intervals by nursery technicians. The animals were housed in individual cages that contained a terry-cloth surrogate mother such as described by Harlow (1961). The four animals constituting the study group were placed together for approximately 30 minutes each day to avoid isolation effects. The animals were taken from their mothers at birth, because we were particularly concerned that whatever sexually dimorphic behavior patterns might be observed would not be the result of differential treatment of the sexes by the mother. The behavior displayed by these two pseudohermaphrodites has been reported previously (Young et al., 1964).

All other animals, experimental and control, have been permitted to remain with the mother for the first 3 months of life. At that time the infant is taken from the mother, placed in a separate cage, and weaned to solid food. Peer groups are formed consisting of four to six animals each. The animals continue to be housed individually, but each weekday the members of a group are brought together in a 6 ft.-by-10 ft. experimental room for observation. Each subject in a group of peers is observed for 5 consecutive minutes. The behavior of each subject is recorded on an inventory checklist for the 5 minutes during which it is observed. To eliminate a possible time effect, the order of observation within a group is rotated daily. Each group is observed at approximately the same time each day. During the first year of life the subjects are studied for 100 days in the same social setting and for 50 days during the second and each subsequent year. During the interval between yearly tests just described, the animals are tested for social and sexual behavior in pairs. All pair combinations possible within a given peer group are studied.

Our findings have confirmed those reported by Rosenblum

TABLE 2 FREQUENCY OF SOCIAL BEHAVIOR DURING THE FIRST YEAR OF LIFE BY MALE AND FEMALE RHESUS MONKEYS

		Frequency per blocks of 10 trials			
		Threat	Play initiation	Rough-and-tumble play	Chasing play
Males (N = 20)	Mean	24.2	37.5	30.5	8.2
	Median	18.3	29.5	27.6	7.7
	Semi-inter-quartile range	7.9 → 35.8	22.2 → 46.3	16.7 → 40.5	4.4 → 11.8
Females (N = 17)	Mean	6.1	9.2	8.9	1.3
	Median	4.2	8.8	6.6	0.8
	Semi-inter-quartile range	1.9 → 10.0	3.4 → 15.1	2.5 → 13.2	0.1 → 2.4

TABLE 3 TOTAL NUMBER OF MOUNTS DISPLAYED IN 100 DAILY OBSERVATIONS DURING THE FIRST YEAR OF LIFE

Normal males		Normal females	
Animal number	Total frequency of mounting	Animal number	Total frequency of mounting
839	19	830	0
1242	117	831	0
1243	169	1252	1
1617	44	1551	1
1620	11	1642	0
1625	4	1649	0
1636	0	1654	0
1657	5	1769	0
1658	12	1838	0
1662	1	2362	1
1954	18	2369	0
1958	28	2539	0
1960	40	2551	0
2354	4	2569	0
2356	12	2575	0
2358	2	2577	0
2359	15	2580	0
2552	8		
2555	3	Median	0
2557	25		
Median	12.0		

TABLE 4 TOTAL NUMBER OF
MOUNTS DISPLAYED IN PSEUDOHERMA-
PHRODITIC FEMALES IN 100 DAILY OB-
SERVATIONS DURING THE FIRST YEAR
OF LIFE

Animal number	Total frequency of mounting
829	20
829	7
836"	4
1239	9
1616	9
1619	22
1640	33
1656	0
Median	9.0

" Data obtained between 10½ and 16 months of age rather than
3½ to 9 months as in all other cases.

(1961) and Harlow (1965) with respect to sexual dimorphism in
play behavior of young rhesus. We have compared the frequency
of occurrence of threat, play initiation, rough-and-tumble play,
and chasing play for 20 normal males and 17 females during the
first year of life (Table 2). The mean performance level for males
in each successive block of 10 daily trials over the 100 days of
observation is clearly above that of the female. Males also show a
greater frequency of mounting behavior than do females (Table
3). This higher level of performance is maintained by males during the second year of life as well as for all the behavior items
mentioned above.

Our purpose in studying the rhesus monkey was not simply
to confirm the observation that differences in sexual behavior and
other behaviors not directly associated with reproduction existed
between male and female but to determine whether or not these
differences could be accounted for by the organizing action of
testosterone. Our observations of female pseudohermaphrodites
over the past few years substantiate our initial hypothesis. Not
only is sexual behavior, such as mounting, increased in the
female pseudohermaphrodite compared with that of untreated
female rhesus, but their play behavior also resembles that of the
genetic male rather than that of the genetic female (Table 4 and
Figure 1).

The augmentation of mounting behavior of the pseudoher-

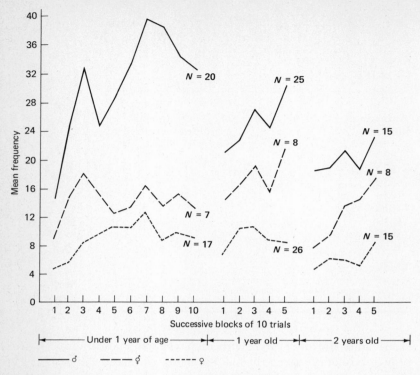

Figure 1. Frequency of rough-and-tumble play by infant and juvenile monkeys studied from 3 months of age to approximately 2½ years of age.

maphrodite compared with the normal female seems to be a specific effect of androgenic stimulation during the prenatal period of development. When large amounts of testosterone propionate are injected into each member of three pairs of adult female rhesus monkeys, mounting activity is not increased (Phoenix et al., 1967). Recently we have extended these tests of adult females by adding a fourth pair to the experiment. Our procedure, briefly, was to test compatible pairs of females by bringing them together in a neutral observation cage for 10 minutes each weekday. Following 1 or 2 weeks of such tests, the subordinate member of each pair was injected for two weeks with 5 mg of testosterone propionate daily followed by two additional weeks with 10 mg daily of the same hormone. One week later, exactly the same sequence of injections was administered to the more dominant member of the pair, and the daily observations were continued. Our analysis of the results obtained from these observations shows that dominant females mounted their partners about 0.8 times per test without androgen treatment. When they were injected with testosterone, the average frequency for these same females increased to 1.2 mounts per test, but the increase was not statistically significant. The subordinate females mounted less than once in every 10 tests prior to treatment with testosterone, and no increase was observed during treatment. The results suggest that testosterone does not augment mounting behavior in the adult female primate regardless of her dominance status in the testing situation, and the lack of effect in the adult clearly contrasts with the marked effect of prenatally administered androgen on the mounting behavior of the developing infant female pseudohermaphrodite.

We find no differences in the kind or frequency of social or sexual behavior displayed by normal males and males whose mothers were injected with testosterone propionate during pregnancy. We have not discounted the possibility, however, that differences may eventually appear.

From our work with the female pseudohermaphrodite monkey we feel reasonably certain that not only are patterns of sexual behavior determined by the presence of testosterone during development, but that other behaviors not directly associated with reproduction are also influenced by the action of androgens during the period of psychosexual differentiation.

We do not know the limits of this organizing action. It may, in fact, extend to behaviors we had not initially anticipated as being influenced by hormone action. We have suspected the frequency of display of aggression and fighting in general to be related to the presence of testosterone during psychosexual development and this indirectly to dominance. We have barely started to tease out the complex social interactions that account for dominance in a group. In other areas, too, we have just begun. For example, we are investigating the role of prenatal testosterone on what may be loosely termed parental behavior. In fact, our approach to the broad problem of the organizing action of prenatal testosterone has led us to look more closely and carefully at sex differences and similarities as they exist in the untreated population.

The simple cataloguing of sex differences is not being pursued as an end in itself. The aim rather is to investigate the array of behaviors which come under hormonal influence during the period of psychosexual differentiation. What has been found thus far in our investigations broadens our initial hypothesis such that we now suggest that testosterone not only organizes the tissues that mediate patterns of sexual behavior but many other sex-related behaviors. In this regard it is important to emphasize that the organizing actions of testosterone are not manifested on certain types of classes of behaviors independently of the species. For example, aggressiveness cannot be said to be enhanced by early treatment with androgen. In species like the monkey and the guinea pig a relationship between early androgen and aggressiveness may in fact exist, but in species like the hamster, in which the female is normally more aggressive than the male, early androgen may reduce the level and frequency of aggressive displays. Correspondingly, urinary postures which are sex-related in dogs (Martins and Valle, 1948; Berg, 1944) and other Canidae may be influenced in a male direction by early androgen, but urinary postures in general cannot be said to be susceptible to the same kind of influence. In short, androgens can be shown to act organizationally only upon those behaviors which exist as dimorphisms in the species. Those behavioral characteristics which the sexes display with equal frequency (such as huddling, grooming, withdrawing, and fear-grimacing—to mention only a few in the rhesus monkey) are not influenced in any detectable manner by the early administration of androgens.

The term "organizing action of testosterone" is used in the sense of setting a bias on a system such that differential sensitivity and responsiveness are built into the mechanism. Being ignorant of the specific body parts that constitute the control mechanisms we have referred simply to the tissues that mediate, in this instance, sexual behavior. From what is known about the role of the hypothalamus in the control of sexual behavior it is an easy step to assume that testosterone acts to organize tissues of the hypothalamus. Learning that an ovary implanted in a male rat castrated on the day of birth would ovulate and produce corpora lutea, Harris (1964) has suggested (in view of the evidence of hypothalamic control of the pituitary) that castration on the day of birth in the rat prevents masculinization of the hypothalamus, and the work of Barraclough and Gorski (1962) supports such a view. Our findings of modified play behavior in the female pseudohermaphroditic rhesus monkey suggest that other areas of the central nervous system in addition to the hypothalamus are also modified by the prenatal treatment with testosterone. It is premature to conjecture just how widespread modification of central neural tissues might be, but the neural modifications obviously have relatively extensive effects on behavior.

The phenomena with which we are dealing are broad and their implications probably not yet fully appreciated. As more investigators from more disciplines become involved with the problem, its total scope and limits will become delineated.

In describing the research that has been done, we have for the most part referred to the organizing action of *testosterone*. This was done primarily to simplify presentation. We have not established that it is testosterone per se and none of its metabolites that produces the many effects we have observed. We do not know, nor do we claim, that in the intact genetic male it is testosterone alone to the exclusion of other fetal morphogenic substances that masculinizes the nervous system controlling patterns of behavior. Those investigators familiar with hormone action are especially aware of the complex interrelationships that exist and of the need for caution in assuming that the injected material itself is producing the effect observed. This limitation does not detract from the generality of the findings, but rather suggests the need for additional research to spell out the complete and specific hormonal condition that accounts for the observed behavioral modifications.

REFERENCES

Barraclough, C. A., and R. A. Gorski. 1962. Studies on mating behaviour in the androgen-sterilized female rat in relation to the hypothalamic regulation of sexual behaviour. *J. Endocrinol.*, **25:** 175–182.

Beach, F. A., and A. M. Holz. 1946. Mating behavior in male rats castrated at various ages and injected with androgen. *J. Exptl. Zool.*, **101:** 91–142.

Berg, I. A. 1944. Development of behavior: The micturition pattern in the dog. *J. Exptl. Psychol.*, **34:** 343–368.

Dantchakoff, V. 1938. Rôle des hormones dans la manifestation des instincts sexueles. *Compt. Rend.*, **206:** 945–947.

Feder, H. H. 1967. Specificity of testosterone and estradiol in the differentiating neonatal rat. *Anat. Rec.*, **157:** 79–86.

Feder, H. H., and R. E. Whalen. 1965. Feminine behavior in neonatally castrated and estrogen-treated male rats. *Science*, **147:** 306–307.

Gerall, A. A., and I. L. Ward. 1966. Effects of prenatal exogenous androgen on the sexual behavior of the female albino rat. *J. Comp. Physiol. Psychol.*, **62:** 370–375.

Goy, R. W., W. E. Bridson, and W. C. Young. 1964. Period of maximal susceptibility of the prenatal female guinea pig to masculinizing actions of testosterone propionate. *J. Comp. Physiol. Psychol.*, **57:** 166–174.

Goy, R. W., J. C. Mitchell, and W. C. Young. 1962. Effect of testosterone propionate on O_2 consumption of female and female pseudohermaphroditic guinea pigs. *Am. Zoologist*, **2:** 525 (Abstr.).

Grady, K. L., C. H. Phoenix, and W. C. Young. 1965. Role of the developing rat testis in differentiaton of the neural tissues mediating mating behavior. *J. Comp. Physiol. Psychol.*, **59:** 176–182.

Gray, J. A., S. Levine, and P. L. Broadhurst. 1965. Gonadal hormone injections in infancy and adult emotional behavior. *Animal Behavior*, **13:** 33–43.

Harlow, H. F. 1961. The development of affectional patterns in infant monkeys. In *Determinants of Infant Behaviour* (B. M. Foss, Ed.). Wiley, New York, pp. 75–97.

Harlow, H. F. 1965. Sexual behavior in the rhesus monkey. In *Sex and Behavior* (F. A. Beach, Ed.). Wiley, New York, pp. 234–265.

Harris, G. W. 1964. Sex hormones, brain development and brain function. *Endocrinology*, **75:** 627–647.

Kennedy, G. C. 1964. Mating behaviour and spontaneous activity in androgen-sterilized female rats. *J. Physiol. (London).* **172:** 393–399.

Martins, T., and J. R. Valle. 1948. Hormonal regulation of the micturition behavior of the dog. *J. Comp. Physiol. Psychol.,* **41:** 301–311.

Neumann, F., and W. Elger. 1965. Physiological and psychical intersexuality of male rats by early treatment with an anti-androgenic agent (1,2α-methylene-6-chloro-Δ-hydroxyprogesterone-acetate). *Acta Endocrinal. Suppl.,* **100:** 174 (Abstr.).

Neumann, F., and W. Elger. 1966. Permanent changes in gonadal function and sexual behavior as a result of early feminization of male rats by treatment with an anti-androgenic steroid. *Endocrinology,* **50:** 209–225.

Phoenix, C. H., and K. L. Grady. 1964. Inhibitory effects of estradiol benzoate administered prenatally on the sexual behavior of female rats. *Anat. Rec.,* **148:** 395 (Abstr.).

Phoenix, C. H., R. W. Goy, A. A. Gerall, and W. C. Young. 1959. Organizing action of prenatally administered testosterone propionate on the tissue mediating mating behavior in the female guinea pig. *Endocrinology,* **65:** 369–382.

Phoenix, C. H., R. W. Goy, and W. C. Young. 1967. Sexual behavior: General aspects. In *Neuroendocrinology,* Vol. II (L. Martini and W. F. Ganong, eds.). Academic Press, New York, pp. 163–196.

Resko, J. A., H. H. Feder, and R. W. Goy. 1968. Androgen concentrations in plasma and testis of developing rats. *J. Endocrinol.,* **40:** 485–491.

Rosenblum, L. 1961. The development of social behavior in the rhesus monkey. Unpublished doctoral dissertation, Univ. of Wisconsin Libraries, Madison.

Swanson, H. H. 1966. Modification of sex differences in open field and emergence behaviour of hamsters by neonatal injections of testosterone propionate. *J. Endocrinol.* **34:** vi–vii.

Swanson, H. H. 1967. Alteration of sex-typical behavior of hamsters in open field and emergence by neo-natal administration of androgen or oestrogen. *Animal Behavior,* **15:** 209–216.

Tedford, M. D., and W. C. Young. 1960. Ovarian structure in guinea pigs made hemaphroditic by the administration of androgen prenatally. *Anat. Rec.,* **136:** 325 (Abstr.).

Wells, L. J., and G. van Wagenen. 1954. Androgen-induced female pseudohermaphroditism in the monkey (*Macaca mulatta*): Anatomy of the reproductive organs. *Carnegie Inst. Wash. Publ.* **235; Contribut. Embryol.,** **35:** 95–106.

Whalen, R. E. 1964. Hormone-induced changes in the organization of sexual behavior in the male rat. *J. Comp. Physiol. Psychol.,* **57:** 175–182.

Whalen, R. E., and R. D. Nadler. 1963. Suppression of the development of female mating behavior by estrogen administered in infancy. *Science,* **141:** 272–275.

Young, W. C. 1961. The hormones and mating behavior. In *Sex and Internal Secretions* (W. C. Young, Ed.). Williams & Wilkins, Baltimore, 3rd ed., pp. 1173–1239.

Young, W. C., R. W. Goy, and C.H. Phoenix. 1964. Hormones and sexual behavior. *Science,* **143:** 212–218.

Early childhood experiences and women's achievement motives

LOIS WLADIS HOFFMAN

The failure of women to fulfill their intellectual potential has been adequately documented. The explanations for this are so plentiful that one is almost tempted to ask why women achieve at all. Their social status is more contingent on whom they marry than what they achieve; their sense of femininity and others' perception of them as feminime is jeopardized by too much academic and professional success; their husband's masculinity, and hence their love relationship as well as their reciprocal sense of femininity, is threatened if they surpass him; discrimination against women in graduate school admittance and the professions puts a limit on what rewards their performance will receive; their roles as wives and mothers take time from their professional efforts and offer alternative sources of self-esteem. Perhaps most important, they have an alternative to professional success and can opt out when the going gets rough. A full-scale achievement effort involves painful periods of effort and many a man would drop out if that alternative were as readily available as it is to women. (Indeed, the Vietnam war and the new distrust of the old goals have provided young men with just such an opportunity and many have grabbed it.) But women's underachievement must have roots deeper even than these, for the precursors of the underachieving women can be seen in the female child.

Even at preschool age girls have different orientations toward intellectual tasks than do boys. Little girls want to please; they work for love and approval; if bright, they underestimate

From *The Journal of Social Issues*, 1972, **28**(2). Reprinted by permission.

their competence. Little boys show more task involvement, more confidence, and are more likely to show IQ increments. Girls have more anxiety than boys, and the anxiety they have is more dysfunctional to their performance. There are also differences in the specific skills of each sex: Males excel in spatial perceptions, arithmetical reasoning, general information, and show less set-dependency; girls excel in quick-perception of details, verbal fluency, rote memory, and clerical skills.

Boys and girls enter the world with different constitutional make-ups, and recent studies show that parents treat boys and girls differently even from birth. Social roles are first—and most impressively—communicated through parent-child relations and events in early childhood may have an impact that cannot later be duplicated in effectiveness.

As a result, interest in women's intellectual achievement has led a number of people to look to the child development data for insights. A few of the limitations of these data will be discussed first, for a number of extravagant generalizations are being drawn from them.

LIMITATIONS OF CHILD DEVELOPMENT DATA
Relativity

Child development data are often relative to a given group. Thus a statement about girls who are "high on aggression" usually means high relative to the other girls studied. If they are compared to boys who are "high on aggression" even in the same study, the actual aggressive behavior may be very different. Boys are considerably more aggressive than girls; a girl who is high on aggression may resemble a boy whose aggressive behavior is coded as average. She may also differ from the boys with respect to the form of aggression and the personality syndrome of which it is a part. It should not be surprising then to discover that the antecedent conditions of high aggression are different in boys and girls. They might very well be different even if the dependent variables were identical, but the fact is that they are not. We are comparing oranges with apples and discovering to our surprise that they grow on different trees.

This problem not only applies to the dependent variables, but also to the independent variables studied, usually parent behavior or the parent-child relationship. To use an actual finding, Kagan and Moss (1962) found that maternal protectiveness during the first three years was negatively related to adult achievement behavior for girls. This was not true for boys and in fact the relationship was positive although not statistically significant. This is an important finding to which we will return, but here it should be pointed out that we cannot tell from these correlations whether or not the actual maternal behavior is different for high-achieving boys and girls. Girls are subject to more overprotection than boys, and the same amount of protective behavior may be relatively low for a girl but average or high for a boy.

Baumrind (1970) has pointed out that obtaining data on the differential treatment (or behavior) of boys and girls is difficult because, even in behavioral observations, when the observer knows the sex of the child, "an automatic adjustment is made which tends to standardize judgments about the two sexes."

Generalizability

The problem of generalizing results obtained with one population to another occurs throughout the social sciences. It is particularly acute when the variables involve relative terms. "High parental coerciveness" in a middle-class sample may not be considered high in a lower-class sample. Furthermore, most empirical generalizations hold only within certain contexts. Variations in social class, parent education, rural-urban residence, family structure, and ethnicity—as well as changes over time—may make the generalizations inapplicable.

As an interesting case in point, it is impossible to generalize white sex differences to blacks, for the patterns of sex differences are very different in the two groups. Studies of blacks will be important in interpreting the etiology of sex differences in intellectual performance, for in many ways the black male resembles the white female. For both, school performance has been largely irrelevant to adult goals and there are interesting similarities in the patterns of achievement scores that may reflect this (Tulkin, 1968; Jensen, 1970). In a study of conformity and perceptual judgments by Iscoe, Williams, and Harvey (1964), black males and white females were more influenced by others than were black females and white males. Similarities between black males and white females argue against constitutional explanations, for these two groups share neither hormones nor race—but they do share environmental handicaps.

Maturation

Another difficulty in interpreting sex differences among children pertains to differences in the maturity of boys and girls. The newborn girl is one month to six weeks developmentally ahead of the boy. At school entrance she is about one year ahead, depending on the index of growth used. Growth does not proceed equally on all fronts and the intellectual growth rate is not related to the physical (Bayley, 1956). These different degrees of maturity complicate the comparison between the sexes.

Conceptualization

Ambiguous concepts are a problem in many fields. The so-called inconsistencies in the child development data often upon close examination turn out to be inconsistencies in the researcher's summaries and concluding statements rather than in the actual findings. If examined in terms of the operational definitions, contradictory studies sometimes turn out to be dealing with different phenomena that have been given the same label. Among the particularly troublesome concepts that are important in the sex-difference literature are identification and dependency (Bronfenbrenner, 1960; Maccoby and Masters, 1970).

FEMALE ACHIEVEMENT ORIENTATIONS

There are very few studies that have empirically connected socialization experiences to sex differences in achievement orientations. As a matter of fact, there are few studies of sex differences in childrearing practices in general, and existing data—most of which were originally collected for other purposes—are subject to the limitations mentioned above. Promising new approaches sensitive to identifying sex differences may be found in the studies of parent-child interaction with neonates (Moss, 1967; Moss and Robson, 1968; Moss, Robson, and Pedersen, 1969; Lewis, 1969; Goldberg and Lewis, 1969; Kagan, 1969; Kagan, Levine, and Fishman, 1967). These are mainly longitudinal studies which will make their most valuable contributions in the future, but some have already examined relationships between maternal behavior and cognitive orientations.

Probably the richest current area in the study of sex differences has to do with cognitive styles. Witkin, Dyk, Faterson, Goodenough, and Karp (1962) as well as other investigators have been interested in differences in perceptions of and approaches to problems. For example, some people are more affected by background stimuli than others. In a task in which the subject is asked to line up a rod until it is perpendicular, the fact that the frame around the rod is tilted will affect the judgment of some respondents more than others. Those most affected by the tilting frame are said to be field dependent. This body of research has revealed a number of personality traits that are associated with performance on the task, and a number of cognitive skills such as mathematical ability that seem to be closely tied to field independence. These personality traits describe differences between the sexes; the corresponding cognitive abilities similarly differentiate.

For example, Maccoby (1963, 1966)[1] has pointed out that girls are more conforming, suggestible, and dependent upon the opinions of others. These traits in turn have been related to field dependency, inability to break the set of a task, and IQ's that tend to decrease rather than increase over the years. She suggests that these same traits in females might also account for their superior performance on spelling and vocabulary tests, and their inferior performance on tests involving analytic thinking, spatial ability, and arithmetic reasoning. Additional discussion on this issue can be found in Kagan (1964), Sherman (1967), Silverman (1970), and Kagan and Kogan (1970).

The actual linkage between these personality traits and the cognitive styles has not been established, nor has the etiology of sex differences in personality. Some of the infancy studies mentioned above are making inroads. Thus the finding that mothers spend more time in face-to-face verbalizations with infant girls (Kagan, 1969; Moss, 1967; Goldberg and Lewis, 1969) may be tied to the observation that female infants are more verbally responsive and to the later superiority of females in verbal ability. Verbal responsiveness may also result from the fact that girls' hearing is superior to that of boys (Garai and Scheinfeld, 1968). Also relevant is a study with 10-year-olds in which observations of mother–daughter interaction in task solving showed that girls good in math or spatial relations were left to solve tasks by themselves while the mothers of girls higher on verbal skills (the more typical female pattern) were more intrusive with help, suggestions, and criticism (Bing, 1963).

The present paper will focus on an area that is even less explored: the question of motivation for top intellectual performance. There are data that the very brightest women more often than comparable men stop short of operating at their top intellectual level. Terman and Oden (1947) have shown that gifted girls did not as adults fulfill their potential as often as gifted boys. Rossi (1965a, 1965b) has summarized data indicating that even those few women who do go into science and the professions rarely achieve eminence.[2]

---

[1] These reviews by Maccoby and reviews by Kagan (1964), Becker (1964), Glidewell, Kantor, Smith, and Stringer (1966), Oetzel (1966), Garai and Scheinfeld (1968), Silverman (1970), Kagan and Kogan (1970), and Bardwick (1971) will be referred to throughout the paper where a point is supported by several studies that are adequately reported in the review.

[2] Simon, Clark, and Galway (1970), on the other hand, have reported that the woman PhD who is employed full time publishes as much as her male colleagues.

These data reflect in part the factors mentioned earlier—alternative choices in life that have been available to women but not to men, barriers to career opportunities that exist because of women's family roles, and discrimination in the professions which limits the rewards obtainable. The concern here is not with these factors, however, but with a deeper, more psychologically based motivation that occurs in women. The most relevant data come from the work of Horner (1968, 1972) who has demonstrated with a projective story completion measure a "fear of success" among able college women. Furthermore, women who indicate fear of success show poorer performance in a competitive task than when the same task is performed alone. In interpreting her results, Horner suggests that this fear exists in women because their anticipation of success is accompanied by the anticipation of negative consequences in the form of social rejection or loss of femininity.

The idea that the affiliative motive can be dysfunctional to performance is supported by another of Horner's findings. Men who were motivated both to achieve and to affiliate showed a performance decrement when asked to compete with another man. Horner suggests this decrement may have resulted for a conflict of motives since "out-performing a competitor may be antagonistic to making him a friend."

AFFILIATIVE NEEDS AND ACHIEVEMENT

There is a great deal of evidence that females have greater affiliative needs than males (Oetzel, 1966; Walberg, 1969) and therefore the conflict between affiliation and achievement probably will occur more often for women. It seems that, apart from direct concerns with whether or not their behavior is sufficiently "feminine," academic and professional women frequently allow their concern with affective relationships to interfere with the full use of their cognitive capacities. In group discussion and in intellectual argument, women often seem to sacrifice brilliance for rapport.

However, while the findings of the Horner studies (1972) and our observations of professional women focus attention on the dysfunctions of affiliative motivations for performance, there are data indicating that the desire for love and approval can also have a positive effect. In fact, the Crandalls (V. J. Crandall, 1963; V. C. Crandall, 1964) as well as others (Garai and Scheinfeld, 1968) have suggested that achievement behavior in girls is motivated not by mastery strivings as with boys, but by affiliative motives.

In two very different studies, nursery school and elementary school girls' achievement efforts were motivated by a desire for social approval to a greater extent than were boys'. In the nursery school study the attempt was also made to motivate the children by appeals to mastery strivings; this technique succeeded with boys but failed with girls (Lahtinen, 1964). In the study with elementary school children, achievement motives in boys were related positively to achievement test scores. Among the girls, affiliative motives, not achievement motives, were so related (Sears, 1962, 1963). Other studies with nursery school and elementary school children found affiliative behavior and achievement efforts positively related in girls, but boys showed no such relationship (Tyler, Rafferty, and Tyler, 1962; Crandall, Dewey, Katkovsky, and Preston, 1964). Similarly with adult women, the achievement arousal techniques that are effective with males have failed with females (Veroff, Wilcox, and Atkinson, 1953; Horner, 1968), but appeals to social acceptability have been successful (Field, 1951).

There are also several studies that indicate that throughout grade school boys are more motivated than girls to master challenging tasks when social approval is not involved. When given the opportunity to perform an easy or more difficult task, to work on a puzzle they had already solved or one they had failed, to pursue further or escape a difficult problem, boys are more likely to choose the more difficult and challenging, girls to choose the task that promises easy success or to leave the scene (Crandall and Rabson, 1960; Moriarty, 1961; McManis, 1965; Veroff, 1969).

From these studies it appears that female achievement behavior even at preschool or early grade school ages is motivated by a desire for love rather than mastery. When achievement goals conflict with affiliative goals, as was the case in Horner's projective responses and in the competitive situation in which her fear-of-success girls showed less competent performance, achievement behavior will be diminished and/or anxiety results. This does not mean that academic performance is lower for females in general since it is often compatible with affiliative motives. In elementary schools, excellence is rewarded with love and approval by parents, teachers, and peers. Even in the lower socioeconomic class, sociometric studies show that academic excellence in girls is rewarded with popularity (Glidewell et al., 1966; Pope, 1953). In college, however, and in professional pursuits, love is less frequently the reward for top performance. Driving a point home, winning an argument, beating others in competition, and attending to the task at hand without being side-tracked by concern with rapport require the subordination of affiliative needs.

In short, the qualities needed for sustained top performance—especially as an adult—are not typically part of a girl's
make-up. She wants approval and so she performs well in school.
She works for good grades. And indeed throughout grammar
school, high school, and college, she obtains higher grades
than boys (Oetzel, 1966; Garai and Scheinfeld, 1968). If over-
achievement is thought of as grades exceeding IQ's, then girls
as a group are more overachieving than boys. But girls are less
likely to become involved in their task; they are less motivated
by strivings for mastery. In McClelland's sense of *achievement*
(McClelland, Atkinson, Clark, and Lowell, 1953)—competition
with a standard of excellence—they fall short.[3]

This affiliative need may be particularly germane to
achievement patterns because it may be rooted in early experiences when the child is learning patterns of effectance. When
little boys are expanding their mastery strivings, learning instrumental independence, developing skills in coping with their
environment and confidence in this ability, little girls are learning that effectiveness—and even safety—lie in their affectional
relationships. The idea expressed by Kagan (1964) that boys try to
"figure the task" and girls try to "figure the teacher" seems
rooted in early childrearing practices and reinforced by later
experiences.

STATEMENT OF THEORY
It is the thesis here that the female child is given inadequate
parental encouragement in early independence strivings. Furthermore, the separation of the self from the mother is more delayed or incomplete for the girl because she is the same sex with
the same sex-role expectations, and because girls have fewer
conflicts with their parents. As a result, she does not develop
confidence in her ability to cope independently with the environment. She retains her infantile fears of abandonment; safety
and effectiveness lie in her affective ties. These points will now
be elaborated and supportive data brought in where available.

The Development of Independence,
Competence, and Self-Confidence
All infants are dependent; as the child matures, his independence strivings increase. Observers have often been im-

---

[3] Women have obtained scores on McClelland's test of achievement motivation under neutral conditions that are as high or higher than those obtained by
men under arousal conditions; however, researchers have questioned the validity
of the measure for women (see McClelland et al., 1953; and Horner, 1968).

pressed with what White (1960) calls the *effectance motive*—the child's need to have an effect upon his environment. Thus the child grasps and releases, reaches and pulls, and in the course of doing this he learns about his environment and his ability to manipulate it. He develops cognitive abilities, and he develops a sense of effectiveness—a sense of competence through increasingly successful interaction with his environment.

As the infant matures, the feats he undertakes get scarier. Increasingly they involve separating the self from the mother and leaving the security of that unity. Early independence explorations seem to take place most successfully with the parent present; the child moves toward independence so long as the "safety man" is in sight. As he gains confidence, the parent's presence becomes less and less necessary.

Very likely this period—somewhere between a year and three or four years of age—is critical in the development of independence and competence (Erikson, 1959; Veroff, 1969; White, 1960; Stendler, 1963). By critical, we mean a period when independence and competence orientations are more efficiently learned than at other times. There is a rapid building up of notions about the self and about the world.

Although theories differ as to the exact timing and differential importance of the events occurring in this period, all would probably agree on the minimal requirements for the development of independence and competence. Thus if the infant is deprived of affection, rejected, or prematurely pushed toward independence, he will not have a secure base from which to build true independence. The dependency that results from a short shrift in early affective ties is probably of a distinct kind (Stendler, 1963). We do not think it is more characteristic of girls, nor that it is sufficiently common to the nonpathogenic middle-class family to be useful in understanding prevalent female achievement orientations.

Even with an adequate affective base, independent behavior does not happen automatically. It requires not only opportunities for independent behavior but also actual parental encouragement. Evidence for this can be found in Baumrind's research (Baumrind and Black, 1967; Baumrind, 1971) which indicates that competence comes not from permissiveness but from guidance and encouragement. The first steps a child takes are exciting but also frightening, and cues from the mother can greatly influence the subsequent behavior. The mother's delight is part of her independence training; her apprehension constitutes training in dependence.

Further, if the child's early independence behaviors are to

be followed by more, these ventures must be reasonably in accord with his abilities. Repeated successes such as these will have the important effect of developing in the child a sense of competence. There may be a delicate timing mechanism—premature independence can backfire; but the parent who withholds independence opportunities too long and indeed does not encourage independent behavior will also fail to produce an independent child. (It is possible that the appropriate timing is different for boys than girls due to differences in abilities and maturation rates.)

The awareness that the mother is a separate person whose wishes are not the same as his serves to increase the child's striving for autonomy and independence. Both Erikson and White see the period between one and three as the battle for autonomy. At this age the child's motoric explorations often require parental interference. The span of consecutive action is such that interference can be frustrating for the child and completions gratifying. Toilet training usually occurs around this time. The child thus enters into conflict with his mother; out of this conflict, if it does not involve his humiliation and defeat, the child will emerge with "a lasting sense of autonomy and pride" (Erikson, 1959) and "a measure of confidence in his own strength" (White, 1960).

THE EMPIRICAL FINDINGS
Independence Training: Sex Differences

Early exploratory behaviors in which the child interacts effectively with his environment are seen here as crucial in building up a sense of competence. In this respect males have a number of advantages.

Infant studies.   Studies of neonates suggest a higher activity level on the part of the male, while females demonstrate greater tactile sensitivity and a lower pain threshold (Garai and Scheinfeld, 1968). From these predispositions alone we could expect more exploratory behavior on the part of male infants, but to compound the matter observations of mothers with neonates show that even controlling for the differences in activity levels, mothers handle and stimulate males more than females (Moss, 1967, undated). And a study by Rubenstein (1967) suggests that such maternal attentiveness facilitates exploratory behavior.

Kagan and Lewis and their associates have also reported differences in maternal behavior toward male and female infants (Kagan, Levine, and Fishman, 1967; Goldberg and Lewis, 1969). Whether the maternal behavior is primarily a response to infant predispositions or a cause of the differences is not definitely established, but there is some evidence that both influences occur. That maternal behavior is not entirely a response to the infant is indicated by relationships found between the mother's infant care and her orientations prior to the child's birth. For example, Moss (1967) reports that mothers were interviewed two years before they gave birth and rated on their attitudes toward babies. A positive attitude toward babies was found to relate significantly to the amount of responsiveness later shown to her 3-week-old infant. This same investigator also found mutual visual regard—one of the earliest forms of mother-infant communication—to be related to maternal attitudes expressed before the birth (Moss and Robson, 1968). On the other hand, that maternal behavior is not the sole determinant of the infant's behavior is indicated by the fact that the sex differences in tactile stimulation and pain thresholds mentioned above have been established for infants less than four days old and still in the hospital nursery (Garai and Scheinfeld, 1968; Silverman, 1970). An interaction hypothesis seems most tenable in the light of the present data.

One of Moss's mother-infant interaction findings is particularly pertinent to the theory presented in this paper (1967, undated). He reports data on the mother's responsiveness to the infant's cries and notes that this sequence—baby cries and mother responds with the needed care—is important in shaping the infant's response to the mother as a supplier of comfort. The more closely the mother's caretaking behavior is related to the infant's cries, the more effectively will the child "regard the mother as having reinforcing properties and respond to her accordingly" (Moss, undated, p. 10). The correlation obtained between maternal contact and infant irritability was statistically significant for females but not for males. The mothers did not attend to the female infants more than the male (less, in fact) but their attention was more closely linked to the infant's state of need as expressed by crying. This finding if borne out by further research could be very important for several reasons. First, it could signify the beginning of a pattern of interaction between mothers and daughters in which the daughters quickly learn that the mother is a source of comfort; and the mother's behavior is reinforced by the cessation of crying. The sheer presence of the mother would soon signal the satisfaction of the infant's needs. Second, there is agreement among most investigators that there are critical periods in infancy when learning takes place so efficiently that long-range behaviors are effected by simple but pertinently timed events; this might be such a critical period. Third, even if this is not a critical period, the finding may reflect an orientation of mothers toward daughters that is often repeated beyond the infancy period.

In any case, one thing appears certain from this body of research on early mother-infant interaction: There are sex differences in both maternal and infant behavior during the first year of life. That sex-role learning is begun so early should not be surprising. Sex is a primary status—the first one announced at birth. The mother is very much aware of it. Her early behaviors toward the infant are not deliberate efforts to teach the child his proper sex role, but she has internalized society's view and acts accordingly. She acts toward her son as though he were sturdy and active and she is more likely to show pleasure when his behavior fits this image. Her daughter is her doll—sweet and delicate and pink. The mother's behavior reflects this perception, and if the child exhibits behavior consistent with the female stereotype, such as dependency, she is not as likely to discourage it as she would with a son.

Independence training in childhood. Moving from early infancy, we find studies that link independence training and the parent's achievement orientations to the child's competence (Baumrind and Black, 1967) and achievement orientations (Winterbottom, 1958; Rosen and D'Andrade, 1959), but few examining sex differences in the independence and achievement training children receive. It is our view that because of parental attitudes toward male and female children which reflect their culturally assigned roles, males receive more effective independence training and encouragement.

An adaptation of the Winterbottom measure for use with parents of younger children was developed by Torgoff (1958). Using this measure, Collard (1964) asked mothers of 4-year-olds to indicate the ages they thought parents should expect or permit certain child behaviors. For example, the parents were asked at what age they believed parents should: (a) begin to allow their child to use sharp scissors with *no* adult supervision, (b) begin to allow their child to play away from home for long periods of time during the day without first telling his parents where he will be. The answers to these questions yielded two measures— *independence granting* and *achievement induction.* Mothers of girls responded with later ages than mothers of boys. This difference was significant for the independence-granting items and it was particularly strong in the middle class. The achievement induction scores were not significantly different for the two sexes, but close inspection of the data revealed that, for the middle class, mothers of girls indicated an earlier age for only two of the

18 items making up the scale. One of the two exceptions was "sharing toys" which may have more to do with interpersonal relationships than with achievement.

Parental anxiety and protectiveness. Still another difference in the independence training received by boys and girls may stem from parental ambivalence: Parents may show more unambivalent pleasure in sons' achievements than in daughters'. The young child's first motoric adventures can produce anxiety in the mother as well as the child, just as they produce pleasure for both. It seems likely that for the parent of a boy there is a particular pride in the achievement and less of a feeling of the child's fragility; as a result, there is a clearer communication of pleasure in the achievement per se. A beaming mother when the child takes his first steps may have a very different effect than the mother who looks anxious while holding out loving arms. In the former case, the task itself becomes the source of pleasure (in reinforcement terms the reward is closer to the act). In the latter case, the mother is saying in effect, "You may break your neck en route, but I will give you love when you get here." The mother's indications of anxiety as the child moves toward independence make the child doubt his own competence, for mothers are still omniscient to the young child.

There is some indirect evidence for this view. Despite the greater maturity and sturdiness of the female infant (Garai and Scheinfeld, 1968), parents think of them as more fragile. Furthermore, behavioral observations of infants have shown that male infants are handled more vigorously (Moss, 1967). The setting of later ages for granting autonomy to girls, as indicated in the Collard (1964) study mentioned earlier, suggests that parents are more protective, if not more anxious, toward girls. For example, parents report allowing boys to cross busy streets by themselves earlier, though they are not motorically more advanced than girls and their greater motoric impulsivity would seem to make this more dangerous. And we do know that infants pick up the subtle attitudes of their caretakers. This was demonstrated in the well-known study of Escalona (1945) in which the infant's preference for orange or tomato juice depended heavily on the preference of the nurse who regularly fed him. The infant had no way of knowing his nurse's preference except through sensing her attitude as she fed him.

Another kind of parent behavior that is detrimental to the development of independence might be called *over-help*. Mastery requires the ability to tolerate frustration. If the parent responds too quickly with aid, the child will not develop such tolerance. This shortcoming—the tendency to withdraw from a difficult task rather than to tackle the problem and tolerate the temporary frustration—seems to characterize females more than males. This has been demonstrated in the test situations mentioned earlier, and Crandall and Rabson (1960) have also found that, in free play, grade school girls are more likely than boys to withdraw from threatening situations and more frequently to seek help from adults and peers. The dysfunctions of this response for the development of skills and a sense of competence are clear. There are no data to indicate that over-help behavior is more characteristic of parents of girls, but such a difference seems likely in view of the greater emphasis placed on the independence training of boys.

Clearly more research is needed to identify differences in the independence and achievement training—and in any over-protection and over-help—that parents provide boys and girls. Even if the differences we have described are definitely established, it will still need to be shown that this pattern of parental protectiveness and insufficient independence training is a major contributor to an inadequate sense of personal competence in girls. It should be pointed out, however, that this inference is consistent with the findings that girls are more anxious than boys, more likely to underestimate their abilities, and more apt to lack confidence in their own judgment when it is contrary to that of others (Sarason, 1963; Sarason and Harmatz, 1965; Sears, 1964; Crandall, Katkovsky, and Preston, 1962; Hamm and Hoving, 1969). There is also evidence that the above pattern is reinforced by the later socialization experiences of girls. Several investigators report that while dependency in boys is discouraged by parents, teachers, peers, and the mass media, it is more acceptable in girls (Kagan and Moss, 1962; Kagan, 1964; Sears, Rau, and Alpert, 1965). Data from the Fels study (Kagan and Moss, 1962) are particularly interesting in this respect, reporting that childhood dependency predicted to adult dependency for females but not males, the converse being true for aggression. Their interpretation is that pressure is exerted on the child to inhibit behaviors that are not congruent with sex-role standards (Kagan, 1964).

Establishing A Separate Self: Sex Differences

Same-sex parent as primary caretaker.   Separation of the self is facilitated when the child is the opposite sex of the primary caretaker. Parson (1949, 1965) and Lynn (1962, 1969), as well as others, have pointed out that both males and females form their first attachment to the mother. The girl's modeling of the mother and maintaining an identity with her is consistent with her own sex role, but the boy must be trained to identify with his father or to learn some abstract concept of the male role. As a result, the boy's separation from the mother is encouraged; it begins earlier and is more complete. The girl, on the other hand, is encouraged to maintain her identification with the mother; therefore she is not as likely to establish an early and independent sense of self. If the early experiences of coping with the environment independently are crucial in the development of competence and self-confidence, as suggested previously, the delayed and possibly incomplete emergence of the self should mitigate against this development.

There are no studies that directly test this hypothesis. As indirect evidence, however, there are several studies showing that the more identified with her mother and the more feminine the girl is, the less likely she is to be a high achiever and to excel in mathematics, analytic skills, creativity, and game strategies. For example, Plank and Plank (1954) found that outstanding women mathematicians were more attached to and identified with their fathers than their mothers. Bieri (1960) found that females higher on analytical ability also tended to identify with their fathers. Higher masculinity scores for girls are related positively to various achievement measures (Oetzel, 1961; Milton, 1957; Kagan and Kogan, 1970), as are specific masculine traits such as aggressiveness (Sutton-Smith, Crandall, and Roberts, 1964; Kagan and Moss, 1962). The relation between cross-sex identification and cognitive style for both boys and girls is discussed also by Maccoby (1966).

For several reasons the above studies provide only limited support for our view. First, there is some evidence, though less consistent, that "overly masculine" males, like "overly feminine" females, are lower on various achievement-related measures (Maccoby, 1966; Kagan and Kogan, 1970). Second, the definitions and measures of femininity may have a built-in anti-achievement bias. Third, the question of the mother's actual characteristics has been ignored; thus the significant factor may not be closeness to the mother and insufficient sense of self, as here proposed. The significant factor may be identifying with a mother who is herself passive and dependent. If the mother were a mathematician, would the daughter's close identification be dysfunctional to top achievement?

Clearly the available data are inadequate and further research is needed to assess the importance of having the same sex as the primary caretaker for personality and cognitive development.

Parent-child conflict. Establishing the self as separate from the mother is also easier for boys because they have more conflict with the mother than do girls. Studies of neonates suggest, as mentioned above, that males are more motorically active; this has also been observed with older children (Garai and Scheinfeld, 1968; Moss, 1967; Goldberg and Lewis, 1969). Furthermore, sex differences in aggressive behavior are solidly established (Oetzel, 1966; Kagan, 1964), and there is some evidence that this is constitutionally based (Bardwick, 1971). Because of these differences, the boy's behavior is more likely to bring him into conflict with parental authority. Boys are disciplined more often than girls, and this discipline is more likely to be of a power-assertive kind (Becker, 1964; Sears, Maccoby, and Levin, 1957; Heinstein, 1965). These encounters facilitate a separation of the self from the parent. (While extremely severe discipline might have a very different effect, this is not common in the middle class.)

One implication of this is that girls need a little maternal rejection if they are to become independently competent and self-confident. And indeed a generalization that occurs in most recent reviews is that high-achieving females had hostile mothers while high-achieving males had warm ones (Bardwick, 1971; Garai and Scheinfeld, 1968; Maccoby, 1966; Silverman, 1970). This generalization is based primarily on the findings of the Fels longitudinal study (Kagan and Moss, 1962). In this study "maternal hostility" toward the child during his first three years was related positively to the adult achievement behavior of girls and negatively to the adult achievement behavior of boys. Maternal protection, on the other hand, as mentioned earlier, related negatively to girl's achievement and positively to boy's.

In discussions of these findings "maternal hostility" is often equated with rejection. There is reason to believe, however, that it may simply be the absence of "smother love." First, the sample of cooperating families in the Fels study is not likely to include extremely rejecting parents. These were primarily middle-class parents who cooperated with a child development study for 25 years. They were enrolled in the study when the mother was pregnant, and over the years they tolerated frequent home visits, each lasting from 3 to 4 hours, as well as behavioral observations of their children in nursery school and camp. Second, we have already pointed out that what is "high hostility" toward girls, might not be so labeled if the same behavior were expressed toward boys. It is interesting to note in this connection that "high hostility" toward girls during these early years is related positively to "acceleration" (i.e., the tendency to push the child's cognitive and motoric development) and negatively to maternal protectiveness. Neither of these relationships is significant for the boys (Kagan and Moss, 1962, p. 207). Further, the mothers who were "hostile" to their daughters were better educated than the "nonhostile." In addition to being achievers, the daughters were "less likely to withdraw from stressful situations" as adults. The authors themselves suggest that the latter "may reflect the mother's early pressure for independence and autonomy" (p. 213).

Our interpretation of these findings then is that many girls experience too much maternal rapport and protection during their early years. Because of this they find themselves as adults unwilling (or unable) to face stress and with inadequate motivation for autonomous achievement. It is significant that the relationships described are strongest when the early years are compared to the adult behavior. Possibly the eagerness to please adults sometimes passes as achievement or maturity during the childhood years.

While excessive rapport between mother and son occurs, it is less common and usually of a different nature. The achievement of boys may be in greater danger from too much conflict with parents—there being little likelihood of too little.

The danger for girls of too much maternal nurturance has been pointed out by Bronfenbrenner (1961a, 1961b) and is consistent with data reported by Crandall, Dewey, Katkovsky, and Preston (1964). The finding that girls who are more impulsive than average have more analytic thinking styles while the reverse pattern holds for boys also fits this interpretation (Sigel, 1965; Kagan, Rosman, Day, Phillips, and Phillips, 1964). That is, impulsive girls may be brought into more conflict with their mothers, as in the typical pattern for boys. Maccoby (1966) has suggested that the actual relationship between impulsivity and analytic thinking is curvilinear: The extreme impulsivity that characterizes the very impulsive boys is dysfunctional, but the high impulsivity of the girls falls within the optimal range. In our view, the optimal range is enough to insure some conflict in the mother-child relationship but not so much as to interfere with the child's effective performance.

Inadequate Self-Confidence and Dependence On Others

Since the little girl has (a) less encouragement for independence, (b) more parental protectiveness, (c) less cognitive and social pressure for establishing an identity separate from the mother, and (d) less mother–child conflict which highlights this separation, she engages in less independent exploration of her environment. As a result, she does not develop skills in coping with her environment nor confidence in her ability to do so. She continues to be dependent upon adults for solving her prolems and because of this she needs her affective ties with adults. Her mother is not an unvarying supply of love but is sometimes angry, disapproving, or unavailable. If the child's own resources are insufficient, being on her own is frustrating and frightening. Fears of abandonment are very common in infants and young children even when the danger is remote. Involvement in mastery explorations and the increasing competence and confidence that results can help alleviate these fears, but for girls they may continue even into adulthood. The anticipation of being alone and unloved then may have a particularly desperate quality in women. The hypothesis we propose is that the all-pervasive affiliative need in women results from this syndrome.

Thus boys learn effectance through mastery, but girls are effective through eliciting the help and protection of others. The situations that evoke anxiety in each sex should be different and their motives should be different.

The theoretical view presented in this paper is speculative but it appears to be consistent with the data. In the preceding sections we have reviewed the research on sex differences in early socialization experiences. The theory would also lead us to expect that owing to these differences females would show less self-confidence and more instrumental dependency than males.

The data on dependency are somewhat unclear largely because the concept has been defined differently in different studies. These findings have been summarized by Kagan (1964), Oetzel (1966), Garai and Scheinfeld (1968), and the concept of dependency has been discussed by Maccoby and Masters (1970). The balance of the evidence is that females are more dependent, at least as we are using the concept here, and this difference appears early and continues into maturity. Goldberg and Lewis (1969) report sex differences in dependency among 1-year-olds, but Crandall and his associates (Crandall, Preston, and Rabson, 1960; Crandall and Rabson, 1960) found such differences only among elementary school children and not among preschoolers. It should be noted, however, that even differences that do not show up until later can have their roots in early experiences. For example, independence training at a later age may require a sense of competence based on early successes if it is to be effective.

The findings on self-confidence show that girls, and particularly the bright ones, underestimate their own ability. When asked to anticipate their performance on new tasks or on repetition tasks, they give lower estimates than boys and lower estimates than their performance indicates (Brandt, 1958; Sears, 1964; Crandall, Katkovsky, and Preston, 1962; Crandall, 1968). The studies that show the girls' greater suggestibility and tendency to switch perceptual judgments when faced with discrepant opinions are also consistent with their having less self-confidence (Iscoe, Williams, and Harvey, 1963; Allen and Crutchfield, 1963; Nakamura, 1958; Hamm and Hoving, 1969; Stein and Smithells, 1969).[4] Boys set higher standards for themselves (Walter and Marzolf, 1951). As mentioned earlier, difficult tasks are seen as challenging to males, whereas females seek to avoid them (Veroff, 1969; Crandall and Rabson, 1960; Moriarty, 1961; McManis, 1965). Thus the research suggests that girls lack confidence in their own abilities and seek effectance through others (Crandall and Rabson, 1960). Affective relationships under these conditions would indeed be paramount.

The findings indicating that this is the case—that affective relationships are paramount in females—were summarized earlier in this paper. The data suggest that they have affiliative needs and that achievement behavior is motivated by a desire to please. If their achievement behavior comes into conflict with affiliation, achievement is likely to be sacrificed or anxiety may result.

IMPLICATIONS

If further research provides support for the present developmental speculations, many questions will still need answering before child-rearing patterns used with girls can be totally condemned. Even from the standpoint of achievement behavior, I would caution that this paper has only dealt with the upper end of the achievement curve. Indices of female performance, like the female IQ scores, cluster closer to the mean and do not show the extremes in either direction that the male indices show. The same qualities that may interfere with top performance at the highest achievement levels seem to have the effect of making the girls conscientious students in the lower grades. Is it possible for the educational system to use the positive motivations of girls to help them more fully develop their intellectual capacities rather than to train them in obedient learning? The educational system that rewards conformity and discourages divergent thinking might be examined for its role in the pattern we have described.

---

[4] Girls do not conform more to peer standards which conflict with adult norms (Douvan and Adelson, 1966), even though they conform more when group pressure is in opposition to their own perceptual judgments.

Although childrearing patterns that fail to produce a competent and self-confident child are obviously undesirable, it may be that boys are often prematurely pushed into independence. Because this paper has focused on achievement orientations, it may seem that I have set up the male pattern as ideal. This is not at all intended. The ability to suppress other aspects of the situation in striving for mastery is not necessarily a prerequisite for mental health or a healthy society. The more diffuse achievement needs of women may make for greater flexibility in responding to the various possibilities that life offers at different stages in the life cycle. A richer life may be available to women because they do not single-mindedly pursue academic or professional goals. And from a social standpoint, a preoccupation with achievement goals can blot out consideration of the effect of one's work on the welfare of others and its meaning in the larger social scheme.

A loss in intellectual excellence due to excessive affiliative needs, then, might seem a small price to pay if the alternative is a single-minded striving for mastery. But the present hypothesis suggests that women's affiliative needs are, at least in part, based on an insufficient sense of competence and as such they may have a compelling neurotic quality. While I have not made the very high achievement needs more characteristic of males the focus of this paper, they too may have an unhealthy base. By unraveling the childhood events that lead to these divergent orientations we may gain insights that will help both sexes develop their capacities for love and achievement.

REFERENCES

Allen, V. L., and Crutchfield, R. S. Generalization of experimentally reinforced conformity. *Journal of Abnormal and Social Psychology*, 1963, **67**, 326–333.

Bardwick, J. M. *The psychology of women: A study of biosocial conflict.* New York: Harper & Row, 1971.

Baumrind, D. Socialization and instrumental competence in young children. *Young Children,* December 1970, 9–12.

Baumrind, D. Current patterns of parental authority. *Developmental Psychology Monograph*, 1971, 4 (1, Pt. 2).

Baumrind, D., and Black, A. E. Socialization practices associated with dimensions of competence in preschool boys and girls. *Child Development,* 1967, **38**, 291–327.

Bayley, N. Growth curves of height and weight by age for boys and girls, scaled according to physical maturity. *Journal of Pediatrics,* 1956, **48**, 187–194.

Bayley, N. Developmental problems of the mentally retarded child. In I. Phillips (Ed.), *Prevention and treatment of mental retardation.* New York: Basic Books, 1966.

Becker, W. Consequences of different kinds of parental discipline. In

M. L. Hoffman and L. W. Hoffman (Eds.), *Review of child development research*. Vol. 1. New York: Russell Sage, 1964.

Bieri, J. Parental identification, acceptance of authority and within-sex differences in cognitive behavior. *Journal of Abnormal and Social Psychology*, 1960, **60**, 76–79.

Bing, E. Effect of childrearing practices on development of differential cognitive abilities. *Child Development*, 1963, **34**, 631–648.

Brandt, R. M. The accuracy of self-estimate: A measure of self concept. *Genetic Psychology Monographs*, 1958, **58**, 55–99.

Bronfenbrenner, U. Freudian theories of identification and their derivatives. *Child Development*, 1960, **31**, 15–40.

Bronfenbrenner, U. Some familial antecedents of responsibility and leadership in adolescents. In L. Petrullo and B. M. Bass (Eds.), *Leadership and interpresonal behavior*. New York: Holt, Rinehart and Winston, 1961a.

Bronfenbrenner, U. Toward a theoretical model for the analysis of parent–child relationships in a social context. In J. Glidewell (Ed.), *Parent attitudes and child behavior*. Springfield, Illinois: Thomas, 1961b.

Coleman, J. S. *The adolescent society*. Glencoe, Illinois: Free Press, 1961.

Collard, E. D. Achievement motive in the four-year-old child and its relationship to achievement expectancies of the mother. Unpublished doctoral dissertation, University of Michigan, 1964.

Crandall, V. C. Achievement behavior in young children. *Young Children*, 1964, **20**, 77–90.

Crandall, V. C. Sex differences in expectancy of intellectual and academic reinforcement. In C. P. Smith (Ed.), *Achievement-related motives in children*. New York: Russell Sage, 1968.

Crandall, V. J. Achievement. In H. W. Stevenson (Ed.), *Child Psychology: The 62nd Yearbook of the National Society for the Study of Education*. Part I. Chicago: University of Chicago Press, 1963.

Crandall, V. J., Dewey, R., Katkovsky, W., and Preston, A. Parents' attitudes and behaviors and grade school children's academic achievements. *Journal of Genetic Psychology*, 1964, **104**, 53–66.

Crandall, V. J., Katkovsky, W., and Preston, A. Motivational and ability determinants of young children's intellectual achievement behaviors. *Child Development*, 1962, **33**, 643–661.

Crandall, V. J., Preston, A., and Rabson, A. Maternal reactions and the development of independence and achievement behavior in young children. *Child Development*, 1960, **31**, 243–251.

Crandall, V. J., and Rabson, A. Children's repetition choices in an intellectual achievement situation following success and failure. *Journal of Genetic Psychology*, 1960, **97**, 161–168.

Douvan, E. M., and Adelson, J. *The adolescent experience*. New York: Wiley, 1966.

Erikson, E. H. Identity and the life cycle. *Psychological Issues*, 1959, **1**, 1–171.

Escalona, S. K. Feeding disturbances in very young children. *American Journal of Orthopsychiatry*, 1945, **15**, 76–80.

Field, W. F. The effects of thematic apperception upon certain experimentally aroused needs. Unpublished doctoral dissertation, University of Maryland, 1951.

Garai, J. E., and Scheinfeld, A. Sex differences in mental and behavioral traits. *Genetic Psychology Monographs*, 1968, **77**, 169–299.

Glidewell, J. C., Kantor, M. B., Smith, L. M., and Stringer, L. A. Socialization and social structure in the classroom. In L. W. Hoffman and M. L. Hoffman (Eds.), *Review of child development research*. Vol. 2. New York: Russell Sage, 1966.

Goldberg, S., and Lewis, M. Play behavior in the year-old infant: Early sex differences. *Child Development*, 1969, **40**, 21–31.

Hamm, N. K., and Hoving, K. L. Conformity of children in an ambiguous perceptual situation. *Child Development*, 1969, **40**, 773–784.

Heinstein, M. *Child rearing in California*. Bureau of Maternal and Child Health, State of California, Department of Public Health, 1965.

Horner, M. S. Sex differences in achievement motivation and performance in competitive and non-competitive situations. Unpublished doctoral dissertation, University of Michigan, 1968.

Horner, M. S. Toward an understanding of achievement related conflicts in women. *Journal of Social Issues*, 1972, **28**(2).

Iscoe, I., Williams, M., and Harvey, J. Modifications of children's judgements by a simulated group technique: A normative developmental study. *Child Development*, 1963, **34**, 963–978.

Iscoe, I., Williams, M., and Harvey, J. Age, intelligence and sex as variables in the conformity behavior of Negro and While children. *Child Development*, 1964, **35**, 451–460.

Jensen, A. R. The race × sex × ability interaction. Unpublished manuscript. University of California, Berkeley, 1970.

Kagan, J. Acquisition and significance of sex-typing and sex-role identity. In M. L. Hoffman and L. W. Hoffman (Eds.), *Review of child development research*. Vol. 1. New York: Russell Sage, 1964.

Kagan, J. On the meaning of behavior: Illustrations from the infant. *Child Development*, 1969, **40**, 1121–1134.

Kagan, J., and Kogan, N. Individuality and cognitive performance. In P. H. Mussen (Ed.), *Carmichael's manual of child psychology*. Vol. 1. New York: Wiley, 1970.

Kagan, J., Levine, J., and Fishman, C. Sex of child and social class as determinants of maternal behavior. Paper presented at the meeting of The Society for Research in Child Development, March 1967.

Kagan, J., and Moss, H. A. *Birth to maturity*. New York: Wiley, 1962.

Kagan, J., Rosman, B. L., Day, D., Phillips, A. J., and Phillips, W. Information processing in the child: Significance of analytic and reflective attitudes. *Psychological Monographs*, 1964, **78**, 1.

Lahtinen, P. The effect of failure and rejection on dependency. Unpublished doctoral dissertation, University of Michigan, 1964.

Lewis, M. Infants' responses to facial stimuli during the first year of life. *Developmental Psychology*, 1969, **1**, 75–86.

Lynn, D. B. Sex role and parental identification. *Child Development*, 1962, **33**, 555–564.

Lynn, D. B. *Parental identification and sex role*. Berkeley: McCutchan, 1969.

Maccoby, E. E. Woman's intellect. In S. M. Farber and R. H. L. Wilson (Eds.), *The potential of woman*. New York: McGraw-Hill, 1963.

Maccoby, E. E. Sex differences in intellectual functioning. In E. E. Maccoby (Ed.), *The development of sex differences*. Stanford, California: Stanford University Press, 1966.

Maccoby, E. E., and Masters, J. C. Attachment and dependency. In P. H. Mussen (Ed.), *Carmichael's manual of child psychology*. Vol. 2. New York: Wiley, 1970.

McClelland, D. C., Atkinson, J. W., Clark, R. A., and Lowell, E. L. *The achievement motive*. New York: Appleton-Century-Crofts, 1953.

McManis, D. L. Pursuit-rotor performance of normal and retarded children in four verbal-incentive conditions. *Child Development*, 1965, **36**, 667–683.

Milton, G. A. The effects of sex-role identification upon problem solving skill. *Journal of Abnormal and Social Psychology*, 1957, **55**, 208–212.

Moriarty, A. Coping patterns of preschool children in response to intelligence test demands. *Genetic Psychology Monographs*, 1961, **64**, 3–127.

Moss, H. A. Laboratory and field studies of mother–infant interaction. Unpublished manuscript, NIMH, undated.

Moss, H. A. Sex, age, and state as determinants of mother–infant interaction. *Merrill-Palmer Quarterly*, 1967, **13**, 19–36.

Moss, H. A., and Robson, K. S. Maternal influences in early social visual behavior. *Child Development*, 1968, **39**, 401–408.

Moss, H. A., Robson, K. S., and Pedersen, F. Determinants of maternal stimulation of infants and consequences of treatment for later reactions to strangers. *Developmental Psychology*, 1969, **1**, 239–247.

Nakamura, C. Y. Conformity and problem solving. *Journal of Abnormal and Social Psychology*, 1958, **56**, 315–320.

Oetzel, R. M. The relationship between sex role acceptance and cognitive abilities. Unpublished masters thesis, Stanford University, 1961.

Oetzel, R. M. Annotated bibliography and classified summary of research in sex differences. In E. E. Maccoby (Ed.), *The development of sex differences*. Stanford, California: Stanford University Press, 1966.

Parson, T. *Essays in sociological theory pure and applied*. Glencoe, Illinois: Free Press, 1949.

Parson, T. Family structure and the socialization of the child. In T. Parsons and R. F. Bales (Eds.), *Family socialization and interaction process*. Glencoe, Illinois: Free Press, 1965.

Plank, E. H., and Plank, R. Emotional components in arithmetic learning as seen through autobiographies. In R. S. Eissler et al. (Eds.), *The psychoanalytic study of the child*. Vol. 9. New York: International Universities Press, 1954.

Pope, B. Socio-economic contrasts in children's peer culture prestige values. *Genetic Psychology Monographs*, 1953, **48**, 157–220.

Rosen, B. C., and D'Andrade, R. The psychosocial origins of achievement motivations. *Sociometry*, 1959, **22**, 185–218.

Rossi, A. S. Barriers to the career choice of engineering, medicine, or science among American women. In J. A. Mattfeld and G. G. Van Aken (Eds.), *Women and the scientific professions: Papers presented at the M.I.T. symposium on American Women in Science and Engineering, 1964*. Cambridge, Massachusetts: M.I.T. Press, 1965(a).

Rossi, A. S. Women in science: Why so few? *Science*, 1965(b), **148**, 1196–1202.

Rubenstein, J. Maternal attentiveness and subsequent exploratory behavior in the infant. *Child Development,* 1967, **38,** 1089–1100.

Sarason, I. G. Test anxiety and intellectual performance. *Journal of Abnormal and Social Psychology,* 1963, **66,** 73–75.

Sarason, I. G., and Harmatz, M. G. Test anxiety and experimental conditions. *Journal of Personality and Social Psychology,* 1965, 1, 499–505.

Sears, P. S. Correlates of need achievement and need affiliation and classroom management, self concept, and creativity. Unpublished manuscript, Stanford University, 1962.

Sears, P. S. The effect of classroom conditions on the strength of achievement motive and work output of elementary school children. Final report, cooperative research project No. OE-873, U.S. Dept. of Health, Education and Welfare, Office of Education, Washington, D.C., 1963.

Sears, P. S. Self-concept in the service of educational goals. *California Journal of Instructional Improvement,* 1964, **7,** 3–17.

Sears, R. R., Maccoby, E. E., and Levin, H. *Patterns of child rearing.* Evanston, Illinois: Row, Peterson, 1957.

Sears, R. R., Rau, L., and Alpert, R. *Identification and child rearing.* Stanford, California: Stanford University Press, 1965.

Sherman, J. A. Problems of sex differences in space perception and aspects of intellectual functioning. *Psychological Review,* 1967, **74,** 290–299.

Sigel, I. E., Rationale for separate analyses of male and female samples on cognitive tasks. *Psychological Record,* 1965, **15,** 369–376.

Silverman, J. Attentional styles and the study of sex differences. In D. L. Mostofsky (Ed.), *Attention: Contemporary theory and analysis.* New York: Appleton-Century-Crofts, 1970.

Simon, R. J., Clark, S. M., and Galway, K. The woman Ph.D.: A recent profile. Paper prepared for a workshop of the New York Academy of Sciences, New York, February 1970.

Stein, A. H., and Smithells, J. Age and sex differences in children's sex role standards about achievement. *Developmental Psychology,* 1969, **1,** 252–259.

Stendler, C. B. Critical periods in socialization. In R. G. Kuhlen and G. G. Thompson (Eds.), *Psychological studies of human development.* New York: Appleton-Century-Crofts, 1963.

Sutton-Smith, B., Crandall, V. J., and Roberts, J. M. Achievement and strategic competence. Paper presented at the meeting of the Eastern Psychological Association, April 1964.

Terman, L. M., and Oden, M. H. *The gifted child grows up.* Stanford, California: Stanford University Press, 1947.

Torgoff, I. Parental developmental timetable. Paper presented at the meeting of the American Psychological Association, Washington, D.C., August 1958.

Tulkin, S. R. Race, class, family, and school achievement. *Journal of Personality and Social Psychology,* 1968, 9, 31–37.

Tyler, F. B., Rafferty, J. E., and Tyler, B. B. Relationships among motivations of parents and their children. *Journal of Genetic Psychology,* 1962, **101,** 69–81.

Veroff, J. Social comparison and the development of achievement motivation. In C. P. Smith (Ed.), *Achievement-related motives in children.* New York: Russell Sage, 1969.

Veroff, J., Wilcox, S., and Atkinson, J. W. The achievement motive in high school and college age women. *Journal of Abnormal and Social Psychology,* 1953, **48,** 108–119.

Walberg, H. J. Physics, femininity, and creativity. *Developmental Psychology,* 1969, **1,** 47–54.

Walter, L. M., and Marzolf, S. S. The relation of sex, age, and school achievement to levels of aspiration. *Journal of Educational Psychology,* 1951, **42,** 258–292.

White, R. W. Competence and the psychosexual stages of development. In M. Jones (Ed.), *Nebraska Symposium on Motivation.* Lincoln, Nebraska: University of Nebraska Press, 1960.

Winterbottom, M. R. The relation of need for achievement to learning experiences in independence and mastery. In J. W. Atkinson (Ed.), *Motives in fantasy, action, and society.* Princeton: Van Nostrand, 1958.

Witkin, H. A., Dyk, R. B., Faterson, H. F., Goodenough, D. R., and Karp, S. A. *Psychological differentiation.* New York: Wiley, 1962.

The effect of the infant's sex on the caregiver

ANNELIESE F. KORNER

This selection is taken from a longer article by Korner entitled "The effect of the infant's state, level of arousal, sex, and
ontogenetic stage on the caregiver." [Ed.]

There is very little doubt, judging from the growing literature, that at a very early age, male and female infants are treated
differently by their caregivers. The infant's biological sex thus
exerts an influence on parental behavior. A recent study by Thoman, Leiderman, and Olson (1972) suggested that differences in
maternal treatment as a function of the sex of the child start right
after birth. Primiparous mothers at least talked to and smiled at
their baby girls significantly more during feeding than they did
with boys. Earlier, Moss and Robson (1968) found that in response to fretting 3-month-old infants, mothers were apt to respond to girls by talking, looking, and offering a pacifier, while
they tended to hold close their baby boys or to offer them distractions. Lewis (1972), also with a sample of 3-month-old infants,
found very similar differential responses in mothers; they vocalized more frequently to girls and they held boys more often
than girls. Lewis (1972) concluded that in the interaction between mothers and infants, boys are apt to receive more proximal
and girls more distal stimulation.

At the same time, sex differences in infants have been noted
in the earliest months of life (e.g., Lewis, Kagan, & Kalafat, 1966;
Moss, 1967; Watson, 1969). The question is whether the sex dif-

Anneliese F. Korner, from "The effect of the infant's state, level of arousal,
sex, and ontogenetic stage on the caregiver." In Michael Lewis and Leonard· A.
Rosenblum (Eds.), *The Effect of the Infant on Its Caregiver.* Copyright © 1974
by John Wiley & Sons, Inc. Reprinted by permission of John Wiley & Sons, Inc.

ferences noted are entirely a function of differential treatment of the sexes by caregivers, or whether, as Olley (1971) pointed out, differential parental behaviors are also in response to subtle sex differences in the infants. To answer this question, the obvious time to study sex differences is right after birth, when differential maternal treatment has not as yet had a chance to have much impact.

I recently reviewed what little evidence there is of sex differences in newborns (Korner, 1973). The scant evidence may in part be a function of the fact that investigators of neonates often do not analyze their data for sex differences, as if it were unthinkable that such differences might exist. Many studies that assessed sex differences did not yield significant results. Yet there are a few studies which point to sex differences in newborns, particularly in certain target areas. It is the cumulative evidence from these studies, rather than the results of any single study, that makes the hypothesis tenable that innate behavioral sex differences do exist.

Tentatively, the female emerges as more receptive to certain types of stimuli, and as orally more sensitized. At the same time, she is in no way less active or expressive. There is also suggestive evidence that the male may be endowed from birth with greater physical strength and muscular vigor. Let me review the evidence.

There are several studies suggesting that the female may have greater tactile sensitivity. For example, Bell and Costello (1964) found females to be more responsive to the removal of a covering blanket and to an air jet stimulation applied to the abdomen. Wolff (1969), in a longitudinal study of a small sample of infants, observed that girls aged 2 weeks were more sensitive to skin contact than boys. Lipsitt and Levy (1959) found significantly lower electrotactual thresholds in females than in males.

In the visual modality an interesting discrepancy appears, depending on whether sex differences are assessed with respect to active visual behavior or photic receptivity on EEG. The female's response to photic stimulation appears to be significantly faster than that of males. In testing the mean photic latency of Oriental, Caucasian, and Negro neonates, Engel, Crowell, and Nishijima (1968) found significantly shorter latencies in females in each of the three races. By contrast, we were unable to find sex differences in visual tracking of moving objects, in the frequency and duration of the state of alert inactivity (Korner, 1970), or in the visual responsiveness in response to maternal types of ministrations (Korner & Thoman, 1970).

No sex differences have been demonstrated in auditory receptivity. Eisenberg (1972), who has tested the auditory responsiveness of hundreds of neonates under carefully controlled conditions, has found no sex-dependent differences. In our study of individual differences (Korner, 1970), we found no sex differences in response to an 80-dB buzzer. Similarly, Engel et al. (1968) were unable to find such differences in the latency of response on EEGS to acoustic stimulation.

Female neonates also appear to be more responsive to sweet taste, which is the first of several examples that they are what I call "orally more sensitized." Nisbett and Gurwitz (1970) found that when females were given sweetened formula, they increased their consumption of milk significantly more than did males. Females were more responsive to the taste of the formula at each body weight level tested. This finding incidentally has interesting parallels in the animal literature. Consistently, female rats consume more glucose and saccharin solutions than males (Valenstein, Kakolewski, & Cox, 1967; Wade & Zucker, 1969).

While there seem to be no sex differences in the frequency of hand-mouth and hand-face contacts and of finger sucking, or in the efficiency or perseverance of these behaviors (Korner & Kraemer, 1972), all of which are more or less activity-related behaviors, we found highly significant sex differences in the style of hand-to-mouth approaches. In one of our film analyses, it was determined for each hand-to-mouth approach whether the hand approached the mouth and the mouth only opened on contact, or whether the mouth approached the hand, with head straining forward to meet the hand. Females engaged in significantly more mouth searching than males ($p < .01$).

When we analyzed for sex differences in the spontaneous behaviors that occurred in the context of various sleep states, we found highly consistent and suggestive sex-related trends which were, however, at best of only marginal statistical significance (Korner, 1969). Wolff (1966), who was the first to systematically monitor these spontaneous behaviors, postulated that since no known stimulus evokes these behaviors, they may represent the discharge of a neural energy potential, which occurs in inverse proportion to the degree of afferent input. In our study we calculated the mean hourly rate of spontaneous startles, reflex smiles, erections, and episodes of rhythmical mouthing in each of three sleep states, namely, regular sleep, irregular sleep, and drowse. In each state the mean hourly rate of startles of males exceeded that of females ($p < .10$). By contrast, females exceeded in reflex smiles and rhythmical mouthing in all the states in which these behaviors occur. Since the overall rate of spontaneous discharge behaviors was almost identical for males and females when erections were excluded, it appears that females make up in smiles and reflex sucks what they lack in startles. If indeed these behaviors represent the discharges of a neural energy potential, it appears that females tend to discharge this potential more frequently via the facial musculatures, particularly the mouth region, whereas males tend to discharge it more frequently through total and vigorous body activation.

Our finding that females engage in more frequent reflex smiles than males finds confirmation in observations by Freedman (1971). In our sample, the rate of reflex smiles during irregular sleep was almost triple that of males ($p < .06$). Even though the hourly rate of rhythmical mouthing in females was almost twice that of males, this difference was not statistically significant.

Females seem to exceed males in still another rhythmical oral behavior. Balint (1948) found that females during bottle feedings showed a rhythmical clonus of the tongue more frequently than males.

By contrast to the oral behaviors which, according to Wolff (1966) probably are of central, neural origin, no sex differences have been observed in the frequency or rate of ordinary spontaneous sucking (Hendry & Kessen, 1964; Korner et al., 1968) or of nutritive or nonnutritive sucking (Dubignon, Campbell, Curtis, & Partington, 1969). This type of sucking is strongly influenced by the overriding and sex-unrelated biological function of hunger (Hendry & Kessen, 1964; Korner et al., 1968), and by high arousal (Bridger, 1962).

Bell and Darling (1965) demonstrated that males were able to lift their heads higher from the prone position, suggesting that they may be endowed with greater muscular strength. Possibly, the males' greater tendency to startle, with the total body activation this entails, can also be taken as an index of greater muscular vigor.

When it comes to spontaneous active and expressive behaviors, I believe no sex differences have been reported for newborns. Several studies, some of which used large samples of neonates, monitored neonatal activity, and none of them found reliable sex differences in the frequency of motions (Brownfield, 1956; Campbell, 1968; Korner et al., 1968; Pratt, 1932). In one of our film analyses, we scored separately small, small multiple, global, and diffuse motions, and none of these were more relied upon by either sex (Korner et al., 1968). While Moss (1967) found significant differences in fussing by 3 weeks of age, boys being more irritable than girls, no such differences have been demonstrated in crying immediately after birth (Fisichelli & Karelitz, 1963; Korner et al., 1968). Similarly, no sex differences have been found in the reduction of crying in response to maternal types of soothing interventions (Korner & Thoman, 1972).

If we accept from this evidence that there are in fact behavioral sex differences detectable shortly after birth, the question is: What can they possibly be due to and how might they affect the caregiver? As to the first part of this question, aside from possible genetic determinants, the most plausible explanation for these differences is that they are hormonal in origin. As Hamburg and Lunde (1966) have pointed out, the hormones responsible for sexual differentiation *in utero* may sensitize the organism's central nervous system in such a way that sex-linked behaviors emerge at a later time, even when the circulation of these hormones is no longer detectable within the system. As to the second part of this question, I believe that, while sex role expectations and sex role taboos are the primary reasons why males and females are treated differently from birth, the behavioral sex differences of the infants themselves may also exert a subtle influence on the caregiver. For example, the mother's repeatedly reported tendency to provide boys with more proximal, tactile stimulation may be, in part at least, an inadvertent, unconscious compensatory response to the male's lesser cutaneous sensitivity. It may also express an effort on her part to provide containment for her more startle-prone male newborn. Also, the male's greater muscular strength and sturdiness and his bigger size (Garn, 1958) may make the mother less hesitant to handle him, particularly if she is an inexperienced mother.

The female newborn's oral sensitivity probably is not a passing matter. Moss (1967) found that 3-month-old girls mouthed significantly more than boys. In light of the neonatal data, one wonders whether this was spontaneous sucking or an attempt to mouth and incorporate objects. Since infants learn through their mouths, one could ask whether female infants learn more frequently through this channel and whether there are qualitative differences in this kind of learning between males and females. Judging from Honzig and McKee's (1962) review of several studies, it appears that girls seek comfort through oral means more often than do boys. From age 1 on, girls are both more frequent and more persistent thumbsuckers than boys. Perhaps mothers intuitively sense a girl's affinity for oral comforting. This could at least in part explain why they offer pacifiers to girls more often than to boys (Moss & Robson, 1968).

REFERENCES

Balint, M. Individual differences of behavior in early infancy and an objective way of recording them. *Journal of Genetic Psychology*, 1948, **73**, 57–117.

Bell, R. Q., & Costello, N. Three tests for sex differences in tactile sensitivity in the newborn. *Biologia Neonatorum*, 1964, **7**, 335–347.

Bell, R. Q., & Darling, J. F. The prone head reaction in the human neonate: Relation with sex and tactile sensitivity. *Child Development*, 1965, **36**, 943–949.

Bridger, W. H. Ethological concepts and human development. *Recent Advances in Biological Psychiatry*, 1962, **4**, 95–107.

Brownfield, E. D. An investigation of the activity and sensory responses of healthy newborn infants. *Dissertation Abstracts*, 1956, **16**, 1288–1289.

Campbell, D. Motor activity in a group of newborn babies. *Biologia Neonatorum*, 1968, **13**, 257–270.

Dubignon, J., Campbell, D., Curtis, M., & Partington, M. W. The relation between laboratory measures of sucking, food intake, and perinatal factors during the newborn period. *Child Development*, 1969, **40**, 1107–1120.

Eisenberg, R. Personal communication, 1972.

Engel, R., Crowell, D., & Nishijima, S. Visual and auditory response latencies in neonates. In B. N. D. Fernando (Ed.), *Felicitation Volume in Honor of C. C. DeSilva*, Ceylon: Kularatne and Company, Ltd., 1968, pp. 1–10.

Fisichelli, V. C., & Karelitz, S. The cry latencies of normal infants and those with brain damage. *Journal of Pediatrics*, 1963, **62**, 724–734.

Freedman, D. G. Personal communication, 1971.

Garn, S. M. Fat, body size, and growth in the newborn. *Human Biology*, 1958, **30**, 265–280.

Hamburg, D. A., & Lunde, D. T. Sex hormones in the development of sex differences in human behavior. In E. E. Maccoby (Ed.), *The Development of Sex Differences*, Stanford, California: Stanford University Press, 1966, pp. 1–24.

Hendry, L. S., & Kessen, W. Oral behavior of newborn infants as a function of age and time since feeding. *Child Development*, 1964, **35**, 201–208.

Honzig, M. P., & McKee, J. P. The sex difference in thumbsucking. *Journal of Pediatrics*, 1962, **61**, 726–732.

Korner, A. F. Neonatal startles, smiles, erections, and reflex sucks as related to state, sex and individuality. *Child Development*, 1969, **40**, 1039–1053.

Korner, A. F. Visual alertness in neonates: Individual differences and their correlates. *Perceptual and Motor Skills*, 1970, **31**, 67–78.

Korner, A. F. Sex differences in newborns with special reference to differences in the organization of oral behavior. *Journal of Child Psychology and Psychiatry*, 1973, **14**, 19–29.

Korner, A. F., Chuck, B., & Dontchos, S. Organismic determinants of spontaneous oral behavior in neonates. *Child Development*, 1968, **39**, 1145–1157.

Korner, A. F., & Kraemer, H. C. Individual differences in spontaneous oral behavior. In J. F. Bosma (Ed.), *Third symposium on oral sen-*

sation and perception: The mouth of the infant. Springfield, Illinois: C. C. Thomas, 1972, pp. 335–346.

Korner, A. F., & Thoman, E. B. Visual alertness in neonates as evoked by maternal care. *Journal of Experimental Child Psychology,* 1970, **10,** 67–78.

Korner, A. F., & Thoman, E. B. The relative efficacy of contact and vestibular-proprioceptive stimulation in soothing neonates. *Child Development,* 1972, **43,** 443–453.

Lewis, M. State as an infant-environment interaction: An analysis of mother-infant interactions as a function of sex. *Merrill-Palmer Quarterly,* 1972, **18,** 95–121.

Lewis, M., Kagan, J., & Kalafat, J. Patterns of fixation in infants. *Child Development,* 1966, **37,** 331–341.

Lipsitt, L. P., & Levy, N. Electrotactual threshold in the human neonate. *Child Development,* 1959, **30,** 547–554.

Moss, H. A. Sex, age, and state as determinants of mother-infant interaction. *Merrill-Palmer Quarterly,* 1967, **13,** 19–36.

Moss, H. A., & Robson, K. The role of protest behavior in the development of mother-infant attachment. Paper presented at the meeting of the American Psychological Association, San Francisco, 1968.

Nisbett, R. E., & Gurwitz, S. B. Weight, sex, and the eating behavior of human newborns. *Journal of Comparative and Physiological Psychology,* 1970, **73,** 245–253.

Olley, J. G. *Sex differences in human behavior in the first year of life.* Major area paper, Department of Psychology, George Peabody College for Teachers, Nashville, Tennessee, 1971.

Pratt, K. C. Note on the relation of activity to sex and race in young infants. *Journal of Social Psychology,* 1932, **3,** 118–120.

Thoman, E. B., Leiderman, P. H., & Olson, J. P. Neonate-mother interaction during breast-feeding. *Developmental Psychology,* 1972, **6,** 110–118.

Valenstein, E. S., Kakolewski, J. W., & Cox, V. C. Sex differences in taste preferences for glucose and saccharin solutions. *Science,* 1967, **156,** 942–943.

Wade, G. N., & Zucker, I. Hormonal and developmental influence on rat saccharin preferences. *Journal of Comparative and Physiological Psychology,* 1969, **69,** 291–300.

Watson, J. S. Operant conditioning of visual fixation in infants under visual and auditory reinforcement. *Developmental Psychology,* 1969, **1,** 508–516.

Wolff, P. H. The causes, controls and organization of behavior in the neonate. *Psychological Issues,* 1966, **5**(1), Monograph 17.

Wolff, P. H. The natural history of crying and other vocalizations in early infancy. In B. M. Foss (Ed.), *Determinants of infant behavior.* Vol. IV. London: Methuen, 1969, pp. 113–138.

Development of gender constancy and selective attention to same-sex models

RONALD G. SLABY
KARIN S. FREY

Social learning theorists have suggested that children acquire their sex-role–related behaviors largely through observational learning. Mischel (1970) has claimed that children attend to, learn from, and imitate same-sex models more than opposite-sex models largely because they perceive same-sex models to be more similar to themselves. He reviewed evidence indicating that subjects who are led to believe that a model's interests and attributes are similar to their own are more likely to acquire the model's behaviors than subjects who perceive a model to be dissimilar. Presumably, then, children can be expected to give preferential attention to same-sex models when they come to understand that they share with the model the common attributes of their own gender.

Results of previous research, though not entirely consistent, provide some support for Mischel's claim. Maccoby, Wilson, and

From *Child Development*, 1975, **46.** Copyright © 1975 by The Society for Research in Child Development, Inc. Reprinted by permission.

This research was partially supported by the Developmental Psychology Laboratory and by the Child Development and Mental Retardation Center of the University of Washington. An earlier version of this paper was presented at the Biennial Meeting of the Society for Research in Child Development, Denver, April 1975. The authors wish to thank Madeline Dodge, director of the Developmental Psychology Laboratory Preschool, as well as the children who participated in the study and their parents, for their kind cooperation. In addition, deep thanks are extended to Rich Borton for serving as the observer, Halbert B. Robinson for his valuable critique of an earlier draft, and Diana Arezzo Slaby for her generous contributions in all phases of this study.

Burton (1958) found that adult subjects preferentially attended to the same-sex model when a male and a female model were simultaneously presented on film. Under similar experimental conditions Maccoby and Wilson (1957) found that adult subjects learned relatively more of the behaviors displayed by the model of their own sex. Grusec and Brinker (1972) found that after 5- and 7-year-old children had watched a male and a female model simultaneously presented, the boys remembered significantly more of the behaviors of the male model than of the female model, and the girls showed a less clear tendency to remember more of the behaviors of the female model than of the male model. In a recent review of children's spontaneous imitation of male and female models, Maccoby and Jacklin (1974) cited 23 studies, seven of which found that both boys and girls showed greater same-sex than cross-sex imitation while the remaining 16 found no significant interaction of sex of subject with sex of model. In none of these studies, however, was there an assessment of the extent to which the children perceived themselves to be similar to the model of the same sex and different from the model of the opposite sex.

Cognitive-developmental theorists have pointed out that a child's understanding of sex similarity may change with his cognitive growth, thereby adding an important qualification to the social learning position on sex-role development. Kohlberg (1966) stated that the young child progresses through a sequence of stages in eventually coming to the understanding that one's gender is a constant and meaningful human attribute. According to Kohlberg, the particular effect of male and female models on the young child depends largely on his stage of gender constancy. For example, male and female models may take on differential personal importance for a young child when the child comes to understand that (a) he or she and every other individual are either male or female, (b) boys invariably become men and girls become women, and (c) the human attribute of being either male or female will not change with changing situations and personal motivations.

Although the evidence for developmental changes in children's concept of gender is fragmentary, developmental changes in related areas of cognitive functioning have been demonstrated. De Vries (1969) found that between 3 and 6 years of age, children develop the belief that the generic identity of a living being is invariant. Children's belief in the constancy of animal identity was tested by first showing them a cat that was apparently transformed (by means of a mask) into a "dog" or a "rabbit," and then questioning them regarding the nature of the cause and reality of the change. Evidence was found for a developmental sequence in the acquisition of "animal constancy" as measured by a reproducible Guttman scale. Furthermore, with mental age controlled, animal constancy was more strongly correlated with scores on other tests of cognitive constancy, including a version of the gender-constancy test, than with scores of the ability to discriminate among animals or the understanding of the use of masks. These findings were interpreted as an indication that the development of constancy could not be attributed to the acquisition of simple knowledge related to the constancy tasks but, rather, reflected cognitive structural change.

DeVries (1969, 1974) has also demonstrated that children's understanding of the constancy of gender shows sequential development. Furthermore, factor analyses of 143 bright, average, and retarded children's performances on 15 cognitive-developmental tasks and their mental age as measured by the Stanford-Binet intelligence scale revealed that gender constancy and animal constancy formed a factor that was moderately correlated with children's conservation of mass and number and was relatively independent of children's mental age (DeVries, 1974).

The primary purpose of the present research was to assess the relationship of young children's concept of gender to their selective attention to models of the same or opposite sex. Children were shown a film that simultaneously presented a male and a female model. The amount of time the children watched each model was recorded. It was predicted that preference for same-sex models would increase with more advanced levels of gender constancy. A secondary purpose was to assess the developmental sequence in children's acquisition of the concept of gender. It was predicted that children's answers to questions concerning various aspects of gender constancy would show sequential characteristics as indicated by a reproducible Guttman scale.

METHOD

Subjects.   Subjects were 55 children with a mean age of 50 months and ranging in age from 26 to 68 months. Twenty-three were boys and 32 were girls; 43 were enrolled in the University of Washington Developmental Psychology Laboratory Preschool and 12 were referred by students in an introductory psychology course; a majority were white and had middle-class backgrounds. One girl was not included because she asked to leave the experiment after viewing only a few seconds of the film. The experimenter was a white female adult.

Procedure.   In Session 1 the experimenter brought each subject individually to an experimental room and administered the gender-constancy interview. Props for the interview included a set of four rubber dolls (a man and a woman doll approximately 13 cm tall, and a boy and a girl doll approximately 8 cm tall) and four 8 × 8 cm color photographs of the face and upper torso of two adult males and two adult females. Subjects were asked to answer the following 14 question and counterquestion items:

1 and 2. (For a boy doll and for a girl doll):
Is this a girl or a boy?
Is this a [*opposite sex of subject's first response*]?

3–8. (For a man doll, for a woman doll, for two men's photographs, and for two women's photographs):
Is this a woman or a man?
Is this a [*opposite sex of subject's first response*]?

9. Are you a girl or a boy?
Are you a [*opposite sex of subject's first response*]?

10. When you were a little baby, were you a little girl or a little boy?
Were you ever a little [*opposite sex of subject's first response*]?

11. When you grow up, will you be a mommy or a daddy?
Could you ever be a [*opposite sex of subject's first response*]?

12. If you wore [*opposite sex of subject, i.e., "boys' " or "girls' "*] clothes, would you be a girl or a boy?
If you wore [*opposite sex of subject*] clothes, would you be a [*opposite sex of subject's first response*]?

13. If you played [*opposite sex of subject*] games, would you be a girl or a boy?
If you played [*opposite sex of subject*] games, would you be a [*opposite sex of subject's first response*]?

14. Could you be a [*opposite sex of subject*] if you wanted to be?

Question 14 was followed by an inquiry about whether the child was referring to a real or a pretend situation. If the child indicated he had been referring to a pretend situation, the question was asked again in terms of the real possibility of a switch in gender status.

Questions were grouped into three sets representing different aspects of the gender concept: *gender identity* (questions

1–9); *gender stability* over time (questions 10–11); and *gender consistency* across various situations and motivations (questions 12–14). Each questions was scored "plus" only if the subject answered both the question and the counterquestion "correctly" (i.e., showing gender constancy); otherwise it was scored "minus." Subjects were given a plus for each question set only if they received a plus for all questions in the category; otherwise they received a minus.

The film viewing of Session 2 was conducted 2–6 weeks after the gender-constancy interview of Session 1. The experimenter brought each child individually to the same experimental room as in Session 1 and asked the subject if he wanted to see a movie. She then seated the subject, started the projector, and sat down behind the subject. If the subject turned around to ask the experimenter a question about the movie, she replied, "You watch the movie and find out."

The 5½-min silent color film depicted a white adult male and female concurrently engaging in simple, parallel activities. They built a fire, popped corn, played musical instruments, and drank juice. Both models were on the screen at all times, the man on the left and the woman on the right. Subjects were seated 3.35 m from the movie screen on which the projected area was 91 cm wide × 71 cm high. The distance between the film models prevented viewers, who were sitting near the screen, from fixating on both models simultaneously. The screen hung in front of a one-way mirror such that a small portion of the mirror extended below the bottom edge, permitting concealed observation of the subject's eye movements. An observer in the adjacent room recorded on two separate clocks the amount of time each subject fixated on the right side and the left side of the screen during the movie. The amount of time that the subject fixated on the middle of the screen or looked away from the screen was not recorded. The sex of the subject was apparent to the observer, but he was not aware of the nature of the film or of the subject's responses in the gender-constancy interview. The subjects made very distinct eye movements when changing the object of their attention. With the use of videotaped eye movements of four pilot subjects, test-retest reliability was found to be high ($r = .91$).

Results

Gender constancy.   The percentage of boys and girls answering both the question and the counterquestion "correctly" for each item in the gender-constancy interview are presented in Table 1. The results indicate that questions *within* each of the categories—gender identity (1–9), gender stability (10–11), and

TABLE 1   PERCENTAGE OF BOYS AND GIRLS
ANSWERING BOTH THE QUESTION AND COUNTER-
QUESTION "CORRECTLY" FOR EACH ITEM IN
THE GENDER-CONSTANCY INTERVIEW

Question set and item number	Boys	Girls	Sexes combined
Gender identity			
1	100	98	98
2	96	100	98
3	100	100	98
4	100	94	96
5	100	97	98
6	100	97	98
7	100	94	96
8	100	97	98
9	91	91	91
Gender stability			
10	83	72	76
11	74	72	73
Gender consistency			
12	52	44	47
13	48	44	45
14	48	62	56

gender consistency (12–14)—were of approximately equal difficulty. Furthermore, all items pertaining to gender identity were
less difficult than all items pertaining to gender stability, which
in turn were less difficult than all items pertaining to gender
consistency.

Table 2 presents the Guttman scale for gender constancy,
based on subjects' answers to the sets of questions pertaining to
gender identity, gender stability, and gender consistency. A
scalogram analysis revealed that these three question sets formed
a reproducible Guttman scale (coefficient of reproducibility = .98; minimal marginal reproducibility = .70). Fifty-four
of the 55 subjects showed one of the four stage-type patterns of
response (stage 1, − − −; stage 2, + − −; stage 3, + + −; or stage
4, + + +). The one girl who showed a non–stage-type pattern of
responses (+ − +) was assigned to stage 2 for purposes of further
analysis. No subjects showed any of the three other possible
non–stage-type patterns of response.

In addition to their scalability, the four stages of response
were found to meet several other criteria for developmental se-
quentiality. Mean stage scores and success on each question set
both increased with age. Subjects' age (in months) was correlated

TABLE 2 SCALE OF GENDER
CONSTANCY, BASED ON THREE QUESTION SETS

Type	Question set			% of children (total = 100)			Age (in months)	
	Gender identity	Gender stability	Gender consistency	Boys	Girls	Combined	Mean	Range
Stage								
1	−	−	−	9	16	13	34	26–39
2	+	−	−	26	16	20	47	35–62
3	+	+	−	17	31	25	53	36–68
4	+	+	+	48	34	40	55	41–67
Non-stage								
A	+	−	+	0	3	2	35	—
B	−	+	−	0	0	0	—	—
C	−	+	+	0	0	0	—	—
D	−	−	+	0	0	0	—	—

positively and significantly with their stage of gender constancy (for all children, $\tau = .484$, $z = 4.399$, $p < .001$; for boys, $\tau = .530$, $z = 2.463$, $p < .025$; and for girls, $\tau = .487$, $z = 3.357$, $p < .001$).

Attention to models. Analyses were performed on two measures of subjects' attention to film models: total duration of attention to both male and female models, and percentage of model-watching time spent selectively attending to the male rather than to the female model. For purposes of analyses of variance, children were assigned to one of two major levels of gender constancy: low (stages 1 and 2), and high (stages 3 and 4). It was reasoned that children who were unable to identify males and females consistently (stage 1) and children who did not fully understand the invariance of gender over time (stage 2) would be unlikely to attend differentially to adult male and female models of a different age level from the subjects. Children who did understand gender constancy over time but did not fully understand the invariance of gender across various situations (stage 3) and children who understood all of the gender constancies (stage 4), should attend differentially to male and female models, given that the situations in the film were not varied in a way which would cast doubt on the gender of the models.

A 2 (sex of subject) × 2 (level of gender constancy) × 2 (sex of model—both male and female for each subject) analysis of

TABLE 3   MEAN PERCENTAGE OF MODEL-WATCHING
TIME SPENT SELECTIVELY ATTENDING TO MALE MODEL
(RATHER THAN TO FEMALE MODEL)

Sex of subject and statistic	Subject's level of gender constancy	
	Low (stages 1 and 2)	High (stages 3 and 4)
Boys		
Mean	47.9	61.4
SD	8.5	9.6
N	8	15
Girls		
Mean	57.8	50.8
SD	9.9	11.7
N	11	21

variance was performed on the total duration of attention (in seconds). It was found that high-gender-constancy subjects spent significantly more total time attending to models, 88.6 sec, than low-gender-constancy subjects, 69.6 sec, $F(1,51) = 6.08, p < .025$. The subjects as a group spent significantly more total time attending to the male model, 88.0 sec, than to the female model, 70.2 sec, $F(1,51) = 7.30, p < .025$. No other main effects or two-way interactions were significant. There was a significant three-way interaction, $F(1,51) = 5.34, p < .05$. Subsequent t tests, based on the pooled within-cell error variance, revealed that high-gender-constancy boys spent significantly more time watching the male model, 108.2 sec, than they did watching the female model, 86.8 sec, $t(51) = 3.15, p < .01$, and significantly more time watching the male model than did low-gender-constancy boys, 63.0 sec, $t(51) = 3.41, p < .01$. High-gender-constancy girls showed a nonsignificant tendency to spend more time watching the female model, 86.8 sec, than did low-gender-constancy girls, 63.6 sec, $t(51) = 1.62$, N.S. No other parallel comparisons were significant.

Table 3 presents the mean percentages of model-watching time spent selectively attending to the male model rather than to the female model. A 2 (sex of subject) × 2 (level of gender constancy) analysis of variance revealed no significant main effects. However, the sex of subject × level of gender constancy interaction was significant, $F(1,51) = 11.66, p < .005$. Subsequent t tests, based on the pooled within-cell error variance, revealed that high-gender-constancy boys spent a greater percentage of their model-watching time selectively attending to the male model, 61.4%, than did either low-gender-constancy boys, 47.9%, $t(51) = 3.20$, $p < .01$, or high-gender-constancy girls, 50.8%, $t(51) = 2.51$, $p < .02$. Also, low-gender-constancy girls spent a greater percentage of their time watching the male model, 57.8%, than did low-gender-constancy boys, 47.9%, $t(51) = 2.34$, p $< .05$.

Stage and age as correlates of selective attention to models. Kendall rank-order correlations were performed to assess the extent to which stage and age were related to the selective attention to male or female models. For all children, stage of gender constancy was significantly correlated with the percentage of model-watching time spent selectively attending to the same-sex model, $\tau = .245$, $z = 2.225$, $p < .05$. Separate correlations for boys and girls revealed that boys' stage of gender constancy was significantly correlated with their selective attention to the male model, $\tau = .360$, $z = 2.007$, $p < .05$, but that the correlation of girls' stage of gender constancy with their selective attention to the female model did not reach statistical significance, $\tau = .156$, $z = 1.086$, N.S.

As was noted previously, the correlations between age and stage of gender constancy were positive and significant. However, age was not correlated with selective attention to the same-sex model (for all children, $\tau = .042$; for boys, $\tau = .036$; and for girls, $\tau = .014$). Partial correlations were calculated to assess the relationship between stage of gender constancy and percentage of selective attention to the same-sex model when the common variation due to age was partialed out. With age controlled, the correlations between stage of gender constancy and selective attention to the same-sex model were slightly higher than the corresponding correlations without age controlled (for all children, $\tau_{12.3} = .257$; for boys, $\tau_{12.3} = .403$; and for girls, $\tau_{12.3} = .171$). (Since Kendall partial correlations represent only approximate values, significance levels are not given.)

Family variables as correlates of stage and selective attention to models. For a subsample of 15 boys and 20 girls for whom family data were collected, neither stage of gender constancy nor selective attention to the same-sex model were found to be correlated with birth order, number of male siblings, number of female siblings, or family size.

DISCUSSION
The perception of similarity or dissimilarity between oneself and a model has been shown to be an important variable in

the modeling process (e.g., Rosekrans, 1967). The results of the present study, while underscoring the significance of this variable, further suggest that young children's perception of their own gender similarity to an adult model may develop in stages in conjunction with their cognitive understanding that gender is a constant human attribute.

Four levels of gender constancy were identified on the basis of children's answers to questions pertaining to gender identity, gender stability over time, and gender consistency across situations. These four levels showed the characteristics of developmental stages in that they were both sequentially ordered (as indicated by a reproducible Guttman scale which fit the response patterns of 98% of the children) and age related (as indicated by a significant positive correlation between age and the gender-constancy levels). Of the three measured components of gender constancy, it was found that gender identity was the easiest for children to understand and gender consistency the most difficult, with gender stability of intermediate difficulty. With the exception of only one of the 55 children, all the children who completely understood gender consistency also completely understood the other two components; and all the children who completely understood gender stability also completely understood gender identity.

Children's relative preference for attending to the adult model of the same sex as themselves was found to increase as a function of cognitive advances in their understanding of gender constancy. Even with age controlled, their level of gender constancy was predictive of their selective attention to the same-sex model. Gender constancy was a better predictor of selective attention than was age; in fact, age by itself did not predict selective attention to the same-sex model.

Why does a more complete understanding of gender lead children to spend relatively more time watching others of their own sex? At an early age children begin to realize the profound implications of the male-female distinction in our society. However, as they come to understand that everyone including themselves is either a male or a female and that this condition is stable and consistent throughout life, it becomes increasingly relevant for them to learn and to adopt the social rules concerning male-appropriate and female-appropriate behaviors. The process of forming and reforming social rules and fitting one's behavior to these rules has been referred to by Maccoby and Jacklin (1974) as the process of "self-socialization." Perhaps children begin to pay particular attention to the same-sex model in a special effort to learn the social rules appropriate for their own sex—that is, to begin to engage in self-socialization.

Children who have a complete understanding of gender constancy might be expected not only to selectively attend to same-sex individuals under certain circumstances, as they did in this study, but also to play with, to learn from, and to imitate individuals of their own in preference to those of the opposite sex. It is unlikely, however, that children's attainment of gender constancy is the single and critical turning point in development, prerequisite for the adoption of sex-appropriate behaviors. Rather, children come to understand gender constancy gradually through stages, and this progressive understanding may increasingly influence their sex-role development by bringing new and added meaning to the behaviors they observe in male and female models.

Kohlberg (1966) has suggested that children's rules for what is sex appropriate are not based solely on direct observation but, rather, reflect their own interpretation of what they observe and what they are told. Children's level of gender constancy is presumably one of several factors that influence the nature of their interpretation of sex-role information, as well as affecting their model-watching behavior per se. For example, the child who has not attained gender constancy may believe not only that playing with dolls is a sex-inappropriate behavior for boys but also that a boy who engages in this behavior may face the additional consequences associated with being redefined (at least temporarily) as a girl.

Although boys and girls did not differ in either the age of gender-constancy attainment or the sequence of its development, the understanding of gender constancy had different implications for boys' and girls' self-selection of models. At the less advanced levels of gender constancy, girls spent a greater percentage of their model-watching time attending to the male model than did boys.[1] In contrast, at the more advanced levels of gender constancy, boys spent more total time as well as a greater percentage

---

[1] During movie viewing one subject (a girl in stage 2) exclaimed (incorrectly) that the male model was her teacher. She was the only subject to claim to know one of the models, and she spent a greater percentage (79.9%) of her model-watching time selectively attending to the male model than did any other girl. With this subject excluded, an analysis of variance performed on the percentage of selective attention to the male model revealed only one change in the reported findings. Low-gender-constancy girls (55.6%) did *not* differ significantly from low-gender-constancy boys (47.9%) in their percentage of selective attention to the male model, $\tau(50) = 1.87, p < .10$. Thus, this comparison will not be discussed further.

of their model-watching time attending to the male model than did girls. A developmental increase in attention to the same-sex model occurred for both sexes but was significant only for boys.

Perceived similarity is presumably only one of several variables which influence selective attention to male or female models. Desired characteristics of the model, such as his or her perceived power, may be another. Bandura, Ross, and Ross (1963) demonstrated that the perceived power of the model will affect the extent to which the model is imitated. Furthermore, they suggested that many of the preschool-age boys and girls in their study may have shared the strong stereotype that only the adult male model can control potent resources. Thus, it may be that at the more advanced levels of gender constancy boys perceive the male model as both a similar model and a powerful model to attend to, whereas for girls there may be contradictory tendencies to attend to the similar (female) model and the powerful (male) model.

This conceptualization is consistent with Brown's (1957) claim that girls are less strongly identified with the female sex role than boys are with the male sex role. Furthermore, Grusec and Brinker (1972) found that, whereas 5- to 7-year-old boys learned more of an adult male model's behaviors than of an adult female model's behaviors, girls of this age did not show as clear a tendency to learn more of the female model's behaviors than of the male model's behavior. In the present study both boys and girls spent more total time attending to the adult male model than to the female model. This difference may be due to specific characteristics of these particular models, differences in the models' presented behaviors, preference for watching the male model's side (left) of the screen, or other uncontrolled factors. It would be of interest in future sex-role research to assess, independently of gender constancy, the development of children's stereotypes regarding the desirable attributes of male and female models and the extent to which these stereotypes may influence self-selection of models.

Investigation of the cognitive development of gender constancy is relatively new. Previous research has indicated that the development of gender constancy is (a) highly correlated with the level of cognitive understanding of other qualitative attributes, such as human constancy and animal constancy; (b) moderately correlated with the level of cognitive understanding of quantitative attributes, such as conservation of mass and number; (c) relatively independent of mental age as measured by traditional psychometric tests; and (d) highly correlated with chronological age (DeVries 1969, 1974). Although no family background correlates of gender constancy were identified in the present study, Emmerich and Goldman (1972) found mothers' level of education to be positively related to level of gender constancy in economically disadvantaged children, as indicated by their answers to questions of the form, "If Johnny really wants to be a girl, can he be?" This relationship did not hold, however, for the other aspects of gender constancy tested by these investigators.

Though the reliability and generalizability of the present findings remain to be established, the initial results add promise to the investigation of sex-role development through the combination of social and cognitive factors.

REFERENCES

Bandura, A., Ross, D., & Ross, S. A. Vicarious reinforcement and imitative learning. *Journal of Abnormal and Social Psychology*, 1963, **67**, 601–667.

Brown, D. G. Masculinity-femininity development in children. *Journal of Consulting Psychology*, 1957, **21**, 197–202.

DeVries, R. Constancy of generic identity in the years three to six. *Monographs of The Society for Research in Child Development*, 1969, **34** (3, Serial No. 127).

DeVries, R. Relationship among Piagetian, IQ, and achievement assessments. *Child Development*, 1974, **45**, 746–756.

Emmerich, W., & Goldman, K. S. Boy-girl identity task (technical report 1). In V. C. Shipman (Ed.), *Disadvantaged children and their first school experiences.* Princeton, N.J.: Educational Testing Service, 1972.

Grusec, J. F., & Brinker, D. B. Reinforcement for imitation as a social learning determinant with implications for sex-role development. *Journal of Personality and Social Psychology*, 1972, **21**, 149–158.

Kohlberg, L. A cognitive-developmental analysis of children's sex-role concepts and attitudes. In E. E. Maccoby (Ed.), *The development of sex differences.* Stanford, Calif.: Stanford University Press, 1966.

Maccoby, E. E., & Jacklin, C. N. *The psychology of sex differences.* Stanford, Calif.: Stanford University Press, 1974.

Maccoby, E. E., & Wilson, W. Identification and observational learning from films. *Journal of Abnormal and Social Psychology*, 1957, **55**, 76–87.

Maccoby, E. E., Wilson, W., & Burton, R. Differential movie-viewing behavior of male and female viewers. *Journal of Personality*, 1958, **26**, 259–267.

Mischel, W. Sex-typing and socialization. In P. H. Mussen (Ed.), *Carmichael's manual of child psychology.* Vol. 2. New York: Wiley, 1970.

Rosekrans, M. Imitation in children as a function of perceived similarity to a social model and vicarious reinforcement. *Journal of Personality and Social Psychology*, 1967, **7**, 307–315.

PART

II

SEPARATION OF MOTHER AND CHILD, AND ALTERNATIVE CARE

There are two separate topics in Part II, one on working mothers and one on day care. You might think these two topics are inextricably tied because virtually all children in day care have working mothers; however, many children of working mothers are *not* in day care, and I thought it would be confusing in the long run to combine the two topics. There are two questions involved: (1) What is the effect of the child's partial separation from the mother (or other caregiver) that occurs when the mother works? (2) When there is separation, what is the effect of *group* care upon the child as opposed to individual care? Two separate decisions are involved for the individual woman. "Should I work when I have young children (assuming there is a choice)?" "If I work, what kind of care should I seek for my child?" Because the two questions and decisions are separate, the discussions of them have been separated, but I suspect that in your own debates and discussions the two may merge.

SECTION I
WORKING MOTHERS

OVERVIEW

The Effect of Maternal Employment on the Child

Except for the period during World War II when the labor of women was needed and there was fairly common approval of their employment (even women with young children), we have had in this country a fairly long history of opposition to having women work, particularly if they have preschool children (see Smuts, 1959, or Siegel and Haas, 1963, for a review of this history). One of the assumptions underlying such opposition is that separation of mother and child, especially during the preschool years, is seriously detrimental to the child's welfare. This assumption was given great weight in 1951 by a review of studies of institutionalized children, prepared for the World Health Organization by John Bowlby. Bowlby concluded that children living in group-care institutions (such as orphanages) suffered from severe "maternal deprivation," and that such deprivation was the cause of the cognitive deficits and emotional difficulties observed in such children. In fact, the institutionalized children studied suffered from a great many things besides the lack of a single mother figure. They also had little contact with fathers or father figures (or any other adults), few toys, little contact with other children, and were generally "stimulus deprived" as well as "mother deprived." It was the emphasis on the importance of the single mother figure, however, that stood out in the Bowlby review. For many people it was an easy step from there to the assertion that if a single mother figure is so important, obviously women with children should not work, since doing so would deprive the child of a single mother figure.

I hope it is obvious that a conclusion about the ill effects of maternal employment does not necessarily follow from the data on institutionalized children. For one thing, most homes provide far richer and more varied stimulation than was common in the institutions examined in Bowlby's review. For another, children of working mothers are not deprived of their mothers; rather, they experience a condition that is best described as "partial separation," accompanied by "multiple mothering." So the legitimate and important questions we need to ask have to do with the effects of partial separation versus no separation and of multiple mothering versus single mothering. Is it bad for a child to be cared for by more than one person? Does the mother's employment and the partial separation that accompanies it alter her relationship with the child? Does the age of the child when the separation and multiple mothering begins matter? Bowlby's review prompted extensive research on these and related questions (much of which is reviewed excellently and comprehensively by L. J. Yarrow, 1964). My concern here is with the body of research that focuses on the effect of the partial separation of mother and child when the mother works.

WHO ARE THE WORKING MOTHERS?

The work pattern of American women has changed so radically over the past decades, and is still changing so rapidly, that it is difficult to provide up-to-date information. But let me point out a few trends and current characteristics of working women in this country.

First, the number of women with preschool and school-age children who are employed has increased enormously in the past 35 years. In 1940, there were about 1.5 million such women (about one mother in ten); in 1970, there were approximately 12 million, which was about 42 percent of all mothers; and in 1974, there were nearly 14 million, which represented about 47 percent of all mothers. (U.S. Department of Labor, 1973a, 1975) There is every reason to expect that the percentage of working women with children will continue to increase over the next years.

Second, the number of working women with *young* children (under age 6) is also on the increase. For example, in 1970, there were about 19.6 million children under age 6, of whom 28 percent had working mothers. Only four years later, in 1974, there were about 18.5 million children under age 6 and 33 percent of them had working mothers. So in 1974, there were over 6 million children under the age of 6 with working mothers.

Third, during this same period there has been a sharp increase in the number of households headed by divorced, deserted, widowed, or never married women with children. These women are more likely to be employed than are mothers with husbands. Of the 6 million children with working mothers, about

TABLE 1 CHILD-CARE ARRANGEMENTS MADE BY WORKING MOTHERS

	Children under age 3	Children 3–5
Child cared for in the home by someone other than mother	45.9%	48.2%
Child cared for in another home by a relative or nonrelative	41.8%	34.3%
Child cared for in a group center of some kind	4.8%	9.7%
Child looked after him/herself	0.2%	0.3%
Mother cared for the child while she was at work	6.4%	6.9%
Other	1.0%	0.8%

Source: Low and Spindler (1968).

1 million are from families in which the mother is the only parent present, and about 5 million are from intact families.

Who takes care of these 6 million children while the mother is working? Current data on child-care arrangements made by working mothers are very difficult to obtain. Table 1 shows what the figures looked like as of 1965 (Low and Spindler, 1968).

Surveys taken in 1970 (see Emlen and Perry, 1974, for a review) show that the percentage of children in center care increased quite substantially between 1965 and 1970, but center care still made up a total of only about 10 percent of all care arrangements for children under 6 in 1970. There is more recent evidence that center care may be on the upswing. A survey taken of child-care arrangements made by 320 working women in New York City in 1971 (U.S. Department of Labor, 1973*b*) revealed that 40 percent of the children under 2 years of age were being cared for in the child's home by someone other than the mother, about 53 percent were in "family day care," that is, were being cared for in someone else's home, and only about 6 percent were in center care. But for the 3- to 5-year-old children in this same study, the pattern was somewhat different: 21 percent were being cared for at home, 43 percent were in family day care, and about 36 percent were in day-care centers. This higher rate of center use may reflect conditions peculiar to New York City, or it may reflect broader national trends toward more center use as such centers become more available.

Several points should be made about all these facts. First, the number of working mothers with young children is increasing steadily, so there is more reason than ever to have good information about the consequences of such employment for the child. Second, I want to emphasize the facts shown in Table 1: *most* young children of working mothers are *not* in group day-care centers. They are cared for in their own homes or in small family day-care settings in someone else's home. So most such children are not in "institutional" care.

METHODOLOGICAL CONSIDERATIONS

How would you go about discovering whether a mother's working has any effect on the child? Hoffman, in her review in the selections, repeatedly mentions the difficult methodological problems in this area and the lack of methodological sophistication of much of the research. Why are the problems so complex?

The obvious procedure seems to be to select a group of families with working mothers and a group with nonworking mothers and compare the two groups. One might compare the characteristics of the mother's relationship to the child, the type of child-rearing practices she uses, or the child's degree of dependency or emotional stability. One might look at the academic performance or IQ test scores of children of working versus nonworking mothers. A good deal of research of this general design has been done, but it has not resulted in very clear conclusions. The reasons for the lack of clarity in the conclusions lie in the design itself. There are several major pitfalls in this sort of research procedure. Because the set of problems involved is fairly typical of the types of difficulties one encounters in attempting to do adequate research on socially relevant issues, let me go into them in some detail.

First, who is a working mother? If you are selecting a sample of working mothers, how long do they have to have worked before you are willing to classify them as "working"? One month? one year? ten years? What about part-time work? Is that the same thing as full-time work? What about work in the home? Is that the same thing from the child's point of view? For example, I work in my "office" at home every day. Before she began school, our youngest child was cared for by her father during the time I was working. As far as she was concerned, I "went away" for several hours every morning, but she knew exactly where I was and that I was available in an emergency. Is the psychological effect on the child in such an arrangement the same as if I had gone to an office in a distant place for several hours or for the whole day?

More troublesome still is the problem of the work history of potential subjects. Many women do not work all the time; they may have periods of several years when they are at home and periods of work during the early years of individual children. Depending on the time the study is done, such women may be classed as "working" or "nonworking." To give just one example of the sort of pickle this can get the researcher into, Rees and Palmer (1970) report that 15-year-old girls whose mothers were employed compared to 15-year-old girls whose mothers were not employed, had had higher IQs at age 6 and at age 15, but had not been different at age 12. What Rees and Palmer do not report is whether the working mothers had been working when the daughters were 6 and 12. The absence of this information makes the results very nearly uninterpretable.

Obviously the selection of nonworking mothers is going to be equally troublesome. Should you pick women who have never worked, not even before the birth of their children? Is it okay to include women who have worked but are not working now? Ideally, if you want a proper contrast, you would have to compare women who have never worked, or at least not since the birth of the child you are studying, with women who have worked for some extended period and are away from the home while they work. Many of the studies of working mothers have not achieved this kind of contrast; they have included women in the nonworking group who have worked since the birth of the child but are not working now; and they have included women in the working group who have worked for very short periods. As a consequence, it is difficult to draw very clear conclusions from the results.

Even if you are able to solve the problem of defining "working" and "nonworking" mothers, you have a second major difficulty. Suppose you pick two groups with nicely contrasting work histories. Two such groups are likely to differ in many other ways as well. The woman who chooses to work for her own satisfaction is undoubtedly different in many ways from the woman who chooses not to work. A woman who works primarily for financial reasons comes from a family that is different from that of a woman who has no financial need to work. Unless you take these differences into account when selecting your samples, you cannot be sure that the differences found in the children, or in the mother-child relationships, are due to the fact that the mother works. They could be due to the fact that fathers are less likely to be present in homes with working mothers, to lower income, or to any one of the many other variables that differentiate the home in which the mother works from the home in which she does not.

There are several ways to solve these problems. One way is to choose very large samples of working and nonworking mothers so that you can look at subgroups as well as the group as a whole. Yarrow, Scott, de Leeuw, and Heinig, whose paper is included in this section, have used this strategy in their study. Another way is to select matched pairs of working and nonworking mothers. That is, you try to match each working woman with a nonworking woman on all the characteristics that you suspect will matter, so that as nearly as possible the two groups differ only in the employment status of the mother. There are very few studies of this kind, primarily because such matching is extremely difficult, but there are some (see, for example, Siegel, Stolz, Hitchcock, and Adamson, 1959; Hoffman, 1963).

The third methodological issue has to do with how one locates the sample of working mothers in the first place. Opponents of employment for mothers are likely to emphasize studies in which the families selected were among those whose children had been referred to child guidance clinics (see Poznanski, Maxey, and Marsden, 1970). Typically, researchers using this strategy select, from children who are already showing difficulties, a group whose mothers are working and compare them to a group whose mothers are not working. If the children of the working mothers have some common disturbance, the conclusion is drawn that this type of disturbance is a typical result of maternal employment (see, for example, Rouman, 1957). You should keep in mind that research of this kind does *not* tell you anything about the majority of children of working mothers. It does not even tell you what percentage of children of working mothers are in child guidance clinics with difficulties of any kind. What the research may tell you is that *when* children of working mothers have emotional or cognitive difficulties, those difficulties tend to be of a particular kind compared to the emotional or cognitive difficulties that may be characteristic of disturbed children from homes in which the mother does not work.

A final methodological problem, according to Hoffman, has as much to do with the analysis of data as it does with the design of the research. Psychologists have tended to treat "working" as if it were a single variable—a characteristic of mothers like having blue eyes. But it is *not* something simple, and not the same "event" from one woman to another. Is the mother's work at a professional level, or is she working at a routine clerical or industrial job? Does she like her work and find it satisfying, or does she dislike it? Has the mother been able to find adequate alternative care for her child? Is there a father in the home? Are the household chores shared with the father, or does the mother have all of these duties as well as her outside-the-home job? What is the social class or educational level of the mother? What is the attitude toward maternal employment within the ethnic and social class group in which she lives? All these factors will affect the mother's attitudes toward her work as well as her interactions with her children. Most research in this area does not provide sufficient information about variables of this sort.

Similarly, the effect of maternal employment on the child will vary as a function of the child's characteristics. The effect may be quite different on girls than on boys, as Hoffman suggests in her review. And the social class level of the family may also affect the results. Only recently have researchers begun to report their findings separately for boys and for girls, as well as for separate social class levels.

The point to remember after all these cautions about methodological problems have been given, is that it is difficult to do adequate research in this area, but not impossible. This is demonstrated in the paper by Yarrow and colleagues and by others described in Hoffman's review. But you should keep the various pitfalls in mind as you review the literature.

THE EVIDENCE

The available information is reviewed so well in the Hoffman paper that there is little need to reiterate her comments and conclusions. Let me merely emphasize a few points I think are particularly important.

First, the effects of maternal employment seem to be different on boys than on girls, although the somewhat confusing results for boys make one hungry for more and better data. In general, the effects on girls seem to be positive, whereas the effects on boys are mixed, and there are some hints of negative effects.

Second, the mother's feeling about her role—whether she is working or not—seems to be an important mediating variable, as the paper by Yarrow and associates clearly shows. In their study the children who showed the poorest general adjustment were those who had mothers who were at home full time but wished they were working. Other evidence, reviewed by Hoffman, supports this finding. So it is clear that working per se is not the critical factor.

Another mediating variable, which Hoffman does not emphasize very strongly, but which I think is probably fairly critical for very young children, is the nature of the alternative care provided for the child. Moore (1964) has provided perhaps the best data; his findings indicate that children of working mothers who were in *stable* alternative care showed no negative effects. But children of working mothers who experienced unstable alternative care arrangements showed several signs of disturbance, including greater dependency, greater attention seeking, and more anxiety about being separated from the mother. Hoffman points out, however, that there are some methodological difficulties with this study that make the interpretation less clear-cut than one would like. This issue obviously will need to be explored further.

Several other issues have had too little research attention. There is not enough information on the impact of maternal employment on very young versus older children. This is particularly critical now as a greater proportion of women with young children enter the labor force. Is there some particular age at which separation of mother and child is detrimental? Does the nature of substitute care matter more for very young children? There is equally little information about the possible effects of different patterns of maternal employment. Is there more effect if the mother has been continuously employed, or is it disruptive if the mother has a more erratic or variable work history? One could argue that an on-again-off-again work pattern could be most disruptive to a child because it would probably be accompanied by varying alternative care patterns or other unstable conditions. Unfortunately, we have little or no data with which to address such questions.

Despite the gaps in the literature and the methodological problems, it seems fair to conclude at this point that if a woman is satisfied with her working role and adequate alternative care is arranged, there is not likely to be any negative effect on the child; indeed, in some instances, particularly for girls, there appear to be some clear benefits.

QUESTION FOR DEBATE AND DISCUSSION
1. Assume that you are the mother of a 1-year-old infant. An opportunity for a job you are interested in comes along. Should you take it? What factors enter into your decision?

ADDITIONAL REFERENCES USEFUL
IN PREPARATION FOR DEBATE OR DISCUSSION

Etaugh, C. Effects of maternal employment on children: A review of recent research. *Merrill-Palmer Quarterly,* 1974, **20,** 71–98.
A review that parallels Hoffman's to some extent, but is organized differently, and includes somewhat different material. If you are particularly interested in this topic, you would find new and useful information in this paper.

Hoffman, L. W., and Nye, F. I. *Working mothers.* San Francisco: Jossey-Bass, 1974.

A first-rate book that includes papers on a series of issues related to the working mother. If you are interested in the topic, this is the first place to look for up-to-date discussions.

Poznanski, E., Maxey, A., and Marsden, G. Clinical implications of maternal employment: A review of research. *Journal of the American Academy of Child Psychiatry,* 1970, **9,** 741–761.

Reviews the maternal employment literature from a generally psychoanalytic perspective. These authors are much less in favor of mothers' employment than are either Etaugh or Hoffman, so the paper should give you some of the alternative interpretations of the data that are possible.

Yarrow, L. J. Separation from parents during early childhood. In M. L. Hoffman and L. W. Hoffman (Eds.), *Review of child development Research.* Vol. 1. New York: Russell Sage Foundation, 1964, 89–136.

An excellent overall review of the literature on all aspects of parent-child separation, including the question of maternal employment.

REFERENCES

Bowlby, J. *Maternal care and mental health.* Monograph Series, No. 2. Geneva: World Health Organization, 1951.

Emlen, A. C., and Perry, J. B., Jr. Child-care arrangements. In L. W. Hoffman and F. I. Nye. *Working mothers.* San Francisco: Jossey-Bass, 1974, 101–125.

Hoffman, L. W. Mother's enjoyment of work and effect on the child. In F. I. Nye and L. W. Hoffman (Eds.), *The employed mother in America.* Chicago: Rand McNally, 1963.

Low, S., and Spindler, P. G. *Child care arrangements of working mothers in the United States.* Children's Bureau publication 461. Washington, D.C.: United States Government Printing Office, 1968.

Moore, T. Children of full-time and part-time mothers. *International Journal of Social Psychiatry,* 1964, **2,** 1–10.

Poznanski, E., Maxey, A., and Marsden, G. Clinical implications of maternal employment: A review of research. *Journal of the American Academy of Child Psychiatry,* 1970, **9,** 741–761.

Rees, A. N., and Palmer, F. H. Factors related to change in mental test performance. *Developmental Psychology Monograph,* 1970, **3**(2, Pt. 2).

Rouman, J. School children's problems as related to parental factors. *Journal of Educational Research,* 1957, **50,** 105–112.

Siegel, A. E., and Haas, M. B. The working mother: A review of research. *Child Development,* 1963, **34,** 513–542.

Siegel, A. E., Stolz, L. M., Hitchcock, E. A., and Adamson, J. M. Dependence and independence in the children of working mothers. *Child Development,* 1959, **30,** 533–546.

Smuts, R. W. *Woman and work in America.* New York: Columbia University Press, 1959.

U.S. Department of Labor, Women's Bureau, Employment Standards Administration. *Day care facts.* Pamphlet 16 (rev.), 1973*a.*

U. S. Department of Labor, Women's Bureau, Employment Standards Administration. *Employer personnel practices and child care arrangements of working mothers in New York City.* 1973*b.*

U. S. Department of Labor, Bureau of Labor Statistics. Children of working mothers, March, 1974. *Special Labor Force Report,* 174, 1975.

Yarrow, L. J. Separation from parents during early childhood. In M. L. Hoffman and L. W. Hoffman (Eds.), *Review of child development research.* Vol. 1. New York: Russell Sage Foundation, 1964, pp. 89–136.

Child rearing in families of working and nonworking mothers

MARIAN RADKE YARROW
PHYLLIS SCOTT
LOUISE DE LEEUW
CHRISTINE HEINIG

In the history of research on child development and child rearing, social concerns have often stimulated particular areas of inquiry. An instance is the work of the 1930's and 1940's on the influence of early institutionalization upon children. Society's concerns about the impact of hospitalization, orphanage placement and the like posed empirical questions which research recast and redefined as basic problems in socialization. In similar fashion the rapidly increasing employment of mothers has currently prodded investigation of the effects of this changed mother role on the rearing of children. Judged by frequency of occurrence in American family structure, maternal employment is a significant socialization variable: two out of five mothers of school-age children were reported in the labor force in the 1957 survey.[1]

The initial questions directed to research on this problem, motivated from the social welfare concerns, were broad and atheoretical: "What happens to children whose mothers work?" The questions were framed with the strong suggestion that the

From *Sociometry*, 1962, **25**(2). Reprinted by permission.

A grant from the Elizabeth McCormick Memorial Fund to the American Association of University Women made possible the work of Miss Christine Heinig and Miss Phyllis Scott.

[1] National Manpower Council, *Womanpower*, New York: Columbia University Press, 1957.

working mother was a "problem," creating conditions of child neglect, juvenile delinquency, disorganized family life, etc. The studies resulting from the practical orientation produced a confusion of findings. In her review of the research literature on maternal employment, Stolz[2] suggests that the inconclusive nature of findings may be laid to the failure of investigators to specify the circumstances surrounding mothers' employment (whether in broken or intact families, motivated from economic stress or personal satisfactions in work, with young or older children, with or without good substitute care) and to the failure of investigators to include adequate control groups.

The inconclusive results can also be explained by the fact that most studies have failed to conceptualize maternal employment in terms of theoretically relevant variables. For example, inherent in the situation of a mother's work outside the home are mother-child separation, multiple mothering, and changed mother-father roles, all of which are familiar variables of developmental research. It is apparent that maternal employment is not a single condition or variable of mothering; it is rather a set of conditions which may vary greatly from case to case.

The research questions in the present investigation are two: (1) When structural variables of the family environment (such as family class and composition, presence of mother, father, and supplemental mother figures) are controlled, do working and nonworking mothers provide different child-rearing environments? (2) Do working and nonworking mothers who differ in their attitudes and feeling about their adult roles differ in their maternal roles?

Personal variables which characterize the mother as an individual have generally been ignored in studies of child rearing. It is hypothesized that the mother's gratifications and frustrations in her other adult (non-mother) roles, her achievement needs, and her feelings of self-fulfillment influence her functioning as a mother and affect what is mediated to the child by her child-rearing practices. Since employment status may be ultimately bound up with the mother's self attitudes and values, the study of employed and nonemployed mothers who differ in attitudes offers an opportunity for an initial test of the more general hypothesis concerning the significance of this class of variables in socialization studies. The particular personal factors studied are those relating to the meaning of working or not working, i.e., the woman's sex role ideology, her basic preferences regarding work-

[2] Lois M. Stolz, Effects of Maternal Employment on Children: Evidence from Research, *Child Development*, 31 (December 1960), pp. 749–782.

ing or not, the motivations supporting her present work status, and her motivations in her role as mother.

Choice of dependent variables was made on the basis of existing opinion and theory concerning the possible consequences of maternal employment for the rearing of children. Working is presumed to result in "deficiencies" in mothering: less dedication and less effectiveness, deviations in supervision and control of the child, exaggeration of the child's dependency needs, greater stress on achievement, altered sex role training, and decreased participation of mother with child.[3] Mothers' reports of practices and philosophies constitute the data on child rearing.

SAMPLE

The subjects of this study are 50 employed and 50 nonemployed mothers. The classification of *working* required at least 28 hours of work per week in steady employment extending over the past year. To be classed in the *nonworking* group, the mother could not have engaged in any paid employment over the past year. Unfortunately the two groups have similar work histories: all having worked at some time. Half of the nonworking mothers had worked after marriage, before the birth of a child.

Subjects of the employed and nonemployed groups were matched in family characteristics. Families were white, intact, with a male wage earner present. There were one to four children per family, with at least one child (about whom the mother was interviewed) between 4 and 11 years of age.

PROCEDURES

In selecting the sample it was the objective to choose social class groups in which employment is not a traditional role for married women, but in which both a traditional woman's role and a changed role exist and are tolerated, and in which differing values and sentiments about women's employment are held. We wished to have groups in which working or not working is more likely to be a matter of individual choice than of dire economic necessity. Narrowing the class range should also reduce variations in child-rearing values and practices, leaving remaining variations more clearly attributable to personal maternal factors or the maternal work role. Middle and upper middle class families and upper working class families living in middle class neighborhoods were included in the sample (Groups I, II, III, IV on the Hollingshead Index of Social Position).

[3] *Ibid.*

Family structural variations associated with maternal employment (separation of mother from child, substitute "mothers," changes in father and mother roles) were greatly reduced in range. Substitute care was primarily for the out-of-school hours, when, for the great majority, paid help or a relative (grandmother, aunt, occasionally an older sibling) cared for the children. Fathers retained wage earner roles in the homes of both groups.

The subjects were located in the Greater Washington area, in twelve public schools selected in terms of social class criteria. The location of eligible families in eight of the schools was facilitated by data on family characteristics from another study.[4] For these families, a letter, followed by a telephone call, determined willingness to cooperate in the study. For the other schools, it was necessary to canvass each home (with knowledge only of the age of the children) to enlist interest and determine eligibility. After preliminary screening on race and social class, approximately 650 families were further screened on family characteristics, using a brief set of polling-type questions. An eligible mother who did not consent to an interview after she had been informed of the nature of the study was counted as a refusal. Twenty-one percent of the working mothers and 17 percent of the mothers not employed did not consent to participate. Illness, imminent moving and the like, accounted for a few of the refusals. The other women indicated they preferred not to be research subjects. The social characteristics of the 100 interviewed mothers are presented in Table 1.

Interview Procedure

The subjects were interviewed in their homes. A schedule was followed as closely as was consistent with the responses of the subject. The interview dealt, in sequence, with the mother's past and present employment status, her motives for working or not working, and her attitudes concerning role differences of men and women as these relate to dependency and achievement needs and to primary responsibility to the home. Interview questions about child rearing included the kind of substitute care provided for the children in the mother's absence, mother's opinions about her own employment or nonemployment in relation to the rearing of her children, and mother's philosophy and practices in the areas of discipline, and control, dependency and indepen-

[4] Thomas L. Gillette, "The Working Mother: A Study of the Relationship Between Maternal Employment and Family Structure As Influenced by Social Class and Race," unpublished doctoral dissertation, University of North Carolina, 1961.

TABLE 1 CHARACTERISTICS OF
EMPLOYED AND NONEMPLOYED MOTHERS

Characteristics		Working mothers N = 50	Non-working mothers N = 50
Index of social position	I	16	13
	II	14	16
	III	8	14
	IV	12	7
Number of children in family	Mean	2.14	2.36
Sex of children	Girls	27	27
	Boys	37	37
Age of children[a]	9–11 years	36	38
	6–8 years	21	19
	4–5 years	7	7
Age of mother	29–39	28	24
	40–50	22	26
Education of mother			
Some college or college graduate		30	26
Some high school or high school graduate		20	24
Mother's occupation			
Professional		13	—
Semiprofessional or managerial		12	—
Clerical or secretarial		19	—
Service trades		6	—

[a] Mothers were interviewed with regard to the children who met the criteria of the sample; i.e., keeping the age between 4 and 11 years, and having age and sex comparable in working and nonworking samples.

dency training, warmth and involvement with the child and sex role training.

Independent Variables

Analyses of child-rearing variables were made in terms of the following group comparisons: (1) working and nonworking mothers of similar social and family circumstances, (2) working and nonworking mothers who *preferred* and those *who did not prefer* their present work or nonwork status, (3) working mothers whose *motives* for *working* differed, (4) nonworking mothers whose *attitudes toward the mother role* differed, and (5) working and nonworking mothers who differed in *academic achievement*.

The sixth variable of sex role ideology was not used because there was little variation among the subjects. It was reasoned in designing the study that ideology concerning masculine and feminine roles might be relevant to the mother's career choice and her functioning in the mother role. Therefore, subjects were asked how they felt about the ideological position that "woman's place is in the home," about the relative achievement needs of men and women, and about the acceptability of either sex showing dependency on the other. Responses were rated as predominantly equalitarian or traditional. Only 15 percent of the mothers were rated traditional on two or three of the dimensions, 44 percent were rated traditional in one dimension, and 41 percent were traditional in none of the dimensions. The decision to work or not seems, for the vast majority of the sample, to be outside of this area of ideological consideration, in spite of a rare expression or two, such as, "It is God's will that woman does what man wants."

Independent and dependent variables of child rearing are described in more detail in the presentation of the findings and in the Appendix. Group differences in child rearing were evaluated using Chi squares for qualitative data and "t" tests for quantitative data. A sample of 26 interviews was coded by two raters working independently. A few codes were dropped which did not reach an arbitrary minimum of 80 percent coder agreement. Forty-seven percent of coded categories used in the report were between 80 percent and 89 percent in inter-rater agreement; 53 percent of the coded categories were 90 percent or above in agreement.

Dependent Variables

Several aspects of the child-rearing relationship were explored in the interview. Relative to areas of discipline and control the interviewer attempted to draw out the general tone of control in the home: how strict was the mother and how did mother and father compare on strictness? Both a direct question to the mother and a rating based on answers to all interview questions on control were obtained. Since the two scores were highly correlated, only the mother's direct statement was used in analysis. The mother was questioned about techniques of discipline used more than occasionally with her child. She was questioned in more detail about the child's display of aggressive behavior and her handling of his aggression. An overall evaluation was made of the degree to which discipline and control seemed to be a contested issue between mother and child. The interview questions forming the basis for ratings and the nature of the rating scales are given in the Appendix for each of the dependent variables.

The nature of dependency-independency relations between mother and child is not easily tapped by interview questions. Questions were asked about the areas in which the child was granted freedom of decision and action and in which he was given responsibility, and the kinds and amount of attention and help which the child sought from his mother. The child's age was taken into consideration in judging the degree to which these factors signified dependence of child and independency training by the mother.

The mother's sensitivity, emotional satisfaction and involvement with her children and her confidence in her mother role were judged by criteria applied to the total interview or sections of questioning rather than to specific questions.

The underlying philosophy and operation of rearing were appraised in the following terms: Did the mother have clearly formulated principles regarding child rearing or did she proceed in a kind of haphazard performance of child care-taking acts as the needs arose? How did principles of rearing carry over into practice? Were the limits set for the child clear or unclear in practice?

Working might make a difference in household schedule, therefore the amount of time pressure or close scheduling was rated. Because of possible differences between working and nonworking women in attitudes toward sex roles, the mother's philosophy about the rearing of boys and girls, and the practices of the family in carrying out household duties, whether according to traditional sex-typed patterns or not, were obtained.

Finally, prior to data analysis, a model of "good" mothering was constructed which combined a set of variables of philosophy and practice. The "good" mother is described in terms of eight variables measured by the interview. (1) At a cognitive level, the "good" mother gives evidence of some formulated principles that guide her rearing practices. (2) She recognizes the importance of supporting the individual potentialities and the growing independence of the child. (3) She shows reasonable consistency between her principles and reported practices. (4) The "good" mother's practices provide clear limits for her child. (5) She establishes controls which are accepted without continuing conflict between parent and child. (6) The "good" mother shows sensitivity to the individual child's needs. (7) She has a feeling of confidence about her child rearing (though she is not necessarily without problems) and (8) she expresses warmth and emotional satisfaction in her relationship with her child. A summary score (0 to 8) of "adequacy of mothering" was derived from ratings on these eight variables.

FINDINGS
Work Status

As indicated in Table 2, the classification of mothers by whether or not they are employed is almost unrelated to child-rearing patterns. These working and nonworking mothers, who are of similar cultural background and family circumstances, are very much alike in philosophy, practices and apparent relationships with their children. In only one comparison is the difference between the groups statistically significant at the 5 percent level. This difference is in the mother's confidence about her role as mother. Working mothers (42 percent) more frequently than nonworking mothers (24 percent) express misgivings and anxious concern about their role, often by explicit questioning and worry as to whether working is interfering with their relationships and the rearing of their children.

Absence of differences in certain of the variables is particularly interesting. The working and nonworking mothers do not express differing points of view on sex role training. About 40 percent of the total sample present opinions or philosophies which emphasize differences in the rearing of boys and girls in such respects as handling of aggression, activity, social relationships; 40 percent reject the idea of rearing differences; the others are uncertain. Using household responsibilities that are assigned to boys and girls as a measure of sex role typing, families of working and nonworking mothers again do not differ (40 percent in the working group, 42 percent in the nonworking assign tasks in terms of traditional sex roles). It may seem reasonable to expect that a working mother will have greater need to schedule time carefully and may, therefore, inject more time-tension into family routines. There is only a suggestive difference in the expected direction; pressured scheduling is prominent among 26 percent of the working and 12 percent of the nonworking group. Working and nonworking mothers do not differ on the summary measure of adequacy of mothering.

Role Preference

More important in differentiating mothers according to child-rearing practices than the fact of working or not working is how the work variable is combined with other maternal characteristics (Table 2). When work (or nonwork) is analyzed according to whether it is a goal in itself or a means to certain goal attainments, associations with child rearing take on more meaningful patternings. The mothers clearly differed in their desire to work or not to work outside the home. Replies to two questions determined their classification as preferring or not preferring their pre-

TABLE 2 PARENT-CHILD RELATIONSHIPS BY WORK STATUS AND

Parent-child variables	All mothers
Discipline	
1. Mother's strictness	—
2. Father stricter than mother	—
3. Disciplinary techniques	—
4. Mother's permissiveness of aggression	—
5. Child's rebellious behavior	W < NW (.10)
6. Control an issue between mother and child	—
Independence training	
1. Nurturing independence	—
2. Household responsibilities	—
3. Child's dependence on mother	—
Emotional relationships	
1. Sensitivity to child's needs	W < NW (.10)
2. Emotional satisfaction in relationships with child	—
3. Planned activities with child:	
by mother	—
by father	—
4. Confidence in child rearing	W < NW (.05)
Rearing environment	
1. Formulated principles of rearing	—
2. Clarity of limits set for child	—
3. Consistency between principles and practices	—
4. Scheduling	W > NW (.10)
5. Traditional philosophy re sex role training	—
6. Traditional sex-typed household functions	—
7. Adequacy of mothering (summary rating)	—

[a] The probability that an observed relationship could have occurred by chance is

sent status: (1) If given the choice, would the mother want to work, and (2) how would she rank a number of alternatives involving job, marriage, and children? Seventy-six percent of the working mothers and 82 percent of the nonworking mothers indicated preference for their present situations. The resulting four subgroups were compared in their child-rearing characteristics.

The questions about these groups can be asked in two ways: (1) Do working and nonworking mothers who are similarly satisfied (or dissatisfied) with present status differ in child rearing? (2) How do working mothers who prefer to work and those

SATISFACTION OF MOTHER[a]

Working vs. nonworking mothers		Satisfied vs. dissatisfied	
Satisfied	Dissatisfied	Working	Non-working
—	—	S < D (.05)	—
—	—	—	—
—	—	—	—
—	W < NW (.05)	—	—
—	W < NW (.01)	S < D (.10)	S < D (.05)
—	—	S < D (.10)	—
—	—	S < D (.10)	—
—	—	S < D (.02)	—
W < NW (.05)	—	—	—
—	W > NW (.10)	—	S > D (.02)
—	—	—	—
—	—	—	—
—	W > NW (.10)	—	D < S (.01)
—	—	—	—
—	W > NW (.10)	S < D (.05)	S > D (.05)
—	—	—	S > D (.01)
—	—	—	—
—	—	—	—
W < NW (.10)	W > NW (.02)	—	S > D (.01)

indicated in parentheses.

who do not prefer to work compare, and, likewise, how do nonworking mothers who prefer to work and those who do not prefer to work compare on child rearing?

Dissatisfaction with present role appears to contribute to mothering functions, and especially among mothers who are not employed. The subgroups differ as follows. If mothers are in their *preferred* work or nonwork *roles,* working or not working makes little difference in their child rearing. There are only two suggestive differences: Thirty-four percent of satisfied nonworking mothers and 11 percent of satisfied working mothers are rated as showing high sensitivity to children's needs. There is a difference of borderline significance giving the nonworking satisfied mothers higher scores on adequacy of mothering. When *dissatisfied* working and nonworking mothers are compared, differences appear in areas of control, emotional satisfaction, confidence in child rearing and on scores on adequacy of mothering, favoring the dissatisfied working mothers. For example 67 percent of dissatisfied nonworking mothers and 18 percent of dissatisfied working mothers report a more or less continuing "battle" for control between mother and child. High ratings in confidence in the mother role occur more often among the working than the nonworking dissatisfied mothers (50 percent and 11 percent, respectively). In the closely related measure of emotional satisfaction in relationship with the child there are similar differences favoring the working over the nonworking dissatisfied mothers. The sum of ratings shows significantly lower scores on adequacy of mothering for the dissatisfied nonworking mothers than for the dissatisfied working mothers.

The same data may be examined with work status controlled. Among *working* mothers there is some support for the idea that there are more internal inconsistencies in child rearing among the dissatisfied than among the satisfied mothers. Three-fourths of the dissatisfied mothers compared with two-fifths of the satisfied mothers report clear limit setting for the child. At the same time, however, control is more often rated a continuing issue in the family for the dissatisfied than for the satisfied mothers. More dissatisfied working mothers describe their children as dependent while at the same time tending to exert more verbal pressure toward independent behavior and to assign more responsibilities to their children than do the satisfied mothers.

Among *nonworking* mothers, several dimensions of child-rearing behavior are clearly related to role preference. Clarity in limit setting is more characteristic of the satisfied mothers (61 percent of this group as compared with 22 percent in the dissatisfied group). A significantly higher proportion of dissatisfied mothers show extreme inconsistency between principles and practices (57 percent of the dissatisfied mothers as compared with 6 percent of the satisfied mothers). Control remains a continuing "issue" between mother and child for 67 percent of the dissatisfied and 32 percent of the satisfied mothers. Lack of emotional satisfaction in relationships with her child is more frequent among dissatisfied than satisfied mothers (78 percent and 35 percent, respectively). Similarly, high confidence in the mother role, expressed in 90 percent of the satisfied group, is rare (11 percent) among the dissatisfied mothers. The generally inferior mothering by the dissatisfied nonworking group is reflected in significantly lower summary scores on adequacy of mothering.

Motives for Working and Not Working

Although it is understandable that a woman's career dissatisfactions may enter into her relationships with her child, it is not so clear why this should be more the case in the nonworking than in the working group. A possible explanation may lie in understanding why the women were working or not working, regardless of their expressed preference. The mothers in this sample were working either primarily as a means of achieving certain *family and child-rearing goals* that were not available without the mother's working, or as a means of *self-fulfillment*. Mothers (52 percent) who spoke of family goals were interested in cultural advantages, social status, educational and health goals for the family. They included both mothers who preferred and those who did not prefer to work. Mothers (48 percent) who found self-fulfillment through working referred to use of their educational training, feelings of contributing to society, needing to be with people, etc. These mothers preferred to work.

Since working but preferring not to is related to valued family benefits, the situation for these reluctant working mothers does not appear to represent great frustration. Certainly one would expect these mothers to be less frustrated than women who have reason to resent the necessity for their working as a circumstance forced upon them by their husbands' failures or as a circumstance in which the work itself involves personal hardship. The absence of differences in child rearing associated with family motivations and self-fulfillment motivation is, therefore, not surprising (Table 3).

Among nonworking women reasons for not working reflect either a *love of mothering* (48 percent), *a duty of mothering* (36 percent), or a desire for "freedom," or an "easier" life (15 percent). "Freedom" is for avocations and "volunteer" work but also, on the less noble side, it is freedom regarded selfishly. As one woman said, she "had it made"; now that husband and children could get their own breakfasts and get off to work and school, the day was for herself. Because of the heterogeneity of motives in the "freedom" group, it was not used in further analyses.

Mothers classified by "love" and by "duty" express different feelings toward the mother role. The "love" mothers are oriented entirely toward mothering; the "duty" mothers speak of child rearing as a responsibility that carries with it various hardships and deprivations. The classification of "love" and "duty" in

TABLE 3 PARENT-CHILD RELATIONSHIPS BY WORK STATUS,

Parent-child variables	Family vs. self motives: working mother only	Love vs. duty motives: non-working mothers only
Discipline		
1. Mother's strictness	—	—
2. Father stricter than mother	F > S (.10)	—
3. Disciplinary techniques	—	—
4. Mother's permissiveness of aggression	F > S (.10)	—
5. Child's rebellious behavior	—	L < D (.10)
6. Control an issue between mother and child	—	L < D (.10)
Independence training		
1. Nurturing independence	—	L > D (.05)
2. Household responsibilities	—	—
3. Child's dependence on mother	—	—
Emotional relationships		
1. Sensitivity to child's needs	—	L > D (.02)
2. Emotional satisfaction in relationships with child	—	L > D (.05)
3. Planned activities with child:		
by mother	—	—
by father	—	—
4. Confidence in child rearing	—	L > D (.02)
Rearing environment		
1. Formulated principles of rearing	—	—
2. Clarity of limits set for child	—	—
3. Consistency between principles and practices	—	—
4. Scheduling	—	—
5. Traditional philosophy re sex role training	F < S (.05)	—
6. Traditional sex-typed household functions	—	—
7. Adequacy of mothering (summary rating)	—	L > D (.05)

[a] The probability that an observed relationship could have occurred by chance is

MOTIVATION, AND EDUCATION OF MOTHER[a]

Working vs. nonworking mothers		High school vs. college attendance	
High school attendance	College attendance	Working mothers	Non-working mothers
—	—	—	—
W > NW (.05)	—	H > C (.02)	—
—	—	—	—
—	—	—	—
W < NW (.01)	—	—	—
—	—	—	—
—	—	—	—
W > NW (.05)	—	—	H < C (.05)
W > NW (.10)	—	—	—
—	—	—	—
—	W < NW (.10)	H < C (.02)	H < C (.01)
—	—	—	—
—	W > NW (.10)	—	—
—	W > NW (.02)	—	—
—	—	—	—
—	—	—	—
—	—	—	H < C (.05)
—	W < NW (.02)	—	H < C (.02)
—	—	—	—
—	—	—	—
—	—	—	—
—	—	—	H < C (.05)

indicated in parentheses.

general parallels the classification of satisfied and dissatisfied
nonworking mothers, although "duty" mothers appear in both the
satisfied and dissatisfied groups. Differences in child rearing are
similar in both classifications; the less favorable qualities appearing in the "duty" and the dissatisfied mothers.

The data on the nonworking mothers support the position
that the mother's motivations and fulfillments in non-mother
roles are related to her behavior in the child-rearing role. It is
necessary, in a sense, first to look at maternal employment and
nonemployment as dependent variables before making predictions concerning associated child-rearing variables.

Mothers' Education

If work status is ignored, college-trained and high school-
trained mothers (within the class range of our sample) do not
differ on child-rearing measures. But, when work status and educational level and child rearing are considered together, suggestive interactions appear (Table 3). *Nonworking* college mothers
and nonworking high school mothers appear to differ in more
ways in child rearing than do *working* college mothers and working high school mothers. In the *nonworking* groups, college
mothers are significantly more often rated high in independence
training (30 percent and 8 percent for college and high school,
respectively), in sensitivity (50 percent and 8 percent), in consistency between principles and practice (85 percent and 54 percent), and in clarity in limit setting (69 percent and 39 percent).
The higher mean scores for college mothers on the "adequacy of
mothering" summary score reflect the differences on the individual items. The *working* groups differ only on ratings of sensitivity
to child's needs (40 percent and 10 percent of high school and
college mothers, respectively, are rated low on sensitivity), and
on the father's being the stricter parent (70 percent and 34 percent of high school and college groups are so rated). The data
suggest that employment may be selective of certain kinds of
mothers, or that working has the effect of "leveling" social class
differences in child rearing. The mothers of high school background who are using working as a means of social mobility
(more lessons, education, travel for family) may also be altering
their child-rearing practices.

When working and nonworking mothers are compared
within each educational group, it appears that families of different social class backgrounds make different types of adaptations
to the mother's working. Mothers of high school background
more often report the father as the stricter parent when these
mothers work (70 percent) than when they do not work (33 percent). Children are less likely to be reported as rebellious by

working mothers (10 percent) than by nonworking mothers (46 percent) in the high school group. Similarly, they are more likely to be assigned a heavy load of household responsibilities (30 percent as compared with 8 percent). The working mothers are more likely to stress independence training (80 percent as compared with 54 percent). In other words, children of the working mothers with *high school* backgrounds are under firmer control and are called upon to perform with more responsibility and independence.

The picture for the college-trained group is not the same. The college working mother compared with her nonworking peers is not more likely to describe the father as the stricter parent; there is instead a tendency in the opposite direction (the father is the stricter parent in 30 percent and 50 percent of the working and nonworking groups, respectively). Assignment of responsibilities and nurturance of independence are not stressed by the college-trained working mothers as they are by the working mothers with high school background. (The differences, though not significant, are in the opposite direction from the high school group.)

A variable which has not shown differences in any other comparisons but which appears in the working-nonworking comparisons of college-trained women is that of planned shared time and activities with the child. In the families of college working mothers both parents apparently attempt to compensate for out-of-the-home time by planned time together with the child. Forty percent of the college working mothers report giving planned time to the child. It is reported for 38 percent of the fathers. The nonworking college group have 16 percent and 8 percent in the comparable categories. In families of high school background there is no difference in this variable between working and nonworking groups.

Subcultural or social class analyses may be extremely important in attempting to pin down the kinds of influences that the widespread employment of mothers may have on the socialization of large populations of children. The present data suggest that rearing influences cannot be predicted across class and cultural boundaries (any more than they can be predicted across motivational differences among mothers), and that the nature of influences for different social groups will vary and will grow out of the values and needs of the particular groups.

SUMMARY AND CONCLUSIONS

Qualities of child rearing by mothers who are employed and those who are not employed outside the home have been studied. One hundred mothers of intact families, of the middle and upper middle class white urban population were interviewed. Families of working and nonworking mothers were matched on family composition and social class.

Mothers' employment status is not related to child-rearing characteristics. The data, however, support the hypothesis that mothers' fulfillments or frustrations in non-mother roles are related to child rearing. When mothers' motivations regarding working are taken into account, the nonworking mothers who are dissatisfied with not working (who want to work but, out of a feeling of "duty," do not work) show the greatest problems in child rearing. They describe more difficulties in the area of control, less emotional satisfaction in relationships with their children, and less confidence in their functioning as mothers. They have lower summary scores on "adequacy of mothering." Working mothers who prefer to work and those who do not wish to work show few group differences in child-rearing practices, probably because the working mothers (of this sample) who prefer not to work are nonetheless achieving certain valued family goals by means of their employment.

Among high-school-trained mothers, differences between working and nonworking mothers appear in the following areas of rearing: firmer control over children, assignment of greater responsibilities to children, and delegation of the stricter disciplinary role to the father appear more frequently in families of working than nonworking mothers. In the college-trained working and nonworking group, these differences do not appear. The college working parents tend to compensate for time away from children by more planned, shared activities with their children than is found in the college nonworking group. The data on educational groups suggest that maternal employment brings different kinds of familial adaptations depending on the value systems of the particular cultural subgroups in which the mother is combining mother and worker roles.

The findings of the present study confirm and elaborate observations by other investigators[5] of the importance of social, familial and personal factors in determining the kind of success the mother achieves in her dual roles. The specific differences in child-rearing practices reported in the present study are perhaps

---

[5] *Ibid.;* Ruth E. Hartley, What Aspects of Child Behavior Should be Studied in Relation to Maternal Employment? In Alberta E. Siegel, editor, *Research Issues Related to the Effects of Maternal Employment on Children,* University Park, Pennsylvania: Social Science Research Center, 1961; Lois Hoffman, "Effects of Maternal Employment on the Child," *Child Development,* 32 (March 1961), pp. 187–197; Alberta E. Siegel "Characteristics of the Mother Related to the Impact of Maternal Employment or Non-employment," in Alberta E. Siegel, editor, *op. cit.*

less important in our conclusions (until they are replicated) than is the general pattern of significant subgroupings of mothers in relation to child rearing.

The findings of this study have relevance for studies of child rearing more generally in pointing to the interplay of rearing practices (as they are usually defined) and maternal motivations within differing subcultures. These variables need further scrutiny in studies of child-rearing antecedents of child behavior and personality.

Effects of maternal employment on the child: a review of the research

LOIS WLADIS HOFFMAN

In a previous review of the literature on the effects of maternal employment on the child, we pointed out that the earlier view that maternal employment had a great many effects on the child, all of them bad, had been replaced by a new outlook—that maternal employment had no effects at all (Hoffman, 1963a). We assumed that maternal employment did have an effect. What the effect was might depend on the nature of the employment, the attitude of the working mother, her family circumstances, the social class, whether employment is full or part time, the age and sex of the child, the kinds of child care arrangements that are set up, and a whole host of other conditions, but until the research questions had been properly defined and explored, we were not prepared to concede that there was no effect. While studies of maternal employment as a general concept yielded little, it was suggested that examining the effects under specified conditions might prove more fruitful. To demonstrate, we tried to show that when the relationships between maternal employment and a child characteristic were examined separately for various subgroups, interesting patterns were revealed. Thus, juvenile delinquency did seem to relate to maternal employment in the middle class, although it did not in the lower class. Part-time maternal employment seemed to have a positive effect on adolescent children, although this was not equally true for full-time employment

Lois Wladis Hoffman, "Effects of maternal employment on the child—a review of the research." In *Developmental Psychology*, 1974, **10**. Copyright © 1974 by the American Psychological Association. Reprinted by permission.

or for younger children. The lack of consistent findings with respect to the effects on the child's independence or academic achievement was tied to the failure to examine these relationships separately for each sex. and the mother's attitude toward employment was seen as an important aspect of the situation that would affect her child-rearing behavior and thus mediate the impact of her employment on the child.

It was our hope that such speculations would give rise to new empirical investigations, but the intervening years have produced few studies of maternal employment. About the same time our review was published three others appeared: Stolz, 1960; Siegel and Haas, 1963; and Yudkin and Holme, 1963. Perhaps the overall impression given was not that maternal employment required more careful study, but that it should not be studied at all. Most of the more recent studies reviewed here were only incidentally interested in the effects of maternal employment on the child, and the few that focused on this variable were modest in scope.

On the other hand, it was previously noted that segments of the American population that contributed more than an equal share of the working mothers—blacks and single-parent families in particular—were not studied at all. A few investigators have begun to fill this gap (Kriesberg, 1970; Rieber & Womack, 1968; Smith, 1969; Woods, 1972).

Moreover, there have been some methodological improvements. Few studies today would lump boys and girls together, and most consider relationships separately for each social class. Several studies have, in fact, focused only on one class—the professional mother being a particularly popular subject currently (Birnbaum, 1971; Garland, 1972; Hoffman, 1973; Holmstrom, 1972; Jones, Lundsteen, & Michael, 1967; Poloma, 1972; Rapoport & Rapoport, 1972). These studies have, in turn, revealed the need to consider both the education of the parents and the nature of the mother's job. The new studies indicate that the mother who works as a professional has a very different influence than one who works in a less intellectually demanding and less prestigious position. Since women's jobs often underuse their talents and training, education and the nature of the job are important singly and also in interaction.

Even methodologically, however, the studies leave much to be desired. Very few controlled on family size or ordinal position, although these variables relate to both maternal employment and most of the child characteristics studied. Failure to match on these may give an advantage to the working mother, since her family is smaller, and small family size contributes positively to cognitive abilities, particularly in the lower class (Clausen & Clausen, 1973). The need to control on more than one variable simultaneously is apparent in a number of reports, while the crudeness of the social class control is a problem in others.

But the most distressing aspect of the current research situation is the lack of theory. The typical study uses the sniper approach—maternal employment is run against whatever other variables are at hand, usually scores on intelligence tests or personality inventories. Even when a study indicates a complex pattern of findings or results counter to the accumulated research, no attempt is made to explain the pattern or reconcile the discrepancy.

Furthermore, the typical study deals only with two levels—the mother's employment status and a child characteristic. The many steps in between—family roles and interaction patterns, the child's perceptions, the mother's feelings about her employment, the child-rearing practices—are rarely measured. As previously noted (Hoffman & Lippitt, 1960), the distance between an antecedent condition like maternal employment and a child characteristic is too great to be covered in a single leap. Several levels should be examined in any single study to obtain adequate insight into the process involved.

To help counteract the generally atheoretical aspect of so much of the maternal employment research, the present review tries to organize the data around five basic approaches.

HYPOTHESES ABOUT THE EFFECTS OF MATERNAL EMPLOYMENT ON THE CHILD

What is the process by which maternal employment might affect the child? The ideas, whether implicit or explicit, that seem to guide the research and discussion can be classified into five general forms:

1. Because the mother is employed, she, and possibly her husband, provide a different model of behavior for the children in the family. Children learn sex role behavior largely from their parents. To the extent that a different role is carried out by the working mother than the non-working mother, the child has a different conception of what the female role is. The self-concept of girls is particularly affected.

2. The mother's emotional state is influenced by whether or not she is employed, and this affects her interaction with her children.

3. Employed and nonemployed mothers probably use different child-rearing practices, not only because the mother's emotional state is different but also because the situational demands are different.
4. Because of her regular absences from the home, the working mother provides less personal supervision of her child than does the nonworking mother; and it is usually assumed that the supervision is less adequate.
5. Again, because of the working mother's regular absences from the home, the child is deprived, either emotionally or cognitively, or perceives her absence as rejection.

In the sections that follow we examine each of these hypotheses and report the relevant research.

The ultimate dependent variables that have been studied—that is, the child characteristics that are the focus of attention—can be classified as follows: (a) the child's social attitudes and values; (b) the child's general mental health and social adjustment and independence or dependence specifically; and (c) the child's cognitive abilities, achievement motivation, and intellectual performance. These are considered throughout the article. In addition, however, data on maternal employment and the child's academic achievement are reviewed in a separate section because much of these data are from simple two-level studies in which it is impossible to say what hypotheses are involved.

The Working Mother as Role Model

Hartley (1961) has observed that one experience common to all children of working mothers is that they "are exposed to a female parent who implements a social role not implemented by the female parents of other children" (p. 42). Since the child learns sex roles from observations of his parents, maternal employment influences his concept of the female role. More importantly, since one of the earliest statuses assigned to the child is that of gender, maternal employment presumably affects the female child's concept of herself and the behavior expected of her.

There is an impressive array of data to support this theory. Hartley (1961) found that elementary-school-age daughters of working mothers, in comparison to daughters of nonworking mothers, are more likely to say that both men and women typically engage in a wide variety of specified adult activities, ranging from using a sewing machine to using a gun and from selecting home furnishings to climbing mountains. That is, the daughters of working mothers indicated more similarity in the participation of men and women. They saw women as less restricted to their homes and more active in the world outside.[1]

That the division of labor between husband and wife is affected by maternal employment is well established. Husbands of employed women help more in household tasks including child care. While considerable traditionalism remains and working women engage in more domestic tasks than do their husbands, the division of household tasks is nonetheless more egalitarian when the mother is employed (Blood & Hamblin, 1958; Hall & Schroeder, 1970; Holmstrom, 1972; Kligler, 1954; Szolai, 1966; Walker, 1970b; Weil, 1961). Furthermore, this difference is reflected in the children's perceptions, as seen in Hoffman's (1963b) study of children in the third through sixth grades and Finkelman's (1966) more recent study of fifth- and sixth-graders. Children 5 years of age and older whose mothers work are more likely to approve of maternal employment (Duvall, 1955; Mathews, 1933), and King, McIntyre, and Axelson (1968) reported that ninth-graders whose mothers worked viewed maternal employment as less threatening to the marital relationship. These investigators also found that the greater the father's participation in household tasks, the more accepting of maternal employment were the adolescent boys and girls.

Furthermore, daughters of working mothers view work as something they will want to do when they are mothers. This was reported by Hartley (1960) in her study of elementary school children and in four studies of adolescent girls (Banducci, 1967; Below, 1969; Peterson, 1958; Smith, 1969). It was also found in college women (Almquist & Angrist, 1971; Zissis, 1964) and as a background factor among working professional women (Astin, 1969; Birnbaum, 1971).[2] Douvan (1963) and Roy (1963) found that adolescent daughters of working mothers were, in fact, more likely to be already employed.

Another closely related group of findings dealt with the attitudes toward women's roles in general. Are working mothers' children less likely to endorse a traditional or stereotypic view of

---

[1] When asked to indicate which activities women liked and disliked, the daughters of working mothers reported more liking and less disliking of all activities—household, work, and recreation.

[2] Studies of children usually deal with maternal employment at the time of the study. Adult subjects, on the other hand, typically report past employment, for example, "when you were growing up," and one does not know how old the child was at the time of the employment. The age of the child is also ambiguous in studies in which samples have been selected in terms of a characteristic of the mothers, since the ages of the children may vary.

women? Douvan (1963) found that the daughters of working mothers scored low on an index of traditional femininity.[3] Vogel, Broverman, Broverman, Clarkson, and Rosenkrantz (1970) studied the relationship between the sex role perceptions held by male and by female college students and their mothers' employment. Sex role perceptions were measured by having subjects describe the typical adult male and the typical adult female by checking a point along a continuum between two bipolar descriptions. Previous work with this scale had indicated which descriptions were more typically assigned to each sex and also which traits were seen as positive or negative. In general, the positively valued stereotypes about males included items that reflected effectiveness and competence; the highly valued female-associated items described warmth and expressiveness. Both male students and female students with employed mothers perceived significantly smaller differences between men and women, with the women being more affected by maternal employment than were the men. Furthermore, the effect of maternal employment was to raise the estimation of one's own sex; that is, each sex added positive traits usually associated with the opposite sex—daughters of working mothers saw women as competent and effective, while sons of working mothers saw men as warm and expressive.

This result is consistent with that of an interesting study by Baruch (1972a). College women were administered a measure developed by Goldberg (1967) in which subjects are presented with a number of journal articles and asked to judge the quality of the article and of the author. Half of the articles are given female names as authors, and half are given male names. Previous research by Goldberg had indicated that college women tend to attach a lower value to the articles attributed to women authors. Baruch found that the daughters of employed women were significantly different from the daughters of full-time housewives in that they did not downgrade the articles attributed to women. Thus, the daughters of working mothers were less likely to assume lower competence on the part of women authors: "it is women whose mothers have not worked who devalue feminine competence" (Baruch, 1972a, p. 37). Meier (1972) also found among college students that maternal employment was positively related to favoring social equality for women. The most

---

[3] The fact that daughters of working mothers are lower on traditional femininity should be kept in mind in evaluating studies like Nelson's (1971) that use pencil-and-paper personality inventories. Many of these inventories are biased toward the very questionable assumption that traditional femininity is the healthy criteria for girls (Constantinople, 1973; Henshel, 1971; Lunneborg, 1968).

equalitarian ideology was held by daughters of women in high-status occupations.

The relationship between maternal employment and sex role ideology is not perfectly clear, however, particularly when a multidimensional sex role ideology scale is used. For example, Baruch, in the above study, developed a 26-item Likert-type scale to measure attitudes toward careers for women. Scores on this scale, which dealt with the desirability of a career orientation in women, the compatibility of the career and family roles, the femininity of the career woman, and women's ability to achieve intellectual excellence, were not related to maternal employment per se. Rather, a positive attitude toward the dual role resulted when the respondent's mother worked and also had successfully integrated the two roles.

With a somewhat comparable sample—wives of graduate students in the Boston area—Lipman-Blumen (1972) found no relationship between employment of the wife's mother and responses on a measure of sex role ideology. This scale consisted of six items dealing with whether women belong in the home carrying out domestic duties and child care, with men responsible for the financial support of the family. In an earlier study, Hoffman (1963c) used two separate scales: one dealing with husband–wife division of labor and the other with attitudes toward male dominance. These two scales were administered to mothers, not daughters, and to a less educated sample than Lipman-Blumen's, representing also a broader range of social class. The expected relationship was found on the first scale: That is, working mothers favored a less traditional division of labor than nonworking mothers, but no relation was obtained between employment and attitudes toward male dominance.

Not only is the role represented by the working mother different in content from the role represented by the nonworking mother, but the motivation to model the working mother appears to be stronger. Thus, Douvan (1963) found that adolescent daughters of working mothers were more likely to name their mothers as the person they most admired; and Baruch (1972b) found that college women with working mothers were more likely to name their mothers as the parent they most resembled, and the one they would most want to be like.

It is clear that the effects of maternal employment considered in this light must be different for males and females. For one thing, although maternal employment might affect all children's concepts of the woman's role, it should affect only the girls' self-concept, unless the mother's working also reflects something about the father. Douvan found that lower-class adolescent boys whose mothers work full time are less likely than those whose mothers do not work to name their father as the person they most admire. In the lower class, the mother's employment may communicate to the child that the father is an economic failure. McCord, McCord, and Thurber (1963) also found in their study of lower-class boys from intact families that the sons of women who were employed during the boys' preadolescent years were significantly more likely than were the sons of full-time housewives to indicate disapproval of their fathers. Since these two studies were done, maternal employment has become much more prevalent, and it might therefore be expected that the finding would no longer be obtained. However, two recent Canadian studies reported the same pattern. Kappel and Lambert (1972) found in their study of children 9 to 16 years old that the sons of full-time working mothers in the lower class evaluated their fathers lower than did the sons of other full-time working mothers and lower than did the sons of the part-time or nonworking mothers in any class.[4] Propper (1972) found that in a predominantly working class sample, the adolescent sons of full-time working mothers were less likely than were the sons of nonworking mothers to name their father as the man they most admired. The finding by Vogel and his colleagues (1970) discussed previously suggests, on the other hand, that at least among middle-class males the father whose wife works may be seen as a more nurturant figure, possibly because of his taking over some of the child care roles. In any case, maternal employment more clearly defines the mother's role change than the father's, and thus the effect on the daughter may be more pronounced.

Nevertheless, there have been few studies of the effect of maternal employment on the daughter's self-esteem, and they have not always found the expected results. Thus Baruch (1972b) found no relationship between maternal employment and the self-esteem of college women as measured by the Coopersmith Self-Esteem Inventory. She reported that the daughters of working mothers with positive career attitudes tended to have higher self-esteem, but this relationship was not statistically significant. Kappel and Lambert (1972), using a semantic-differential-style self-esteem measure with 3,315 9- to 16-year-old Canadian children, found that the daughters of nonworking mothers were lower in self-esteem than were the daughters of part-time working mothers but higher than were the daughters of full-time working mothers. The daughters of full-time working mothers did

---

[4] This finding was obtained from Tables 3 and 5 of the Kappel and Lambert study and was not discussed by the authors.

have higher self-esteem than did those of the nonworking group, however, when any one of the following conditions existed: The mother worked for self-oriented reasons, was very satisfied with work, or was a professional.

Despite the inconclusive findings on self-esteem, for girls maternal employment seems to contribute to a greater admiration of the mother, a concept of the female role that includes less restriction and a wider range of activities, and a self-concept that incorporates these aspects of the female role. Douvan (1963) found the adolescent daughters of working mothers to be relatively independent, autonomous, and active, and there are suggestions from other studies that this may be true for younger girls as well (Hoffman, 1963a). For boys, maternal employment might influence their concept of the female role, but what the effects are on their attitudes toward their father and themselves depends very much on the circumstances surrounding the mother's employment.

It would seem, then, that the daughter of a working mother would have higher academic and career aspirations and show a higher level of actual achievement. Considerable evidence for this comes from studies of college women. Almquist and Angrist (1971) found that career-oriented college women were more likely to be the daughters of working women; and Tangri (1969) found that college women who aspired to careers in the less conventionally feminine areas were more likely to be the daughters of working women. In studies of highly educated professional women, both Ginzberg (1971) and Birnbaum (1971) found maternal employment a significant background factor.

Studies of the achievement motivation or academic success of younger children provide neither overwhelming support nor clear refutation of the role-model explanation. On the whole the data are consistent with such a theory, but the investigations have not been designed to pinpoint the process by which the independent and dependent variables are linked. Thus, many studies have not examined the relationships separately for male and female subjects—an essential step for applying the results to the role-model hypothesis. For example, Powell (1963) obtained projective-test measures of achievement motivation from subjects four times, at ages 9, 10, 11, and 12. The children of working mothers had higher achievement motives, but the relationship was significant only at age 9. However, even though Powell was working from a modeling theory, the data were not reported separately by sex. Jones et al. (1967), using a similar measure, compared sixth-grade children of professionally employed mothers with a matched sample whose mothers were full-time housewives. The children of professional women showed a higher achievement motive, but the difference was not statistically significant. The relationship might have been stronger in these two studies if the girls had been examined alone.

In some cases the predicted child behavior may not be found because there is a counterinfluence at work. For example, the study by Kappel and Lambert (1972) suggests that when the mother's employment involves conflict and difficulties, as is sometimes the situation with full-time employment, the daughter's self-esteem is not enhanced.

In other cases, the empirical data seem to support the role-model rationale, but other processes may be at work that could also explain the result. For example, the study by Jones et al. (1967) showed that children of professional mothers were better readers than were the children of full-time housewives. Although their subjects were matched by socioeconomic status, the professional mothers were better educated than were the housewives, more time was spent with the child in reading activities, and their homes included more books. One wonders whether modeling was the process involved or the more stimulating home environment that the professionally employed mothers provided. In short, while the parental roles in the employed-mother family may serve as an influence in a particular direction, other factors associated with maternal employment might exert influence in the same direction. As noted earlier, the conceptual gap between maternal employment and a child trait is too great to be covered in simple two-level studies. A better test of the hypothesis would require examining the many intervening steps in the modeling process: (a) the content of the roles, (b) the attitudes toward the roles, (c) the child's motivations to model various aspects of the roles, and (d) the development in the child of the skills needed to implement the appropriate behaviors.

Nevertheless, it does seem clear that when a mother works she provides a different model of behavior for the children in the family, particularly for the girls. Further, the hypothesis that this difference is important for the daughter's concept of sex roles, and thus presumably her self-concept, makes sense. Traditional sex role stereotypes in America assign a lower status to women than to men and include the view that women are less competent. Maslow, Rand, and Newman (1960) described as one effect, "the woman in order to be a good female may feel it necessary to give up her strength, intelligence or talent, fearing them as somehow masculine and defeminizing" (p. 208). Another effect has been empirically documented by Horner (1972)—that women who dare to achieve do so with anxiety and ambivalence about their success. The role of working mother is less likely to lead to traditional sex role stereotypes and more likely to communicate competence and the value of the woman's contribution to the family. She may have higher status in the family and represent to her daughter a person who is capable in areas that are, in some respects, more salient to a growing girl than are household skills.

To summarize: Considering the four major dependent variables from the standpoint of the role-model theory, the data indicate that maternal employment is associated with less traditional sex role concepts, more approval of maternal employment, and a higher evaluation of female competence. This in turn should imply a more positive self-concept for the daughters of working mothers and better social adjustment, but there are only indirect data on this. There is some support for the idea that daughters of working mothers are more independent because of modeling their more independent mothers. Evidence also suggests that the daughters of working mothers have higher achievement aspirations, but it has not yet been demonstrated that the actual abilities of the child are affected by the different role model provided by the working mother.

The Mother's Emotional State

Morale. The assumption that the mother's emotional state is influenced by whether or not she is employed and that this affects her adequacy as a mother underlies several different approaches. One type of hypothesis, for example, relies on the commonly accepted belief that good morale improves job performance. Since this theory has validity in the industrial setting (Roethlisberger & Dickson, 1939), why not in the home? In fact, there is some support for it. Yarrow, Scott, deLeeuw, and Heinig (1962) examined, by means of interviews with mothers of elementary school children, the child-rearing patterns of four groups of mothers: (a) mothers who worked and preferred to work, (b) mothers who worked and preferred not to work, (c) nonworking mothers who preferred to work, and (d) nonworking mothers who preferred not to work. Among the nonworking mothers, satisfaction with their lot made a significant difference: The satisfied nonworking mothers obtained higher scores on a measure of adequacy of mothering. However, satisfaction did not differentiate the working mothers. One should keep in mind that when this study was conducted it was more socially acceptable to say, "Yes, I am working, but I wish I could be home all the time with my children," than it was to say, "Yes, I am home all day with my children, but I wish I were out working." Thus, some of the dissatisfied workers may not have been as dissatisfied as they indicated. By the same token, the dissatisfaction of the home-maker may have been more extreme, and her dissatisfaction more closely linked to the mothering role itself; that is, the very role with which she was indicating dissatisfaction included mothering. Indeed, of all four groups, the lowest scores on ade-quacy of mothering were obtained by the dissatisfied homemaker (the highest, by the satisfied homemaker). Furthermore, the in-vestigators considered the motives for choosing full-time homemaking: those women who stressed duty as the basis for the choice had the lowest scores of all.

The question of the dissatisfied nonworking mother is in-teresting. Would the working mother who enjoys her work be dissatisfied as a full-time homemaker? In the practical sense, this may be the real issue; and the Yarrow et al. (1962) data suggest that the satisfied working mother may not be as adequate a parent as the satisfied nonworking mother but she is more adequate than the dissatisfied nonworking mother. Birnbaum (1971) in an in-teresting study compared professionally employed mothers with mothers who had graduated from college "with distinction" but had become full-time homemakers, that is, women who had the ability to pursue professional careers had they so chosen. Both groups were about 15 to 25 years past their bachelor's degree at the time they were interviewed. With respect to morale, the pro-fessional women were clearly higher. The nonworking mothers had lower self-esteem, a lower sense of personal competence—even with respect to child care skills—felt less attractive, ex-pressed more concern over identity issues, and indicated greater feelings of loneliness. The nonworking mothers were even more insecure and unhappy in these respects than was a third sample of professional women who had never married. Asked what they felt was missing from their lives, the predominant answer from the two groups of professional women was time, but for the house-wives it was challenge and creative involvement.

The mothers were also compared with respect to orientation toward their children. In response to the question, "How does having children change a woman's life?" the full-time homemakers stressed the sacrifice that motherhood entailed sig-nificantly more often than did the professional women. The pro-fessional women answered more often in terms of enrichment and self-fulfillment. Although both groups mentioned the work involved and the demanding aspects of motherhood, the homemakers stressed duty and responsibility to a greater extent. The homemakers indicated more anxiety about their children, especially with regard to the child's achievements, and they stressed their own inadequacies as mothers. In response to a projective picture showing a boy and his parents with a crutch in the background, the homemakers told more dramatic, depressed, and anxious stories. With respect to the growing independence of their children, the professional women responded positively, while the homemakers indicated ambivalence and regret. They seemed to be concerned about the loss of familiar patterns or their own importance.

There are no direct data in the Birnbaum (1971) study on the children themselves, but the pattern of the able, educated, full-time homemakers suggests that they would have shortcomings as mothers, particularly as their children approached adolescence. At that time, when the child needs a parent who can encourage independence and instill self-confidence, the anxieties and concerns of these women and their own frustrations would seem to operate as a handicap.

There are additional studies suggesting that when work is a source of personal satisfaction for the mother, her role as mother is positively affected. Kligler (1954) found that women who worked because of interest in the job were more likely than were those who worked for financial reasons to feel that there was improvement in the child's behavior as a result of employment. Kappel and Lambert (1972) found that the 9- to 16-year-old daughters of full-time working mothers who indicated they were working for self-oriented reasons had higher self-esteem and evaluated both parents more highly than did either the daughters of full-time working mothers who were working for family-oriented reasons or the daughters of nonworking mothers. In this study the measures of the mother's motives for working and the child data were obtained independently. In the studies by Yarrow et al. (1962), Birnbaum (1971), and Kligler, the mother was the source of all of the data. Woods (1972) found that in a study of fifth-graders in a lower-class, predominantly black urban area where almost all of the mothers were employed, mothers who reported a positive attitude toward employment had children who obtained scores on the California Test of Personality indicating good social and personal adjustment.

Role strain.   Another dimension of morale that has been studied focuses on the strain of handling the dual roles of worker and mother. The general idea is that whatever the effect of maternal employment under conflict-free circumstances, the sheer pressure of trying to fill these two very demanding roles can result in a state of stress that in turn has a negative effect on the child. Thus, the main thrust of Kappel and Lambert's (1972) argument is that part-time employment and full-time employment, when it involves minimal conflict, have a positive effect; full-time employment under most conditions, however, involves strain and therefore has adverse effects. In Douvan's (1963) study of adolescent children in intact families, the only group of working-mother children who indicated adjustment problems were the children of full-time working mothers in the lower class. This group of working mothers was the one for whom the strain of the dual role seemed to be the greatest.

In contrast, Woods (1972) found the children of full-time workers to be the best adjusted. Her sample, however, was all lower class from a population in which most mothers were employed and included many single-parent families. Under these circumstances, the full-time employed mothers may have been financially better off than were the others and may have had more stable household arrangements to facilitate their employment. The mother's positive attitude toward employment related to the child's adjustment, as noted above, but also her satisfaction with child care arrangements contributed to a positive attitude toward employment. In a sense then, although full-time employment of lower-class mothers did not seem to have adverse effects on the child as suggested in the other two studies, strain as manifested in dissatisfaction with child care arrangements may have exerted such an influence.[5] To some extent the attitude toward employment generally may reflect the mother's feeling of role strain.

Guilt. Still another possible emotional response to employment is that the working mother feels guilty about her work because of the prevailing admonishments against maternal employment. While this may result in some appropriate compensation for her absence from home, it may also be overdone.

There is evidence that working mothers are very concerned about whether or not their employment is "bad" for their children, and they often feel guilty. Even Birnbaum's (1971) happy professional mothers indicated frequent guilt feelings. Kligler (1954) also noted that the working mothers experienced anxiety and guilt and tried to compensate in their behavior toward their children. Some evidence for guilt on the part of the working mother and the effects of this on the child is provided in a study by Hoffman (1963b). Third- through sixth-grade children of working mothers were studied, with each working-mother family matched to a nonworking-mother family on father's occupation,

---

[5] The study does not indicate whether the woman's satisfaction reflected the objective conditions or not. The mother's perceptions and the child's report of the situation were significantly but not highly related.

sex of child, and ordinal position of the child. The data included questionnaires filled out by the children, personal interviews with the mothers, teacher ratings, and classroom sociometrics. The working mothers were divided into those who indicated that they liked working and those who disliked it. Working mothers who liked work, compared to the nonworking matched sample, had more positive interaction with the child, felt more sympathy and less anger toward the child in discipline situations, and used less severe discipline techniques. However, the children of these working mothers appeared to be less assertive and less effective in their peer interactions. Their intellectual performance was rated lower by teachers, and their scores on the school intelligence tests were lower. Also, these children helped somewhat less in household tasks than did the children of nonworking mothers. Thus, the overall pattern seemed to indicate that the working mother who liked work not only tried to compensate for her employment but may have actually overcompensated. These data were collected in 1957 when popular sentiment was opposed to maternal employment. As a result the women may have felt guilty about working. In trying to be good mothers, they may have gone too far, since the children's behavior suggested a pattern of overprotection or "smother love."

The mothers who did not like work, on the other hand, showed a very different pattern. They seemed less involved with the child; for example, they indicated less frequent disciplining and somewhat fewer positive interactions, as compared to nonworking mothers. The children helped with household tasks to a greater extent than did the children of nonworking mothers. They were also more assertive and hostile toward their peers. Their school performance as rated by their teachers was lower, although they did not perform more poorly on the school intelligence tests. The total pattern suggested that these children were somewhat neglected in comparison to the nonworking matched sample. The working mothers who disliked work had less reason to feel guilty, since they were working for other than self-oriented reasons.

Effects on the child.   A complicated picture is presented if the data on the working mother's emotional state are considered in relation to the child characteristics cited earlier as most often linked to maternal employment: (a) the child's attitudes, (b) mental health and social adjustment and independence–dependence specifically, and (c) cognitive abilities and orientations. First, with respect to the attitude toward maternal employment itself, there are some indications that the tendency of working mothers' children to have a positive attitude is enhanced when the employment is accompanied by a minimum of conflict and strain for the mother (Baruch, 1972a; King et al., 1968).

Moving on to the more complex dependent variables, it appears that when maternal employment is satisfying to the mother, either because it is more easily incorporated into her activities or because it is intrinsically gratifying, the effects on the child may be positive. The effects are more clearly positive—as indicated by various measures such as an "adequacy of mothering" score, the child's self-esteem, the child's adjustment score on the California Test of Personality, and attitudes toward parents—when this situation is compared either to that of the full-time housewife who would really prefer to work (Yarrow et al., 1962) or to maternal employment when it is accompanied by strain and harassment (Douvan, 1963; Kappel & Lambert, 1972; Woods, 1972). There are even indications that in some situations, as when the children are approaching adolescence and older or when the mother is particularly educated and able, the working-mother role may be more satisfying than is the role of full-time housewife and that this may make the working mother less anxious and more encouraging of independence in her children (Birnbaum, 1971). On the other hand, there is also evidence that the working mother with younger children who likes work might feel guilty and thus overcompensate, with adverse effects for the child in the form of passivity, ineffectiveness with peers, and low academic performance (Hoffman, 1963b). Thus the data about the mother's emotional state suggest that the working mother who obtains satisfaction from her work, who has adequate arrangements so that her dual role does not involve undue strain, and who does not feel so guilty that she overcompensates is likely to do quite well and, under certain conditions, better than does the nonworking mother.

Child-Rearing Practices

Concern here is with whether the child of a working mother is subject to different child-rearing practices and how these in turn affect his development. To some extent this topic is covered in other sections. In discussing the different role models presented in the working-mother families, for example, we indicated that the child-rearing functions are more likely to be shared by both parents. The fact that the child then has a more balanced relationship with both parents has generally been viewed with favor. The active involvement of the father has been seen as conducive to high achievement in women, particularly when he is supportive of independence and performance (Ginzberg, 1971;

Hoffman, 1973), and to the social adjustment of boys (Hoffman, 1961) as well as to the general adjustment of both boys and girls (Dizard, 1968).

Data also indicate that the working mother's family is more likely to include someone outside the conjugal family who participates in the child care (Hoffman, 1958; U.S. Department of Labor, 1972). This situation undoubtedly operates as a selective factor, since the presence of, for example, the grandmother makes it easier for the mother to go to work; but the effects of this pattern have not been widely examined. The specific issue of multiple mothering and frequent turnover in baby sitters is discussed later in the article, primarily in terms of effects on the infant and the young child when these issues are most meaningful.

In discussing the guilt sometimes felt by the working mothers, it was suggested that they sometimes try to compensate for their employment, in some cases overdoing it. There is considerable evidence that working mothers particularly in the middle class do try to compensate. In some studies, this is made explicit by the respondents (Jones et al., 1967; Kligler, 1954; Rapoport & Rapoport, 1972), while in others it is revealed in the pattern of working–nonworking differences obtained. As examples of the latter, Yarrow and her colleagues (1962) found that the college-educated working mothers compensated by having more planned activities with children, and the professional mothers in Fisher's (1939) early study spent as many hours with their children as did the full-time homemakers. Finally, Jones et al. found that the mothers employed as professionals spent more time reading with their sixth-grade children than did nonworking mothers, though this was part of a generally greater stress on educational goals, not just compensation for employment.

When the working mother tries to make up for her employment, she often makes certain implicit judgments about what the nonworking situation is like. These may be quite inaccurate. The working mothers in Hoffman's (1963b) study who required less household help from their children than did the nonworking mothers are a case in point. And, in general, the nonworking mother is not necessarily interacting with her child as much as is imagined or as pleasantly. There is a great deal of pluralistic ignorance about the mothering role, and many mothers may be measuring themselves against, and trying to match, an over-idealized image. It is possible that the nonworking mother spends relatively little time in direct positive interaction with her child, and thus the working mother's deliberate efforts might end up as more total positive interaction time. With respect to the amount of time spent in total child care, comparisons indicate that the nonworking women spend more time (Robinson, 1971;

Walker & Woods, 1972). These reports, however, are geared toward other purposes and are not helpful in providing information about parent–child interaction. In most cases, working and nonworking women are compared without regard to whether or not they are mothers. Obviously the nonworking women include more mothers, and thus they do, as a group, spend more time in child care. Even when only mothers are compared, the number of children in the family and the children's ages are not considered, and the kind of child care is often not specified. Just how much of the day does the nonworking mother spend interacting with the child? This is an unfortunate gap in our knowledge.

Independence training. Several studies have focused on whether the working mother encourages independence and maturity in her children more than does the nonworking mother. The answer seems to depend on the age of the child and the social class or education of the mother. In the work of Yarrow and her colleagues (1962), the working mothers who had not gone to college were more likely to indicate a stress on independence training and to assign the children a greater share of the household responsibilities. The college-educated working mothers did not show this pattern and in fact showed a nonsignificant tendency in the opposite direction. The subjects in this study were similar to Hoffman's (1963b) respondents in that the children were of elementary school age; thus it is interesting that the college-educated working mothers in the former study exhibit a pattern similar to the working women who liked work in the latter study. Burchinal and Lovell (1959) reported for somewhat older children that working mothers were more likely to stress independence, and a stress on independence and responsibility can be inferred as more characteristic of the working mothers in the national sample study of adolescent girls reported by Douvan (1963), although the data rely more on what the girl is like than on parental child-rearing practices. Birnbaum's (1971) study of professionally employed mothers also suggests an encouragement of independence. The age of these children varied. The study by Von Mering (1955) is often cited as evidence that professional mothers stress independence training in elementary-school-age children, but since there were only eight mothers in the sample, such conclusions do not seem justified.[6]

[6] Propper (1972) found that the adolescent children of working mothers were more likely to report disagreements with parents but were not different from the children of nonworking mothers with respect to feelings of closeness to parents, parental interest, or support. The overall pattern may indicate more tolerance of disagreement by the working mothers rather than a more strained relationship. This interpretation fits well with the general picture of working mothers encouraging independence and autonomy in adolescent children.

A longitudinal study of lower-class boys from intact families, begun in the 1930s, suggests that the relationship between maternal employment and independence training is contingent upon the family milieu (McCord et al., 1963). Data obtained when the boys were between 10 and 15 years old showed that among the families judged to be stable by a composite index, working mothers were less overprotective and more supportive of independence than were nonworking mothers. These differences were not obtained for the unstable families, and the sons of the working mothers in this group proved to be the most dependent subjects in the entire sample. Because their mothers did not seem to be the most encouraging of dependency, their dependent behavior was interpreted by the authors as a response to feelings of rejection rather than to parental patterns of independence training.

The data are quite sketchy, but the general picture is that except for the working mothers of younger children (elementary school age) who are educated or enjoy work and possibly the working mothers in unstable families, working mothers stress independence training more than do nonworking mothers. This is consistent with what one would expect. It has already been indicated that the more educated working mothers try to compensate for their employment. Thus they would be expected to avoid pushing the younger children into maturity, stressing the nurturant aspects of their role to make up for their absence at work. As the child grows older, independence is called for. To the nonworking mother the move from protector and nurturer to independence trainer is often very difficult. For the working mother, on the other hand, the child's growing independence eases her role strain. Furthermore, the psychological threat of becoming less essential to the child is lessened by the presence of alternative roles and sources of self-worth.

The evidence for the effect of this pattern on the child is not definitely established. Two of the studies, Hoffman's (1963b) and McCord et al.'s (1963), examined data at each of the three levels: employment status, child-rearing behavior, and child characteristics; but the findings are ambiguous. Hoffman did not directly examine the relationship between maternal behavior and the child characteristics; McCord and her colleagues did and failed to find a significant association between independence training and independence. None of the other relevant maternal employment studies obtained separate data on the child-rearing patterns and the child characteristics. On the other hand, several child development studies that have no data on maternal employment have found that parental encouragement of independence relates to high achievement motivation, competence, and achievement behavior in both males and females (Baumrind & Black, 1967; Hoffman, 1972; Winterbottom, 1958).

Household responsibilities. Most of the data indicate that the child of the working mother has more household responsibilities (Douvan, 1963; Johnson, 1969; Propper, 1972; Roy, 1963; Walker, 1970a). The exception to this generalization is again the mothers of younger children who are more educated or who enjoy work. Although working mothers may sometimes deliberately avoid giving the child household responsibilities, such participation by children has generally been found to have a positive, not a negative, effect (Clausen, 1966; Johnson, 1969; Woods, 1972). Obviously, this does not mean overburdening the child, but expecting the child to be one of the effectively contributing members of the family seems conducive to the development of social adjustment and responsibility.

Parental control. What other effects of maternal employment on child-rearing practices might be expected? One hypothesis might be that the working mother leaves her child more often without care or supervision. This is the focus of the next section, but by and large, there is little evidence that this is the case. On the other hand, because of the demands imposed by the dual role of worker and mother, the working mother might be stricter and impose more conformity to a specified standard. That is, just as reality adaptation might lead her to encourage the child in independence and to take on household responsibilities, she might also be expected to demand more conformity to rules so that the household can function smoothly in her absence. There is some evidence for this pattern among the less educated groups. Yarrow et al. (1962) found that the children of working mothers in their noncollege group were generally under firmer parental control than were the children of nonworking mothers. Woods (1972) found more consistency between principles and practice in the discipline used by the full-time working mothers in her lower-class, predominantly black sample. However, Yarrow et al. found greater inconsistency in their college-educated working mothers.

Still another possibility is that the working mother is milder in discipline because of conscious efforts to compensate the child or because of higher morale. Hoffman's (1963b) working mothers, especially those who liked work, used less severe discipline and indicated less hostility in the discipline situation than did the nonworking mothers. It should be noted that the focus in this study was not on the content of the discipline but on its severity.

Thus the data do not indicate whether the children were under more or less firm control but only that the discipline used was milder.

There are a few studies, such as those that compared the child-rearing views of working and nonworking mothers and found no meaningful differences (Kligler, 1954; Powell, 1963), that are not reviewed here, but we have included most of the available data on maternal employment and child-rearing practices. It is surprising how few investigations of maternal employment have obtained data about actual child-rearing behavior. Most of the studies have simply related employment to a child characteristic and then later speculated about any relationship that might be found. If the daughters of working mothers are found to be more independent or higher achievers, one cannot tell if this is a product of the working mother as model, the fact that the father is more likely to have had an active part in the girl's upbringing, the result of the fathers in working-mother families being more likely to approve of and encourage competence in females, or whether it is because these girls were more likely to have been encouraged by their mothers to achieve independence and assume responsibilities. All of these intervening variables have been linked to female independence and achievement (Hoffman, 1972, 1973).

Maternal Absence and Supervision

The most persistent concern about maternal employment has to do with the sheer absence of the mother from the home while she is working and the fear that this represents a loss to the child in terms of supervision, love, or cognitive enrichment. Much of the earlier research on maternal employment and juvenile delinquency was based on this hypothesis: The mother was working, the child was unsupervised, and thus he was a delinquent. There is some support for this theory, despite the fact that maternal employment and delinquency do not relate as expected. In the study of lower-class boys carried out by Glueck and Glueck (1957), regularly employed mothers were no more likely to have delinquent sons than were nonemployed mothers. However, inadequate supervision seemed to lead to delinquency whatever the mother's employment status, and employed mothers, whether employed regularly or occasionally, were more likely to provide inadequate supervision. McCord and McCord (1959) also found a tie between supervision and delinquency in their longitudinal study of lower-class boys (which, unlike the Gluecks', included only intact families), but there was little difference between the working and nonworking mothers with respect to adequacy of supervision (McCord et al., 1963). Furthermore, the tie between the adequacy of supervision and social adjustment conceptualized more generally is not conclusively established. In the study by Woods (1972) of lower-class fifth-grade children, inadequate supervision did not have a statistically demonstrable adverse effect on boys, although unsupervised girls clearly showed lower school adjustment scores on tests of social relations and cognitive abilities.[7] Delinquency per se was too rare in this sample for any comparison, and the relationship between maternal employment and the adequacy of supervision was not examined.

Even less is known about the linkage of these three variables—maternal employment, supervision, and delinquency—in the middle class. Although middle-class working mothers express concern about finding adequate supervision for their children and although a number of publications stress the inadequacy of supervision in families in which the mother works (Low & Spindler, 1968), it is not clearly established that the children end up with less supervision in either social class. Furthermore, although the adequacy of supervision seems related to delinquency in the lower class, this relationship is not established for the middle class. Nye (1958), for example, found a curvilinear relationship—both high and low supervision moderately associated with delinquency. It may seem obvious that these three variables should be linked in both the middle and the lower class, but there is little empirical documentation.

Ignoring now the issue of supervision, what is the relationship between maternal employment and delinquency? In our previous review, we suggested that there did seem to be a relationship between maternal employment and delinquency in the middle class. This relationship was found by Nye (1963) using a self-report measure of delinquent behavior and Gold (1961) who used police contact as the measure; in both studies the relationship was obtained for the middle class and not for the lower

[7] The sex differences in the Woods study are both intriguing and difficult to interpret. In most child development studies, the girls show ill effects from too much supervision or control, while the boys typically suffer from too little (Becker, 1964; Bronfenbrenner, 1961; Hoffman, 1972). This may reflect the higher level of control generally exercised over girls, so that the low end of the scale for girls is not as low as for boys, either objectively or subjectively. However, there have been very few child development studies of the lower class, and it is possible that the lack of supervision is more extreme than in the typical child development sample. Thus the middle-class girl who is unsupervised relative to other middle-class girls may not represent the level of neglect encountered by Woods.

class.[8] Glueck and Glueck (1957), studying only lower-class subjects, found no tendency for the sons of regularly employed women to be delinquent despite the fact that their sample included broken homes, a variable that relates to both delinquency and maternal employment. They did find the sons of the "occasionally" employed women to be delinquent, but the occasionally employed group was clearly more unstable than were those in which the mother worked regularly or not at all. They were more likely to have husbands with poor work habits and emotional disturbances, poor marriages, or to be widowed or divorced. The Gluecks saw the occasionally employed mother as working "to escape household drudgery and parental responsibility," but, in another view, the question is not why they went to work, since their employment was obviously needed by the circumstances of their lives, but why they resisted regular employment. The delinquency of their sons seemed more a function of family instability, the inadequacies of the father, or something about the mothers not being employed more regularly, rather than a function of maternal employment per se.

Two studies already mentioned supplement these ideas. McCord et al. (1963) found no tendency for maternal employment to be associated with delinquency when the family was stable, but in the unstable families the sons of working mothers did have a higher delinquency rate. The higher frequency of delinquency was clearly not simply due to the instability; family instability did relate to delinquency, but maternal employment in the unstable family further increased the risk.

Woods' (1972) study, which included results of psychological tests and information gathered from teachers and school and community records, found that the full-time, steadily working mother seemed to be a positive factor in the child's social adjustment. The subjects were 142 fifth-graders, all the fifth-graders in the school, and 108 had working mothers. Clearly, in this context, in which maternal employment is the common, accepted pattern, its meaning to parents and children is quite different. The author suggests that full-time maternal employment is a requirement of family well-being in the economic circumstances of these families and as such is respected and appreciated.

Woods' (1972) interpretation is consistent with our own earlier hypotheses about the meaning of maternal employment particularly among blacks (Hoffman, 1963a) and with other data

---

[8] There are two other recent studies (Brown, 1970; Riege, 1972) in which no relationship was found between maternal employment and juvenile delinquency. Since there was no separate examination by social class or attention to relevant mediating variables, these studies are not illuminating in this discussion.

(Kriesberg, 1970). A basic theme throughout both the earlier review and the present one is that the context within which maternal employment takes place—the meaning it has for the family
and the social setting—determines its effects. In addition, the
positive influence of full-time maternal employment in the lower
class raises the question again of why some lower-class women
resist full-time employment when their situation obviously calls
for it. What characterizes these nonworking or irregularly employed mothers? They may have less ego strength, less competence in terms of physical or emotional health, training or
intellectual ability, or more children. The Gluecks' (1957) data
indicate that the occasionally employed mothers were the most
likely to have a history of delinquency themselves. In short, in
addition to the value of the mother's employment to the family,
the differences may reflect selective factors, and the employed
mothers in these circumstances may be healthier, more competent,
or in better circumstances with respect to family size.[9]

Consistent with Woods (1972) interpretation is the fact that
the children in the study with extensive responsibility for the
household tasks and the care of siblings showed higher school
achievement.[10] Like their mothers they were cooperating with
realistic family demands. The author is aware, however, that the
causality might be reversed, that is, that mothers give competent
children more responsibilities. There are also other interpretations: For example, firstborn children particularly in lower income families usually show higher academic performance, and
they are also the ones more likely to be given household tasks.

To summarize, the hypothesis that maternal employment
means inadequate supervision has been primarily invoked to
predict higher delinquency rates for the children of working
mothers. There are data, although not very solid, that in the lower
class, working mothers provide less adequate supervision for
their children and that adequacy of supervision is linked to delinquency and social adjustment, but there is no evidence that the
children of working mothers are more likely to be delinquent.
The data suggest instead that full-time maternal employment in

[9] There are data that indicate that children from large families, particularly
in the lower class, show lower school performance than do children from smaller
families (Clausen & Clausen, 1973). Perhaps, then, it is not that full-time employment has a positive effect but that the full-time employed mothers have fewer
children and the positive effect is a function of smaller family size.

[10] These findings seem somewhat inconsistent with Douvan's (1963)
suggestion that the lower-class daughters of full-time working mothers were over-
burdened with household responsibilities. Douvan's subjects were older, and
thus it is possible that they were more heavily burdened than were the fifth-
graders and more resentful of their duties. Douvan's sample was also white, while
Woods' was predominantly black.

the very low social class groups represents a realistic response to economic stress and thus, because of selective factors or effects, may be correlated with more socially desirable characteristics in the child. Adequacy of supervision has rarely been studied in the middle class, although here there is some evidence for a higher delinquency rate among working mothers' children.

Maternal Deprivation

The school-age child.   For school-age children, there is very little empirically to link maternal employment to maternal deprivation. Although Woods (1972) suggests that full-time employment may represent rejection to the middle-class child, there is no evidence of this. While it has been commonly assumed that maternal employment is interpreted by the child as rejection, the evidence, as indicated above, suggests that the children of working mothers tend to support the idea of mothers working. Furthermore, as maternal employment becomes the norm in the middle as well as in the lower class, it seems even less likely that the sheer fact that a mother is working would lead to a sense of being rejected.

The evidence as to whether the working mother actually does reject the school-age child has already been covered in earlier sections of this review. The general pattern is that the working mother, particularly in the middle class, makes a deliberate effort to compensate the child for her employment (Hoffman, 1963b; Jones et al., 1967; Kligler, 1954; Poloma, 1972; Rapoport & Rapoport, 1972; Yarrow et al., 1962) and that the dissatisfied mother, whether employed or not and whether lower class or middle class, is less likely to be an adequate mother (Birnbaum, 1971; Woods, 1972; Yarrow et al., 1962). The idea that maternal employment brings emotional deprivation to the school-age child has not been supported (Hoffman, 1963a; Peterson, 1958; Propper, 1972; Siegel & Haas, 1963; Yudkin & Holme, 1963). In part this may be because the working mother is often away from home only when the child is in school; and if her work is gratifying in some measure, if she does not feel unduly hassled, or if she deliberately sets about to do so, she may even spend more time in positive interaction with the child than does the nonworking mother. While this can sometimes be overdone and compensation can turn into overcompensation (Hoffman, 1963b), it may also be one of the important reasons why maternal employment has not been experienced by the school-age child as deprivation. In drawing action conclusions from the research, it is important to keep this in mind. The absence of negative effects does not mean that the mother's employment is an irrelevant variable; it may mean that mothers have been sufficiently concerned to counterbalance such effects effectively.

Infancy. More recently attention has focused on the possible adverse effects of maternal employment on the infant and the very young child. The importance of attachment and a one-to-one relationship in the early years has been stressed by Spitz (1945), Bowlby (1958, 1969), and others (Yarrow, 1964). Although most of this research has been carried out on children in institutions with the most dramatic effects demonstrated among children whose infancy was spent in grossly deprived circumstances, it nevertheless seems clear that something important is happening during these early years and that there are critical periods when cognitive and affective inputs may have important ramifications throughout the individual's life. Concern has been generated about this issue because of the recent increase in maternal employment among mothers of infants and young children and also because of the new interest in day care centers as a means of caring for the preschool children of working mothers. As these two patterns emerge, the effects of maternal employment must be reevaluated. In this section we review the evidence that has been cited on one side or the other of these issues. As we shall see, however, we really know very little.

The research on maternal deprivation suggests that the infant needs a one-to-one relationship with an adult or else he may suffer cognitive and affective loss that may, in extreme conditions, never be regained. The importance of interactions in which the adult responds to the child and the child to the adult in a reciprocal relationship has been particularly stressed (Bronfenbrenner, 1973). There is some evidence of a need for cuddling (Harlow & Harlow, 1966) and a need for environmental stimulation (Dennis & Njarian, 1957; Hunt, 1961). These studies are often cited as evidence for the importance of the mother's full-time presence in the home when the infant is young.

Extending these findings to the maternal employment situation may be inappropriate, however. Not only were the early Bowlby (1953, 1958) and Spitz (1945) data obtained from studies of extremely barren, understaffed institutions, but later research suggested that the drastic effects they had observed might be avoided by increasing the staff–child ratio, by providing nurses who attended and responded to the infants' cries, smiles and vocalizations, and by providing a more stimulating visual environment. Further, the age of the child, the duration of the institutionalization, and the previous and subsequent experiences of the child all affect the outcome (Rheingold, 1956; Rheingold &

Bayley, 1959; Rheingold, Gewirtz, & Ross, 1959; Tizard, Cooperman, Joseph, & Tizard, 1972; Yarrow, 1964). Most important, however, institutionalization is not the same as day care, and day care is not the same as maternal employment. The inappropriateness of the studies of institutionalized infants to maternal employment has also been noted by Yudkin and Holme (1963), by Yarrow (1964), and by Wortis (1971).

In addition, there is no evidence that the caretaker has to be the mother or that this role is better filled by a male or a female. There is some evidence that the baby benefits from predictability in handling, but whether this is true throughout infancy or only during certain periods is not clear, nor is it clear whether the different handling has any long-lasting effects. Studies of multiple mothering have produced conflicting results (Caldwell, 1964). Child psychologists generally believe that there must be at least one stable figure to whom the infant forms an attachment, but this is not definitely established, and we do not know whether the periodic absence from the infant that is likely to go along with the mother's employment is sufficient to undermine her potential as the object of the infant's attachment.

Nevertheless, a number of child development studies suggest that within the normal range of parent–child interaction, the amount of expressive and vocal stimulation and response the mother gives to the infant affects his development (Emerson & Schaffer, 1964; Kagan, 1969; Lewis & Goldberg, 1969; Moss, 1967). Furthermore, although the attempts to increase cognitive performance through day care programs have not been very successful, attempts to increase the mother–infant interaction in the home appear to have more enduring effects (Bronfenbrenner, 1973; Levenstein, 1970, 1971). While there is no evidence that employment actually affects the quantity or quality of the mother–infant interaction, the voluntary employment of mothers of infants and young children has not heretofore been common, and it has rarely been studied. It is therefore important to find out whether the mother's employment results in less (or more) personal stimulation and interaction for the infant.

In addition to the importance of stimulation and interaction and the issue of emotional attachment for the infant, there are less fully explored questions about the effects on the mother. Bowlby (1958) and others (Hess, 1970) believe that the mother–child interaction is important for the development of the mother's "attachment," that an important source of maternal feeling is the experience of caring for the infant. Yudkin and Holme (1963), who generally approve of maternal employment in their review, stress this as one of the real dangers of full-time maternal employment when the child is young:

> We would consider this need for a mother to develop a close and mutually satisfying relationship with her young infant one of the fundamental reasons why we oppose full-time work for mothers of children under 3 years. We do not say that it would not be possible to combine the two if children were cared for near their mothers so that they could see and be with each other during the day for parts of the day, and by such changes in households as will reduce the amount of time and energy needed for household chores. We are only stating that this occurs very rarely in our present society and is unlikely to be general in the foreseeable future and that the separation of children from their mothers for eight or nine hours a day, while the effects on the children may be counteracted by good substitute care, must have profound effects on the mother's own relationship with her young children and therefore on their relationship in the family as they grow older [pp. 131–132].

The issue of day care centers is not discussed in this review in any detail; however, our ignorance is almost as great here. While the cognitive advances expected from the Head Start day care programs were not adequately demonstrated (Bronfenbrenner, 1973), neither were there negative effects of these programs (Caldwell, Wright, Honig, & Tannenbaum, 1970). Obviously, the effects of day care centers for working mothers' children depend on the quality of the program, the time the child spends there, what happens to the child when he is not at the day care center, and what the alternatives are.

Arguments on either side of the issue of working mothers and day care often use data from studies of the kibbutzim in Israel, since all kibbutzim mothers work and from infancy on the child lives most of the time in the child centers. Some investigators have been favorably impressed with the devlopment of these children (Kohn-Raz, 1968; Rabkin & Rabkin, 1969), while others have noted at least some deleterious consequences (Bettelheim, 1969; Spiro, 1965). In fact, however, these data are probably quite irrelevant. According to Bronfenbrenner (1973), these children spend more time each day interacting with their parents than do children in the more conventional nuclear family arrangement, and the time they spend together is less subject to distractions. The whole living arrangement is different, including the nature of the parents' work and the social context within which interaction takes place. The mother participates a great deal in the infant care, breast-feeding is the norm, and both parents play daily with the child for long periods and without other diversions even as he matures. Thus, the Israeli kibbutz does not provide an example of maternal deprivation, American day care, or maternal employment as it is experienced in the United States.

There have been few direct attempts to study the effects of the mother's employment during the child's infancy. These few have had two special problems with which to cope: (a) Observed differences in infancy are difficult to interpret in terms of long-range adjustment; and (b) because the pattern of going to work when one had an infant was previously unusual, there were often special surrounding circumstances that made it difficult to ferret out the effects of employment per se. One way to handle the first problem is to compare older children with respect to their mothers' earlier employment. For example, Burchinal (1963) examined intelligence scores and school adjustment for a large sample of children in the seventh and eleventh grades. Children whose mothers had been employed when the child was 3 years old or younger were compared to children whose mothers were employed only when the child was older or whose mothers were never employed. Very few statistically significant results were obtained.

The second problem plagued the study by Moore (1963). In an intensive, longitudinal study, Moore compared children of elementary school age in Great Britain with respect to their mothers' employment history, with particular consideration given to the nature of the child care arrangements that the working mother established. However, the groups contrasted were different in ways other than whether or not the mother was employed at certain points in the child's life. Thus, one observed difference was that the children who had been left by their mothers from early infancy showed more dependent attachment to their parents than did any other children in the study and they also exhibited other symptoms of insecurity such as nail-biting and bad dreams; however, Moore also indicated that the mothers who started work early in the child's life did not themselves seem as attached to the child. While this latter observation could have been a result of the mother's not having had as much close contact with the child, it is also possible that these mothers were different from the start and the child's disturbance reflected this more than it reflected the mothers' employment. Since these mothers had sought employment when few mothers of infants worked, they may have been a more psychologically distinct group than one would now find. Indeed, Moore's case studies reveal patterns of emotional rejection, and in some cases the mother explicitly went to work to escape from the child. Furthermore, the mothers who went to work full time before their children were 2 years old often had difficulty finding good mother substitute arrangements, and the data indicate that the stability of the child care arrangements was an important factor affecting the child's adjustment.

Obviously the effects of maternal employment on the infant depend on the extent of the mother's absence and the nature of the substitute care—whether it is warm, stimulating, and stable. However, while studies of maternal employment and the school-age child by and large offer reassurance to the working mother, we have very little solid evidence concerning the effect on the younger child.

MATERNAL EMPLOYMENT AND
THE CHILD'S ACADEMIC ACHIEVEMENT

Probably the child characteristics that have most often been examined in relation to maternal employment are those pertaining to academic achievement. These are reviewed separately, since in most cases the data are too skimpy to be interpreted in terms of the five approaches discussed above. Included are studies of academic aspirations (usually whether or not the child plans to go to college), achievement motivation, intelligence test scores, and school performance. Most of the studies lack a guiding theory or even post hoc interpretations; the investigator rarely tries to explain why his data are consistent or inconsistent with other studies. The result is a hodgepodge of findings. The more recent studies have analyzed the data separately for sex and social class, and this has resulted in complex patterns, but there is no apparent order in these patterns. Until this issue is tackled with more theoretical sophistication, there will be little illumination.

College Plans

Why would one expect college plans to be affected by the mother's employment? Possibly because it means extra money in the house, one might predict that the children of the employed women, if the husbands' incomes were equated, would be more likely to plan on college. In fact, mothers often indicate they are working to help finance their children's college education. Possibly, daughters, modeling an active, occupation-oriented mother, would be more likely to seek college when their mothers worked. This second hypothesis might be affected by what kind of work the mother engaged in, particularly what kind of work in relation to her education, and also by how the mother felt about her employment. None of these necessary additional pieces of data are available in the pertinent studies, so an interpretation of the results is impossible.

Roy (1963) found that among rural high school students the children of working mothers were more likely to plan to go to college than were the children of nonworking mothers. This was true for both sexes, although a general impression from the tables is that the relationship was stronger for girls. (The report does not indicate if this sex difference was statistically significant.) On the other hand, the children of working mothers in the town sample were less likely to go to college. (Here the difference for girls appeared very slight.) The research supported the investigator's point that even within the same generally rural area, residence in the town or on farms was a meaningful distinction, but the data are insufficient for interpreting the results.

Banducci (1967) also examined the relationship between desires and plans for college and maternal employment, reporting the data separately by sex and father's occupation. His sample consisted of 3,014 Iowa high school seniors living with both parents. Three occupational levels were considered—laborer, skilled worker, and professional—presumably representing socioeconomic levels generally; "professional" in this study did not necessarily connote high educational achievement. For most subjects, males and females, maternal employment was positively associated with desires and plans for college. But for the group classified as professional, the opposite relationship prevailed: The daughters of working mothers were significantly less likely to expect to go to college, and the sons of working mothers were less likely to expect to go or to aspire for college, the latter relationship being significant. How can we interpret this curious pattern of findings? Did the presence of a working mother indicate the lower socioeconomic end of the professional group? Were the working mothers in this group employed in a family business, and thus the family was less education oriented? As indicated below, the sons of these women also had lower grade point averages, so there was something different about them, but whether an effect of maternal employment or some other peculiarity of this particular subsample was uncovered, it is impossible to say with the available information.

The several studies of college and professional women that indicate maternal employment is associated with more ambitious career goals have already been cited (Almquist & Angrist, 1971; Birnbaum, 1971; Ginzberg, 1971; Tangri, 1969).

Achievement Motives

There are two studies of children's achievement motives in relation to maternal employment. Both measured achievement motives by scoring projective responses according to the scheme developed by McClelland and Atkinson (Atkinson, 1958). Powell (1963) obtained achievement motivation scores and maternal employment data longitudinally for subjects at each of the following ages: 9, 10, 11, and 12. The children of employed mothers showed higher achievement motivation at each age level, significantly for age 9. Several years after the Powell study was published, Jones et al. (1967) carried out a similar study with sixth-graders. They found a parallel but nonsignificant relationship. No mention was made of the earlier study. How valuable it would have been if they had replicated Powell's work by presenting data for 9-, 10-, 11-, and 12-year-olds! Neither study analyzed the data separately for boys and girls, although, as indicated earlier, Powell's "modeling" hypotheses would suggest that the relationship might have been stronger for girls than for boys.

IQ Scores

Two studies of the lower socioeconomic class indicate that maternal employment and IQ scores are positively related. Woods (1972) in her study of fifth graders found that full-time maternal employment was associated with higher intelligence test scores as measured by the California Test of Mental Maturity, and Rieber and Womack (1968), studying preschoolers, found that more of the children of working mothers fell in the highest quartile on the Peabody Picture Vocabulary Test. Both of these studies included blacks and single-parent families, and the latter also included families of Latin American background.

The researchers who examined the relationship between maternal employment and intelligence test scores in more middle-class samples found more complex results. Hoffman (1963b) found that in a sample of white, intact families, the children of working mothers who liked work had lower IQ scores than did the matched children of nonworking mothers. The children of the working mothers who disliked work, however, were not different from the nonworking matched group.

Rees and Palmer (1970) presented a particularly interesting and complicated analysis of longitudinal data from a number of different studies. Their samples varied, but by and large they represented a higher socioeconomic group than the above three studies. Data were analyzed separately for boys and girls, with important differences appearing. In general, maternal employ-

ment related to high IQ in girls and low IQ in boys. Using as the
independent variable the mother's employment status when the
child was 15, they found that the daughters of working mothers
had higher IQs at age 6 and around age 15, although there was no
relationship for age 12. Was the working mother of the 15-year-
old also working when the child was 6? We do not know. The
relationships for the boys were the opposite. The data were interpreted by the investigators as reflecting a general association
between nontraditional femininity and higher IQ in girls: That is,
the working mother represented to her daughter a less traditional
view of femininity.[11] This theory suggesting a negative relationship between traditional femininity and achievement in girls has
been discussed more fully by Maccoby (1966) and by Hoffman
(1972); and data tying maternal employment to nontraditional
feminity were discussed earlier in this review.

Academic Performance

Hoffman (1963b) found that the elementary-school-age
children of working mothers showed lower school performance
than did the matched sample with nonworking mothers, using
teacher ratings of performance to measure the dependent variable. Nolan (1963) found no difference for rural elementary
school children and a difference favoring the children of working
mothers in high school, but this study did not even control on
social class. Neither of these studies reported the data separately
by sex.

Two more recent studies of elementary school children
were carried out in which attention was directed to whether or
not the mother was employed in a professional capacity. In one,
the reading achievement of the sixth-grade children of professionally employed mothers was compared to the reading
achievement of full-time housewives' children who were
matched by social class, sex, age, and IQ (Jones et al., 1967). The
study indicates that the children of the professional mothers were
more proficient. It also suggests why, for these parents spent
more time in reading activities with the children and had more
plans for the children's education, there were more books in the
home, and the mothers were better educated. The data were not
analyzed separately for boys and girls. It is important to point out
as one implication of this study that matching on social class is not
the same as matching on education, and matching on the father's
occupation is not the same as matching on income or life-style.

---

[11] Another finding of their analysis consistent with this interpretation is that
girls who had a brother either just older or just younger also had higher IQs.

The difference between employed mothers and professionally employed mothers is also indicated in the study by Frankel (1964) of intellectually gifted high school boys. High and low achievers matched on IQ scores were compared. The low achievers were more likely to have working mothers, but the high achievers were more likely to have professional mothers. Although the socioeconomic status as conventionally measured did not differentiate the groups, the education of the mothers (and possibly both parents) did. While the higher achievement of the children of professional mothers is easily interpreted, it is not clear why the low achievers tended to have nonprofessional working mothers. Frankel described these women impressionistically as dissatisfied and hostile. This judgment may or may not be valid, but it would be worthwhile to compare women working at various levels of jobs in terms of both selective factors and the effects of employment on the mother's psychological state. It might be noted that in Levine's (1968) study of women's career choice, the mother's education was found to be more important than whether or not the mother worked; Tangri (1969) found the mother's employment the more important.

Moving into the high school age, most studies found no differences in school achievement. Thus neither Nye (1963) nor Nelson (1969) reported significant differences, nor did Keidel (1970) in a comparison that matched on academic ability. In Burchinal's data (1963) one of the few relationships that remained significant despite controls introduced on socioeconomic status was the lower school grades of the eleventh-grade boys whose mothers were currently working. Roy (1963) also found adolescent sons of working mothers to have lower school grades, although only in his town sample. Banducci also reported differences in grades: Sons of working mothers in the socioeconomic class called professional had significantly lower grades than did the sons of nonworking mothers, but in the class labeled "skilled worker" the opposite relationship prevailed, the sons of working mothers having significantly higher grades than did the sons of the nonworkers. No other differences in school grades were significant. Of the several comparisons by Banducci (1967) of scores on the Iowa Tests of Educational Development, a standardized achievement measure, the sons of working mothers in the lowest socioeconomic group, laborers, had higher scores than did the nonworking-mother sons in that class. Brown (1970) found lower scores on the California Achievement Test for the middle-class eighth- and ninth-grade sons of working mothers.

Farley (1968) compared the self-reported grade point averages of students in an introductory sociology course at Cornell

University. The males who indicated their mothers were employed also reported significantly higher grades. There was no relationship for females. No variables were controlled. If the data were more solidly established, it would be interesting, since several studies indicate that maternal employment is prevalent in the backgrounds of women who pursue professional careers, but whether their college grades were better has not been established.

SUMMARY OF THE FINDINGS
ON ACADEMIC ACHIEVEMENT

Although there are some indications that maternal employment is positively associated with high school children's college plans, the opposite relationship has occasionally been shown. Per capita family income has not been controlled in these studies, however, and maternal employment may sometimes reflect low income as well as indicate augmented income.

There is evidence, however, that college-educated daughters of working mothers have higher career aspirations and achievements. Furthermore, in one study using longitudinal data, daughters of working mothers obtained higher intelligence test scores at 6 and 15 years of age. Two of the hypotheses discussed in this article, the modeling theory and the idea that independence training is stressed by working mothers, are particularly pertinent to the achievement of girls, and both predict higher achievement for the daughters of working mothers.

On the other hand, we suggested in an earlier review (Hoffman, 1963a) that sons of working mothers may not fare so well. This view receives a modest amount of support, and the data suggest that the sons of working mothers in the middle class show lower academic performance. In the lower class, however, better academic performance is associated with maternal employment for both sexes.

GENERAL SUMMARY

The research reviewed in this article has been organized around five general hypotheses that seem to be implicitly involved in the expectation that maternal employment affects the child, with an additional section dealing with effects on academic achievement. These hypotheses are not mutually exclusive, and the various processes in fact interact—sometimes reinforcing one another, sometimes counteracting. An aim of the social scientist interested in this topic should be to ascertain the conditions under which one process or another would operate and how these would interact. It is important to understand the effects of maternal employment at this level so that predictions and action implications are meaningful in the face of a changing society.

REFERENCES

Almquist, E. M., & Angrist, S. S. Role model influences on college women's career aspirations. *Merrill-Palmer Quarterly,* 1971, **17,** 263–279.

Astin, H. S. *The woman doctorate in America.* New York: Russell Sage Foundation, 1969.

Atkinson, J. W. (Ed.) *Motives in fantasy, action, and society.* Princeton, N.J.: Van Nostrand, 1958.

Banducci, R. The effect of mother's employment on the achievement, aspirations, and expectations of the child. *Personnel and Guidance Journal,* 1967, **46,** 263–267.

Baruch, G. K. Maternal influences upon college women's attitudes toward women and work. *Developmental Psychology,* 1972a, **6,** 32–37.

Baruch, G. K. Maternal role pattern as related to self-esteem and parental identification in college women. Paper presented at the meeting of the Eastern Psychological Association, Boston, April 1972b.

Baumrind, D., & Black, A. E. Socialization practices associated with dimensions of competence in preschool boys and girls. *Child Development,* 1967, **38,** 291–327.

Becker, W. C. Consequences of different kinds of parental discipline. In M. L. Hoffman & L. W. Hoffman (Eds.), *Review of child development research.* New York: Russell Sage Foundation, 1964.

Below, H. L. Life-styles and roles of women as perceived by high-school girls. Unpublished doctoral dissertation, Indiana University, 1969.

Bettelheim, B. *The children of the dream.* London: Macmillan, 1969.

Birnbaum, J. A. Life patterns, personality style and self-esteem in gifted family oriented and career committed women. Unpublished doctoral dissertation, University of Michigan, 1971.

Blood, R. O., & Hamblin, R. L. The effect of the wife's employment on the family power structure. *Social Forces,* 1958, **36,** 347–352.

Bowlby, J. A. Some pathological processes engendered by early mother-child separation. In M. J. E. Senn (Ed.), *Infancy and childhood.* New York: Josiah Macy, Jr. Foundation, 1953.

Bowlby, J. A. The nature of the child's tie to his mother. *International Journal of Psychoanalysis,* 1958, **39,** 350–373.

Bowlby, J. A. *Attachment.* New York: Basic Books, 1969.

Bronfenbrenner, U. Some familial antecedents of responsibility and leadership in adolescents. In L. Petrullo & B. M. Bass (Eds.), *Leadership and interpersonal behavior.* New York: Holt, Rinehart & Winston, 1961.

Bronfenbrenner, U. Is early intervention effective? Paper presented at the biennial meeting of The Society for Research in Child Development, Philadelphia, March 1973.

Brown, S. W. *A comparative study of maternal employment and nonemployment.* (Doctoral dissertation, Mississippi State University) Ann Arbor, Mich.: University Microfilms, 1970, No. 70–8610.

Burchinal, L. G. Personality characteristics of children. In F. I. Nye &

L. W. Hoffman (Eds.), *The employed mother in America*. Chicago: Rand McNally, 1963.

Burchinal, L. G., & Lovell, L. Relation of employment status of mothers to children's anxiety, parental personality and PARI scores. Unpublished manuscript (1425), Iowa State University, 1959.

Caldwell, B. M. The effects of infant care. In M. L. Hoffman & L. W. Hoffman (Eds.), *Review of child development research*. New York: Russell Sage Foundation, 1964.

Caldwell, B. M., Wright, C. M., Honig, A. S., & Tannenbaum, J. Infant day care and attachment. *American Journal of Orthopsychiatry*, 1970, **40**, 397–412.

Clausen, J. A. Family structure, socialization, and personality. In L. W. Hoffman & M. L. Hoffman (Eds.), *Review of child development research*. Vol. 2. New York: Russell Sage Foundation, 1966.

Clausen, J. A., & Clausen, S. R. The effects of family size on parents and children. In J. Fawcett (Ed.), *Psychological perspectives on fertility*. New York: Basic Books, 1973.

Constantinople, A. Masculininity–femininity: An exception to a famous dictum? *Psychological Bulletin*, 1973, **80**, 389–407.

Dennis, W., & Najarian, P. Infant development under environmental handicap. *Psychological Monographs*, 1957, **71** (7, Whole No. 436).

Dizard, J. *Social change in the family*. Chicago: University of Chicago, Community and Family Study Center, 1968.

Douvan, E. Employment and the adolescent. In F. I. Nye & L. W. Hoffman (Eds.), *The employed mother in America*. Chicago: Rand McNally, 1963.

Duvall, E. B. Conceptions of mother roles by five- and six-year-old children of working and non-working mothers. Unpublished doctoral dissertation, Florida State University, 1955.

Emerson, P. E., & Schaffer, H. R. The development of social attachments in infancy. *Monographs of the Society for Research in Child Development*, 1964, **29** (3, serial No. 94).

Farley, J. Maternal employment and child behavior. *Cornell Journal of Social Relations*, 1968, **3**, 58–70.

Finkelman, J. J. Maternal employment, family relationships, and parental role perception. Unpublished doctoral dissertation, Yeshiva University, 1966.

Fisher, M. S. Marriage and work for college women. *Vassar Alumnae Magazine*, 1939, **24**, 7–10.

Frankel, E. Characteristics of working and nonworking mothers among intellectually gifted high and low achievers. *Personnel and Guidance Journal*, 1964, **42**, 776–780.

Garland, T. N. The better half? The male in the dual profession family. In C. Safilios-Rothschild (Ed.), *Toward a sociology of women*. Lexington, Mass.: Xerox College Publishing, 1972.

Ginzberg, E. *Educated American women: Life styles and self-portraits*. New York: Columbia University Press, 1971.

Glueck, S., & Glueck, E. Working mothers and delinquency. *Mental Hygiene*, 1957, **41**, 327–352.

Gold, M. *A social-psychology of delinquent boys*. Ann Arbor, Mich.: Institute for Social Research, 1961.

Goldberg, P. Misogyny and the college girl. Paper presented at the meeting of the Eastern Psychological Association, Boston, April 1967.

Hall, F. T., & Schroeder, M. P. Time spent on household tasks. *Journal of Home Economics*, 1970, **62**, 23–29.

Harlow, H., & Harlow, M. H. Learning to love. *American Scientist*, 1966, **54**, 244–272.

Hartley, R. E. Children's concepts of male and female roles. *Merrill-Palmer Quarterly*, 1960, **6**, 83–91.

Hartley, R. E. What aspects of child behavior should be studied in relation to maternal employment? In A. E. Siegel (Ed.), *Research issues related to the effects of maternal employment on children.* University Park, Penn.: Social Science Research Center, 1961.

Henshel, A. Anti-feminist bias in traditional measurements of masculinity-femininity. Paper presented at the meeting of the National Council on Family Relations, Estes Park, Colorado, August 1971.

Hess, H. Ethology and developmental psychology. In P. Mussen (Ed.), *Carmichael's manual of child psychology*, New York: Wiley, 1970.

Hoffman, L. W. *Effects of the employment of mothers on parental power relations and the division of household tasks.* Unpublished doctoral dissertation, University of Michigan, 1958.

Hoffman, L. W. The father's role in the family and the child's peer group adjustment. *Merrill-Palmer Quarterly*, 1961, **7**, 97–105.

Hoffman, L. W. Effects on children: Summary and discussion. In F. I. Nye & L. W. Hoffman (Eds.), *The employed mother in America.* Chicago: Rand McNally, 1963*a*.

Hoffman, L. W. Mother's enjoyment of work and effects on the child. In F. I. Nye & L. W. Hoffman (Eds.), *The employed mother in America.* Chicago: Rand McNally, 1963*b*.

Hoffman, L. W. Parental power relations and the division of household tasks. In F. I. Nye & L. W. Hoffman (Eds.), *The employed mother in America.* Chicago: Rand McNally, 1963*c*.

Hoffman, L. W. Early childhood experiences and women's achievement motives. *Journal of Social Issues*, 1972, **28**(2), 129–155.

Hoffman, L. W. The professional woman as mother. In R. B. Kundsin (Ed.), *A conference on successful women in the sciences.* New York: New York Academy of Sciences, 1973.

Hoffman, L. W., & Lippitt, R. The measurement of family life variables. In P. Mussen (Ed.), *Handbook of research methods in child development.* New York: Wiley, 1960.

Holmstrom, L. L. The two-career family. Paper presented at the conference of Women: Resource for a Changing World, Radcliffe Institute, Radcliffe College, Cambridge, April 1972.

Horner, M. S. Femininity and successful achievement: A basic inconsistency. In J. M. Bardwick, E. Douvan, M. S. Horner, & D. Gutman, *Feminine personality and conflict.* Belmont, Calif.: Brooks/Cole, 1972.

Hunt, J. McV. *Intelligence and experience.* New York: Ronald Press, 1961.

Johnson, C. L. *Leadership patterns in working and nonworking mother middle class families.* (Doctoral dissertation, University of Kansas) Ann Arbor, Mich.: University Microfilms, 1969, No. 69–11, 224.

Jones, J. B., Lundsteen, S. W., & Michael, W. B. The relationship of the professional employment status of mothers to reading achievement of sixth-grade children. *California Journal of Educational Research*, 1967, **43**, 102–108.

Kagan, J. Continuity of cognitive development during the first year. *Merrill-Palmer Quarterly,* 1969, **15,** 101–119.

Kappel, B. E., & Lambert, R. D. Self worth among the children of working mothers. Unpublished manuscript, University of Waterloo, 1972.

Keidel, K. C. Maternal employment and ninth grade achievement in Bismarck, North Dakota. *Family Coordinator,* 1970, **19,** 95–97.

King, K., McIntyre, J., & Axelson, L. J. Adolescents' views of maternal employment as a threat to the marital relationship. *Journal of Marriage and the Family.* 1968, **30,** 633–637.

Kligler, D. The effects of employment of married women on husband and wife roles: A study in culture change. Unpublished doctoral dissertation, Yale University, 1954.

Kohn-Raz, R. Mental and motor development of kibbutz, institutionalized, and home-reared infants in Israel. *Child Development,* 1968, **39,** 489–504.

Kriesberg, L. *Mothers in poverty: A study of fatherless families.* Chicago: Aldine, 1970.

Levenstein, P. Cognitive growth in preschoolers through verbal interaction with mothers. *American Journal of Orthopsychiatry,* 1970, **40,** 426–432.

Levenstein, P. Verbal interaction project: Aiding cognitive growth in disadvantaged preschoolers through the Mother-Child Home Program July 1, 1967—August 31, 1970. Final report to Children's Bureau, Office of Child Development, U.S. Department of Health, Education and Welfare, 1971. (Mimeo)

Levine, A. G. Marital and occupational plans of women in professional schools: Law, medicine, nursing, teaching. Unpublished doctoral dissertation, Yale University, 1968.

Lewis, M., & Goldberg, S. Perceptual-cognitive development in infancy: A generalized expectancy model as a function of the mother-infant interaction. *Merrill-Palmer Quarterly,* 1969, **15,** 81–100.

Lipman-Blumen, J. How ideology shapes women's lives. *Scientific American,* 1972, **226**(1), 34–42.

Low, S., & Spindler, P. *Child care arrangements of working mothers in the United States.* (Children's Bureau Publication 461) Washington, D.C.: U.S. Government Printing Office, 1968.

Lunneborg, P. W. Stereotypic aspect in masculinity-femininity measurement. Paper presented at the meeting of the American Psychological Association, San Francisco, September 1968.

Maccoby, E. E. Sex differences in intellectual functioning. In E. E. Maccoby (Ed.), *The development of sex differences.* Stanford, Calif.: Stanford University Press, 1966.

Maslow, A. H., Rand, H., & Newman, S. Some parallels between sexual and dominance behavior of infra-human primates and the fantasies of patients in psychotherapy. *Journal of Nervous and Mental Disease,* 1960, **131,** 202–212.

Mathews, S. M. The development of children's attitudes concerning mothers' out-of-home employment. *Journal of Educational Sociology,* 1933, **6,** 259–271.

McCord, W., & McCord, J. *Origins of crime.* New York: Columbia University Press, 1959.

McCord, J., McCord, W., & Thurber, E. Effects of maternal employment on lower-class boys. *Journal of Abnormal and Social Psychology,* 1963, **67**, 177–182.

Meier, H. C. Mother-centeredness and college youths' attitudes toward social equality for women: Some empirical findings. *Journal of Marriage and the Family,* 1972, **34**, 115–121.

Moore, T. Children of working mothers. In S. Yudkin & H. Holme (Eds.), *Working mothers and their children.* London: Michael Joseph, 1963.

Moss, H. A. Sex, age, and state as determinants of mother-infant interaction. *Merrill-Palmer Quarterly,* 1967, **13**, 19–36.

Nelson, D. D. A study of school achievement among adolescent children with working and nonworking mothers. *Journal of Educational Research,* 1969, **62**, 456–457.

Nelson, D. D. A study of personality adjustment among adolescent children with working and nonworking mothers. *Journal of Educational Research,* 1971, **64**, 1328–1330.

Nolan, F. L. Effects on rural children. In F. I. Nye & L. W. Hoffman (Eds.), *The employed mother in America.* Chicago: Rand McNally, 1963.

Nye, F. I. *Family relationships and delinquent behavior.* New York: Wiley, 1958.

Nye, F. I. The adjustment of adolescent children. In F. I. Nye & L. W. Hoffman (Eds), *The employed mother in America.* Chicago: Rand McNally, 1963.

Peterson, E. T. The impact of maternal employment on the mother-daughter relationship and on the daughter's role-orientation. Unpublished doctoral dissertation, University of Michigan, 1958.

Poloma, M. M. Role conflict and the married professional woman. In C. Safilios-Rothschild (Ed.), *Toward a sociology of women.* Lexington, Mass.: Xerox College Publishing, 1972.

Powell, K. Personalities of children and child-rearing attitudes of mothers. In F. I. Nye & L. W. Hoffman (Eds.), *The employed mother in America.* Chicago: Rand McNally, 1963.

Propper, A. M. The relationship of maternal employment to adolescent roles, activities, and parental relationships. *Journal of Marriage and the Family,* 1972, **34**, 417–421.

Rabkin, L. Y., & Rabkin, K. Children of the kibbutz. *Psychology Today,* 1969, 3(4), 40.

Rapoport, R., & Rapoport, R. The dual-career family: A variant pattern and social change. In C. Safilios-Rothschild (Ed.), *Toward a sociology of women.* Lexington, Mass.: Xerox College Publishing, 1972.

Rees, A. N., & Palmer, F. H. Factors related to change in mental test performance. *Developmental Psychology Monograph,* 1970, 3(2, Pt. 2).

Rheingold, H. The modification of social responsiveness in institutional babies. *Monographs of the Society for Research in Child Development,* 1956, **21**(2, Serial No. 63).

Rheingold, H., & Bayley, N. The later effects of an experimental modification of mothering. *Child Development,* 1959, **30**, 363–372.

Rheingold, H., Gewirtz, J. L., & Ross, H. W. Social conditioning of vocalizations in the infant. *Journal of Comparative and Physiological Psychology,* 1959, **52**, 68–73.

Rieber, M., & Womack, M. The intelligence of preschool children as related to ethnic and demographic variables. *Exceptional Children*, 1968, **34**, 609–614.

Riege, M. G. Parental affection and juvenile delinquency in girls. *The British Journal of Criminology*, 1972, **12**, 55–73.

Robinson, J. B. Historical changes in how people spend their time. In A. Michel (Ed.), *Family issues of employed women in Europe and America*. Leiden, Netherlands: E. J. Brill, 1971.

Roethlisberger, F. J., & Dickson, W. J. *Business Research Studies*. Cambridge, Mass.: Harvard Business School, Division of Research, 1939.

Roy, P. Adolescent roles: Rural -urban differentials. In F. I. Nye & L. W. Hoffman (Eds.), *The employed mother in America*. Chicago: Rand McNally, 1963.

Siegel, A. E., & Haas, M. B. The working mother: A review of research. *Child Development*, 1963, **34**, 513–542.

Smith, H. C. *An investigation of the attitudes of adolescent girls toward combining marriage, motherhood and a career*. (Doctoral dissertation, Columbia University) Ann Arbor, Mich.: University Microfilms, 1969, No. 69–8089.

Spiro, M. E. *Children of the kibbutz*. New York: Schocken Books, 1965.

Spitz, R. A. Hospitalism: An inquiry into the genesis of psychiatric conditions in early childhood. *Psychoanalytic Studies of the Child*, 1945, **1**, 53–74.

Stolz, L. M. Effects of maternal employment on children: Evidence from research. *Child Development*, 1960, **31**, 749–782.

Szolai, A. The multinational comparative time budget: A venture in international research cooperation. *American Behavioral Scientist*, 1966, **10**, 1–31.

Tangri, S. S. Role innovation in occupational choice. Unpublished doctoral dissertation, University of Michigan, 1969.

Tizard, B., Cooperman, O., Joseph, A., & Tizard, J. Environmental effects on language development: A study of young children in long-stay residential nurseries. *Child Development*, 1972, **43**, 337–358.

U.S. Department of Labor, Women's Bureau, *Who are the working mothers?* (Leaflet 37) Washington, D.C.: U.S. Government Printing Office, 1972.

Vogel, S. R., Broverman, I. K., Broverman, D. M., Clarkson, F. E., & Rosenkrantz, P. S. Maternal employment and perception of sex roles among college students. *Developmental Psychology*, 1970, **3**, 384–391.

Von Mering, F. H. Professional and non-professional women as mothers. *Journal of Social Psychology*, 1955, **42**, 21–34.

Walker, K. E. How much help for working mothers?: The children's role. *Human Ecology Forum*, 1970a, **1**(2), 13–15.

Walker, K. E. Time-use patterns for household work related to homemakers' employment. Paper presented at the meeting of the Agricultural Outlook Conference, Washington, D.C., February 1970b.

Walker, K. E., & Woods, M. E. Time use for care of family members. (Use-of-Time Research Project, working paper 1) Unpublished manuscript, Cornell University, 1972.

Weil, M. W. An analysis of the factors influencing married women's actual or planned work participation. *American Sociological Review*, 1961, **26**, 91–96.

Winterbottom, M. R. The relation of need for achievement to learning experiences in independence and mastery. In J. W. Atkinson (Ed.), *Motives in fantasy, action, and society.* Princeton, N.J.: Van Nostrand, 1958.

Woods, M. B. The unsupervised child of the working mother, *Developmental Psychology,* 1972, **6**, 14–25.

Wortis, R. P. The acceptance of the concept of the maternal role by behavioral scientists: Its effects on women. *American Journal of Orthopsychiatry,* 1971, **41**, 733–746.

Yarrow, L. J. Separation from parents during early childhood. In M. L. Hoffman & L. W. Hoffman (Eds.), *Review of child development research.* New York: Russell Sage Foundation, 1964.

Yarrow, M. R., Scott, P., deLeeuw, L., & Heinig, C. Child-rearing in families of working and nonworking mothers. *Sociometry,* 1962, **25**, 122–140.

Yudkin, S., & Holme, A. *Working mothers and their children.* London: Michael Joseph, 1963.

Zissis, C. A study of the life planning of 550 freshman women at Purdue University. *Journal of the National Association of Women Deans and Counselors,* 1964, **28**, 153–159.

SECTION 2
DAY CARE

OVERVIEW

Day Care

For some, the phrase *day care* is a rallying cry for social change. Women's groups see day care for their children as an essential step in the freeing of women from the roles of homemaker and child rearer. Welfare groups see day care as a necessary adjunct to the elimination of the poverty cycle: If women who are heads of households are to be able to work to support themselves, they must have some kind of good, inexpensive care for their children. Student groups at colleges and universities have asked that day care be provided for their children to enable mothers to attend school on an equal basis with fathers, or at least with less difficulty than has existed in the past. More prosaically, some kind of day care is a necessity for those millions of women who work and have young children. Most such women are not particularly interested in the "liberation" of women, or in the breaking of the poverty cycle. They need to work, for a variety of reasons, and for them *day care* is a solution to a pressing personal problem.

For others, *day care* elicits a frightening image of vast numbers of babies cared for in institutional settings by people other than mothers. The fears and concerns expressed in discussions of day care may appear foolish to some, but they are real and deserve careful discussion and examination. The major concerns appear to be threefold: (1) To place a child in day care means to separate that child from his family, which may weaken his attachment to that family. I have already discussed this question in some detail in the section on working mothers because this general concern is voiced about any situation in which the child and the mother are separated. (2) If the mother is going to work anyway, day care—that is, care of the child *away* from the home in some kind of group setting—may be worse than other kinds of care because it is "institutional" group care. We know from research on other kinds of institutions that institutional care can and often does result in intellectual retardation and emotional "stunting." As I mentioned in the preceding section, Bowlby's paper (1951) for the World Health Organization on institutionally reared infants and children placed great emphasis on the dire consequences of "maternal deprivation" for the child. But he also placed emphasis on the harmfulness of the institutional setting; any setting in which the child did not have a one-to-one relationship with a single adult was seen as potentially damaging to the child. And most day-care settings do not include a one-to-one relationship between a child and a single adult. There are often many children and comparatively few adults; hence the fear that day care will result in some of the same effects as were seen by Bowlby and others. The paper by Blehar in this section touches on some of these concerns. (3) When children are in groups for protracted periods, as they are in day-care settings, the danger of infectious diseases being transmitted may be increased.

These fears cannot simply be rejected as old-fashioned. They are based on past experience and past analyses of research as well as on old cultural traditions and biases. If day care is to become a major part of our services to families, it is important that these questions be discussed and dealt with honestly. Is group care necessarily bad for a child? If not, what conditions are needed in a group-care arrangement in order to prevent ill effects and foster good effects? Does group care necessarily result in higher rates of infection? How can the effect be avoided or ameliorated? Is the child's relationship with his family altered by a group-care experience? Is the family "weakened" in some way?

Before looking at the research on such questions, let me take you on a guided trip through the information on types and uses of day care.

KINDS OF DAY CARE

As I pointed out in the overview chapter on working mothers, *most* children cared for by someone other than the mother are not cared for in organized day-care centers at all. A large percentage are cared for in their own homes by someone other than the mother, and the remainder outside their homes in various arrangements. In the current discussion I am concerned primarily about those children who are cared for by someone outside their own home. Good *current* information on the type of care arranged for such children is extremely hard to come by. The Office of Child Development, several years ago, suggested the following figures (Grotberg, 1971):

Children in day-care centers   575,000
Children in family day care   712,000

Clearly these figures are now much too low. There are about 6 million children under age 6 whose mothers work. There is every reason to suppose that *at least* half of these children are being cared for outside of their own homes, so there are approximately 3 million children to account for. One of the difficulties is that federal agencies, which collect most of the statistics on such questions, are likely to have data only from *licensed* centers and day-care homes. In 1972 there were about 1 million children in such licensed centers and homes (U.S. Department of Labor, 1975). But many children are placed in *un*licensed centers and homes, and such day-care arrangements simply do not show up in most of the Department of Labor statistics. My own guess is that of the 3 million or so children cared for outside of their homes, fewer than a million are in day-care centers, another million or more are in family day-care homes, and the remainder are cared for by relatives, have no care, or are in some other kind of setting.

What are the differences between day-care centers and family day care? The centers are what you probably think of when the phrase *day care* is mentioned. Commonly there are 10 to 15 (or more) children cared for in a group in a non-home setting. Ordinarily, for each group of 10 to 15 children there is at least 1 qualified teacher and often 3 or 4 aides who have had varying degrees of training.

Some private day-care centers contain a number of groups of 10 to 15 children each in the same building, with a total of 60 to 100 children. Some centers are in buildings especially designed for such use; more commonly, however, centers have been established in converted space, such as church basements, old stores, or former homes.

A family day-care home, on the other hand, is simply a private home. The mother in this home takes in 1 to 4 or more children, in addition to her own, to care for during the day. In a sense, this is comparable to all-day baby-sitting, except that it is done in the sitter's home rather than the child's, and there are often two or more unrelated children brought to the home for care.

It is critical that you keep in mind, as you read the following pages, that nearly all the research data on the effects of *day care*

are based on observations and testing of children in day-care *centers;* there is almost no information on the consequences of family day care, despite the fact that it is a more common arrangement for young children. There are some existing stereotypes of family day care, however, which depict such care as unstimulating, with large numbers of children cared for by untrained adults. What evidence is available about family day care suggests that this picture is probably very much exaggerated. Emlen's review of family day-care research (Emlen and Perry, 1974) and his own studies of family day-care homes in Portland, Oregon (Emlen, 1972; Emlen, Donoghue, and LaForge, 1971), suggest that the average number of children in family day-care homes is typically about 3, of whom one is usually the caregiver's own child. In only 5 percent of the cases Emlen studied in Portland were there more than 6 children in the day-care home. And most of the children in the families he surveyed were in the same family day-care home for protracted periods of time. In other research, Prescott (1973) observed that there were more occasions of one-to-one contact between child and caregiver in day-care homes than in centers, and that opportunities for cognitive engagement were at about the same level as in the more "open structured" day-care centers. Thus the care provided in family day care can be, and often is, stable and individualized. Still, we need a great deal more information about what happens in day-care homes and about the consequences of such care for the child.

One other fact you should know: Unlike the situation in some other countries (particularly in Europe), about half of all licensed day care in this country is run for profit and not subsidized by any government agency. Some government subsidy may exist in the form of financial assistance to poverty-level families with young children, but there is little direct aid to day-care centers from any government group. Of the nonprofit centers, most are run by religious groups or churches, or by voluntary or community organizations. A small subset of day-care centers are run for research purposes, but these centers are a distinct minority. Unfortunately, however, a substantial portion of the data on day care and its effects comes from just such centers, although in recent years there has been more research attention given to the "ordinary" as opposed to the "research" centers.

PURPOSES OF DAY CARE
At least two purposes for day care can be distinguished in the discussions of and legislation for day care. On the one hand,

there is a need to provide service for families in which all the adults work. These families want a stable, reliable caregiving arrangement for their children that will provide the equivalent of good home care. Alternatively, day care may be seen as a potential vehicle for providing educational benefits to the enrolled children, particularly children from poverty environments. The day-care center described in the Robinson and Robinson paper reflects such an orientation, as does the Syracuse center begun by Bettye Caldwell (Caldwell et al., 1970; Lally, 1973). For these researchers, day care is envisaged as an early, intensive, compensatory education program that has the potential not just to ameliorate problems that already exist but to prevent the development of problems.

The two goals are not necessarily incompatible. Few parents who are looking for a reliable service would object to having their child in a day-care center that offered extensive enrichment experiences. The distinction between the two sets of goals, or the two sorts of programs, is important for two reasons, however. First, enriched educational day care is vastly more expensive than the "good baby-sitting" kind of care. Second, the preponderance of research on day care done in this country has been done in intensively educational centers. In the past several years, researchers exploring the effects of day care on attachment processes have sometimes studied more "typical," less "enriched" centers, but nearly all the information on the effects of day care on cognitive development comes from studies of children in experimental, highly enriched centers. Almost no information on either of these issues has been collected in *family* day care. These major gaps in our information should be kept in mind as you read the rest of this overview and as you look at the selections in this section. What we know about day care is limited, at best, and that limited amount may not be equally true of the several types of centers or of family day-care homes.

EFFECTS OF DAY CARE ON THE CHILD'S EMOTIONAL AND SOCIAL DEVELOPMENT

In the past several years there has been quite a burst of studies on the impact of day-care experience on various facets of social and emotional development. The greatest focus has been on the impact of day care on the child's attachment to the natural mother, and here the findings are somewhat equivocal. On the negative side, Blehar (whose paper is in the selections) found that 3-year-olds in day care showed a kind of anxious attachment to the mother that suggested there might be some disruption of the attachment to her. The 2-year-olds in Blehar's study showed more indifference or detachment toward the mother, which may be interpreted either as a sign of healthy adjustment to the day-care experience or as a sign of a fairly significant restriction in the child's attachment. Others have *not* found evidence of similar disruptions. Ragozin (also included in the selections), for example, observed day-care children both in the artificial "strange situation" that Blehar used and in the natural setting of a day-care center itself where the child was being left by the parent and picked up again at the end of the day. In the natural setting she found no age differences in the children's behavior at separation and reunion, but all the children did show heightening of attachment behaviors at reunion with the mother at the end of the day, indicating that the attachment to her was still strong. In the "strange situation" (in which the child is alternately with the mother, alone, with a stranger, or with mother and stranger) Ragozin did observe age differences in the children's behavior, with the younger children showing more distress at separation. But the age differences she found paralleled those found by others in home-reared children.

Doyle (1975), also using the strange situation format, found no basic difference between home-reared and day-care children, except that the home-reared children looked more at the stranger when she entered the setting than did the day-care infants. Presumably this is the result of a greater "novelty" effect of a stranger for the home-reared child. Saunders (1972) similarly found no difference in response to strangers.

Cornelius and Denney (1975), using a laboratory setting in which the child was observed with the mother, with the mother and a confederate adult, and with the mother and a confederate child, observed no general effect of day care. Day-care children, compared to home-reared children, did not show more proximity to the mother and did not show more attention-seeking. Cornelius and Denney did, however, observe one interesting interaction effect in this setting: among the home-reared children, boys were significantly less proximity-seeking than were girls, but this difference did not exist for the center children. This finding suggests the possibility that day-care children may be less stereotypically sex-typed than are home-reared children. This is an intriguing finding, worth additional exploration, although I should emphasize that other researchers have not found this kind of interaction effect.

Finally, in an older study (Caldwell, Wright, Honig, and Tannenbaum, 1970), Caldwell and her associates reported that there were no differences in attachment to the mother between children in day care from infancy and those reared at home. In this study, attachment to the mother was assessed through interviews with the mother and some observations in the home.

How is one to make sense out of the conflicting findings? More specifically, how can one explain the Blehar results since her findings are discrepant? The simplest explanation appears to be in terms of the staff-to-child ratio in the various centers used in the different studies. In Blehar's study the day-care centers all had staff-to-child ratios of about 1 : 7 or 1 : 8. In the studies reporting no disruption of attachment patterns, the staff-to-child ratios were more on the order of 1 : 4 (Doyle, 1975; Caldwell et al., 1970; see also Ragozin's selection in this section). In order to determine if the staff-to-child ratio is really as critical as it appears it could be, some research to directly compare centers with varying ratios is badly needed. Other dimensions on which day-care centers may differ, such as the number of children in the center and the amount of play space, also need to be explored in future research.

Another interesting study in this area has focused not on the child's attachment, but on other features of social and emotional development of day-care children. Schwarz, Strickland, and Krolick (1974) observed two groups of children who had entered a new day-care center at the same time (The Children's Center, Syracuse, the site of a number of studies). The youngsters were all about 4 years old when they entered the new center. Some had been in other day-care centers within the Children's Center complex since early infancy; others had been reared at home until age 4. This set of circumstances made it possible to look at some of the potential effects of long-term day-care experience compared to short-term experience at a later age.

The children were rated on a series of nine scales (using a forced-distribution method, which gets around some of the problems of ratings) by their teachers and again later in the year by a group of graduate student observers. The two sets of ratings were highly correlated, suggesting that the variations in children's behavior were quite consistent through the year.

Infant-care children, compared to those who had entered day care at age 4, were rated as significantly different on three scales: they were less cooperative with adults, more aggressive, and more motorically active. There were no differences in playfulness, ability to abstract, success at problem solving, spontaneity, or getting along with peers. There was a slight difference on tolerance for frustration, with infant-care children being somewhat less tolerant of frustration.

There are obviously many possible interpretations of these

findings. It is possible, as Schwarz and associates (1974) point out, that the reduced cooperativeness with adults results from a weakened socialization because of the frequent separation of child and parent. Or the findings may result from the pluralistic socialization of the children in infant day care because the different adults such children must deal with may have had varying expectations. In any case, these effects do not seem to be the result of day-care experience per se but of *early* day-care experience, since those who entered the day-care setting at age 4 did not become more aggressive or less cooperative over the course of the year. I should also emphasize that such differences need not suggest that the early care group is somehow seriously maladjusted. Braun and Caldwell (1973) studied another group of youngsters in the same center and noted that a psychiatrist making "blind" judgments about the overall emotional health of the children found no differences in adjustment between children who entered day care before and after age 3.

In all of this, it is important to bear in mind that in no instance is it possible unequivocally to attribute the differences observed to day care. It is always possible that families choosing to place their child in day care in infancy are systematically different from those who do not make that choice; so it may be the family differences, not the day care, which produce the observed effects in the children. The Schwarz et al. study is somewhat less vulnerable to this alternative interpretation than usual, however, because in this instance all the families did eventually choose to place their child in day care. So there was no moral or other objection to day care among those whose children entered at age 4. Still, we need to be careful in interpreting the findings, and we do need to know more about the long-range effects of such experience. Does the greater aggressiveness of the infant-center children persist to school age? Does the lack of cooperativeness with adults create difficulties in school?

A number of psychiatrists and other researchers and theorists have been concerned about the potential long-range effects of day-care experience. Meers (1972), for example, has suggested that the potential for long-term psychiatric damage is greatest for very young children in group care. He argues that we simply do not yet know enough to specify safeguards in such settings. The data reviewed above do not show any kind of major short-term dislocation of children in day care, but it is true that we know less than we would like about long-term effects. In European countries which have had infant day-care programs for several decades, psychologists have not done the research that might show whether there were long-term difficulties for children so reared. There are a few long-range studies of children reared in groups on kibbutzim in Israel (Kaffman, 1961, 1965; Rabin, 1958), and these do not show any negative consequences over the long run. Wolins (1969a, 1969b) has explored the same kind of question in his studies of adolescent children who had been reared in various kinds of 24-hour group-care settings. He could find no evidence of any widespread emotional disturbance resulting from the group rearing. In those instances where emotional difficulties seemed to be present, they could be attributed to the disrupted family conditions that led to the placement of the child in a group-rearing situation.

The cumulative evidence, more extensive than several years ago but still scant, suggests that early attachments probably are not disrupted by day-care experience, at least where there is a sufficiently good adult-to-child ratio, but that there may be other effects of early group rearing we should explore further. Long-term effects are much more difficult to discuss because the data base is extremely poor, but my reading of the evidence does not suggest as much pessimism as Meers has stated. Still, the possibility of long-term negative outcomes of early day care cannot be ruled out, and there is a clear need for good research in this area.

EFFECTS OF DAY CARE ON
THE CHILD'S INTELLECTUAL DEVELOPMENT

The data on the child's intellectual development are quite clear. In virtually every study done in this country and in most studies abroad, group-care children are superior in intellectual development to a home-reared comparison group. This effect is illustrated in the Robinson and Robinson paper, but their findings are not unique. Caldwell (1971) examined the intellectual status of the children in the Syracuse center and found that center infants showed an increase in IQ of about 17 points, whereas the matched controls showed a decrease of about 6 points. Later data from the same center (Lally, 1973) show a spread of about 15 points between center and control children after three years in the center. Children in the Greensboro program were also significantly higher on IQ tests than those in the control group (Keister, 1970), as were the children in the Howard University experimental program (Cisin, 1970). Doyle (1975), whose results on attachment I have mentioned earlier, also found that day-care children were higher in IQ, as measured by the Cattell Infant Scale, than were home-reared children.

Generally speaking, the greatest gains in the experimental programs have been made by infants or children from poverty-level families. Middle-class children have shown either smaller gains or no gains at all compared to the control group (Robinson and Robinson, in the 1971 paper in the selections; Keister, 1970).

Studies in Europe and Israel provide similar evidence. Kibbutz-reared children score higher than home-reared counterparts in most studies (Rabin, 1958). In Wolin's study of five different group-rearing settings, three of the five groups were higher in cognitive functioning than their home-reared controls, and two showed no difference.

Again, however, some caution is in order. Let me reemphasize the fact that nearly all the positive findings about the impact of day care on children's cognitive development have emerged from expensive, experimental programs. There is almost no information about the effects of the more typical neighborhood day-care center, and still less on the effect of family day care. The only study I know on family day care that touches on intellectual development is one by Saunders and Keister (1972, described in Williams, 1974), who tested a group of twelve children in family day care, all of whom had been in day care before 12 months of age, and compared them to a group of ten children in day-care centers in the same city. Over a 3- to 15-month period, three of the family day-care children showed an increase of 10 points or more on the Bayley mental scale, four showed a decrease of 10 points or more, and five showed no change. Of the center-care children, eight showed an increase of at least 10 points, one showed a decrease, and one showed no change on the Bayley.

The comparison in this case seems to favor the center-care children. It certainly suggests that we need to know a great deal more about family day care and the conditions under which it *might* result in some slowing of cognitive development. There is an extensive literature on the effects of *institutional* group rearing, such as in orphanages, which indicates that substantial retardation of intellectual development can occur when the group-rearing setting is severely deprived of both animate and inanimate stimulation (Yarrow, 1964). So group care per se does not invariably produce cognitive benefits. *Good* group care frequently does have that effect, but there is a clear need for more information on the conditions that create or define "good" care.

EFFECTS OF DAY CARE ON THE CHILD'S HEALTH

Several studies suggest that children in day care are somewhat more likely to get colds or other respiratory disorders, presumably because of the greater contact with others and the consequent increase in the possibility of infection. Glezen, Loda, Clyde, Senior, Schaeffer, Conley, and Denney (1971) (studying the children in the Chapel Hill Center described by Robinson and

Robinson in the selections) report that the children who had attended the center, particularly those who had been in the center as infants, showed slightly higher rates of respiratory illnesses than was typical for the metropolitan area in which the center was located. Keister (1970) reported similar findings from the Greensboro project. She found that the center children had more diaper rash and more colds or runny noses than had the control group of home-reared children. And Doyle (1975) reported that the center-care children in her study had a somewhat higher rate of flu than did the home-reared controls.

If these findings hold for other centers—and there is every reason to suppose that they would—then provision must be made for appropriately increased medical surveillance and care for children in group-care settings.

Conclusions

There is certainly more information bearing on the whole range of issues I have raised here than there was three years ago when I wrote this chapter for the first edition of this book. There has been a sharp increase in interest in the practical and theoretical questions at issue in day care, and there is every reason to suppose that there will continue to be research addressed to these issues. In particular, I devoutly hope that there will be some good work done on family day care and its effects, since we know so little about this very common child-care arrangement. For now, however, we must do the best with what we have.

On the whole it still seems to me that *good* center day care need not have any detrimental effects, and for some children it seems to have clear benefits. Increasingly it is obvious that one of the characteristics of "good" care is an adult-to-child ratio of 1 : 3 to 1 : 5; ratios much smaller than this seem to be associated with some negative effects.

But you should always keep in mind that the findings on which I base that conclusion are almost entirely from studies of centers, particularly from intensive experimental centers. Too little is known about the run-of-the-mill neighborhood day-care center and about the family day-care home. And too little is known about the long-term effects of even good center care. Perhaps by the time this chapter is revised again the picture will be still clearer.

QUESTIONS FOR DEBATE AND DISCUSSION

1. If you were the person in the federal government who had to decide whether to fund day-care programs on a nationwide basis,

  a. Would you say Yes, No, or Maybe? Why?
  b. What standards do you think you would need to set, if any?
  c. What evidence would you like to have before making any decision?
2. Assume you are a parent with a year-old child. Some alternative care for your child is needed because the adults in the family work. Would you chose center day care? If so, why? If not, why not? What information would you want to have about a center before placing your child in it?

ADDITIONAL REFERENCES USEFUL
IN PREPARATION FOR DEBATE OR DISCUSSION

Emlen, A. C., and Perry, J. B., Jr. Child-care arrangements. In L. W. Hoffman and F. I. Nye (Eds.), *Working mothers*. San Francisco, Calif.: Jossey-Bass, 1974, pp. 101–125.

A discussion of the demand for day care and of the several varieties of care arrangements made by mothers. The best source I know for a review of family day care.

Grotberg, E. (Ed.) *Day care: Resources for decisions*. Office of Economic Opportunity, Office of Planning, Research and Evaluation, 1972.

An excellent overview (although now not completely up to date) of research on day care and various theoretical perspectives on day care, including a paper by Meers critical of some of the assumptions underlying day care. It is available from Day Care and Child Development Council of America, Inc. (1401 K St., N.W., Washington, D.C., 20005) for $4.50. Not available elsewhere as far as I know.

Robinson, N. M., and Robinson, H. B. A cross-cultural view of early education. In I. J. Gordon (Ed.), *Early childhood education*, 71st Yearbook of the National Society for the Study of Education. Chicago: University of Chicago Press, 1972, pp. 291–316.

In this paper the Robinsons outline some of the factors that lead to different kinds of early child-care programs in various countries. The chapter includes a discussion of programs other than day care, but it should give a good overall perspective.

REFERENCES

Bowlby, J. *Maternal care and mental health*. Monograph Series, No. 2. Geneva: World Health Organization, 1951.

Braun, S. J., and Caldwell, B. M. Emotional adjustment of children in day care who enrolled prior to or after the age of three. *Early Child Development and Care*, 1973, **2**, 13–21.

Caldwell, B. M. Impact of interest in early cognitive stimulation. In H. E. Rie (Ed.), *Perspectives in child psychopathology.* New York: Aldine-Atherton, 1971.

Caldwell, B. M., Wright, C. M., Honig, A. S., and Tannenbaum, J. Infant day care and attachment. *American Journal of Orthopsychiatry,* 1970, **40,** 397–412.

Cisin, I. A group day care program for culturally deprived children and parents. George Washington University, Washington, D.C.: Progress Report, Office of Child Development, U.S. Department of Health, Education and Welfare, 1970.

Cornelius, S. W., and Denney, N. W. Dependency in day-care and home-care children. *Developmental Psychology,* 1975, **11,** 575–582.

Doyle, A. B. Infant development in day care. *Developmental Psychology,* 1975, **11,** 655–656.

Emlen, A. C. Family day care research: A summary and a critical review. Paper presented for "Family Day Care West—A Working Conference," Pacific Oaks College, Pasadena, California, February 1972.

Emlen, A. C., Donoghue, B. A., and LaForge, R. Child care by kith: A study of the family day care relationships of working mothers and their neighborhood caregivers. Report submitted to the Office of Child Development, U.S. Department of Health, Education and Welfare, 1971.

Emlen, A. C., and Perry, J. B., Jr. Child-care arrangements. In L. W. Hoffman and F. I. Nye (Eds.), *Working mothers.* San Francisco, Calif.: Jossey-Bass, 1974, pp. 101–125.

Glezen, W. P., Loda, F. A., Clyde, W. A., Jr., Senior, R. J., Schaeffer, C. I., Conley, W. G., and Denny, F. W. Epidemiological patterns of acute lower respiratory diseases of children in a pediatric group practice. *Journal of Pediatrics,* 1971, **78,** 397–406.

Grotberg, E. A review of the present status and future needs in day care research. A working paper. Prepared for the interagency panel on early childhood research and development, Office of Child Development, Department of Health, Education and Welfare, 1971.

Kaffman, M. Inquiry into the behavior of 403 kibbutz children. *American Journal of Psychiatry,* 1961, **117,** 732–738.

Kaffman, M. Comparative psychopathology of kibbutz and urban children. In P. Neubauer (Ed.), *Children in collectives.* Springfield, Ill.: Charles C. Thomas, 1965, pp. 261–269.

Keister, M. W. *"The good life" for infants and toddlers.* Washington, D.C.: National Association for the Education of Young Children, 1970.

Lally, J. R. The family development research program. A program for prenatal infant and early childhood enrichment. Progress report submitted to the Office of Child Development, U.S. Department of Health, Education and Welfare, 1973.

Meers, D. R. International day care: A selective review and psychoanalytic critique. In E. Grotberg (Ed.), *Day care: Resources for decisions.* Office of Economic Opportunity, Office of Planning, Research and evaluation. 1972.

Prescott, E. A comparison of three types of day care and nursery school-home care. Paper presented at the biennial meetings of The Society for Research in Child Development, Philadelphia, 1973.

Rabin, A. I. Infants and children under conditions of intermittent mothering in the kibbutz. *American Journal of Orthopsychiatry,* 1958, **28,** 577.

Saunders, M. M. Some aspects of the effects of day care on infants' emotional and personal development. Unpublished doctoral dissertation, University of North Carolina at Greensboro, 1972. Abstracted in T. M. Williams (Ed.), *Infant care. Abstracts of the literature.* Supplement, Washington, D.C.: Consortium on Early Childbearing and Childrearing, Child Welfare League of America, Inc. 1974.

Saunders, M. M., and Keister, M. E. Family day care: Some observations. Unpublished manuscript, 1972. Abstracted in T. M. Williams (Ed.), *Infant care. Abstracts of the literature.* Supplement. Washington, D.C.: Consortium on Early Childbearing and Childrearing, Child Welfare League of America, Inc. 1974.

Schwarz, J. C., Strickland, R. G., and Krolick, G. Infant day care: Behavioral effects at preschool age. *Developmental Psychology,* 1974, **10,** 502–506.

U.S. Department of Labor, *1975 Handbook on women workers.* Bulletin 297, Women's Bureau, Employment Standards Administration, 1975.

Wolins, M. Group care: Friend or foe? *Social Work,* 1969a, **14,** 35–53.

Wolins, M. Young children in institutions: Some additional evidence. *Developmental Psychology,* 1969b, **2,** 99–109.

Yarrow, L. J. Separation from parents during early childhood. In M. L. Hoffman and L. W. Hoffman (Eds.), *Review of child development research.* Vol. 1. New York: Russell Sage Foundation, 1964, pp. 89–136.

Longitudinal development of very young children in a comprehensive day-care program: the first two years

HALBERT B. ROBINSON
NANCY M. ROBINSON

In September 1966 the Frank Porter Graham Child Development Center of the University of North Carolina at Chapel Hill opened a day care center offering comprehensive services to a small number of infants and very young children. This center was established as a pilot facility for a much larger multidisciplinary research project. The latter was to be devoted in part to a longitudinal intervention study of a sizable cohort of children ranging in age from birth to 13 years given education and comprehensive day care under conditions as optimal as could reasonably be devised (Robinson, 1969). This study presents the assessment of the development of the 11 children admitted in 1966 and the 20 enrolled in 1967 and 1968. The data reflect the results of a com-

From *Child Development*, 1971, **42**. Copyright © 1972 by The Society for Research in Child Development, Inc. Reprinted by permission.

Support for this research and for the facility was furnished by the U.S. Children's Bureau, MCH and CC research grant H-79; by the National Institute of Child Health and Human Development, grant 2P01-HD-03110, by a grant from the Carnegie Corporation of New York, and by the University of North Carolina. Our sincere thanks to Harriet Rheingold and to Carol Eckerman, who carried out most of the infant testing; to Barbara Semonche, who carried out the special language assessment; and to Frances Campbell, who completed some of the final tests. Special debts are acknowledged to the center staff and in particular to Ann Peters, a cofounder of the center, whose sustained determination and compassion profoundly influenced its operation during this period.

plex experimental plan which combined several rather unusual characteristics:

1. Almost all Ss admitted as infants were selected before their birth, with the conditions only that the sample be roughly balanced for sex and race and that no gross anomalies be detected during the neonatal period. They entered day care when the mother returned to work, which ranged from 4 weeks to 6 months after the birth of the child.
2. The sample was broadly representative of the community's socioeconomic spectrum of Caucasian and Negro children of working mothers.
3. Comprehensive daytime care was given, including complete health care; children attended the center whether sick or well.
4. A carefully structured educational program, beginning in early infancy, constituted a strong focus of the center. Pilot curricula were developed in language, sensorimotor skills, perception and reading, scientific and numerical concepts, music, art, and French.
5. The basic organizational pattern consisted of two cottages of up to 16 children of all ages represented in the center for basic activities such as eating, sleeping, and free play. All center children in the same family were housed together. Grouping by developmental level for instruction and play occurred for approximately 3 hours each day, children ages 2½–4½ going from their cottage to an educational unit.
6. Child-focused work with parents occurred through daily conversations with staff, frequent contact with the pediatrician, and home visits by the public health nurse. There were also occasional newsletters, parent meetings, and parties.

SUBJECTS
Center Sample
During this pilot phase of the study, infants and 2-year-olds were admitted in order to provide for some heterogeneity. Most infants were selected through routine interviewing of all employed women receiving prenatal care in the university hospital, the only hospital in Chapel Hill. A few infants, and all older children, were admitted after applications by families not initially contacted prior to the birth of the child. Four infant siblings

born to families already having a child in the center were automatically admitted. Efforts were made to keep each of the three annual waves (1966, 1967, 1968) as varied and balanced as possible in race, sex, and socioeconomic status.

During the fall of 1966 four children were admitted between the ages of 2.0 months and 5.5 months (mean age, 3.8 months) and seven others between 26 and 36 months (mean age, 28.7 months). In the fall of 1967, seven infants between 1.5 and 5.5 months old were admitted (mean age, 2.7 months), and five children who were 23–28 months of age (mean age, 25.6 months). In 1968, all eight new Ss were infants, 1.1–4.0 months (mean age, 2.1 months). Of the 31 children, 12 (7 Caucasian and 5 Negro) were admitted at age 2; 19 (8 Caucasian and 11 Negro) were admitted as young infants. One additional child, however, was a congenital athyreotic admitted before his condition was diagnosed at age 3 months. Borderline retarded, he is omitted from this report. One boy admitted at age 2 was withdrawn when his family moved 18 months later. He is included in the comparison with community controls, but not in the longitudinal analysis. By the end of the 2½-year period covered by this report, the 31 Ss ranged in age from a few weeks to 4½ years.

Twenty-four families were represented. Total incomes of the 12 Caucasian families (i.e., all adults with legal responsibility for child) ranged from $4,500 to above $40,000, the median family income for the 15 children being $10,976. Incomes of the 12 Negro families ranged from zero (unmarried student mothers) to $10,000, the median for the 16 children being $3,519. Median education for the Caucasian mothers was 14.5 years and for the Caucasian fathers, 16.5 years. Median education of the Negro mothers was 12.0 years, and of the Negro fathers, 11.0 years. One Caucasian child and four Negro children had no father in the home.

The dramatic differences between the Caucasian and Negro families in the sample are, in large part, a reflection of the disparities in this community. Its Caucasian wage earners are largely university staff and merchants, while its Negro population has traditionally performed supportive services. Community acceptance was also an issue, however. The early appeal of the center was to the poorer Negro parents, attracted by the low cost, and to the more affluent Caucasian parents, attracted by the potential benefits for their children. Eventually, however, the center's reputation began to attract blue-collar Caucasian parents and middle-class Negro parents. Included in the 1968 sample are, for example, the infant sons of a white policeman and of a Negro social worker.

Control Groups

Two separate control groups were studied. One was followed from early infancy onward and is compared with center infants; the other was tested only once and was compared with center children who were at that time 2½–4½ years old.

From 1967, when pediatric services became available as part of the center's program, control groups of infants were selected by the same prenatal interviewing methods as center infants, an attempt being made to equate the annual waves as closely as possible on sex, race, number of siblings, education and occupation of parents, and number of rooms in the house. These groups were evaluated medically and psychologically on the same schedule as the center population, and additional health records were kept in conjunction with medical studies being carried out in the center. Complete medical supervision was given to the control children, in part to enlist the families' cooperation, but more important, to attempt to equalize medical care, the better to evaluate the effects of the enriched daily experience of the center children. Eleven control group infants were followed during the period of this report.

By 1968, the 16 oldest center Ss were 2½–4½. Four of these children had entered in 1966 as infants; 12 had entered in 1966 or 1967 at age 2. None had attended less than 1 year. As a rough comparison, a completely different group of noncenter children was matched with them individually on the basis of race, sex, parents' education and occupation, and the age at which the center child had last been given the Stanford-Binet and PPVT (see below). The controls were chosen from applicants to the center for whom there had not been space ($N = 5$), from friends of the family of the child for whom matching was sought ($N = 9$), and from another local day care center ($N = 2$). Mean CA of each group was 41 months, the mean within-pair age difference being 1.8 months. Exceedingly close matching on occupation and education of both parents was achieved, except that 6 control mothers were not currently employed.

BEHAVIORAL MEASURES

The data reported here represent only the results of standardized testing over the period being considered. Tests were scheduled every 3 months to age 18 months, the Bayley mental scale, the Bayley motor scale, and the Bayley behavior profile (Bayley, 1961) being completed on each occasion. Table 2 lists most of the subsequent tests administered to age 4½. In addition, several language-assessment measures were administered in June 1968 to the 14 oldest children (ages 2–7 to 4–3) and three additional tests (WPSSI, Frostig, Caldwell preschool inventory) were given at age 4.

Testing through age 18 months was conducted by the staff of the University of North Carolina Laboratory of Infant Behavior to which the infants were transported by a caretaker from the center or by the mothers of the control infants. Testing of center children 2 and over was conducted at the center by a member of its staff. The control children for the special one-time comparison with the older Ss were seen in their own homes or regular day care settings by the same examiner who tested the older center children. The Stanford-Binet and Peabody Picture Vocabulary Test (PPVT) were administered. Effort was made to establish rapport through an initial period of play and the presence, when apparently desirable, of a trusted adult. For almost all of the Negro children, whose homes had no telephones, the testing visit constituted the second to the fourth contact with the examiner, who had played with the child during each previous visit. Nevertheless, these comparison data suffer the obvious drawbacks of the greater familiarity of the examiner with the center Ss and the unknown practice effects of their previous testing.

TEST RESULTS
Subjects Admitted as Infants

Test results for all children admitted as infants are shown in Table 1, together with those for the control infants. A 2×5 analysis of variance (Dixon, 1965) nested on treatments (center-control) with repeated measures on comparisons over time and using a general linear hypothesis to handle missing data values was applied to the infant test scores. Analysis of the Bayley mental scale scores yielded a between-groups F ratio of 7.99 (df 1/116, $p = .01$) for the treatments, an F ratio of 2.72 (df 4/116, $p = .05$) for the comparisons over time, and a nonsignificant interaction ($F = 1.45$, df 4/116). For the Bayley motor scale, the only significant F ratio (4.75, df 1/109, $p = .05$) occurred in the comparison of center and control groups. A t test of the mental scale scores at 18 months was significant at the .01 level, but a t test of motor scale scores at that age failed to reach significance at the .05 level. A t test of the small samples tested on the Stanford-Binet at 24 months also failed to reach significance.

In other words, scores for center and control Ss were significantly different on both tests, but a significant trend over time was found only on the mental scale, consisting of an initial rise for both groups, and a drop for the control group at the 18-month level. The suddenness of that drop probably accounts for the lack of significance in the interaction. The scores on the Bayley motor

TABLE 1 TEST RESULTS FOR Ss
ADMITTED AS INFANTS AND CONTROLS

	Bayley mental scale				
Group	6 Mo	9 Mo	12 Mo	15 Mo	18 Mo
Center					
N	17	18	19	10	11
$\overline{X}$	108.00	115.94	112.16	116.60	115.18
SD	8.95	14.71	9.91	9.19	8.95
Control					
N	11	11	11	10	8
$\overline{X}$	105.90	113.27	110.91	110.70	99.75
SD	10.15	12.23	9.97	8.79	11.61
	Bayley motor scale				
Group	6 Mo	9 Mo	12 Mo	15 Mo	18 Mo
Center					
N	17	18	18	8	7
$\overline{X}$	110.94	109.22	99.61	107.62	107.29
SD	14.06	11.90	14.45	9.29	16.71
Control					
N	11	11	11	10	8
$\overline{X}$	103.82	105.00	101.09	103.60	94.00
SD	13.11	11.45	14.96	10.95	7.17
	Stanford-Binet				
Group	24 Mo	30 Mo			
Center					
N	4	4			
$\overline{X}$	116.25	117.25			
SD	8.67	4.76			
Control					
N	4	—			
$\overline{X}$	99.75	—			
SD	11.23	—			

scale favored the center group but were less consistently different over time.

Subjects Admitted at Age 2

The test results for children admitted to the center at age 2 are described in Table 2. Additional tests administered to the 1966 group at age 4–0 yielded the following mean scores and standard deviations: Wechsler primary and Preschool Inventory full scale IQ 124.6 (SD 12.4), verbal IQ 126.0 (8.8), performance

TABLE 2   TEST SCORES OF CHILDREN ADMITTED AT AGE 2

Test	Admitted 1966 (N = 6)					Admitted 1967 (N = 5)	
	2–6	3–0	3–6	4–0	4–6	2–6	3–0
Stanford-Binet							
$\bar{X}$	112.3	124.5	132.7	—	127.2	118.4	123.8
SD	23.5	20.2	17.5	—	13.4	23.1	13.9
PPVT							
$\bar{X}$	93.8	100.8	114.0	111.5	108.5	111.4	107.2
SD	15.5	19.7	7.2	6.9	6.9	17.9	10.8
ITPA							
$\bar{X}$	104.3	124.5	122.2	—	—	—	115.0
SD	14.0	17.0	12.8	—	—	—	15.0
Leiter							
$\bar{X}$	—	128.0	128.3	—	126.8	106.6	130.0
SD	—	19.6	16.4	—	8.7	26.1	14.9
Draw-a-Man							
$\bar{X}$	—	—	96.8	—	98.5	—	—
SD	—	—	15.3	—	9.9	—	—

IQ 117.7 (14.5); Frostig test of visual perception IQ 100.0 (20.9) and Caldwell preschool inventory, median percentile 90 (middle-class norms).

Scores on most primarily verbal measures were high, as shown by the Stanford-Binet (Terman and Merrill, 1960), the verbal scale of the WPPSI (Wechsler, 1967), the Caldwell pre-school inventory (Caldwell, 1967), and, as an exception, the non-verbal Arthur Adaptation of the Leiter scale (Arthur, 1952). Peabody Picture Vocabulary Test (Dunn, 1959) scores were consistently lower than the other measures.

On the nonverbal measures, most of the children's scores fell below their verbal scores. On the Frostig test of visual per-ception (Frostig, Lefever, and Whittlesey, 1964), the draw-a-man test (Harris, 1963), and portions of the Illinois Test of Psycholin-guistic Abilities (McCarthy and Kirk, 1961), this lower perfor-mance was evident. Sensorimotor items (motor encoding, visual-motor sequential) were consistently the lowest of the mean ITPA scores, with the exception of the visual-motor association test, which is "motor" only to the extent that a pointing response is required. Similarly, on the WPPSI, the mean subscale scores for the 7 children tested at age 4 ranged from a high of 16.43 on arithemetic to a low of 12.29 on geometric designs, the single exception being a mean score of 9.71 on the highly motoric

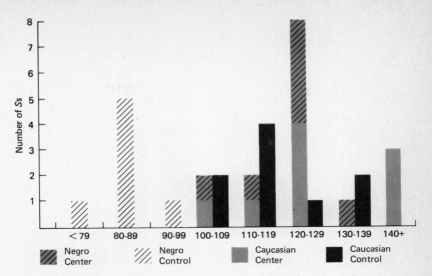

Figure 1. Stanford-Binet IQs of center and control children ages 2½–4½.

mazes. The WPPSI performance IQ was approximately ½ SD below the mean verbal IQ.

The language assessment in June 1968 likewise revealed advanced verbal behavior. Of the 12 children given the Templin-Darley scale (Templin and Darley, 1960), the score of each S was at or above CA level, the mean speech age exceeding the mean CA (42 months) by approximately 22 months. On the action-agent test (Gesell, 1940), 10 of the 12 scored at age level or better, three S s exceeding the CA by at least 6 months. On the Michigan Picture Language Inventory (Lerea, 1958; Walski, 1962) given to the seven oldest children, mean standard score of expression was +.96, while the mean comprehension standard scores was +.65.

Test results for the 16 older center children and 16 matched controls are shown in Figures 1 and 2. The most striking findings on both tests are the differences, on the order of two standard deviations, between the center Negro children and their controls. Mean Stanford-Binet IQs were 119.7 for these seven center children and 86.1 for their controls; both groups showed a marked clustering of scores (SDs 8.16 and 6.59, respectively). On the PPVT, center Negro children attained a mean IQ of 107.4 (SD 10.03) while that of the control Negro children was only 77.6 (SD 13.75). There was no overlap of scores between these groups on either test.

Differences between the nine Caucasian center children and their controls appeared on the Stanford-Binet but not on the

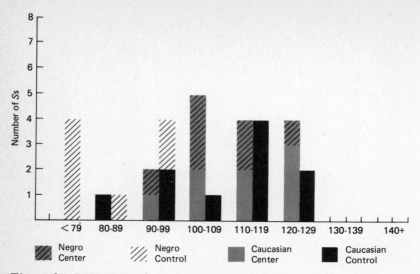

Figure 2. PPVT IQs of center and control children ages 2½–4½.

PPVT. Mean IQs on the Stanford-Binet were 129.7 (SD 17.00) and 116.9 (SD 11.71), respectively. On the PPVT, mean IQ of the center Caucasian group was actually lower (108.1, SD 12.42) than that of the controls (110.2, SD 12.81).

According to an analysis of variance (Dixon, 1965) of Stanford-Binet scores, F ratios were highly significant for the comparisons of racial groups ($F = 22.27$, df 1/28, $p < .001$) and center control groups ($F = 28.89$, df 1/28, $p < .001$), the significant interaction ($F = 5.81$, df 1/28, $p = .05$) highlighting the much greater magnitude of the difference between the Negro groups. In the analysis of scores on the PPVT, there were also significant effects of race ($F = 14.29$, df 1/28, $p = .001$) and of the center/control variable ($F = 9.90$, df 1/28, $p = .01$). The interaction term ($F = 13.14$, df 1/28, $p < .01$) demonstrated that the significant differences were limited to the Negro groups. Center Ss who were 3–6 and older attained somewhat higher scores on both tests than did center Ss 3–0 and younger (mean Stanford-Binet IQs 129.1 and 121.5, respectively; mean PPVT IQs 113.5 and 102.1), but a t test of these Stanford-Binet differences was not significant, and the PPVT difference ($t = 2.346$, df 14) was significant at only the .05 level. The control group showed no such age trends. Practice effects cannot be ruled out. Sex differences were not significant.

DISCUSSION
Within the serious limitations which characterize the data, a number of tentative suggestions emerge:

1. Enriched group care of the young infant, when carefully designed and fully staffed, may enhance cognitive development, especially during the time when verbal abilities are beginning to emerge. The differences between experimental and control groups which were apparent at the 18-month level suggest that the period before this may be a crucial one. Earlier concern about the possibility of detrimental cognitive effects of "institutionalization" (i.e., any form of group care) is apparently unjustified. On the contrary, a decline in scores was found for the control group, while the center's group maintained its status on cognitive measures at about 1 SD above the mean of the national normative sample.

2. High quality group care combined with educational efforts during ages 2–4 years may have its major impact upon culturally disadvantaged children. Although the center Caucasian (more advantaged) children in the study obtained higher scores on the Stanford-Binet than the control Caucasian children, the really dramatic differences occurred between the center Negro (less advantaged) children and their controls. Indeed, the center Negro children attained a mean Stanford-Binet of approximately 120, as opposed to the control Negro mean IQ of approximately 86. The crucial variables of the day care, educational, and health programs cannot be identified in this pilot study, but that the "package" made a difference in the lives of the children is unmistakable.

3. The major impact of the program was in verbal rather than motoric areas. The nonverbal scores of the center children were "normal" but not particularly advanced.

The lack of well-standardized instruments to assess social-emotional functioning of young children is a major handicap to a study of this nature. A series of attempts to devise a problem-behavior checklist or interview with the mothers was unsuccessful because of the inability of some poorly educated mothers, even with considerable prompting, to think in differentiated terms about their children's behavior. Overall evaluation by a team of psychoanalytically oriented clinicians yielded interesting individual assessments which were based on limited observations of center children and did not yield useful research data. Similarly, detailed behavioral ratings by the staff, useful in many ways for longitudinal research, are not reported here because they yielded only within-group comparisons. There was unanimous agreement among all the staff, who were of diverse cultural and educational backgrounds, that as a group the children were extremely amicable, stable, and outgoing, and that none exhibited behavior deviant from the normal range of childhood behavior patterns.

A study such as the present one raises many more questions than it can answer. What are the long-range residuals of a program such as that provided by the center? In the long run, will the development of children who enter as infants differ significantly from that of children admitted at age 2, later, or not at all? What elements within the program are most effective? Can these elements be packaged and delivered more economically than through comprehensive full-day programs? What positive impact may the availability of reliable day care have on the stability of families, and on the mother's employment and personal adjustment? What are the immediate and delayed effects on the children's relationships with their parents? Major longitudinal research efforts will be required to answer these compelling questions.

REFERENCES

Arthur, G. A. *The Arthur adaptation of the Leiter international performance scale.* Washington, D.C.: Psychological Service Center Press, 1952.

Bayley, N. Manual of directions for infant scales of development (temporary standardization). (Mimeographed.) Bethesda, Md.: National Institute of Neurological Diseases and Blindness, Colloborative Research Project, 1961.

Caldwell, B. M. *The preschool inventory.* Princeton, N.J.: Educational Testing Service, 1967.

Dixon, W. J. (Ed.) General linear hypothesis (BMDO5V). Biomedical Computer Program. Los Angeles, UCLA Health Sciences Computing Facility, 1965.

Dunn, L. M. *Peabody Picture Vocabulary Test manual.* Minneapolis: American Guidance Service, 1959.

Frostig, M., Lefever, D. W., and Whittlesey, J. R. B. A development test of visual perception for evaluating normal and neurologically handicapped children. *Perceptual and Motor Skills,* 1964, **12**, 383–394.

Gesell, A. *The first five years of life.* New York: Harper & Row, 1940.

Harris, D. B. *Measuring the psychological maturity of children: a revision and extension of the Goodenough draw-a-man test.* New York: Harcourt, Brace & World, 1963.

Lerea, L. Assessing language development. *Journal of Speech and Hearing Research,* 1958, **1**, 75–85.

McCarthy, J. J., and Kirk, S. A. *Illinois test of psycholinguistic abilities.* (Exp. ed.) Urbana: University of Illinois, Institute of Research on Exceptional Children, 1961.

Robinson, H. B. From infancy through school. *Children,* 1969, **16**, 61–62.

Templin, M. C., and Darley, F. L. *The Templin-Darley tests of articulation.* Iowa City: University of Iowa Bureau of Education Research and Service, 1960.

Terman, L. M., and Merrill, M. A. *Stanford-Binet intelligence scale.* Boston: Houghton Mifflin, 1960.

Walski, W. Language development of normal children, four, five, and six years of age as measured by the Michigan Picture Language Inventory. Unpublished doctoral dissertation, University of Michigan, 1962.

Wechsler, D. A. *A manual for the Wechsler preschool and primary scale of intelligence.* New York: Psychological Corp., 1967.

Anxious attachment and defensive reactions associated with day care

MARY CURTIS BLEHAR

Full-day group care for infants and toddlers differs from home care in two major ways. A child in group care is reared by multiple caregivers rather than by one or a few figures, and he is separated daily from his primary mother figure. Bowlby (1969, 1973) hypothesized that an infant is biased genetically to maintain a degree of proximity to his mother figure and predisposed toward becoming attached to her. Does full-time group day care constitute a sufficient departure from the environment to which a child's behavioral systems are preadapted to generate anomalies in the development of attachment? More specifically, can an infant develop an attachment to his mother figure if he spends nine or ten hours a day with substitute caregivers in a group setting? Can a young child who has already become attached to his mother figure sustain a normal relationship with her despite the repeated, long daily separations implicit in day care? There is a dearth of research addressed to these questions.

Caldwell, Wright, Honig, and Tannenbaum (1970) studied

From *Child Development*, 1974, **45**. Copyright © 1974 by The Society for Research in Child Development, Inc. Reprinted by permission.

This study was undertaken as a doctoral dissertation at the Johns Hopkins University. An early version of this paper was presented at the biennial meeting of The Society for Research in Child Development, Philadelphia, March 1973, in a symposium entitled "Anxious Attachment and Defensive Reactions." I wish to thank Mary D. Ainsworth and Julian Stanley for their critical comments and Mary B. Main for her assistance in the data analysis.

the effects of day care on infants who entered care in the first year of life or early in the second year. They focused on a number of variables purporting to reflect the strength of child-mother attachment—affiliation, nurturance, absence of hostility, permissiveness, dependency, happiness, and emotionality. Finding no significant differences between their day-care and home-reared groups, they concluded that full-time day care did not prevent children from developing attachments of normal strength to their mothers.

The present study concerns older children who were at home with their mothers either two or three years before beginning day care. It addresses itself not to the question of day care's effects on attachment formation processes, but to the effects of repeated daily separations on qualitative aspects of established attachment relationships.

Research into children's responses to major separations, lasting weeks or months, has demonstrated adverse effects, the severity of which depends on a number of factors, such as the child's age, the length of the separation, and the availability of responsive substitute caregivers. In one notable study, Robertson and Bowlby (1952) observed three distinct phases in children's reactions to major institutional separation. Initially, there occurred a protest phase followed by a despair phase. If the separation was very long and conditions were depriving, children would manifest a detachment phase, marked by loss of interest in the mother and superficiality in interpersonal relationships. Detachment was interpreted as a defensive behavioral pattern stemming from repression of anxiety and ambivalence occasioned by separation.

Reunion behaviors of children after major separation typically consist of angry rejection of or apparent indifference to the mother, alternating with heightened attachment behaviors (Heinicke & Westheimer, 1965). However, detached children tend to persist in this mode, sometimes indefinitely, before reestablishing a relationship, usually of a permanently anxious quality (Robertson & Bowlby, 1952). Ainsworth (personal communication), having examined Robertson and Bowlby's data, reported that younger children in their sample (between ages 1 and 2½) were more likely to develop detachment than older children (between ages 3 and 4), who were more capable of maintaining an attachment to the mother, albeit of an anxious quality.

Although some disturbance is a predictable outcome of separation once a child has become attached, distress can be attenuated if he has the opportunity to form a close relationship with a substitute figure (e.g., Robertson & Robertson, 1971) or if he remains in a familiar environment while separated from his mother (Yarrow, 1961).

In order to assess the possibility that day care could affect attachment, the strange situation, a technique sensitive to qualitative differences in the mother-child relationship, was chosen. This situation first elicits exploratory behavior, and then, through a series of separations and reunions, heightened attachment behavior. Ainsworth, Bell, and Stayton (1971) classified 1-year-olds into three groups chiefly on the basis of reunion behaviors. The first group was active in seeking and maintaining proximity to and contact with the mother upon reunion. A second group sought little proximity or contact but actively avoided proximity and interaction. A third group mixed seeking proximity and contact with resistance of contact and interaction. Stable relationships were found, both between the infant's strange-situation behavior and his home behavior and between his behavior and maternal behavior. Infants in the first group had histories of harmonious interaction with the mother, while infants in the other groups had histories of disturbed interaction. Ainsworth and Bell (1970) compared avoidant and resistant behaviors observed in the strange situation with detachment and ambivalence others have noted in young children after major separation.

Although Ainsworth has used her situation to study individual differences in attachment, others (Maccoby & Feldman, 1972; Marvin, 1972) have also used it to observe normative patterns of attachment behavior and changes in patterns over the first four years of life. They found a gradual decline in seeking contact with the mother upon reunion and then in seeking proximity to her. Maintaining of contact upon reunion tended to disappear by age 2, and seeking of proximity tended to disappear by age 4. Separation protest declined more sharply around age 3.

In the present study, the strange situation was used to compare responses to separation from and reunion with the mother in groups of day-care and home-reared children. Depending on one's theoretical point of view, there are three predictions that can be made: (1) day-care children will behave no differently from the controls, on the assumption that day care does not affect attachment; (2) day-care children will be less distressed by separation and will exhibit less strongly heightened attachment behaviors upon reunion because of their more frequent experiences with separation; (3) day-care children will exhibit disturbances in attachment related to daily separation, and the type of disturbance will be related to the child's developmental level at the time of entering day care.

METHOD
Subjects
The subjects were 40 middle-class children, all but one white. Twenty were enrolled in full-time group day care and 20 were reared by their mothers at home. Ten of the day-care group had entered centers at a mean age of 25.66 months (SD = 1.18 months) and 10 at a mean age of 34.83 months (SD = 2.45 months). Both groups had been enrolled for approximately the same length of time when observed—4.55 months for the younger group (SD = 2.56 months) and 4.78 months for the older group (SD = 1.69 months). When observed they had mean ages of 30.23 months (SD = 2.20 months) and 39.62 months (SD = 1.98 months), respectively. The mean ages of the home-reared groups at the time of observation were 30.23 months (SD = 1.98 months) and 39.46 months (SD = 1.95 months). Equal numbers of males and females were observed at each age level.

One assumption underlying the comparison was that the groups were equivalent on variables affecting the quality of attachment other than the daily separations implicit in day care. This assumption would be unnecessary in an experimental study which randomly assigned children to day care or home rearing, but such a study would be extremely difficult to carry out. However, all children were from middle-class homes, both in terms of parental education and income. Both parents were present in the home. Measures of the home environment which support the assumption of equivalence between the groups will be reported below. Eighty percent of day-care children and 60 percent of home-reared children were firstborn. Four day-care children had been cared for by babysitters approximately four months before starting group day care. Three home-reared 40-month-olds attended nursery school two or three mornings a week.

Cooperation in collecting a day-care sample was obtained from four private centers that followed traditional nursery school regimes with little emphasis on structured academic programs. The degree of structuring in play and the amount of organized group activities were greater for the older children than for the younger. Children were segregated into groups of 2- and 3-year-olds, 4-year-olds, and 5-year-olds. Two caregivers were assigned to each group, and they did not shift over the course of the week. On the average, caregivers tended to remain in their positions for 3 years. At age 4 and again at age 5, children moved up into a new group with new caregivers. In the 2- and 3-year-old group, the ratio of caregivers to children was 1 : 8 or 1 : 6, depending on the center. A registered nurse was on hand daily at two of the centers. Names of all children attending the centers were provided beforehand by directors, and from this list parents were contacted individually. All but one agreed to cooperate. Pediatricians in private practice supplied names of home-reared children, and all but two parents contacted agreed to participate.

Procedure

The first part of the procedures entailed a 1½-hour home visit to each mother-child pair by the investigator. Its purposes were to establish rapport with the mother, to instruct her about the study, and to assess the general quality of stimulation provided the child by his home environment. Each visit was rated on the Inventory of Home Stimulation, devised by Caldwell (Caldwell et al., 1970). The majority of the items were straightforward and depended on firsthand observation of the home and of mother-child interaction rather than on maternal report alone. For example, it was noted if the mother spoke spontaneously to the child at least twice, if she caressed or kissed him, if books were present and visible, or if he had a pet. A measure of the mother's empathy or social sensitivity was obtained by use of a Q-sort technique devised by Hogan (1969). The mother was rated by the observer immediately after each visit.

Approximately two weeks later, each mother-child pair participated in a standardized strange situation at Johns Hopkins University. The experimental room had a 9 × 9 foot area of clear floor space. One wall contained one-way-vision mirrors. Near the opposite wall stood a child's chair with toys heaped on and around it. Near the window on one side of the room was a chair for the mother and opposite it a chair for the stranger. The situation consisted of eight episodes, each except the first 3 mintues long (see Table 1).

A continuous description of the child's behavior was dictated into recorders, which also picked up the sound of a buzzer every 15 seconds. The transcribed narrative reports were marked off into time intervals. In 65 percent of the cases there were two independent observers, and in the other cases the investigator served as sole observer. The second observer, in all but four instances, was an individual who was unaware of the hypotheses of the study and of the child's group membership. Two women played the role of stranger in all but three cases, when a substitute had to be found. The first woman was stranger for 12 home-reared and nine day-care children, and the second woman was stranger for eight home-reared and eight day-care children. Individual narrative accounts were consolidated for analysis and

TABLE 1 STRANGE-SITUATION EPISODES

Episode No.	Duration	Participants	Description of Episode
1	30 sec, approximately	O, M, C	O ushers M and C into the room. C is set down on the floor
2	3 min	M, C	C is free to explore. M reads a magazine
3	3 min	S, M, C	S enters, sits quietly for a moment, interacts with M, then with C
4	3 min[a]	S, C	M leaves. S remains with C; responds to his advances or comforts him if necessary
5	3 min	M, C	S leaves as M enters M comforts C if he is distressed, then reinterests him in toys
6	3 min[a]	C	M leaves C alone in room
7	3 min[a]	S, C	S enters; attempts to comfort C if distressed; returns to her chair
8	3 min	M, C	M enters as S leaves M behaves as in episode 5

NOTE.—O = observer; M = mother; C = child; S = stranger.
[a] The duration of episode was curtailed if the child became very distressed.

three types of measures were extracted: frequency measures, percentage measures, and scores of social interaction with the mother and the stranger.

Frequency measures and percentages. Four measures were obtained by making counts of the frequency of the following behaviors: exploratory manipulation, crying, oral behavior, and distance interaction with the mother. Exploratory manipulation was defined as shaking, banging, turning over, or other active involvement with a toy. Crying was defined as distressed vocalization, ranging from a fuss to a full-blown cry. Oral behavior was defined as chewing or sucking of fingers or toys. For these behaviors, a frequency count of the 15-second intervals in which they occurred was obtained. Distance interaction was a composite of the absolute frequency of smiling and showing a toy to the mother and the 15-second interval frequency of vocalizations to the mother. Relative frequency of vocalization was used because it was extremely difficult to determine in a time interval when a particular vocalization stopped and another started in those cases where the child talked almost incessantly. The distance interaction measure (taken from Maccoby & Feldman, 1972) was used only in episode 2 when the mother was noninterventive in order to obtain an index of the child's spontaneous interest in her. In episode 3, the presence of the stranger reduced the behavior to a very low level. The following coefficients of interobserver reliability were obtained for the frequency measures: exploratory manipulation, .98; crying, .98; oral behavior, .90; distance interaction, .85.

Percentages of children who approached and who touched the mother in reunion episodes, who exhibited oral behavior, who cried, and who resisted contact and interaction were also used in conjunction with the frequency measures and the social interaction scores.

Social interaction scores.   Another part of the analysis involved detailed codings of socially interactive behavior with the mother and with the stranger on the basis of the narrative reports. Each child was scored on seeking proximity and contact, avoiding proximity and interaction, and resisting contact and interaction. Intensity of search behavior for the mother during separation episodes was also scored. The scoring system was adopted with only minor modifications from Ainsworth et al. (1971). The following is a brief description of the contents of the behavioral categories.

1. Proximity- and contact-seeking behaviors include active approach, clambering up, active gestures such as reaching, partial approaches, and vocal signals.
2. Proximity- and interaction-avoiding behaviors pertain to episodes which normally elicit approach, or greeting. Behaviors include backing away, ignoring, gaze aversion, and looking away. Avoiding the mother is scored only in reunion episodes.
3. Contact- and interaction-resisting behaviors include angry attempts to push away, hit, or kick the adult, squirming to get away from the adult, pushing away toys, or displays of temper when the adult attempts to intervene in the child's ongoing activities.
4. Search behavior includes following mother to the door, trying to open it, going to the mother's chair, looking at her chair, and looking at the door. The behaviors imply that the child is seeking to regain proximity to the absent mother.

TABLE 2 GROUP MEANS FOR INVENTORY OF HOME STIMULATION

	Day Care	Home Care
1. Total score	35.30	35.80
2. Emotional-verbal responsiveness of mother	9.40	8.95
3. Avoidance of restriction and punishment	4.79	5.20
4. Organization of physical and temporal environments	5.85	5.85
5. Provision of appropriate play materials	8.25	8.30
6. Maternal involvement with child	3.40	3.95
7. Opportunities for variety in daily stimulation	3.70	3.85

The behaviors were scored independently by two judges, one of whom was unaware of the child's rearing-group classification, and the following coefficients of interscorer agreement were obtained: seeking proximity to the mother, .97; to the stranger, .98; resistance of mother, .93; of stranger, .92; avoiding of mother, .94; of stranger, .88; search behavior, .98.

Methods of analysis. Analyses of variance were conducted for all measures obtained from the home visit and all measures obtained from the strange situation, except orality. In this case, a nonparametric test was used because of the skewness of the distribution. Separate analyses were performed for behavior to mother and to stranger. There were three independent variables—age, sex, and rearing group—forming a $2 \times 2 \times 2$ factorial design, and one within-subjects repeated measure of episode.

Scores on each behavior to the mother and to the stranger and on frequency measures were obtained for each episode, and a total score for a behavior was obtained by summing scores for the relevant episodes. The interaction of episode with the independent variables was also examined.

RESULTS
Testing the Equivalence of Groups

Table 2 gives the mean scores for the day-care and home-reared groups on the Inventory of Home Stimulation and its subscales. None of the differences was significant. The empathy measure likewise did not discriminate significantly between

TABLE 3   SUMMARY OF *ANOVA* FINDINGS

Source of Variation	Exploratory manipulation	Crying	Distance interaction to M	Proximity to M
Sex	—	—	—	—
Rearing group (Rear. grp.)	—	.05	.025	—
Age	—	—	—	—
Sex × rear. grp.	—	—	—	—
Sex × age	—	—	—	—
Rear. grp. × age	.025	.10	—	.10
Sex × rear. grp. × age	—	—	—	—
Episode (Ep.)	.0005	.001	NA	—
Sex × ep.	—	—	—	—
Rear. grp. × ep.	—	—	—	—
Age × ep.	—	—	—	—
Sex × rear. grp. × ep.	—	—	—	—
Sex × age × ep.	—	—	—	—
Rear. grp. × age × ep.	—	—	—	.025
Sex × rear. grp. × age × ep.	—	—	—	—

NOTE.—M = mother; S = stranger; NA = not applicable.

mothers of the day-care and home-reared children. Although detailed assessments of each mother's sensitivity to her child's signals and communications were not made, the groups' equivalence on the measures obtained suggests that the children observed were receiving normal mothering and stimulation from their home environment adequate for healthy development.

Behavior in the Strange Situation

Table 3 presents a summary of the ANOVA findings. Sex and age differences were relatively few and will not be discussed further. Episode effects are highly significant and in agreement with those reported elsewhere by Ainsworth and Bell (1970). Differences in attachment behavior to the mother between first and later-born children were also examined by ANOVAs and were not significant. However, the data are consistent in showing rearing group differences and interactions of age with rearing group.

Exploratory behavior. Table 3 indicates a significant age × rearing group interaction in the total amount of exploratory manipulation occurring in strange situation, $F(1,32) = 5.83$, $p < .025$. Day-care 40-month-olds were lowest in exploration

Re-sisting M	Avoid-ing M	Prox-imity to S	Re-sisting S	Avoid-ing S	Search
—	.025	.025	—	—	—
.05	.0005	.05	—	.001	—
—	—	.025	—	—	—
—	—	—	—	—	—
—	—	—	—	—	—
—	—	.05	—	—	.05
—	.005	—	—	—	—
—	.10	.10	.025	.0005	.0005
—	—	—	—	—	—
.10	—	—	—	.005	—
—	—	—	—	—	—
—	—	—	—	—	—
—	—	—	.05	.10	—
—	—	—	—	—	—

($\overline{X} = 7.48$) and home-reared 40-month-olds were highest ($\overline{X} = 9.68$). Day-care 30-month-olds were intermediate between their home-reared age counterparts ($\overline{X} = 8.9$ vs. $\overline{X} = 8.2$) and the older home-reared children. All groups decreased in exploration during separation episodes, but these changes were most marked in the older day-care group and least marked in the older home-reared group.

Separation behaviors. A significant main effect, $F(1,32) = 4.60$, $p < .05$, indicates that total crying was higher in day-care children than in home-reared children. However, an age × rearing group interaction, $F(1,32) = 3.78$, $p < .07$, suggests that the main effect may be accounted for chiefly by differences in the 40-month-old groups (40-month-old day-care $\overline{X} = 3.3$ vs. 40-month-old home-reared $\overline{X} = 0.22$). In the 30-month-old groups, day-care children were only slightly higher in amount of crying than home-reared children ($\overline{X} = 1.72$ vs. $\overline{X} = 1.57$).

Oral behavior in episode 7 was also more conspicuous in day-care children than in home-reared children (randomization test for two independent samples: $p < .0005$). Orality occurred most frequently in episode 7, apparently a result of anxiety over

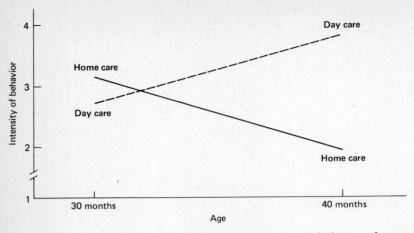

Figure 1. Age × rearing group interaction in search behavior during separation episodes.

the mother's absence compounded by the appearance of the stranger when the mother was expected to return. Forty-five percent of day-care children but only 15 percent of home-reared children engaged in oral behavior in this episode, $\chi^2(1) = 4.29$, $p < .05$.

Search behavior in episodes 4, 6, and 7 was another indicator of separation anxiety since it represented attempts to regain proximity to the absent mother by going to the door or at least looking at her chair. An age × rearing group interaction, $F(1,32) = 5.14$, $p < .05$, depicted in Figure 1, indicates that day-care 40-month-olds searched most for the mother ($\overline{X} = 3.72$) and home-reared 40-month-olds searched least ($\overline{X} = 2.05$). The two 30-month-old groups were much closer together in total amount of search, although the home-reared children showed slightly stronger behavior ($\overline{X} = 3.15$ vs. $\overline{X} = 2.75$). The older day-care children were conspicuous for engaging in active search (i.e., going to the door and attempting to open it) even in episode 4 when children in the other groups tended to maintain exploratory manipulation, and merely looked at the door, if they displayed any search at all.

Behavior to the Mother
Distance interaction. Home-reared children of both ages interacted more with their mothers across a distance in episode 2 than did day-care children ($\overline{X} = 6.08$ vs. $\overline{X} = 4.06$) as is indicated by a main effect, $F(1,32) = 6.66$, $p < .025$. This finding could be interpreted as indicating that day-care children are more inde-

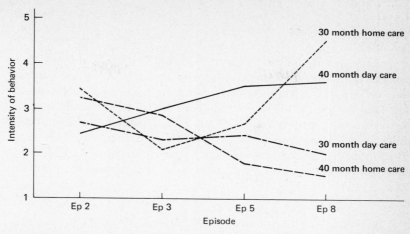

Figure 2. Age × rearing group × episode interaction in proximity seeking to the mother.

pendent of their mothers, at least in their free-play activities, than home-reared children. However, a negative correlation ($r = -.42, p < .01$) between distance interaction in episode 2 and resistant and avoidant behaviors directed toward the mother in later reunion episodes suggests that little interaction of this type before separation is a precursor of negative tendencies, which become more apparent in the reunion episodes and which indicate a disturbance in the mother-child relationship.

   Proximity-seeking behaviors. Figure 2 shows that group differences in seeking the mother's proximity tended to be small in the preseparation episodes 2 and 3, but increased in the reunion episodes, age × rearing group × episode interaction, $F(3,96) = 3.85$, $p < .025$. In episode 5, day-care 40-month-olds showed heightened attachment behavior, whereas their home-reared age counterparts showed little. In episode 8, the older day-care group continued to increase somewhat in proximity seeking, and the older home-reared group declined slightly. Home-reared 30-month-olds showed clear heightening of attachment behaviors in this episode, whereas their day-care counterparts tended to decrease somewhat in proximity seeking. The contrast in this episode between the combined day-care 30-month-old and home-reared 40-month-old group means and the other two means combined is significant (Scheffé test, $p < .025$) and accounts for most of the variance in the interaction. Past strange-situation work (e.g., Ainsworth et al., 1971) has shown that individual differences in seeking the mother's proximity are most clearly highlighted after separation in the reunion episodes, and especially after two separations in the second reunion, episode 8.

The percentage of children in each group who actually approached and touched the mother upon reunion in episode 8 was also calculated. Although two of the findings are only trends, day-care 40-month-olds seemed more likely to do so than their home-reared counterparts (60% vs. 10%, Fisher Exact Test, two-tailed, $p < .10$, approach; 60% vs. 0%, $p < .025$, touch). Day-care 30-month-olds seemed less likely to do so than their home-reared age counterparts ($\overline{X} = 30\%$ vs. 90%, $p < .025$, approach; 10% vs. 60%, $p < .10$, touch).

Resisting and avoiding behaviors. Resistance to the mother tended to be a low-intensity behavior in the children studied. However, day-care children resisted the mother more than home-reared children, $F(1,32) = 5.22, p < .05$. The behavior occurred in only 20 percent of day-care and home-reared 30-month-olds but in 60 percent of the older day-care group. It was completely absent in the older home-reared group. This finding suggests that the older day-care children were somewhat more overtly ambivalent toward the mother than the other groups. Proximity-avoiding behaviors upon reunion were also more conspicuous in day-care children of both ages than in home-reared children ($\overline{X} = 3.2$ vs. $\overline{X} = 1.8$), $F(1,32) = 16.36$, $p < .0005$, although they occurred more markedly in the younger day-care group than in the older group.

Behavior to the Stranger
Day-care children sought less proximity to the stranger than did home-reared children, $F(1,32) = 4.40$, $p < .05$, but an age × rearing group interaction, $F(1,32) = 5.24$, $p < .05$, suggests that the younger home-reared children accounted for this difference by seeking a moderate amount of proximity to the stranger. Resistance to the stranger was higher in day-care 40-month-olds than in the other groups, especially during separation episodes 4 and 7, as a rearing group × age × episode interaction, $F(1,32) = 4.30$, $p < .05$, indicates. In general, day-care children of both ages were more avoidant of the stranger than home-reared children, $F(1,32) = 13.26$, $p < .001$. An interaction of rearing group × episode, $F(2,64) = 6.26$, $p < .005$, indicates that home-reared children were most wary of the stranger in episode 3 and became more accepting of her later on during separation episodes. In contrast, day-care children found the stranger in-

creasingly aversive as the situation proceeded (Scheffé test, $p < .025$).

Differences in the children's responses to the two women who served chiefly as stranger were also examined. These differences tended to be quite small, and none was significant.

DISCUSSION

The above findings demonstrate that day-care children of both ages interacted less with their mothers across a distance before separation in episode 2 than did home-reared children. During separations they cried more and showed more oral behavior and avoidance of the stranger. Upon reunion with the mother, they exhibited more avoidant and resistant behaviors. However, the findings also indicate important age differences. Day-care 40-month-olds showed more heightening of attachment behaviors and more distress as a result of separation than did day-care 30-month-olds, whereas in the home-reared groups, the opposite age trend was found. The work of Maccoby and Feldman (1972) and Marvin (1972) indicates that the home-reared groups behaved in a manner typical of normal children of these ages. However, in comparison to the older home-reared children, children who began day care at 35 months of age explored less, were more distressed by separations, and sought more proximity to and contact with the mother upon reunion, although these bids were mixed with resistance and avoidance. In comparison to the younger home-reared children, children who began day-care at 25 months of age sought little proximity to or contact with the mother upon reunion but showed heightened proximity- and interaction-avoiding tendencies.

The finding of anxious ambivalent attachment behavior in the older day-care children and avoidant behavior in younger day-care children is consistent with age differences reported in children's responses to major separation. During major separation, it is also the younger children (age 1–2½) who are more likely to become detached and to respond to the mother with indifference upon reunion, whereas the older children (age 3–4) are less likely to consolidate detachment and more likely to respond to reunion with the mother in an anxious ambivalent fashion. Thus, the results of the present study suggest that many repetitions of minor separation may have effects similar in form (although not in severity) to major separations.

More recently, Ainsworth (1973) has reported that repetition of the strange-situation procedure after a 2-week interval sensitizes rather than habituates 1-year-olds to separation. This finding also lends credence to the notion that the reunion behaviors of the day-care groups in the present study may be attributable to a sensitizing effect of daily separation.

It is generally acknowledged that detachment is a more serious outcome of major separation than anxious attachment, because as long as a child remains detached, he is limited in his ability to form close interpersonal relationships. Anxious attachment, even if ambivalent, signifies that the child is capable of maintaining a close relationship, and indeed, under favorable conditions he may reestablish a more normal relationship. In the absence of longitudinal data, it is impossible to ascertain the significance for later development of either the anxious attachment observed in the older day-care group or the avoidant behavior observed in the younger day-care group. However, the possibility exists that the mother-avoiding tendencies of the younger children may signal a more substantial disturbance in the child-mother attachment—at least in the short term—than the anxious behavior of the older children, even though at first glance the younger children seem less overtly disturbed.

The finding that day-care children are also more avoidant of strangers than their home-reared peers runs counter to a "common sense" expectation that children who are exposed to a variety of adults would affiliate more readily with strangers than those reared within the more sheltered confines of the nuclear family. Nevertheless, this finding is congruent with those of Tizard and Tizard (1971), who found young children reared in residential nurseries more afraid of strangers than home-reared children, and those of Heinicke and Westheimer (1965), who found previously separated children highly fearful of persons they had seen months before during separations. It is possible that day-care children may react to a stranger's presence in an unfamiliar environment as a cue that separation from the mother is about to take place; or there may be a more general relationship between the anxiety versus security that a child experiences in his primary attachment relationship and the anxiety versus security he demonstrates in dealing with unfamiliar individuals.

The results of the present study are at variance with those of Caldwell et al. (1970), who found no differences between day-care and home-reared children on several behavioral measures purporting to relate to attachment. There are a number of factors which may account for this discrepancy. First, the staff of Caldwell's center may have provided care so highly individualized that the relationship with the substitute caregiver compensated for adverse reactions to separation from the mother. Second, children accustomed to group care from infancy (as Caldwell et al.'s sample was) may not experience the same overt disruption of the relationship with the mother as do children shifted from home care to day care at age 2 or 3. Third, Caldwell and her associates failed to distinguish between those who entered day care relatively early and relatively late. Had interactions between age and rearing group not been examined in the present study, no differences between day-care and home-reared children would have been found on manipulation of toys, search behavior, contact with the mother, or seeking of proximity.

For example, Caldwell et al. compared groups on strength of attachment, measured by the intensity of seeking proximity to the mother. Since the younger day-care children in the present study sought relatively little proximity, whereas the older children sought much proximity, and since the opposite was true in the home-reared groups, day-care and home-reared children would have appeared equally "intensely" attached if age differences had not been taken into account. On the other hand, the present study highlights resistant and avoidant behaviors as indicative of qualitative disturbances in attachment relationships. Absence of proximity seeking in reunion coupled with proximity avoiding is interpreted to reflect a reaction against ambivalence and anxiety rather than weak attachment. Hence, a failure on Caldwell et al.'s part to attend to the relationship between proximity seeking and negative behaviors and their tendency to focus chiefly on strength of proximity seeking may have obscured the effects so conspicuous in the present study.

It may be asked to what extent the results of this study can be attributed to separation rather than to differences which existed between day-care and home-reared groups prior to the day-care experience. The strange-situation procedure has been used previously to highlight differences between home-reared infants who had experienced relatively harmonious relationships with a sensitive mother and those who had experienced disturbed relationships with an insensitive mother. In the case of the present day-care group, there is no evidence that their mothers were any less sensitive or responsive to their children, when at home, than mothers of home-reared children. However, there is some evidence that the quality of the mother's personality (and hence presumably her mothering practices) can influence the intensity and duration of any adverse effects of substitute care (Moore, 1964, 1969). Although the families of the day-care children fell well within the normal range, it is possible that they differed from families of home-reared children on more subtle dimensions, which may have interacted with the experience of day care to create disturbances in attachment.

Hence, further research should attempt to elucidate the relationship between the child's prior experiences and his reaction to day care. It may be that prior disturbed mother-child interaction, more general family instability, or previous experiences of separation, may exacerbate a child's reactions to daily separations. It is also possible that a close relationship with a responsive adult in a center may compensate greatly for separation from the mother, but if this substitute relationship is of such importance, then it becomes critical that children experience stability in their caregivers. In view of the present high turnover of day-care staff, this issue deserves immediate attention, as does the issue of whether alternative methods of care, such as family day care or part-time group care, are more suited to young children's needs than full-time group care. Whether or not research established immediate adverse effects, longitudinal studies of day-care children into adolescence are necessary to show that there are no "sleeper" effects. It is essential that research be designed to deal with day care as a separation experience as well as a multiple-mothering experience, and in this, the classical separation literature can serve as a guide to variables on which day-care and home-reared groups may be compared. It is not sufficient to compare groups on "strength" of attachment measures. Such measures may show that a child is attached to his mother, but they do not deal with the issue of whether day care can affect the security versus anxiety he experiences in this primary relationship.

REFERENCES

Ainsworth, M. D. S. Anxious attachment and defensive reactions in a strange situation and their relationship to behavior at home. Paper presented at the biennial meeting of The Society for Research in Child Development, Philadelphia, March 1973.

Ainsworth, M. D. S., & Bell, S. M. Attachment, exploration, and separation: illustrated by the behavior of one-year-olds in a strange situation. *Child Development,* 1970, **41,** 49–67.

Ainsworth, M. D. S., Bell, S. M., & Stayton, D. Individual differences in strange-situation behavior of one-year-olds. In H. R. Schaffer (Ed.), *The origins of human social relations.* London: Academic Press, 1971.

Bowlby, J. *Attachment and loss.* Vol. 1. *Attachment.* London: Hogarth; New York: Basic, 1969.

Bowlby, J. *Attachment and loss.* Vol. 2. *Separation.* London: Hogarth, 1973.

Caldwell, B. M., Wright, C. M., Honig, A. S., & Tannenbaum, J. Infant day care and attachment. *American Journal of Orthopsychiatry,* 1970, **40,** 397–412.

Heinicke, C. M., & Westheimer, I. *Brief separations.* New York: International Universities Press, 1965.

Hogan, R. Development of an empathy scale. *Journal of Consulting and Clinical Psychology,* 1969, **33**(5), 307–316.

Maccoby, E., & Feldman, S. Mother-attachment and stranger reactions. *Monographs of The Society for Research in Child Development*, 1972, **37**(1, Serial No. 146).

Marvin, R. S. Attachment, exploratory, and communicative behavior of two-, three-, and four-year-old children. Unpublished doctoral dissertation, University of Chicago, 1972.

Moore, T. Children of full-time and part-time mothers. *International Journal of Social Psychiatry*, 1964, **2**, 1–10.

Moore, T. Stress in normal childhood. *Human Relations*, 1969, **22**, 235–250.

Robertson, J., & Bowlby, J. Responses of young children to separation from their mothers. *Courrier: Centre international de l'enfance*, 1952, **2**, 131–142.

Robertson, J., & Robertson, J. *Young children in brief separations*. New York: Quadrangle, 1971.

Tizard, J., & Tizard, B. The social development of two-year-old children in residential nurseries. In H. R. Schaffer (Ed.), *The origins of human social relations*. London: Academic Press, 1971.

Yarrow, L. J. Maternal deprivation: toward an empirical and conceptual evaluation. *Psychological Bulletin*, 1961, **58**, 459–496.

A laboratory assessment of attachment behavior in day-care children

ARLENE S. RAGOZIN

The existence of day care—all-day group care of children in centers—is an established fact. At the present time, however, the number of children cared for in centers is quite small, and there is disagreement about whether group care is an appropriate substitute care arrangement for young children. Particularly for those under 3 years of age, the combination of separation from mother, multiple caretakers, and large numbers of children has been viewed with some concern (Bowlby, 1969).

Questions about the effects of day care often have focused on its influence on children's attachments to their mothers. Although there appears to be a consensus that day care has little effect on *infants'* attachments (Doyle, 1975; Kearsley, Zelazo, Kagan, and Hartmann, 1975; Kessel and Singer, 1973), there are discrepant data on the effects of group care in the *toddler* age range (approximately 1½–3 years). Two studies, which utilized comparable experimental manipulations, obtained essentially opposite results. Comparing Israeli *kibbutz*-reared and American home-reared 2½-year-olds, Maccoby and Feldman (1972) found few significant effects of child-rearing condition. They concluded that "the attachment patterns in the two groups of children are very similar" (p. 79). Blehar's (1974) study of American day-care and home-reared children, in contrast, disclosed rather striking rearing group effects. When separated from mother, day-care children cried more than did the home-reared

This study was based in part upon a dissertation submitted to Harvard University, 1976.

comparison group; when mother was present, day-care children engaged in less distance interaction with mother and in more proximity-resisting or avoiding behavior.

Perhaps the most telling aspect of Blehar's findings was that the developmental course of attachment in day-care children was *opposite* to the age trends in a home-reared comparison group. The age changes in home-reared children were predictable from attachment theory and were roughly consonant with those reported in previous studies (Maccoby and Feldman, 1972; Marvin, 1971). It was expected that there would be age-related increases in exploratory play, as well as decreases in separation distress and proximity-contact seeking. Blehar's home-reared sample followed this pattern, whereas the day-care group displayed age-related increases in distress and proximity-contact seeking, and also decreases in play.

The study to be reported here was designed to provide further data on the effects of day care on the development of attachment in the third year of life. By using the same experimental method that had been used in the Blehar, Maccoby and Feldman, and Marvin investigations, I could compare any age effects found in a day-care sample with those previously reported in home-reared children.

The research also was intended to examine closely the experimental method itself—the widely used Strange Situation procedure (Ainsworth and Wittig, 1969). This procedure consists of a fixed series of 3-minute episodes in which various combinations of child, mother, and adult female stranger are together in an unfamiliar experimental room. The child's behavior to mother under low-stress, preseparation conditions can be observed; then reactions to separations and reunions can be seen.

The rationale behind this technique is that behaviors elicited under experimental conditions reflect the patterns that occur in "real life." The stated or implicit presumption is that under the moderately stressful conditions of the Strange Situation, children's behavior will be an exaggerated version of behavior typically seen under routine, nonstressful circumstances (Ainsworth and Bell, 1970; Ainsworth, Bell, and Stayton, 1971).

Behavioral consistency between laboratory and natural settings may be demonstrated in two ways. In the simpler model, differences between behaviors in laboratory and natural settings would be quantitative: stress in the laboratory would increase the rate at which particular behaviors are emitted. It also is possible that certain qualitative transformations of behavior could occur. For example, leaving the child in an unfamiliar place might lead to the child seeking contact with mother when she returns, whereas leaving him in his familiar day-care center might produce only distal reunion behavior. Systematic relationships between the same behaviors in different settings or between behaviors and their predicted transformations would demonstrate the ecological validity of laboratory procedures and permit generalization of laboratory findings.

Data on the cross-situation consistency of behavior are lacking for day-care children, and they are conflicting in the home-reared population. Although three studies found evidence of cross-situational consistency (Ainsworth, Bell, and Stayton, 1971; Bretherton, 1974; Ross, Kagan, Zelazo, and Kotelchuck, 1975), two others concluded that attachment behavior was situation-specific (Lamb, 1975; Maccoby and Feldman, 1972).

A related question is whether attachment behaviors exhibited in the laboratory are systematically related to other aspects of children's functioning. Specifically, are attachment behaviors related to exploratory behaviors and to peer interaction? Only two studies have addressed this issue: Heathers (1954) found a negative relationship between separation distress and peer interaction in nursery school, while Maccoby and Feldman (1972) failed to detect any relationship between attachment and peer behaviors. No data are available on comparisons of attachment versus play behavior in the 2- to 3-year age range.

METHOD

Subjects.   The sample consisted of 20 children who had been in day-care centers on a full-time basis for at least 4 months. They were middle-class children of highly educated mothers, all but one of whom had attended college. It is noteworthy that two-thirds of the mothers were students, for whom the decision to place children in day care represented a choice rather than an economic necessity. Fifteen of the children came from intact, two-parent families; the rest lived with their mothers.

Subjects were divided into groups of *younger* children $(N = 9; \overline{X} = 23.6$ months; range $= 17$–29 months) and *older* children $(N = 11; \overline{X} = 34.4$ months; range $= 32$–38 months). Age and sex were confounded in this sample; however, since the large majority of attachment studies report few sex differences (see Maccoby and Jacklin, 1974), the groups will be referred to simply by age.

Children in the study attended one of three day-care centers for an average of 39 hours weekly (range $= 30$–55 hours). Two centers were university affiliated; the third, an independent non-profit organization. Although the observers' informal assessments indicated that centers differed in "quality," all had high staff to children ratios—approximately 1 : 4.

Procedure. Children were observed in a Strange Situation procedure that closely followed the one devised by Ainsworth and Wittig (1969). Table 1 provides a description of Strange Situation episodes. The experimental room was located at the University of Washington. It measured 15.5 × 11 feet and contained chairs for mother and stranger at one end. At the other end there was a large pile of toys that had been selected for their appeal to 1- to 3-year-olds. A one-way-vision mirror and microphone gave the unseen observers access to events in the experimental room.

As described more fully elsewhere (Ragozin, 1975), children also were observed in their day-care centers during naturally occurring episodes such as at arrival in the morning, during separation from the mother in the morning, during the day, and at reunion at night.

Response measures. In both settings, discrete, overt behaviors were coded "on the spot" on a modified frequency basis. Behaviors were entered for continuous 6-second intervals; there was no separation of observation and recording periods. Two observers, connected in tandem to a single timing device, simultaneously coded different aspects of a subject's behavior. Proximity-promoting (attachment) and proximity-resisting behaviors were coded with reference to mother and other adults (i.e., to the stranger in the laboratory and to the class of "all other adults" in centers). The attachment measures were three proximity items, touch, give-take, follow-move with, communication, and three responses to separation. Other items were recorded to describe distress, exploratory behavior, and peer-oriented behavior (see Table 2). Although the same general code was used in both laboratory and day-care settings, some items were analyzed for one location only. Follow-move with, for example, was an inappropriate measure in the laboratory. Rate scores, the percentage of intervals in which a given behavior occurred, were used to adjust for individual variation in the length of episodes.

Prior to data collection, interobserver reliability was tested on a group of children in their day-care center. For behaviors that occurred frequently, Kendall's tau was used to assess interobserver reliability; for those items that occurred rarely, a percent agreement measure was used. Tau ranged from .91 to .75; percent agreement, from .96 to .81. On only two items did the reliability fall below .80.

TABLE 1   STRANGE SITUATION (S.S.) PROCEDURE

Episode	Participants	Description
S.S. 1	M, C[a]	C explores room; M completes background information form
S.S. 2	M, C, St[a]	St enters and sits quietly for 1 minute; converses with M for 1 minute; interacts with C for 1 minute
S.S. 3	St, C	M leaves, either slipping out unobtrusively or saying, "I'll be back." St disengages from C and moves to spot on floor 3 feet from C. St is responsive to C (Time variable)
S.S. 4	M, C	M calls, "I'm back" and pauses in doorway. M greets C; then goes to her seat. St leaves unobtrusively at beginning of episode
S.S. 5	C	M leaves saying, "I have to make a phone call. I'll be back." C is left alone (Time variable)
S.S. 6	St, C	St enters, sits on floor, and interacts with C. She distracts or comforts C as appropriate. St gradually disengages from C and moves 3 feet away (Time variable)
S.S. 7	M, C	M opens door, says, "Hello," and pauses. M then interacts freely with C. St leaves unobtrusively at beginning of episode

[a] M = mother, C = child, St = stranger.

Data reduction.   Distinctions among day-care centers and the two days of day care observations were eliminated after preliminary *t* tests revealed few significant differences. The number of dependent variables was reduced by excluding from statistical analyses those behaviors that occurred in very few subjects (less than 30 percent) or that occurred at very low rates (less than 4 percent). Proximity-resisting behaviors, as well as a number of other measures, were thus excluded from the data analysis.

Methods of analysis.   The effects of age and Strange Situation episode on the behavior of day-care children were determined by univariate analyses of variance conducted on all measures which met the above criteria. Age was the between-subjects variable, and episode, the within-subjects repeated measure.

Kendall's tau was used to assess the degree of behavioral consistency between laboratory and day-care situations and also to show the relationship between attachment behaviors expressed in the Strange Situation and peer-and-play measures in day-care absence.

TABLE 2 RESPONSE MEASURES USED IN
STRANGE SITUATION AND DAY-CARE SETTINGS

Code Item	Definition
Behavior to M[a]	
M present	
Proximity	C[a] is within 3 feet of M
Child-initiated proximity	C is responsible for stationing himself within a 3-foot radius of M
Child-initiated distance	C moves outside a 3-foot radius of mother or remains there
Touch	Any nonaggressive form of physical contact by C
Give-take	C gives play object to or takes object from M
Follow-move with	C follows behind or moves with M while she moves
Communication	All vocalizations, smiles, and gestures except those that serve to reduce child-mother proximity
M absent	
Active proximity seeking	C manipulates object in order to get closer to departed M (e.g., C bangs on door)
Passive proximity maintenance	C stays at door by which M left, or C stays at M's last location in room
Call	Any verbalization for or about M
Behavior to St/Ad[a]	
See items under M present	
Distress	
Crying	C whines, cries, etc., for no observable reason or for an obviously attachment-related reason
Exploratory Behavior	
Play	Manipulation of play objects; includes imaginary objects; excludes caretaking objects
Locomotion	Nonsocial movement of at least 3 feet
Behavior to peers	
Proximity	C is within 3 feet of peer
Interaction	All socially neutral or positive interactions

[a] M = mother, C = child, St = stranger, Ad = all adults, other than mother, in day-care centers.

RESULTS

Since the major hypothesis regarding behavior in the Strange Situation was that age trends in the day-care sample would be consistent with those previously reported for home-reared children, only age effects and their interactions with episode will be discussed here. "Significant" results will refer to those with a probability level of .05 or better.

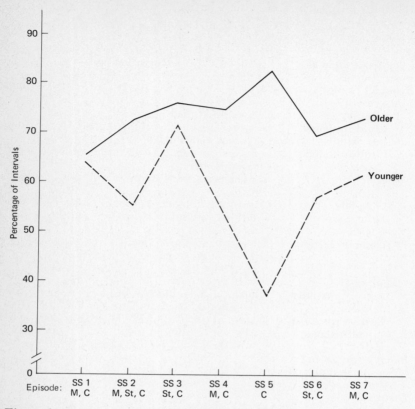

Figure 1. Percentage of 6-second intervals in which day-care children engaged in *play*, by age and Strange Situation episode (*N* = 20).

Exploratory behavior. Manipulative play with objects increased with age (*p* < .01), and the episode manipulations had different effects on the two age groups (age × episode interaction, *p* < .01). As Figure 1 shows, play behavior of younger children dropped markedly when they were left alone in S.S. 5. For older children, play *peaked* in S.S. 5, and generally was unaffected by mother's and stranger's presence and absence. Younger children moved around the experimental room more than did older children (locomotion age effect, *p* < .01).

Distress. As indicated by the amount of crying, the entire Strange Situation procedure was significantly more disturbing to the younger day-care children than to the older group. Although being left alone (S.S. 5) produced the highest rates of crying for all children, the mean rate for the older group was only 4.8 percent, whereas it was 36.1 percent for the younger group.

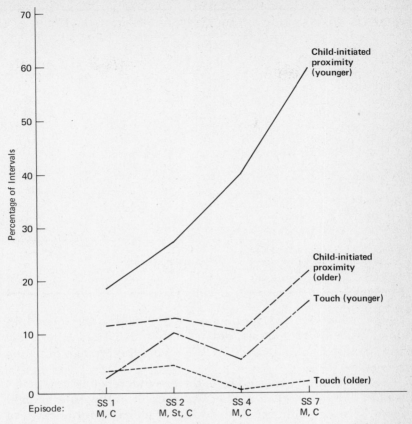

Figure 2. Percentage of 6-second intervals in which day-care children *initiated proximity with* and *touched mother*, by age and Strange Situation episode (*N* = 20).

Moreover, differential effects of episode on younger and older children produced an age × episode interaction (*p* < .001).

    Behaviors to mother. Younger children initiated and maintained proximity to their mothers at a higher rate than did older children (*p* < .01). In the younger day-care group, child-initiated proximity increased with each mother-present episode (S.S. 1, 2, 4, and 7); in the older group, child-initiated proximity remained virtually unchanged through S.S. 4, but increased in S.S. 7 (age × episode interaction, *p* < .01).

    Similarly, younger day-care children touched mothers more than did older children (*p* < .05), and the two groups showed different patterns of response to the episode manipulations. As Figure 2 shows, younger children increased their rate of touching

TABLE 3   DEGREE OF CONCORDANCE BETWEEN BEHAVIOR IN

Measure	S.S. 1 × Arrival	S.S. 2 × Arrival
Exploratory behavior		
Play	.12	−.06
Locomotion	−.16	.09
Behavior to mother	(N = 18)	(N = 18)
Child-initiated prox.	−.35*	−.11
Child-initiated distance	(N = 14)	(N = 18)
	−.11	−.03
Touch	a	.13
Communication	−.16	.02
Behavior to stranger/adult		
Proximity	—	.22
Communication	—	a

Note. N = 20, except as specified.
   [a] Measure fell below criteria for analysis in this episode.
   * $p < .05$, one-tailed test.
   ** $p < .01$, one-tailed test.

mother when the stranger entered (S.S. 2) and in the second re-union (S.S. 7). In contrast, older children exhibited a very low and declining rate of touching throughout the Strange Situation procedure.

As might be expected from the age difference in proximity-contact behaviors when mother was present in the experimental room, younger children also had higher mean scores on each of the three separation response measures in each separation episode. For passive proximity maintenance and calling, these differences reached significance.

Two measures, communication and child-initiated distance, failed to produce age effects or interactions.

Behaviors to stranger.   In comparison to their attachment, distress, and exploratory behaviors, younger and older day-care children were more alike in their response to the stranger. Rates of communication to and child-initiated distance from stranger were similar for the two groups; the rate of child-initiated proximity was higher in the younger group.

Cross-situation consistency of behavior.   The generalizability of Strange Situation findings to the "real life" behavior of day-care children was determined by comparing measures taken in the laboratory with the same measures and hypothesized transformations in analogogous episodes in day-care centers. In

LABORATORY AND DAY-CARE CENTERS: KENDALL'S TAU

S.S. 3 × Separation	S.S. 5 × Separation	S.S. 6 × Separation	S.S. 4 × Reunion	S.S. 7 × Reunion
−.13	−.43**	.02	.37	.16
a	.29*	.02	.13	.44**
—	—	—	.34*	.04
			(N = 15)	(N = 19)
—	—	—	.19	.00
—	—	—	a	.20
—	—	—	−.03	.11
.13	—	−.14	—	—
.22	—	.26	—	—

each case, Kendall's tau was used to determined intraindividual consistency—the degree to which children maintained the same position, relative to other children, in laboratory and day-care settings. Changes in the rate of behavior for the group as a whole would not affect children's rankings relative to one another. All Strange Situation episodes were compared to their day-care analogues (for example, S.S. 1 and 2 were compared with day-care arrival). Positive associations between variables were expected.

The results of the analyses revealed a virtual absence of cross-situation consistency. Of the 32 "same measure" comparisons, only 4 reached significance in the predicted positive direction (see Table 3). Exclusion of the stranger versus familiar adult comparisons—on the grounds that they were not analogous—scarcely alters the conclusion. The transformational analysis proved useless; the number of significant relationships was little more than could have been expected by chance.

Relationships between attachment and peer-play behaviors. Since there was no basis for predicting the direction of any relationships between attachment and peer or play behaviors, two-tailed tests of significance were performed on Kendall's tau, and the results reported indicate patterns or tendencies ($p < .10$).

Comparison of attachment and peer-play behaviors indicated systematic relationships between these different behavioral

TABLE 4 PREDICTION OF BEHAVIORS
IN DAY CARE FROM ATTACHMENT BEHAVIORS IN
THE STRANGE SITUATION: KENDALL'S TAU

Strange Situation Measure	Day-Care Absence	
	Peer Interaction	Play
Behavior to mother		
Child-initiated proximity		
S.S. 1 (M, C)	−.06	.08
S.S. 2 (M, St, C)	−.27†	−.28†
S.S. 4 (M, C)	−.33*	−.29†
S.S. 7 (M, C)	−.32†	−.19
Child-initiated distance		
S.S. 1 ($N = 14$)	.01	.09
S.S. 2 ($N = 18$)	.28	.32†
S.S. 4 ($N = 15$)	.34†	.03
S.S. 7 ($N = 19$)	−.12	.17
Touch		
S.S. 2	−.20	−.19
S.S. 7	−.36*	−.28†
Communication		
S.S. 1	.01	−.01
S.S. 2	.03	−.05
S.S. 4	.09	.15
S.S. 7	−.08	.04
Active proximity		
S.S. 5 (C)	−.24	.14
Passive proximity		
S.S. 5	−.28†	−.31†
Call		
S.S. 5	.07	.34*

Note. $N = 20$, except as specified.
  * $p < .05$, two-tailed test.
  † $p < .10$, two-tailed test.

systems (see Table 4). Attachment behaviors were *negatively* related to peer interaction, with substantial associations occurring in 6 of the 17 comprisons. Similarly, substantial *negative* associations between attachment and play behaviors were found in 5 of 17 comparisons. It should be noted that in both sets of comparisons, proximity-contact behaviors—the "classic" attachment measures—were related to peer and play behaviors. Associations between communication to mother and peer-play behaviors were close to zero. Moreover, the ability of attachment measures to predict both peer and play behaviors was not an artificat of the measures. In day-care absence, peer interaction and play were

essentially independent, as indicated by a low association between these measures (tau = .16).

DISCUSSION
Age trends.   The attachment behavior of 2- and 3-year-old
middle-class day-care children in the Strange Situation was consistent with the age trends previously found in home-reared children (Blehar, 1974; Maccoby and Feldman, 1972; Marvin, 1971).
In each study, manipulative play increased with age; crying,
proximity-contact behavior when mother was present, and attempts to regain mother when she was absent all decreased with
age. For the home-reared children in Blehar's and Marvin's
studies and the day-care children in the present study, there was
less heightening of attachment behavior following separation
with increased age. In fact, declines in proximity-contact behavior between S.S. 1 and S.S. 7 were noted for Blehar's older
home-reared group and this older day-care sample.

There were few differences between the age changes of the
present day-care children and those of home-reared children in
other studies. On only one measure did the age effects reported
here differ markedly from those previously found in home-reared
children. Blehar, Maccoby and Feldman, and Marvin all reported that play declined in mother-absent episodes for both 2-
and 3-year-olds. Although similar episode effects occurred in this
sample of day-care 2-year-olds, they were not found in the
3-year-old group. For older day-care children, play increased in
mother's absence and peaked when children were left all alone.
In some cases, age trends of day-care children differed from those
reported in one study, but not another. For example, Maccoby
and Feldman found age differences in home-reared children's
distal behavior to mother; age differences were not found in the
pesent day-care sample, nor in Blehar's study. In short, there was
clear confirmation of the hypothesis that the development of attachment in 2- to 3-year-old day-care children would parallel that
of home-reared children.

In contrast, Blehar reported that age trends in a sample of
middle-class day-care children were opposite to those found in a
home-reared comparison group. The discrepancies between the
present results and those obtained by Blehar may be attributed to
differences in observation methods (Maccoby and Feldman used
modified frequency coding of discrete behaviors, whereas Blehar
used ratings, as well as frequency counts), to differences in the
samples (in this study mothers were more highly educated), or to
differences in the staff-to-child ratio in day-care centers (in this
study the ratio was about 1 : 4; in Blehar's study, 1 : 6–8). One

might hypothesize that when the staff-to-child ratio falls below 1:5, day-care attendance begins to affect the young child's relationship with his mother.

The self-selection of families into different types of day-care centers also may be a factor. Are there differences in the ongoing child-mother relationship that are responsible for attendance in one or another type of center? Would the mothers in this study have left their children in a center that contained few adults relative to the number of children if it were the only center available? Would they have made other arrangements, such as in-home baby-sitting? Would they have postponed their own career or educational commitments? Ainsworth (1967, 1973) has argued repeatedly that mother's sensitivity to her baby is related to the infant's attachment to her. It may be that such sensitivity is demonstrated in the selection of substitute care arrangements and that mother's sensitivity, rather than staff-to-child ratios, is the critical factor.

Situation-specificity of attachment behavior. Although there had been weak expectations about behavioral consistency between laboratory and field situations, the overwhelming lack of consistency came as a surprise. On the individual level there were few significant positive associations between behaviors in the Strange Situation and day-care centers. Predicted transformations of attachment behaviors were not found. Considering the behavior patterns of the sample as a whole, important differences existed between settings. Analysis showed that while age had an important effect on behavior in the Strange Situation, it failed to make an appreciable difference in the familiar day-care setting (reported in Ragozin, 1976). Further, a number of measures occurred at a rate sufficient for statistical analysis in only one of the settings.

Minimally, these results indicate a conservative approach in generalizing Strange Situation findings for a day-care population. More generally, they raise the question of whether attachment behavior is largely determined by situational variables, or whether any cross-situation consistency may be expected. A middle-ground hypothesis is that attachment behavior under stress is qualitatively different from and independent of attachment behavior under nonstress, but that within each condition there is some degree of intraindividual consistency.

Attachment, peer, and play behavior. Since results of comparisons between attachment and other behaviors generally were below acceptable levels of statistical significance, they must be treated cautiously. It may be that these associations are idiosyncratic to the present sample. Only replication will determine the extent to which the findings are generalizable to other day-care groups and to home-reared samples.

Although specific results differ, this study and Heathers' (1954) both showed that attachment is not an isolated system of behavior. Lower levels of attachment behavior in a moderately stressful situation were associated with greater involvement with peers and play objects in a day-care or nursery-school setting. The age trends in Strange Situation and the relationship between attachment and peer-play behaviors taken together hint at a developmental shift from a focus on mother to a more pronounced orientation to the child's world of toys and peers.

The comparison between attachment and peer-play behavior also suggests an approach to interpreting individual differences in attachment behavior. If attachment is studied in a limited context without measures of children's total functioning, one simply can say that children's behavior is alike or that it differs. In contrast, the comparison between attachment and peer-play behavior tells us that lower levels of attachment behavior are associated with what are apparently desirable behaviors. Consider the different evaluation one would make if attachment and peer-play behavior had been positively associated.

Scientifically, it is inappropriate to value certain patterns of attachment as "better" or "worse." Yet, on the human level, such judgments are unavoidable. By recasting the interpretive issue into behavioral terms—"What are the behavioral correlates of this or that pattern of attachment behavior?"—a matter of private judgment becomes amenable to psychological research.

REFERENCES

Ainsworth, M. D. S. *Infancy in Uganda.* Baltimore: Johns Hopkins Press, 1967.

Ainsworth, M. D. S. The development of infant-mother attachment. In B. M. Caldwell and H. N. Ricciuti (Eds.), *Review of child development research* (Vol. 3). Chicago: University of Chicago Press, 1973.

Ainsworth, M. D. S., and Bell, S. M. Attachment, exploration, and separation: Illustrated by the behavior of one-year-olds in a strange situation. *Child Development,* 1970, **41**, 49–67.

Ainsworth, M. D. S., Bell, S. M., and Stayton, D. J. Individual differences in strange situation behavior of one-year-olds. In H. R. Schaffer (Ed.), *The origins of human social relations.* New York: Academic Press, 1971.

Ainsworth, M. D. S., and Wittig, B. A. Attachment and exploratory behavior of one-year-olds in a strange situation. In B. M. Foss (Ed.), *Determinants of infant behaviour.* London: Methuen, 1969.

Blehar, M. C. Anxious attachment and defensive reactions associated with day care. *Child Development*, 1974, **45**, 683–692.

Bowlby, J. *Attachment and loss* (Vol. 1) *Attachment*. New York: Basic Books, 1969.

Bretherton, I. Making friends with one-year-olds: An experimental study of infant-stranger interaction. Unpublished doctoral dissertation, Johns Hopkins University, 1974.

Doyle, A. Infant development in day care. *Developmental Psychology*, 1975, **11**, 655–656.

Heathers, G. The adjustment of two-year-olds in a novel social situation. *Child Development*, 1954, **25**, 147–158.

Kearsley, R. B., Zelazo, P. R., Kagan, J., and Hartmann, R. Separation protest in day-care and home-reared infants. *Pediatrics*, 1975, **55**, 171–175.

Kessel, F. S., and Singer, S. Day care and the attachment behaviour of disadvantaged "coloured" South African infants: Results of a study that succeeded, ethical implications of a study that failed. Paper presented at the meeting of The Society for Research in Child Development, Philadelphia, March 1973.

Lamb, M. E. Infants, fathers, and mothers: Interactions at 8 months of age in the home and in the laboratory. Paper presented at the meeting of the Eastern Psychological Association, New York, April 1975.

Maccoby, E. E., and Feldman, S. S. Mother-attachment and stranger-reactions in the third year of life. *Monographs of The Society for Research in Child Development*, 1972, **37** (4 Serial No. 146).

Maccoby, E. E., and Jacklin, C. N. *The psychology of sex differences*. Stanford: Stanford University Press, 1974.

Marvin, R. S. Attachment- and communicative-behavior in two-, three-, and four-year-old children. Unpublished doctoral dissertation, University of Chicago, 1971.

Ragozin, A. S. Attachment in day care children: Field and laboratory findings. Paper presented at the meeting of The Society for Research in Child Development, Denver, April 1975.

Ragozin, A. S. Attachment behavior of young children in day care. Unpublished doctoral dissertation, Harvard University, 1976.

Ross, G., Kagan, J., Zelazo, P., and Kotelchuck, M. Separation protest in infants in home and laboratory. *Developmental Psychology*, 1975, **11**, 256–257.

PART III

THE EFFECTS OF POVERTY

OVERVIEW

The Effects of Poverty

This chapter seems to get harder and harder to write, instead of easier and easier. I keep hoping that somehow this tangled mess of issues and problems is suddenly going to become clear, or that new evidence will come along that will show an obvious interpretation of the data, but alas it has not happened yet, and it is unlikely to happen in the future. So I will have to do what I can to create some order for you out of the chaos of results and opinions in this area.

Ten years ago, and perhaps even five years ago, there was more agreement about the effects of poverty than there is now. It was obvious that most children from poverty environments did poorly in school and had lower scores on nearly any kind of standardized test of intellectual functioning that could be devised. Most psychologists a decade ago were in agreement that this lowered or slowed intellectual performance resulted from some kind of "deficit": children reared in poverty were seen as having fewer cognitive skills or as having developed basic cognitive competencies more slowly than had children from more affluent backgrounds. The deficiencies were seen as particularly obvious in the area of language and concept development. Poor school performance, in this view, resulted from the child's deficiencies. The child from a poverty environment was thought of as not "ready" for school in the same way as is a middle-class child. He does not have the same basic language and conceptual skills, and therefore cannot perform the same tasks.

There are still many psychologists and educators who agree with this "deficit" hypothesis, but there are now many who do not. The *facts* of low school performance and poor test performance are not disputed by anyone, to my knowledge, but these facts are interpreted very differently. In the area of language, the "fact" of poorer or slower language development among the poor is also in dispute.

Because of the fundamental disagreement about the characteristics of children reared in poverty environments, it is not possible in this section to focus only on explanations of the effects of poverty. Instead, we must first ask the prior question: What *are* the effects of poverty? or, more precisely, What are the opposing views of the effects of poverty, and what is the evidence for each view? Then we can turn to some of the various theories that have been offered to explain why poverty has the effects it has.

So that you understand who I am talking about when I speak of children of poverty, let me begin with a brief description of the nature of the population of the poor in the United States.

WHO ARE THE POOR CHILDREN?

According to data presented to the 1970 White House Conference on Children and Youth, roughly 10 million children in the United States were being raised in conditions that could be described as poverty-stricken—that is, in 1969, approximately 14 percent of all American children under age 18 were living in families whose yearly income was less than $3000. By 1974, there were still approximately 10 million children living below the poverty level (although the poverty level itself had risen to about $5000 a year), which represented about 15 percent of all children.

The common assumption seems to be that most poverty-stricken families are nonwhite. Not true. Of the 10 million poor children in 1969, 6 million were white, 4 million were nonwhite. But a higher *percentage* of the nonwhite are poor: About 40 percent of all nonwhite children in 1969 were in families with earnings below the poverty line, and only about 10 percent of the white children were in poor families. Thus more of the poor are white, but more of the nonwhite are poor. Another common misconception is that the vast majority of the poor live in cities. Again, not quite true. In 1969 about two-fifths were in rural areas and about three-fifths in urban environments. Bear these facts in mind as you read the descriptions of the poor child. I am not only talking about urban, ghetto-reared minority group children, but also about rural and suburban children and white children in the Appalachian Mountains, Indians on reservations, and many other groups.

CHARACTERISTICS OF POOR CHILDREN
The Traditional Evidence
General intellectual ability. Virtually every study that included IQ or other standard intellectual measures of middle-class and poor children shows middle-class children with significantly higher average IQ's (Lesser, Fifer, and Clark, 1965; Kennedy, Van de Reit and White, 1963; Whiteman and M. Deutsch, 1968; for a review, see C. Deutsch, 1973). Furthermore, there is evidence from several studies that the same differences hold *within* ethnic groups. That is, the overall social-class difference is not just the result of some kind of test bias against blacks or other minority groups, who make up a large proportion of the poor; within each minority group the middle-class children score higher than do the poor children. For example, Kennedy, Van de Reit, and White (1963), in a study of black children selected from all elementary school-age children in five Southern states, found that the average IQ of the middle-class black children was 105 (above average), and the mean IQ of the poverty-level black children was 79 (considerably below average). In a more impressive study, Lesser and his associates (Lesser et al., 1965) tested groups of middle-class and poor first-grade children from Chinese, Jewish, black, and Puerto Rican families in New York City. The test used yielded separate scores for verbal, reasoning, numerical, and spatial abilities. Their results are clear: On every scale, for every ethnic group, there was a difference in favor of the middle-class children—that is, middle-class Chinese children scored higher on verbal, reasoning, numerical, and spatial abilities than lower-class Chinese; the same was true of blacks, Puerto Ricans, and Jews. These findings were later replicated by Stodolsky and Lesser (1967) for Chinese, black, and Irish Catholic children in Boston.

There is also evidence from a number of sources that prolonged living under conditions of poverty results in a steady *lowering* of the IQ score. This phenomenon, which M. Deutsch has called "cumulative deficit," can be seen in various places. In many studies done in the Appalachian Mountains region during the 1930s and 1940s, the consistent finding was that the older children in a community had lower IQs than had the younger children in the same community (this evidence is reviewed in Jones, 1954). Similar findings were obtained by Kennedy and his colleagues (1963) in their study of black children in the South. They found that the 5-year-olds in their sample had a mean IQ of 86, whereas the 13-year-olds had a mean IQ of 65. Some decline in measured IQ is also quite commonly observed in the "control" group children in studies of compensatory education—that is, the urban children who were *not* in experimental preschools or other compensatory programs, but were from equivalently poor families, often show some decline in IQ over the preschool and early elementary school years (Gray and Klaus, 1970).

Overall, then, there is strong evidence that on *standard measures* such as an IQ test poverty-level children on the average score lower. It is important to note, however, that in studies in which children below approximately 2½ years of age have been examined, social-class differences in IQ have *not* been found. Bayley (1965), in a monumental study including 1400 children from all racial and economic backgrounds, found no social-class or racial differences on any of the Infant Scales up to 15 months of age—except that black children were slightly more advanced in motor development. In their paper included in this section, Golden, Birns, Bridger, and Moss report similar findings: their all-black samples from middle-class and poverty environments showed no differences on "infant IQ" tests or in performance on Piaget-style tests up to age 2. By the time the children were 3, however, there were significant social-class differences favoring the middle-class children.

School performance. Again there is good agreement: poor children do not, on the average, do as well in school. One study involving children in western Pennsylvania, for example (Hill and Giammateo, 1963), showed that by grade 3, children from middle-class families, compared to children from poor families, were 8 months ahead in vocabulary, 9 months ahead in reading comprehension, 6 months ahead in arithmetic skills, and 11 months ahead in problem solving. The same type of findings are reported in Coleman's nationwide study of school performance (Coleman, 1966).

I want to emphasize here that these are *average* differences. In nearly every instance the two distributions overlap so that there are children from poor backgrounds who perform extremely well in school and children from middle-class backgrounds who do not, but there is an average difference in performance.

Verbal ability. The measure of verbal ability used most commonly in older studies and in more recent ones is vocabulary size. On such measures, poor children appear to be lower (Stodolsky, 1965; Templin, 1957). In their study of ethnic differences in cognitive functioning, Lesser and his colleagues (1965) demonstrated that the vocabulary differences hold up even when the child is tested in his native language or dialect with all words that show an initial social-class bias eliminated from the test— that is, if all the words the middle-class child is more likely to know merely because he is middle class and all the words the poor child is more likely to know because he is from a poor environment are eliminated, there is still a difference between the two groups. What this seems to mean is that the poor child simply knows fewer of the words to which both groups have access.

There is less aggreement about other measures of language skill, but a number of researchers have found social-class differences, favoring the middle class, in language complexity, ability to comprehend the speech of others, and language fluency (these studies are reviewed in C. Deutsch, 1973).

Problem solving.   A number of studies indicate that the problem-solving strategies used by poor children differ qualitatively from the strategies used by middle-class children and, further, that the middle-class strategies are developmentally the more mature form. For example, if children are given a group of objects or pictures and asked to pick out "those that go together" and to say why they go together, there are several possible strategies. The child may select and justify a superordinate grouping, such as "they are all fruit" or "they are all tools." A second kind of grouping is based on the objects' relationships, such as "the boy and the dog play together." A third alternative is an analytic grouping based on some similar parts of the objects, such as "these two have arms." The available data indicate that with increasing age, there is an increase in analytic responses and a large increase in superordinate groupings along with a decrease in relational groupings (Kagan, Rosman, Day, Albert, and Phillips, 1964). But this age trend seems to take place more slowly in poor children than in middle-class children (Sigel, Anderson, and Shapiro, 1966; Sigel and McBane, 1967).

Cognitive impulsivity.   In problem-solving situations, children differ from one another in their tendency to pause and "reflect" on the answer as opposed to choosing and answering impulsively. Kagan and his associates have devised a number of tests of this dimension (Kagan et al., 1964) and have some evidence that the tendency to be reflective or impulsive is a relatively enduring characteristic. Further, they have demonstrated that among first-graders, children who are relatively more reflective learn to read more readily than do more impulsive children (Kagan, 1965). There are several studies showing poor children to be more impulsive than middle-class children (Bee et al., 1968;

Mumbauer and Miller, 1970), and the greater impulsivity may thus interfere in some way with early reading, which would have more pervasive negative effects on school performance.

Some caution is in order, though, in interpreting these findings. There is quite good evidence for a general developmental shift from impulsivity toward reflection; older children and those with higher mental age (as measured on an IQ test) tend to be more reflective (Plomin and Buss, 1973; Achenbach and Weisz, 1975; Mumbauer and Miller, 1970). So it is possible that the greater cognitive impulsivity observed in many groups of poor children is merely another reflection of a somewhat slower rate of cognitive development. Mumbauer and Miller's findings support this interpretation. They found that poor children were more impulsive than middle-class children, but when IQ differences were controlled, the difference in impulsivity disappeared—that is, among children of equal mental age, poor children were *not* more impulsive than middle-class children. A further look at this question seems to be in order so that we can determine whether impulsivity is an *independent* characteristic of poor children or merely a reflection of other cognitive differences.

Emotional and social characteristics. As you have no doubt gathered from all the details I have already given, much of the research has been focused on the question of differences in cognitive development between poor and middle-class children. There is far less information about differences in personality characteristics, and the data we do have are more confusing. For example, do poor children have less favorable self-concepts? The information is both scanty and mixed. Whiteman and Deutsch (1968) found that children from families high on their "deprivation index" (which assessed the dilapidation of housing, the parents' educational aspirations for the children, number of children in the home, conversation at meals, "cultural experiences" available to the child, and kindergarten attendance) were lower in self-esteem. The children with poor self-concept also tended to do poorly in school compared to equivalently poor children from families with less deprived conditions as measured by the "deprivation index." This observed relationship between deprived homes, poor self-image, and poor school performance makes intuitive sense but has not been consistently supported by later studies. Trowbridge (1972), for example, in a study of almost 4000 children aged 8 to 14 in urban and rural areas, found that the lower-social-class children had consistently *more favorable* self-concepts than had the middle-class children, and this finding held for all ages and for both urban and rural groups. It does appear to be the case that children and adolescents who have unfavorable self-images are likely to do less well in school and are more likely to drop out of school (Berry, 1974), but there appears to be no consistent tendency for the poor child to have a less favorable self-image.

Other findings, not replicated but of interest, are the following: (a) Lower-class children tend to be lower in "achievement motivation," that is, the desire to compete successfully with a standard of excellence (Rosen, 1956). (b) Poor children seem to be somewhat more sensitive to both disapproval and approval. In one study in which approval or disapproval was given for performance of a simple task, Rosenhan (1966) found that the poverty children's performance declined more when they were given disapproval and improved more when they were given approval than did the performance of the middle-class children. (c) Poor children learn experimental tasks more rapidly when they are working for material rewards (such as candy) than when they are working for nonmaterial rewards (such as knowledge of results) (Terrel, Durkin, and Wiesley, 1959; Zigler and deLabry, 1962).

The most consistent finding in the area of personality differences is that poor children are more likely to believe that control of events and their own actions lies outside of themselves, whereas middle-class children are more likely to believe that they have control over their own actions and over other events (Battle and Rotter, 1963; Gruen, Korte, and Baum, 1974; Stephens and Delys, 1973.) Stephens and Delys, in particular, have explored this variable in preschool-age children and have shown that poor children enter preschool and elementary school with different expectancies already established about their own abilities to shape and influence events. Such differences appear to persist in elementary and high school and to influence school performance in various ways.

Health differences.   The subject of health differences is well covered in the excellent paper by Herbert Birch included in the selections. His paper and other evidence make it quite clear that the poorer the family, the poorer is the health status of the child and the mother. In particular, poverty conditions are accompanied by a substantial increase in complications surrounding pregnancy and birth and by poorer diet (Knobloch and Pasamanick, 1963).

The Counter-argument and Counter-evidence
It might appear that the weight of the evidence I've already given leads one inevitably to the conclusion that the poor child

does have some cognitive "deficits" that will affect his ability to perform in school or to learn in other situations. But many psychologists do *not* agree that this is the only possible conclusion from the data given, and have marshaled other evidence to support alternative interpretations. The counter-argument, essentially, is that the poor child is not deficient in basic cognitive skill, but that he is different in cultural patterns, in learning style, and in motivation, and that these differences account for the lower level of school and test performance.

One of the most articulate spokesmen for this alternative position is Herbert Ginsburg, whose book *The Myth of the Deprived Child* is a well-argued and carefully documented counter-argument to the "deficit" view. An excerpt from this book has been included in the selections so you can read for yourselves some of what he says. I will try here only to summarize his position briefly and to suggest the kind of evidence that can be offered to support his argument.

Ginsburg grants that children from poverty environments score lower on standard tests and that they do badly in school, but he does not take this as evidence that they are fundamentally less skilled or less competent. Instead, he takes it as evidence that the tests have not really measured the poor child's competence. The essence of his position is that there is a fundamental difference between competence and performance (see Glick, 1968, for an extensive discussion of this distinction).

The tests and the schools measure performance; they do not necessarily tap the child's fundamental ability. Most people who have worked with poor children have looked at the vast evidence showing that poverty-level children perform poorly and have concluded that the poor performance results from less competence. Ginsburg starts from the other end. He assumes that all children are basically equal in competence, that they all begin life with the same abilities to deal with their world, and that they proceed to do so, developing in the process a fixed sequence of logical abilities. Following Piaget, he emphasizes that the active, exploring child utilizes his particular environment to make cognitive progress and that the specific characteristics of the environment do not matter very much so long as there is sufficient variety of experience to provide the needed input. Given this overall assumption about the nature of cognitive development, it obviously follows that any differences we observe between the poor and the middle-class child are merely surface differences; they do not reflect what Ginsburg assumes to be fundamental equality of underlying competence. Why, then, does the poor child not perform as well? Presumably for several reasons. First, the tests have been designed to test middle-class children and may demand specific information that is more readily available to them. Second, and more importantly, with most measures of performance it is assumed that the child is motivated to do his best and understands that the test is in fact something to be taken seriously. If poor children are less motivated to perform in standard assessment situations or if they do not understand the demands of the situation, they may not perform as well. Thus one could have low performance without low competence.

Michael Cole (Cole and Hall, 1974; Cole and Bruner, 1971) has argued for a similar position. Cole suggests that the poor child comes to the school setting (and presumably to any testing situation as well) with a *different* (but not inferior) set of skills, attitudes, and strategies. Since the school, and the testing settings, are largely run by middle-class teachers and psychologists, the expectations of the settings do not "match" the child's entering behavior and attitudes. In Cole's view, it is this "mismatch" between what the child brings and what the situation demands that produces the observed lowered performance by poor children.

There is quite a lot of research evidence that can be mustered in support of these counterpositions. First, it is clear that the child's motivation and attitude about standard testing situations affect his test scores. Zigler and his associates in several studies (Zigler and Butterfield, 1968; Zigler, Abelson, and Seitz, 1973; Seitz, Abelson, Levine, and Zigler, 1975) have shown that the performance of poor children on standardized tests (Stanford-Binet or the Peabody Picture Vocabulary Test) can be significantly increased if the conditions of testing are altered. For example, if the testing is done under "optimizing" conditions in which easy and hard items are mixed, more time is given, and a greater encouragement is given to the child, preschool-age children show test score increases of about 10 points compared to their scores under standard conditions of test administration. And if the child has had a chance to play with the examiner before the test, disadvantaged preschool children show similar gains of about 10 points on tests given under standard conditions. Thus when testing conditions are altered to reduce strain and anxiety, poor children perform significantly better.

Improvements in test performance may also be obtained for poor black students if the tests are given in their own idiomatic English, rather than in "standard English" (see Cole and Hall,

1974, for a review of some of these studies). Language may mask the child's cognitive competence in other ways. Anastasiow and Hanes (1974), for example, compared the performance of poor black children on several Piagetian tasks with that of poor rural white and middle-class white children. The performance of the poor blacks was consistently lower. *But* if the black child's nonstandard English constructions are considered as correct, the difference disappears. Anastasiow and Hanes argue that differences in the surface structure of the language thus cannot be taken as evidence of differences in underlying cognitive competencies.

Other findings on early language development support the contention that the basic structures of language develop at about the same rate in the poverty-level child as in the middle-class child. Thus while measures of vocabulary typically show social-class differences, measures of the rate of development of grammatical features or sentence complexity typically do *not* show social-class differences (see Dale, 1976, or Ginsburg, 1972, for reviews of this evidence). One can suggest from this that although the specifically experiential part of language (the vocabulary) does differ as a function of social class, the *logical* part of language (namely the grammar) does not. Or, put another way, one can perhaps argue that grammatical skills reflect basic competence more directly than do vocabulary skills, and since poor children apparently do not differ from middle-class children in the rate of grammatical development, this is evidence that their developing logical competencies are equivalent.

A final line of argument on the counter-argument side is the evidence Ginsburg presents (in the excerpt in the selections) on the performance of children from differing backgrounds on Piagetian tests. Ginsburg and others have argued that tests based on Piagetian theory come closer to assessing underlying cognitive competencies than do standardized IQ or achievement tests. The evidence Ginsburg cites shows quite clearly that on Piagetian measures the *sequence* of cognitive development is much the same across cultures and across social-class groups in our own culture.

This argument cuts both ways, however. Although it is true that the sequence remains pretty constant across cultures and social classes, the *rate* of development does not. There is now quite a substantial body of evidence showing that poor children perform consistently less well on tests and measures designed to assess the kinds of basic competencies Piaget talks of. Gaudia (1972) and Almy, Chittenden, and Miller (1966) found that poor children were slower in developing concepts of conservation; Wei, Lavatelli, and Jones (1971) found poor children to be slower in development of classification skills, as did Overton, Wagner, and Dolinsky (1971). If we accept the notion that tests of classification or conservation tap more fundamental processes than do standard IQ tests, then these findings show that poor children are developing basic cognitive skills more slowly. Although they may be on the same track, and may reach the same competency levels eventually, at any given age or grade, many poor children will be at a "lower" developmental level than their middle-class peers. Of course, the difficulty here is that all of the studies of Piagetian concepts are still assessing *performance,* and all the situational and motivational factors that affect performance on standardized tests no doubt affect performance on Piagetian concept tests as well. Research like that of Zigler and his colleagues certainly points to the fact that the gap in cognitive skills between the poor and the middle class is much smaller than earlier "deficit" conceptions would have suggested, but there may still be a gap, with poor children proceeding through the several stages and skills at a somewhat slower rate.

The Third Alternative: Genetic Differences

A word, however brief, must be said about a third possible alternative, namely, that children from poverty environments show poor performance on various kinds of tests and in school because they are simply genetically less bright. Arthur Jensen (1969) in his highly controversial article has suggested something like this. As comment, let me make only three points.

First, no psychologist I know of disputes the assertion that a good portion of the variation in scores on a standard IQ test is determined by genetic differences. Jensen suggests that about 80 percent of the variance is accounted for by heredity; Scarr-Salapatek (1975) suggests that the figure should be more like 50 percent; but virtually everyone agrees that the contribution of genetic differences to measured IQ is substantial. (I should mention that our knowledge of heritability of IQ is almost entirely restricted to studies of whites, so we do not really know much about heritability in other groups.)

Second, it is *not* legitimate to go from statements about heritability of IQ of individuals to statements about groups or group differences. The tendency is to say, "Well, if IQ is inherited that much, inheritance must explain the difference between the poor and the affluent or between blacks and whites." But the argument *simply does not follow.* It is entirely possible for IQ to have as high a degree of heritability as Jensen suggests and still have differences between *groups* that are entirely the result of environment.[1]

Third, how *are* we to account for group differences in IQ (between poor and middle class, or between black and white, for example)? The point I have just made is that we cannot automatically conclude that the difference is genetic in origin just because we know that IQ test scores are highly heritable. But equally, we cannot assume that all of the group differences can be accounted for by environment, either, just because we know that differences in environment have an effect. You must keep in mind that there are no findings that permit you to exclude genetic variation as an explanation of social-class differences in IQ. However, all the evidence on the effects of environmental variations suggests that a good portion of the social-class difference in IQ we observe may be due to environmental variation. Recent research by Scarr-Salapatek and Weinberg (1975) underlines this possibility still further. They have studied a group of black children, nearly all born to lower-class or less-educated mothers, adopted into middle-class, well-educated white families. The adopted children's average IQ was about 15 points higher than what one would have predicted from the natural mother's education or IQ, and the adopted children performed at an average or above average level in school. In this particular study, the environmental factors appeared to be accounting for more of the variance in the children's IQ than did genetic factors. "Cross-fostering" research of this kind may make it possible to draw

[1] Because this is a difficult concept to grasp, let me give an example. In small villages in the rural areas of Mexico, the people are quite a bit shorter than the people in the larger cities, such as Mexico City. Height, as you probably know, is a highly heritable trait; this is as true in the Mexican villages—where the tallest children are born to the tallest parents—as in the city. So there is high heritability within each group. But what about the difference between the groups? Is that difference the result of hereditary differences between the village and city people? The city families do not have more "tall" genes. The group difference is apparently largely the result of diet. When the diet of the village people is improved, the grow as tall as the city people. So you have a situation in which there is high heritability within each group, but the difference between the two groups is largely environmental.

Another delightful example is given by Ken Kaye in his review of Eysenck's book, *The IQ Argument*. Kaye says,

Imagine, for example, that we test all white Americans, but just before giving the test we give away some of the answers to everyone whose name begins with a letter from A to M. Suppose we give away just enough answers so that each person in the A–M group gets a score 15 points higher than he would have otherwise. This raises their average score 15 points above that of the N–Z group. The heritability will still be just as high within each group—because we will have done nothing to increase the variance within either group—but the 15-point difference between the two groups will have nothing to do with heritability (Kaye, 1972).

firmer conclusions about the potential explanations of group differences in IQ.

Synthesis

Excluding the genetic argument for now and concentrating only on the traditional and counter-evidence, how do we put the two alternative positions together? There is good evidence on each side and it is obviously impossible to choose one as completely "true." I suspect we will find, as is often the case in such debates, that the truth lies somewhere in the middle. My own views about a reasonable synthesis or "middle-ground" position have shifted over the past decade, so you should not take my conclusions as gospel. If you are interested in this set of questions and problems, look at the evidence for yourself, and draw your own conclusions. But for what it may be worth as a guide to your thinking, here is my own current synthesis.

First, I think that Ginsburg, Cole, and others have made valid points about the fundamental similarity of thinking among all children. The broad sequence of cognitive development seems to be extremely durable in the face of wide variations in enviornment. Second, it seems clear that poor children, and perhaps more particularly minority group children, enter school and testing settings with somewhat different sets of expectations, motivations, and social skills. These differences undoubtedly affect the teacher-child interaction, particularly since most teachers come from the white middle-class culture. Some of the lowered school performance of poor and minority group children can probably be traced to this source. When a better "match" between the child's characteristics and the style of teaching can be achieved, there may be improvements in performance by such children (see Cole and Hall, 1974, for a review of several unpublished studies of this type). Overall, I can agree with Seitz and her associates when they state that "A consensus has developed that the intellectual competence of economically disadvantaged children is greater than is generally shown by their performance on standardized tests" (Seitz et al., 1975, p. 481).

But I am not persuaded that there is *no* difference in intellectual competence between poor and middle-class children. I have several reasons for concluding that there are some "real" differences in cognitive competence. First, whereas "optimizing" testing conditions do result in improved performance by poor children, even under such conditions the difference between the poor and the middle-class children is not eliminated. For example, Lesser and his colleagues (1965) found performance differences even when carefully optimized testing procedures were used. They not only tested the child in his native language, they also used as many testing sessions as were necessary, did not start the testing until the child was thoroughly familiar with the testing situation and the materials, set no time limits on the tests, and rewrote the tests to include only items with which all groups might reasonably be familiar. Even under these unusually careful methodological conditions, differences between poor and middle-class children were observed in all the ethnic groups studied. They also made an effort to measure the child's motivation and responsiveness to the tester, and found that these factors could not account for the social-class differences they found. To be sure, the tests used are still measures of perhaps "surface performance," but the differences do not disappear when one is careful and fair about the measurement procedures and when motivational factors are equalized as much as possible.

Second, I am struck by the findings of social-class differences in *rate* of progress through the cognitive development stages outlined by Piaget. Poor children do not do less well only on standardized IQ and achievement tests, as I mentioned earlier, they also do less well on measures of multiple classification, conservation, and other measures based on Piaget's theories. I think these findings support the hypothesis that many children from poverty environments develop cognitively *more slowly* than do middle-class children. Such a slower rate of development would be reflected not only in lower IQ scores but also in school performance, and may be a contributor to the differences in style and motivation that Cole and Ginsburg and others have emphasized. For example, if greater cognitive "impulsivity" is a characteristic of children who are developmentally younger, then more poor first-grade children would be impulsive and might therefore have greater difficulty in learning to read. Impulsivity would then be seen not as an exclusive or dominant characteristic of poverty, but as a feature of a particular level of cognitive development.

In sum, I think there is probably a far smaller difference in basic cognitive competence between poor and middle-class children than the traditional "deficit" hypothesis would suggest, but there is *some* difference.

EXPLANATIONS OF THE EFFECTS OF POVERTY
If you have taken the position that poor children are essentially the same as non-poor children in cognitive competence, then there is nothing further to explain. But if you have taken the

position, as I and others have, that some kinds of deficits or a slowing down of cognitive development are associated with poverty circumstances, it becomes important to try to specify what it is about poverty environments that has such an effect. To talk about a poverty environment as having *caused* intellectual retardation is a gross oversimplification. Poverty environments are not all alike and the children who come out of them are not all alike. What we need are some explanations that suggest more precisely what kinds of early environmental experiences may produce the observed effects.

At least three types of explanations have been offered, all focusing on different aspects of the environment.

Health Differences as Cause

Increasing attention has recently been paid to health factors as possible causes of the observed cognitive "deficits" in children from poverty environments. Birch's review (1972) shows that there is increased risk of prenatal and postnatal traumas for poor infants. And as research on animals has accumulated showing that dietary deficiency produces slower development and slower learning in offspring, there has been a sharply increased interest in the possibility that the same relationship may hold for children. There are at least two questions about this literature that must be answered before we can have any sense of the adequacy of health factors as explanations of poor intellectual performance of poor children. (1) Does dietary deficiency in children produce any kind of demonstrable learning problems or deficits? That is, can we generalize from the animal data to children? (2) How widespread is severe or moderate malnutrition among the poor in this country?

When I wrote this section for the first edition of this book, nearly everyone was comfortable with the assertion that protein-calorie malnutrition *does* have detrimental effects on neurological development in children, and that those neurological effects, in turn, affect the child's cognitive development. There are several good reviews of this literature (Vore, 1973; Scrimshaw, 1969; Birch, 1972; Brockman and Ricciuti, 1971), and these reviewers are in agreement that malnutrition *in utero* and during the first months after birth may result in a reduction of the number of brain cells developed. Some investigators have estimated the potential loss in number of brain cells from prolonged prenatal and postnatal malnutrition as high as 60 percent. Animal research also shows that animals malnourished prenatally or in the early postnatal weeks are slower to learn in standard situations; there is some evidence that the same is true for children (Richardson, Birch, and Hertzig, 1973).

There is also a limited body of literature showing that dietary supplements or improvements for children living in poverty circumstances can yield increased scores on standard tests (Ebbs, Brown, Tisdall, Moyle, and Bell, 1942; Ramey, Starr, Pallus, Whitten, and Reed, 1975).

While it may seem very clear and straightforward that malnutrition in the early months of life has detrimental effects on cognitive development in children, the fly in the ointment is a single, impressive study of children born in the Netherlands during a period of famine in World War II (Stein, Susser, Saenger, and Marolla, 1975). Because the Dutch keep excellent records, it was possible to trace the majority of children who had been born during or just after a period of extreme famine (1944–1945), and to see what happened to them over the intervening 20 years. The results do *not* show that this particular group of individuals were lower in performance in any definable way. Stein and her colleagues do agree that there was probably "brain cell depletion" for those infants who experienced severe malnutrition *in utero*. But this early neurological effect seems not to have had any *lasting* effect on the children's ability to function. We need to be cautious about drawing too sweeping conclusions from these results. There was apparently no *post*natal malnutrition for any of these children, and the nutrition for the remainder of their lives was good. So the absence of long-term effects does not mean that postnatal or both prenatal and postnatal malnutrition would have no impact. But the findings suggest that there may be more redundancy in brain cells than we supposed and that the duration of malnutrition would have to be quite lengthy before clear and lasting behavioral results would be seen.

Other research of this kind, if circumstances permit it, would be extremely helpful. For now, this single study must call into question the assumption that poor diet in the early months and years of life may be helping to produce the lowered school and test performance of poverty-level children. This is not to say that *ongoing* malnutrition has no effect. Children who are moderately or severely malnourished may be listless and inattentive, and these qualities must affect not only their learning interactions with the environment but also their performance in school and on tests.

Moderate or severe malnutrition is fairly common among the poor in this country, as Birch suggests (see also Chase et al., 1971; Christakis et al., 1968; Owen and Kram, 1969). In general, the lower the income of the family, the greater the likelihood of poor nutrition, particularly inadequate iron intake (which leads to iron deficiency anemia) and inadequate total caloric intake. Most of the malnutrition noted in studies of children and adults in the United States is moderate to mild; it is not severe enough to require hospitalization of the child. There is *some* evidence that these more moderate levels of malnutrition have effects on the child's concurrent school performance (see, for example, Hertzig, Tizard, Birch, and Richardson, referred to in Birch, 1972), but more research is needed here.

I am no longer as confident as I once was that a large part of the poorer performance of children from low-income families may be laid at the door of inadequate diet. But *some* of the performance deficit may well be the result of generally poorer health and nutritional status.

Insufficient Environmental Stimulation as Cause

A second view of the causal factors in poverty environments focuses primarily on the inanimate environment surrounding the child. What kinds of toys are available? What opportunities for play? We know from research on institutionalized infants that one of the necessary ingredients for normal development is the opportunity to move around, to play with objects, and to explore the environment (see, for example, Dennis, 1960). It seems logical to extrapolate from the institutional environment to the poverty environment and to look to the characteristics of the stimulation available to the infant as a primary cause. The "deprivation index" that Whiteman and Deutsch developed in the study discussed earlier is an example of one effort to specify some kinds of stimulation variables more precisely (although they also include some "animate" stimulation variables in their index). In support of the notion that the amount or variety of stimulation may make a difference, they report that children who are high on the deprivation index show a deterioration in school performance between grades 1 and 5, whereas children from the same neighborhood who are not high on the deprivation index do not show this decline in performance over time.

Further, there is evidence that poverty homes and middle-class homes differ on some dimensions of amount and variety of stimulation. Tulkin (1970), for example, examined 10-month-old infants from working-class and professional families. The working-class infants in his sample had fewer objects to play with and spent less time in free exploration without barriers than did the middle-class infants. Middle-class mothers more often gave their infants objects to play with and the infants played more often. In a longitudinal follow-up of this group of children at ages 5 to 6 years (Tulkin and Covitz, 1975), those children who had had more environmental objects (toys) and had spent less time in the playpen had higher scores on measures of language and IQ at ages 5 to 6. Tulkin does not suggest that the experiences in infancy *caused* the later test performance; rather he suggests that the mothers' behavior with the child and the characteristics of the inanimate environment during the child's infancy are reflections of *enduring* environmental differences between the social-class groups and among families within each social-class group.

Other evidence that differences in variety, complexity, and "responsiveness" of the inanimate envirionment predicts an infant's cognitive functioning comes from a study by Yarrow and his associates (Yarrow, Rubenstein, Pederson, and Jankowski, 1972). They studied 5-month-old infants in their homes, observing both the inanimate and animate stimulation available to the child. The infants were also tested in a variety of ways. The researchers found that the complexity and variety of inanimate stimulation was related to the infants' exploratory behavior and to their goal-directed behaviors. Infants who were surrounded with a wider variety of objects and toys and with objects that were more complex and more "responsive" (for example, objects that changed as a result of the infant's action) showed more exploratory behavior when presented with novel objects and more persistence in trying to reach goals.

Although this research did not include any poverty-level infants, it highlights the fact that aspects of the inanimate environment may indeed be crucial in some areas of cognitive development. Tulkin's research, in turn, shows that there may be differences between poor and middle-class homes (on the average) in precisely those dimensions that affect cognitive growth.

Style of Social Interaction as Cause

Another equally important aspect of the environment experienced by the infant and child is the nature of the animate stimulation. A number of studies give evidence that middle-class mothers and poverty-level mothers differ in the amount they talk to their children, starting when the child is an infant. Kilbride, Johnson, and Streissguth (1971) found such differences in mothers of 2-week-old infants; Tulkin (1970) found the same in mothers of 10-month-old infants. There is also consistent evidence that mothers from lower-class environments (or those with less education) are more critical of their children. They tell the child more often when he has done something wrong and praise him less often when he has done something right (Bee et al., 1969; Streissguth and Bee, 1972; Hess and Shipman, 1965, 1967). So we know there are differences in the patterns of interaction between mother and child in families of differing social class, but do we know whether these differences are related to the child's cognitive development? There are several lines of evidence.

Hess's work on the problem is best known. He has called attention in particular to the "mother's strategies for orienting the child toward selected cues in the environment, the types of regulatory or control techniques she uses, and her patterning of stimuli to organize information for the child" (Hess, 1970, p. 515). Does the mother emphasize that the child should do something "because I say so" (that is, because it is a rule), or does she emphasize that the child should do something because if he does not, someone's feelings will be hurt, or because the consequences of the action will be beneficial to the child, or because of some other "rational" or "social-emotional" reason? Hess and Shipman (1967) have reported that mothers from poverty environments are much more likely to resort to appeals to status or rules; middle-class mothers more often use the rational or social-emotional approach. Further, Hess and his associates have found that these differences in maternal style not only predicted the child's concurrent cognitive functioning, with status and rule orientations on the part of the mother being associated with poorer intellectual performance in the child, but that they also predicted the child's later performance in school (Hess, Shipman, Brophy, and Bear, 1969).

There is very good evidence from other sources, too, that the manner in which parents (most often mothers) relate to their infants and young children and the type and timing of stimulation they provide are related to or predict the child's cognitive development. Yarrow and his associates (1972) found that *animate* stimulation (primarily stimulation from the caregiver) was related to the child's general mental development and to language development. Mothers who provided a greater variety and a greater amount of stimulation to their infants (talking, holding, and so on) had infants who scored higher on the standard infant scales and showed more vocalization in test situations. Clarke-Stewart (1973) has similarly found 9- to 18-month-old children to show more rapid cognitive development on a number of measures when mothers are affectionate, provide social stimulation and play materials, spend time playing with the child, and when their reactions to the infant are *contingent* on the child's behavior. In particular, mothers who provided rich language stimulation had infants who showed more rapid language development.

Tulkin's research (Tulkin, 1970; Tulkin and Covitz, 1975) links these findings to social class. In his research, middle-class mothers were more likely to talk to their infants, and those infants, at age 6, showed higher scores on measures of language skill. Tulkin and Covitz also report that the total amount of time the mother had spent with the infant and the number of play episodes predicted the child's later language development.

I want to emphasize that through all of this discussion I have been talking about *group* differences between poor and middle-class children and families. I do not want you to carry away from this discussion the idea that *all* poor families are alike, any more than that all middle-class families are alike. They are not, and neither are the children who emerge from these families. But what this research does point to are the dimensions of early experience and parent-child interaction that may be related to or predictive of the child's cognitive development. If these dimensions are in fact important, we should find that they predict the child's intellectual progress as well *within* social-class groups as between groups. Generally that is the case. In Hess and Shipman's work, the poor mothers who used the most rational or social-emotional controls had children who were more likely to do well in school than were the children of poor mothers who used primarily rules; among the middle-class families, those in which the mothers were the most rule-oriented had children whose school performance was likely to be least good. Similarly, in Tulkin's research, although the relationships between the mother's behavior with the infant and the child's later cognitive skill were stronger for the middle class mothers, generally the same type of relationships held for both groups.

Obviously we are a long way from being able to specify the precise characteristics of any envirionment that promote or impede normal intellectual development. It is clear, however, that some aspects of both the animate and the inanimate early environment are important and that poor and non-poor families are likely to differ on some of the apparently critical dimensions. What is needed now is a greater number of studies like that of Yarrow and his associates or Clarke-Stewart's, in which the characteristics of the environment are carefully specified and the child's competence is assessed in a variety of ways.

QUESTIONS FOR DEBATE AND DISCUSSION
1. Given all that you have read, what do you think is the validity of a "deficit" description of the poverty child? Are you persuaded by Ginsburg's or Cole's argument? If so, why? If not, why not?
2. How would each of the explanations of the effects of poverty discussed in the Overview affect public policy? What kinds of federal or local programs would be appropriate given the

assumptions in each case? (You might want to take a look at Part IV, "Compensatory Education," before you answer this question. Some public policies have been attempted, so we have some information about the success or failure of several policy approaches.)

ADDITIONAL REFERENCES USEFUL
IN PREPARATION FOR DEBATE OR DISCUSSION

Deutsch, C. P. Social class and child development. In B. M. Caldwell and H. N. Ricciuti (Eds.), *Review of child development research*. Vol. 3. Chicago: University of Chicago Press, 1973, pp. 233–282.

An absolutely first-rate paper, essential reading if you are interested in or involved in some way in this set of issues. She discusses public policy issues, as well as factual matters.

Deutsch, M. (Ed.) *The disadvantaged child*. New York: Basic Books, 1967.

A now somewhat out-of-date book, but with some good papers included.

Ginsburg, H. *The myth of the deprived child*. Englewood Cliffs, N.J.: Prentice-Hall, 1972.

The whole book should be read by anyone proposing to debate the set of issues discussed in this chapter.

Scarr-Salapatek, S. Genetics and the development of intelligence. In F. D. Horowitz (Ed.), *Review of child development research,* Vol. 4. Chicago: University of Chicago Press, 1975, pp. 1–58.

For those of you interested in the genetic argument, this is the best source I can suggest for you. It is somewhat technical but clear and thorough.

Vore, D. A. Prenatal nutrition and postnatal intellectual development. *Merrill-Palmer Quarterly,* 1973, **19,** 253–260.

One of the most recent reviews of the data on nutrition and cognition; useful as a source of other references.

REFERENCES

Achenbach, T. M., and Weisz, J. R. Impulsivity-reflectivity and cognitive development in preschoolers: A longitudinal analysis of development and trait variance. *Developmental Psychology,* 1975, **11,** 413–414.

Almy, M., Chittenden, E., and Miller, P. *Young children's thinking: Studies of some aspects of Piaget's theory.* New York: Teachers College Press, 1966.

Anastasiow, N. J., and Hanes, M. L. Cognitive development and the acquisition of language in three subcultural groups. *Developmental Psychology,* 1974, **10,** 703–709.

Battle, E. S., and Rotter, J. E. Children's feeling of personal control as related to social class and ethnic groups. *Journal of Personality,* 1963, **31,** 482–490.

Bayley, N. Comparisons of mental and motor test scores for ages 1–15 months by sex, birth order, race, and geographical location, and education of parents. *Child Development,* 1965, **36,** 379–411.

Bee, H. L., Nyman, B. A., Pytkowicz, A. R., Sarason, I. G., and Van Egeren, L. A study of cognitive and motivational variables in lower and middle-class preschool children: An approach to the evaluation of the impact of Head Start. Vol. 1. University of Washington Social Change Evaluation Project, Contract 1375, Office of Economic Opportunity, 1968.

Bee, H. L., Van Egeren, L. F., Streissguth, A. P., Nyman, B. A., and Leckie, M. S. Social class differences in maternal teaching strategies and speech patterns. *Developmental Psychology,* 1969, **1,** 726–734.

Berry, G. L. Self-concept and need factors of inner city high school adolescents and dropouts. *Child Study Journal,* 1974, **4,** 21–31.

Birch, H. G. Malnutrition, learning and intelligence. *American Journal of Public Health,* 1972, **62,** 773–784.

Brockman, L. M., and Ricciuti, H. N. Severe protein-calorie malnutrition and cognitive development in infancy and early childhood. *Developmental Psychology,* 1971, **4,** 312–319.

Chase, H. P., Kumar, V., Dodds, J. M., Sauberlich, H. E., Hunter, R. M., Burton, R. S., and Spalding, V. Nutritional status of preschool Mexican-American migrant farm children. *American Journal of Diseases of Children,* 1971, **122,** 316–324.

Christakis, G., Miridjanian, A., Nath, L., Khurana, H. S., Cowell, C., Archer, M., Frank, O., Ziffer, H., Baker, H., and James, C. A nutritional epidemiologic investigation of 642 New York City children. *American Journal of Clinical Nutrition,* 1968, **21,** 107–126.

Clarke-Stewart, K. A. Interactions between mothers and their young children: Characteristics and consequences. Monographs of The Society for Research in Child Development, 1973, **38** (Whole No. 153).

Cole, M., and Bruner, J. S. Cultural differences and inferences about psychological processes. *American Psychologist,* 1971, **26,** 867–876.

Cole, M., and Hall, W. S. The social context of psychoeducational research. Paper presented in the Series on Public Policy, Center for Urban Studies, Harvard University, May 1974.

Coleman, J. S. *Equality of educational opportunity.* Washington, D.C.: United States Government Printing Office, 1966.

Dale, P. S. *Language Development: Structure and function.* (2nd ed.) Hinsdale, Ill.: Dryden Press, 1976.

Dennis, W., Causes of retardation among institutional children: Iran. *Journal of Genetic Psychology,* 1960, **96,** 47–59.

Deutsch, C. P. Social class and child development. In B. M. Caldwell and H. N. Ricciuti (Eds.), *Review of child development research.* Vol. 3. Chicago: University of Chicago Press, 1973, pp. 233–282.

Ebbs, J. H., Brown, A., Tisdall, F. F., Moyle, W. J., and Bell, M. The influence of improved prenatal nutrition upon the infant. *Canadian Medical Association Journal,* 1942, **608.**

Gaudia, G. Race, social class, and age of achievement of conservation on Piaget's tasks. *Developmental Psychology,* 1972, **6,** 158–165.

Ginsburg, H. *The myth of the deprived child.* Englewood Cliffs, N.J.: Prentice-Hall, 1972.

Glick, J. Some problems in the evaluation of preschool intervention programs. In R. Hess and R. Bear (Eds.), *Early education.* Chicago: Aldine, 1968.

Gray, S. W., and Klaus, R. A. The Early Training Project: A seventh-year report. *Child Development,* 1970, **41,** 909–924.

Gruen, G. E., Korte, J. R., and Baum, J. K. Group measures of locus of control. *Developmental Psychology,* 1974, **10,** 683–686.

Hess, R. D. Social class and ethnic influences on socialization. In P. H. Mussen (Ed.), *Carmichael's manual of child psychology.* (3rd ed.) Vol. 2. New York: Wiley, 1970, pp. 457–557.

Hess, R. D., and Shipman, V. C. Early experience and the socialization of cognitive modes in children. *Child Development,* 1965, **34,** 869–886.

Hess, R. D., and Shipman, V. C. Cognitive elements in maternal behavior. In J. P. Hill (Ed.), *Minnesota symposia on child psychology.* Vol. 1. Minneapolis: University of Minnesota Press, 1967.

Hess, R. D., Shipman, V. C., Brophy, J. E., and Bear, R. M. *The cognitive environments of urban preschool children: Follow-up phase.* Chicago: The Graduate School of Education, The University of Chicago, 1969.

Hill, E. H., and Giammateo, M. C. Socioeconomic status and its relationship to school achievement in the elementary school. *Elementary English,* 1963, **50,** 265–270.

Jensen, A. R. How much can we boost IQ and scholastic achievement? *Harvard Educational Review,* 1969, **39,** 1–123.

Jones, H. E. The environment and mental development. In L. Carmichael (Ed.), *Manual of child psychology.* (2nd ed.) New York: Wiley, 1954, pp. 631–696.

Kagan, J. Reflection-impulsivity and reading ability in primary grade children. *Child Development,* 1965, **36,** 609–628.

Kagan, J., Rosman, B. L., Day, D., Albert, J., and Phillips, W. Information processing in the child: Significance of analytic and reflective attitudes. *Psychological Monographs,* 1964, **78** (1, Whole No. 578).

Kaye, K. Review of H. J. Eysenck, The IQ argument: Race, intelligence and education. *Adult Education,* 1972, **22,** 229–233.

Kennedy, W. Z., Van de Reit, V., and White, J. C., Jr. A normative sample of intelligence and achievement of Negro elementary school children in the southereastern United States. *Monographs of the Society for Research in Child Development,* 1963, **28** (6).

Kilbride, H., Johnson, D., and Streissguth, A. P. Early home experience of newborns as a function of social class, infant sex, and birth order. Unpublished manuscript, University of Washington, 1971.

Knobloch, H., and Pasamanick, B. Predicting intellectual potential in infancy. *American Journal of Diseases of Children,* 1963, **106,** 43–51.

Lesser, G. S., Fifer, G., and Clark, D. H. Mental abilities of children from different social class and cultural groups. *Monographs of the Society for Research in Child Development,* 1965, **30** (4).

Mumbauer, C. C., and Miller, J. O. Socioeconomic background and cognitive functioning in preschool children. *Child Development,* 1970, **41,** 471–480.

Overton, W. F., Wagner, J., and Dolinsky, H. Social-class differences and task variables in the development of multiplicative classification. *Child Development,* 1971, **42,** 1951–1958.

Owen, G. M., and Kram, K. M. Nutritional status of preschool children in Mississippi: Food Sources of nutrients in the diets. *Journal of the American Dietary Association,* 1969, **54,** 490–494.

Plomin, R., and Buss, A. H. Reflection-impulsivity and intelligence. *Psychological Reports,* 1973, **33,** 726.

Profiles of Children. (1970 White House Conference on Children) Washington, D.C.: United States Government Printing Office, 1970.

Ramey, C. T., Starr, R. H., Pallus, J., Whitten, C. F., and Reed, V. Nutrition, response-contingent stimulation, and the maternal deprivation syndrome: results of an early intervention program. *Merrill-Palmer Quarterly,* 1975, **21,** 45–54.

Richardson, S. A., Birch, H. G., and Hertzig, M. E. School performance of children who were severely malnourished in infancy. *American Journal of Mental Deficiency,* 1973, **77,** 623–632.

Rosen, B. C. The achievement syndrome: A psychocultural dimension of social stratification. *American Sociological Review,* 1956, **21,** 203–211.

Rosenhan, D. L. Effects of social class and race on responsiveness to approval and disapproval. *Journal of Personality and Social Psychology,* 1966, **4,** 253–259.

Scarr-Salapatek, S. Genetics and the development of intelligence. In F. D. Horowitz (Ed.), *Review of child development research.* Vol. 4. Chicago: The University of Chicago Press, 1975, pp. 1–58.

Scarr-Salapatek, S., and Weinberg, R. A. IQ test performance of black children adopted by white families. Paper presented at the biennial meetings of The Society for Research in Child Development, Denver, 1975.

Scrimshaw, N. Early malnutrition and CNS function. *Merrill-Palmer Quarterly,* 1969, **15,** 375–388.

Seitz, V., Abelson, W. D., Levine, E., and Zigler, E. Effects of place of testing on the Peabody Picture Vocabulary Test scores of disadvantaged Head Start and non-Head Start children. *Child Development,* 1975, **46,** 481–486.

Sigel, I. E., Anderson, L. M., and Shapiro, H. Categorization behavior of lower- and middle-class Negro preschool children: Differences in dealing with representation of familiar objects. *Journal of Negro Education,* 1966, **35,** 218–229.

Sigel, I. E., and McBane, B. Cognitive competence and level of symbolization among five-year-old children. In J. Hellmuth (Ed.), *Disadvantaged child,* Vol. 1. Seattle: Special Child Publications, 1967.

Stein, Z., Susser, M., Saenger, G., and Marolla, F. *Famine and human development. The Dutch hunger winter of 1944–1945.* New York: Oxford University Press, 1975.

Stephens, M. W., and Delys, P. External control expectancies among disadvantaged children at preschool age. *Child Development,* 1973, **44,** 670–674.

Stodolsky, S., Maternal behavior and language and concept formation in Negro preschool children: An inquiry into process. Unpublished doctoral dissertation, Department of Psychology, University of Chicago, 1965.

Stodolsky, S. S., and Lesser, G. Learning patterns in the disadvantaged. *Harvard Educational Review,* 1967, **37,** 546–593.

Streissguth, A. P., and Bee, H. L. Mother-child interactions and cognitive development in children. In W. W. Hartup (Ed.), *The young child: Reviews of research.* Vol. 2. Washington, D.C.: National Association for the Education of Young Children, 1972, pp. 158–183.

Templin, M. C. *Certain language skills in children: Their development and interrelationships.* Minneapolis: University of Minnesota Press, 1957.

Terrel, G., Jr., Durkin, K., and Wiesley, M. Social class and the nature of the incentive in discrimination learning. *Journal of Abnormal and Social Psychology,* 1959, **59,** 270–272.

Trowbridge, N. Self-concept and socio-economic status in elementary school children. *American Education Research Journal,* 1972, **9,** 525–537.

Tulkin, S. R. Mother-infant interaction: Social class differences in the first year of life. Paper presented to the American Psychological Association, Miami, Fla., September, 1970.

Tulkin, S. R., and Covitz, F. E. Mother-infant interaction and intellectual functioning at age six. Paper presented at the biennial meetings of The Society for Research in Child Development, Denver, 1975.

Vore, D. A. Prenatal nutrition and postnatal intellectual development. *Merrill-Palmer Quarterly,* 1973, **19,** 253–260.

Wei, T. T. D., Lavatelli, D. B., and Jones, R. S. Piaget's concept of classification: A comparative study of socially disadvantaged and middle-class young children. *Child Development,* 1971, **52,** 919–927.

Whiteman, M., and Deutsch, M. Social disadvantage as related to intellective and language development. In M. Deutsch, I. Katz, and A. R. Jensen (Eds.), *Social class, race and psychological development.* New York: Holt, Rinehart and Winston, 1968.

Yarrow, L. J., Rubenstein, J. L., Pederson, F. A., and Jankowski, J. J. Dimensions of early stimulation and their differential effects on infant development. *Merrill-Palmer Quarterly,* 1972, **18,** 205–218.

Zigler, E., Abelson, W. D., and Seitz, V. Motivational factors in the performance of economically disadvantaged children on the Peabody Picture Vocabulary Test. *Child Development,* 1973, **44,** 294–303.

Zigler, E., and Butterfield, E. C. Motivational aspects of changes in IQ test performance of culturally deprived nursery school children. *Child Development,* 1968, **39,** 1–14.

Zigler, E., and deLabry, J. Concept-switching in middle-class, lower-class and retarded children. *Journal of Abnormal and Social Psychology,* 1962, **56,** 267–273.

Social class differentiation in cognitive development among black preschool children

MARK GOLDEN
BEVERLY BIRNS
WAGNER BRIDGER
ABIGAIL MOSS

It is of theoretical and practical importance to determine when social-class differences in intellectual performance first emerge and to identify the specific deficiencies which prevent many lower-class children from achieving academically. It might then be possible to discover the causal mechanisms or factors which account for social-class differences in cognitive development. Only on the basis of such information can optimally timed and really effective compensatory education programs be designed.

In a cross-sectional study reported previously (Golden and Birns 1968), we compared 192 black children of 12, 18, and 24 months of age from three socioeconomic-status (SES) groups on

From *Child Development*, 1971, **42**. Copyright © 1971 by The Society for Research in Child Development, Inc. Reprinted by permission.

Revised for publication from a paper presented at the 1969 meeting of The Society for Research in Child Development, Santa Monica, California. The study was supported by grant HDMH-01926 from the National Institute of Child Health and Human Development and by grant MH15458 from the National Institute of Mental Health.

the Cattell Infant Intelligence Scale and the Piaget Object Scale. Children from the following SES groups were studied:

    A. Welfare families: Neither mother nor father was employed or going to school; family on welfare.
    B. Lower-educational-achievement families: Neither parent had any schooling beyond high school.
    C. Higher-educational-achievement families: Either mother or father had some schooling beyond high school (from a few months of secretarial school to completion of medical training).

Ninety-three percent of the Group A children were from fatherless families, in contrast to 5 percent of the B and 0 percent of the C children. Contrary to our expectations, we did not find any social-class differences in either the Cattell or the Object Scale scores during the first 2 years of life.

The present paper is a report of a longitudinal follow-up study in which children in the 18- and 24-month samples of the cross-sectional study were retested on the Stanford-Binet at 3 years of age. The purpose of the follow-up study was to see whether the same pattern of social-class differentiation in cognitive development, emerging during the third year of life, reported for white children was also present in black children (Hindley, 1962; Terman and Merrill, 1937; Willerman, Sledge, and Fiedler, 1969).

In the present study, only black children from different social-class groups were compared. In this respect, it differs from other studies (Knobloch and Pasamanick, 1960; Wachs, Uzgiris, and Hunt, 1967) which include both black and white children, where race and social class may be confounded.

METHOD

Eighty-nine of the original 126 A, B, and C children in the 18- and 24-month samples were retested on the 1960 revision (form L-M) of the Stanford-Binet Intelligence Scale at approximately 3 years of age. Most of the children were retested between 3 and 3½ years of age. A few were a month or so under 3 years or over 4 years of age. The mean chronological ages (CAs in years and months) for the A, B, and C children at the time they were tested on the Binet were 3.2, 3.5, and 3.4 years. The Peabody Picture Vocabulary Test was administered to the mothers in order to see at what age the children's IQ scores began to correlate with mothers' intellectual performance.

Every effort was made to retest as many of the 18- and 24-month children as possible. This included a payment of $10 to the mothers, several letters, and numerous telephone calls. We succeeded in retesting about 70 percent of the children in all three SES groups for both age samples combined. The follow-up rates for Groups A, B, and C were 53, 70, and 80 percent. We were unable to obtain the rest of the children for a variety of reasons, the principal one being that the families had moved and the new address was unknown. Comparisons were made, using the *t* test, between the Cattell scores of children who were retested and those who did not return. There were no significant differences in this respect.

As in the original cross-sectional study, every effort was made to obtain each child's optimal intellectual performance. This included taking as much time as necessary to establish rapport and to elicit responses. Children were seen a second time if the examiner felt that they were not doing their best. It was only necessary to see four out of 89 children twice.

The children in the original cross-sectional study were recruited from well-baby clinics, child health stations, and private pediatricians and through mothers who had participated in the study. Where records were available, children were screened to include only normal healthy children who had no histories of serious prolonged illness, birth complications, or prematurity (birth weight less than 5½ pounds). Where records were not available, this information was obtained from the mothers.

RESULTS

Whereas there were no significant social-class differences on the Cattell at 18 and 24 months of age, when the same children were tested on the Stanford-Binet at 3 years of age, there were highly significant SES differences in intellectual performance (see Table 1). Two independent samples of children, one originally tested at 18 months and the other originally tested at 24 months, showed similar patterns of social-class differences on the Stanford-Binet at 3 years of age. The fact that the same results were obtained at age 3 on two independent samples strengthens the validity of the findings.

The 3-year Binet scores for the 18- and 24-month samples were combined for purposes of data analysis. The combined Binet mean IQs for the A, B, and C Groups were 94, 103, and 112, respectively. A one-way analysis of variance resulted in highly significant SES differences in IQ ($F = 13.25$, $df = 2$, 86, $p < .0005$). Scheffe tests, involving all possible comparisons, yielded the following results: $C > A$, $p < .01$; $C > B$, $p < .05$;

TABLE 1 MEAN IQ SCORES OF CHILDREN
IN THE 18- AND 24-MONTH SAMPLES RETESTED
AT 3 YEARS OF AGE CLASSIFIED BY ABC SES SYSTEM

| Social class | N | 18-month sample | | N | 24-month sample | |
		18 months	36 months		24 months	36 months
C (>high school)	16	110	112	21	102	113
B (≤high school)	10	113	104	21	99	101
A (welfare)	10	110	94	11	96	93

NOTE. The 18- and 24-month scores are based on the Cattell, and the 36-month scores are based on the Stanford-Binet.

and $B > A$, $p < .10$ (Edwards, 1965). Children from middle-income families obtained significantly higher Stanford-Binet IQ scores than children from poor stable families and those from fatherless welfare families. Children from poor stable families obtained higher IQ scores than those from fatherless welfare families, but this difference fell short of the .05 level of significance.

In the original cross-sectional study, we did not employ a more widely used SES measure, such as Hollingshead's Index of Social Status, because it is based on the educational-occupational achievement of the head of the household, which in most cases is the father. In many black families, the mother's achievements in these respects may be higher than the father's. For this reason, we had assumed that the Hollingshead Index would not adequately reflect important differences in social status among blacks. We had also assumed that, by classifying the black children in our sample in terms of Hollingshead's Index, there would be a range in mean IQ scores narrower than the range obtained on the basis of our ABC classification system. Both of these assumptions proved to be quite erroneous.

The children in our sample were classified on the basis of the following modification of Hollinghead's Index of Social Status: (1) middle class or higher, (2) working class, (3) lower class/nonwelfare and (4) lower class/welfare (Hollingshead, 1957). Group 1 corresponds to Hollingshead's Classes I, II, and III combined; Group 2 corresponds to Hollingshead's Class IV; and Groups 3 and 4 represent subclasses of Hollingshead's Class V. In terms of the original ABC classification system, all of the children in Group 1 were in Group C; Group 2 is about equally divided between B and C children; Group 3 children were in

TABLE 2 MEAN IQ SCORES OF CHILDREN IN
THE 18- AND 24-MONTH SAMPLES RETESTED AT 3 YEARS
OF AGE CLASSIFIED BY MODIFIED HOLLINGSHEAD SES SYSTEM

Social class	(N)	18-month sample 18 months	36 months	(N)	24-month sample 24 months	36 months
1 (middle class)	(5)	106	115	(11)	102	115
2 (working class)	(15)	113	110	(23)	101	106
3 (lower class/ nonwelfare)	(5)	114	102	(8)	98	101
4 (lower class/ welfare)	(10)	110	94	(11)	96	93

Group B, with the exception of one child from Group C; and all of the children in Group 4 were in Group A.

When the same children were classified in terms of the modified Hollingshead Index, there were still no significant SES differences on the Cattell at 18 and 24 months of age, but there was a somewhat greater range in mean Stanford-Binet IQ scores than was obtained on the basis of the original ABC classification system. The mean IQ scores for Groups 1, 2, 3, and 4 were 116, 107, 100, and 93, respectively, a spread of 23 IQ points (see Table 2). A one-way analysis of variance resulted in highly significant SES differences in IQ ($F = 8.85$, $df = 2, 85$, $p < .0005$). The range in mean IQ scores obtained on the basis of the modified Hollingshead Index in the present longitudinal study of black children was almost identical to that reported by Terman and Merrill (1937) for 831 white children between 2½ and 5 years of age in their standardization sample, classified into seven SES groups on the basis of the fathers' occupations. Children in Class I (professionals) obtained a mean IQ score of 116, and children in Class VII (laborers) obtained a mean IQ score of 94 (see Table 3). The unique and perhaps significant conbtribution of the present longitudinal study is that the same pattern and degree of social-class differentiation in intellectual performance, emerging during the third year of life, previously reported for white children have now been demonstrated for black children.

Pearson r's were computed between mothers' Peabody Picture Vocabulary scores and children's IQ scores at 18, 24, and 36 months of age. The correlation between the Peabody and 18-month Cattell scores was .10, which is not significant. The correlation between the Peabody and the 24-month Cattell scores was .28, which is significant at the .05 level. The correlation between

TABLE 3 COMPARISONS OF STANFORD-BINET IQ
SCORES OF BLACK CHILDREN IN LONGITUDINAL STUDY
CLASSIFIED BY ABC SYSTEM AND HOLLINGSHEAD'S MODIFIED
SYSTEM, AND WHITE CHILDREN FROM TERMAN AND MERRILL'S
STANDARDIZATION SAMPLE

Social class	N	IQ
Black children in longitudinal study classified by ABC system[a]		
C (>high school)	37	112
B (≤high school)	31	102
A (welfare)	21	93
Black children in longitudinal study classified by modified Hollingshead system[b]		
1 (middle class)	16	116
2 (working class)	38	107
3 (lower class/nonwelfare)	13	100
4 (lower class/welfare)	21	93
Terman and Merrill's white children classified by father's occupation[c]		
I (professional)		116
II (semiprofessional managerial)		112
III (clerical, skilled trades, retails)		108
IV (rural owners)		99
V (semiskilled, minor clerical, small business)		104
VI (semiskilled laborers)		95
VII (unskilled laborers)		94

[a] $N = 89$; $p > .0005$.
[b] $N = 88$; $p > .0005$. One child was excluded because there was not enough information
to classify him in terms of Hollingshead's Index.
[c] $N = 831$.

the Peabody and 3-year Stanford-Binet scores was .32, which is
significant at the .01 level. The pattern of increasing correlations
of children's IQ scores with those of their mothers in our sample
of black families was similar to the pattern previously reported
for white families. Bayley (1965) and Honzik (1957) found that
children's IQ scores do not correlate at all with their mothers'
intelligence or education during the first 18 months of life, but
after 18 months the correlations gradually increase, reaching an
asymptote of about .50 by 5 years of age.

Social-class influences on cognitive development already
appear to be operating between 18 and 24 months of age. These
are reflected in low but significant correlations between children's IQ scores after 18 months of age and mother's intelligence

and education. In the present study, the rank order of the mean IQ scores at 24 months of age correspond perfectly with social class (see Tables 1 and 2), whereas at 18 months of age this is not the case. However, the differences in the mean IQ scores at 24 months are not great enough to produce a significant F. Low significant correlations between social-class factors, such as mother's intelligence and education, reflect a relatively *weak effect*, whereas mean IQ differences between SES groups reflect a relatively *strong effect*. The process of social-class differentiation in cognitive development appears to begin somewhere between 18 and 24 months of age, but the divergence in intellectual ability only becomes great enough to be reflected in statistically significant SES differences in mean IQ scores by about 3 years of age.

DISCUSSION

The results of the present longitudinal study of black children confirm the findings of other investigators (Bayley, 1965; Hindley, 1962; Knobloch and Pasamanick, 1960). When such factors as birth complications and poor nutrition and health are ruled out, social-class differences in intellectual performance have not been demonstrated until the third year of life.

Why should social-class differences in intellectual performance first manifest themselves during the third year of life and not earlier? Since SES differences in cognitive development emerge during a period of rapid language growth, it seems reasonable to assume that these differences may be due to language. There is reason to believe that between 18 and 36 months of age there is a shift from the preverbal or sensorimotor to the verbal or symbolic level of intelligence and that different environmental conditions facilitate or retard development on these two qualitatively different levels of intelligence.

Given an average expectable environment with an opportunity to explore and manipulate objects and a sufficient amount of attention or handling by parents or care-taking adults, children reared under a variety of social conditions can acquire on their own the kinds of perceptual-motor skills measured by infant tests or Piaget-type scales. On the sensorimotor level, the child's construction of reality, to borrow Piaget's terminology (1954), for the most part may not be socially transmitted but, rather, acquired through his own direct experience or activity. To be sure, during the first 18 to 24 months of life, children in New York City learn something about elevators and automobiles while children in a rural village in India learn about elephants and tigers. In this respect, the knowledge which they acquire is different. But children in different cultures, or in black ghettos and middle-class suburbs, learn that objects exist when they are no longer in the perceptual field, that objects fall down and not up, and so forth. The basic knowledge which children acquire about the world on the sensorimotor level—in terms of the dimensions which Piaget has described, such as object permanence and spatial, causal, and temporal relations—may be acquired largely through their own direct experience and hence may be universal. While language may be present, very little of what children learn during the first two years of life is acquired from other people through language. Their ability to understand and express ideas verbally is fairly limited. Their capacity to use language as a tool for symbolic or representational thinking is probably not present to any significant degree during the first two years. During the third year of life, as children become increasingly capable of using language for these purposes, social class—and, in particular, the intellectual, verbal, and educational level of the parents—begins to make a difference in terms of facilitating a child's cognitive development.

In regard to the question of why social-class differences in intellectual performance were not found during the first two years of life, it is possible that social-class differences are present but that infant tests, such as the Cattell, which largely seem to measure perceptual-motor skills, may not be sensitive enough to detect them. Operating on this assumption, we included in the original cross-sectional study (Golden and Birns, 1968) the Object Scale, a new measure of cognitive development based on Piaget. The Object Scale seemed more related to cognitive development, and therefore we had expected to find social-class differences. However, we did not find SES differences on the Object Scale among black children between 12 and 24 months of age. It is possible, of course, that other measures may be more sensitive to social-class influences. There are two recent unpublished studies which report SES differences in cognitive development much earlier than other investigators have found. One of these is a report by Kagan (1966) in which social-class differences in perceptual discrimination, attention, and persistence were observed in infants of about 1 year of age. In another study, Wachs et al. (1967) obtained SES differences as early as the first year of life on several new cognitive measures based on Piaget. More specific details of these studies and replication of the results are necessary, however, before the findings can be properly evaluated.

In the original cross-sectional study, while we did not find social-class differences in the Cattell or Object Scale scores, children in the fatherless welfare families (Group A) seemed more difficult to test and more effort was required to get them to perform at their optimal intellectual level. This was reflected in the fact that significantly more of the welfare children had to be seen on more than one occasion to obtain a valid estimate of their intellectual ability. However, in a subsequent study . . . when children were tested on the Cattell and the Piaget Object Scale under identical conditions, including number of testing sessions, we did not find any differences in intellectual performance in children between 18 and 24 months of age from black welfare (Group A), black middle-income (Group C), and white middle-income families.

To summarize, in a longitudinal follow-up study of 89 black children from different social classes, there were no significant social-class differences on the Cattell or Piaget Object Scale at 18 or 24 months of age. When the same children were retested on the Stanford-Binet at approximately 3 years of age, there was a highly significant 23-point mean IQ difference between children from black welfare and middle-income families. The range in the mean IQ scores of the black children from the two extreme SES groups (93–116) was almost identical to that reported by Terman and Merrill (1937) for 831 white children between 2½ and 5 years of age in their standardization sample. The unique contribution of the present study is that the same pattern of social-class differentiation in cognitive development, emerging during the third year of life, previously reported for white children has now been demonstrated for black children.

REFERENCES

Bayley, N. Comparisons of mental and motor test scores for ages 1–15 months by sex, birth order, race, geographical location, and education of parents. *Child Development*, 1965, **36**, 379–411.

Edwards, A. L. *Experimental design in psychological research.* New York: Holt, Rinehart & Winston, 1965.

Golden, M., and Birns, B. Social class and cognitive development in infancy. *Merrill-Palmer Quarterly of Behavior and Development*, 1968, **14**, 139–149.

Hindley, C. B. Social class influences on the development of ability in the first five years. In *Child and Education: Proceedings of the XIV International Congress of Applied Psychology.* Copenhagen: Munksgaard, 1962.

Hollingshead, A. B. Two factor index of social position. Mimeographed, A. B. Hollingshead, New Haven, Conn., 1957.

Honzik, M. P. Developmental studies of parent-child resemblance in intelligence. *Child Development*, 1957, **28**, 215–228.

Kagan, J. A developmental approach to conceptual growth. In H. J.

Klausmeier and C. W. Harris (Eds.), *Analyses of concept learning.*
New York: Academic, 1966.

Knobloch, H., and Pasamanick, B. Environmental factors affecting
human development after birth. *Pediatrics,* 1960, **26**, 210–218.

Piaget, J. *The construction of reality in the child.* New York: Basic, 1954.

Terman, L. M., and Merrill, M. A. *Measuring intelligence: a guide to the
administration of the new revised Stanford-Binet tests.* Boston:
Houghton-Mifflin, 1937.

Wachs, T. D., Uzgiris, I., and Hunt, J. McV. Cognitive development in
infants of different age levels and from different environmental
backgrounds. Paper presented at the biennial meeting of The Society for Research in Child Development, New York, 1967.

Willerman, L., Sledge, S. H., and Fiedler, M. Infant development, Binet
IQ and social class. Paper presnted at meeting of The Society for
Research in Child Development, Santa Monica, California, 1969.

Health and the education of socially disadvantaged children

HERBERT G. BIRCH

INTRODUCTION

Recent interest in the effect of social and cultural factors upon educational achievement could lead us to neglect certain bio-social factors which through a direct or indirect influence on the developing child affect his primary characteristics as a learner. Such a danger is exaggerated when health and education are administered separately. The educator and the sociologist may concentrate quite properly on features of curriculum, familial environment, motivation, cultural aspects of language organisation, and the patterning of preschool experiences. Such concentration, while entirely fitting, becomes one-sided and potentially self-defeating when it takes place independently of, and without detailed consideration of, the child as a biological organism. To

From *Developmental Medicine and Child Neurology*, 1968, **10**. Reprinted by permission.

A working paper presented at the Conference on Bio-Social Factors in the Development and Learning of Disadvantaged Children held in Syracuse, New York, April 19–21, 1967.

Acknowledgments: The research reported was supported in part by the National Institutes of Health, National Institute of Child Health and Human Development (HD-00719); the Association for the Aid of Crippled Children; and the National Association for Retarded Children.

The background examination of the literature and the detailed spelling out of many problems was carried out in conjunction with Mrs. Joan Gussow and Mrs. Ronni Sandroff Franklin.

This paper was commissioned under United States Office of Education Contract #6-10-240 (ERIC). It was also used at the Conference on Bio-Social Factors in the Development and Learning of Disadvantaged Children, held in Syracuse in April 1967 under the terms of United States Office of Education Contract #6-10-243.

be concerned with the child's biology is not to ignore the cultural and environmental opportunities which may affect him. Clearly, to regard organic factors as a substitute for environmental opportunity (Hunt, 1966) is to ignore the intimate interrelation between the biology of the child and his environment in defining his functional capacities. However, it is equally dangerous to treat cultural influences as though they were acting upon an inert organism. Effective environment (Birch, 1954) is the product of the interaction of organic characteristics with the objective opportunities for experience. The child who is apathetic because of malnutrition, whose experiences may have been modified by acute or chronic illness, or whose learning abilities may have been affected by some "insult" to the central nervous system cannot be expected to respond to opportunities for learning in the same way as does a child who has not been exposed to such conditions. Increasing opportunity for learning, though entirely admirable in itself, will not overcome such biologic disadvantages (Birch, 1964; Cravioto et al., 1966).

There are two considerations with children who have been at risk of a biologic insult. First, such children must be identified and not merely additional but *special* educational opportunities effective for them must be provided. As no socially deprived group can be considered to be homogeneous for any particular disability, groups of children from such backgrounds must be differentiated into meaningful subgroups for purposes of remedial, supplemental, and habilitative education. Secondly, if conditions of risk to the organism can be identified, principles of public health and of current bio-social knowledge should be utilized to reduce learning handicap in future generations.

Concern for the socially disadvantaged cannot in good conscience restrict itself to the provision of either equal or special educational and preschool opportunities for learning. It must concern itself with all factors contributing to educational failure, among which the health of the child is a variable of primary importance.

Such an argument is not new. The basic relationship between poverty, illness, and educational failure has long been known, as has the fact expressed by James (1965) that "poverty begets poverty, is a cause of poverty and a result of poverty." What is new is the nature of the society in which such an interaction occurs. As Galbraith (1958) has put it,

> to secure each family a minimum standard, as a normal
> function of society, would help insure that the misfortunes
> of parents, discerned or otherwise, were not visited on their

children. It would help insure that poverty was not self-perpetuating. Most of the reaction, which no doubt would be almost universally adverse, is based on obsolete attitudes. When poverty was a majority phenomenon, such action could not be afforded. . . . An affluent society has no similar excuse for such rigor. It can use the forthright remedy of providing for those in want. Nothing requires it to be compassionate. But it has no high philosophical justification for callousness.

The pertinence of Galbraith's concern as it applies to the health of children, particularly those in the non-white segments of our population, is underscored by the fact that, according to the Surgeon General Stewart (1967), the United States' standing with respect to infant mortality has been steadily declining with respect to other countries. Though we are the richest country, our 1964 mortality rate of 24.8 per 1,000 live births causes us to rank fifteenth in world standing. Had we had Sweden's rate, the world's lowest, approximately 43,000 fewer infants would have died in that year. Of particular pertinence to the problem of social disadvantage is the fact that the mortality rate for non-white infants is twice as high as that for whites, with the highest rates for the country as a whole in the east south central states, Kentucky, Tennessee, Alabama, and Mississippi. Wegman (1966) notes that "Mississippi again has the dubious distinction of having the highest rate [infant mortality] . . . more than twice that of the lowest state." Most of this difference could be related to the higher Negro population of Mississippi.

The data on infant mortality have been extended to other features of child health by Baumgartner (1965) and by Densen and Haynes (1967), who have pointed out that although detailed and careful documentation of the "degree and magnitude of the health problems" of the Negro, Puerto Rican, and Indian groups are not readily available, a strikingly dangerous picture may be pieced together as a montage from various public health statistics, research studies, and occasional articles. The picture is striking, not merely because it shows these minority groups to be at a significant health disadvantage with respect to the white segment of the population, but because it indicates that the disparity between white and non-white groups is increasing. Thus, while in 1930 twice as many non-white mothers died in childbirth, in 1960 "for every white mother who lost her life in childbirth, four non-white mothers died" (Baumgartner, 1965). In 1940 the number of non-white mothers delivered by poorly trained midwives was 14 times that for white mothers, a discrepancy that rose to 23 times as great by 1960. Gold (1962) pointed out that while the overall death rate for mothers in childbirth had reached an all-time low of 3.7 per 10,000 live births, this change was largely due to the reduction of the mortality rate among white mothers to 2.6. Non-white mothers had a death rate four times as great, 10.3, a rate characteristic of white mothers two decades earlier. In generalizing these findings Baumgartner believes "that the most advantaged non-white family has a poorer chance of having a live and healthy baby than the least advantaged white family."

In our concern with educational disadvantage we must therefore recognize the excessive risk of ill-health relevant to educational handicap that exists in the children with whose welfare and education we are concerned. To this end I shall discuss some selected features of health and how far they differentiate the population of socially disadvantaged children from other children in the U.S.A.

PREMATURITY AND OBSTETRIC COMPLICATIONS

Few factors in the health history of the child have been as strongly associated with later intellectual and educational deficiencies as prematurity at birth and complications in the pregnancy from which he derives (McMahon and Sowa, 1959). Although a variety of specific infections, explicit biochemical disorders, or trauma may result in more clearly identified and dramatic alterations in brain function, prematurity, together with pre- and perinatal complications, are probably factors which most broadly contribute to disorders of neurologic development (Lilienfeld et al., 1955, Pasamanick and Lilienfeld, 1955).

A detailed consideration of health factors which may contribute to educational failure must start with an examination of prematurity and the factors associated with it.

Prematurity has been variously defined either by the weight of the child at birth, by the maturity of certain of his physiologic functions, or by gestational age (Coiner, 1960). Independently of the nature of the definition in any society in which it has been studied, prematurity has an excessive representation in the lower social strata and among the most significantly socially disadvantaged. Prematurity in any social group is simultaneously indicative of two separate conditions of risk. In the first place, fetuses that are primarily abnormal and characterized by a variety of congentical anomalies are more likely to be born before term than are normal fetuses. Second, infants who are born prematurely, even when no congenital abnormality may be noted, are more likely to develop abnormally than are infants born at term.

TABLE 1 PERCENTAGE DISTRIBUTION OF 4,254,784
LIVE BIRTHS BY BIRTHWEIGHT AND ETHNIC GROUP, USA 1957

Birthweight (g)	Total	White	Non-white
1,000 or less	0.5	0.4	0.9
1,001–1,500	0.6	0.5	1.1
1,501–2,000	1.4	1.3	2.4
2,001–2,500	5.1	4.5	8.1
2,501–3,000	18.5	17.5	24.5
3,001–3,500	38.2	38.4	37.2
3,501–4,000	26.8	28.0	19.6
4,001–4,500	7.3	7.8	4.8
4,501–5,000	1.3	1.3	1.3
5,001 or more	0.2	0.2	0.2
Total	100	100	100
Percentage under 2,501 g	7.6	6.8	12.5
Median weight (g)	3,310	3,330	3,170
Number of live births	4,254,784	3,621,456	633,328

From Baumgartner, 1962.

Thus, Baumgartner (1962) has noted that follow-up studies have
"indicated that malformation and handicapping disorders
(neurological, mental, and sensory) are more likely to be found
among the prematurely born than those born at term. Thus, the
premature infant not only has a poorer chance of surviving than
the infant born at term, but if he does survive he has a higher risk
of having a handicapping condition." One consequence of this
association between prematurity and neurological, mental, sensory, and other handicapping conditions is the excessive representation of the prematures among the mentally subnormal and
educationally backward children at school age (Drillien, 1964).

Baumgartner (1962) has presented the distribution of live
births by birthweight for white and non-white groups in the
United States for 1957 (Table 1). For the country as a whole 7.6
percent of all live births weighed 2,500 g. or less. In the white
segment of the population 6.8 percent of the babies fell in this
category, while 12.5 percent of the non-white infants weighed
2,500 g. or less. The frequency at all levels of low birthweight
was twice as great in non-white infants. Baumgartner attributed
the high incidence of prematurity among non-whites to the
greater poverty of this group. The studies of Donnelly et al.
(1964) in North Carolina, of Thomson (1963) in Aberdeen, Scotland, and of Shapiro et al. (1960) in New York suggest that many
factors, including nutritional practices, maternal health, the

mother's own growth achievements as a child, as well as deficiencies in prenatal care and birth spacing and grand multiparity, interact to produce group differences between the socially disadvantaged and more advantageously situated segments of the population.

It has sometimes been argued that the excess of low birthweight babies among the socially disadvantaged is largely a consequence of ethnic differences (i.e., Negroes "naturally" give birth to smaller babies). However, the high association of prematurity with social class in an ethnically homogeneous population such as that in Aberdeen, the finding of Donnelly et al. that within the Negro group higher social status was associated with reduced frequency of prematurity, the findings of Pakter et al. (1961) that illegitimacy adds to the risk of prematurity within the non-white ethnic group, and the suggestion made by Shapiro et al. that a change for the better in the pattern of medical care reduces the prevalence of prematurity, all make the ethnically based hypothesis of "natural difference" difficult to retain.

If gestational age is used instead of birthweight as an indication of prematurity, the non-whites are at an even greater risk than when birthweight is used. In 1958–1959 (Baumgartner, 1962) 18.1 percent of non-white babies born in New York City had a gestational age of 36 weeks or less, in contrast to 8.5 percent for live-born white babies.

Both the data on birthweight and the data on gestational age leave little doubt that prematurity and its attendant risks are excessively represented in the non-white segment of the population. Moreover, an examination in detail of regional data such as that provided by Donnelly et al. for hospital births in university hospitals in North Carolina indicate clearly that in that community the most advantaged non-white has a significantly greater risk of producing a premature infant than the least advantaged segment of the white population.

For equal degrees of prematurity, non-white infants have a somewhat better chance for survival during the first month of life (Erhardt, 1964). However, during the remainder of infancy this likelihood is reversed, particularly for infants weighing between 1,500 and 2,500 g. at birth. Baumgartner, reviewing these data, concludes,

> this observation strongly suggests that inadequate medical care, inadequate maternal supervision, inadequate housing and associated socio-economic deprivations are exerting unfavorable influences on the later survival of those non-white babies who initally appear the more favored. It is apparent

that socio-economic factors not only influence the incidence of low birthweight in all ethnic groups, but greatly influence survival after the neonatal period.

If the low birthweight and survival data are considered distributively rather than categorically, it appears that the non-white infant is subject to an excessive continuum of risk reflected at its extremes by perinatal, neonatal, and infant death, and in the survivors by a reduced functional potential.

THE BACKGROUND OF PERINATAL RISK

Clearly, the risk of having a premature baby or a complicated pregnancy and delivery begins long before the time of the pregnancy itself. A series of studies carried out in Aberdeen, Scotland, on the total population of births of that city (Thomson, 1963; Walker, 1954; Thomson and Billewicz, 1963) indicate that prematurity as well as pregnancy complications are significantly correlated with the mother's nutritional status, height, weight, concurrent illnesses, and the social class of her father and husband. Although the relation among these variables is complex, it is clear that the women born in the lowest socio-economic class and who have remained in this class at marriage were themselves more stunted in growth than other women in the population, had less adequate dietary and health habits, were in less good general health, and tended to be at excessive risk of producing premature infants. The mother's stature as well as her habits were determined during her childhood, tended to be associated with contraction of the bony pelvis, and appeared systematically related to her risk condition as a reproducer. In analyzing the relation between maternal health and physique to a number of obstetrical abnormalities such as prematurity, caesarean section and perinatal death, Thomson (1959) (Table 2) has shown each of these to be excessively represented in the mothers of least good physical grade.

The finding of a relation between the mother's physical status and pregnancy outcome is not restricted to Scotland. Donnelly et al., in their study of North Carolina University Hospital births, [have] shown a clear distribution of height with social class. In class I (the most advantaged whites) 52 percent of the women were less than 5 ft. 5 in. tall. In contrast, in social class IV (the least advantaged non-whites) 75 percent of the women were under 5 ft. 5 in. in height. The proportion of shorter women increased consistently from classes I to IV, and within each class the incidence of prematurity was higher for women who were less than 5 ft. 3 in. tall. Moreover, within any height range the

TABLE 2 INCIDENCE OF OBSTETRIC ABNORMALITIES IN
ABERDEEN PRIMIGRAVIDAE BY MATERNAL HEALTH AND
PHYSIQUE AS ASSESSED AT THE FIRST ANTENATAL
EXAMINATION. (TWIN PREGNANCIES HAVE BEEN EXCLUDED.)

	Health and physique			
	Very good	Good	Fair	Poor; very poor
Prematurity[a] (%)	5.1	6.4	10.4	12.1
Cesarean section (%)	2.7	3.5	4.2	5.4
Perinatal deaths per 1,000 births	26.9	29.2	44.8	62.8
No. of subjects	707	2,088	1,294	223
Percentage tall (5 ft. 4 in. or more)	42	29	18	13
Percentage short (under 5 ft 1 in.)	10	20	30	48

[a] Birthweight of baby 2,500 g. or less (From Thomson, 1959)

least advantaged whites had lower prematurity rates than the
most advantaged non-whites. Thus in the least advantaged
whites less than 5 ft. 3 in. tall, the prematurity rate was 12.1
percent as contrasted with a rate of 19.6 percent for the non-
whites in the same height range. In the tallest of the most disadvantaged whites the rate was 5.6 percent whereas in non-whites
of the same height range who were least disadvantaged the prematurity rate was 10.1 percent.

DIETARY FACTORS—PRE-WAR
AND WARTIME EXPERIENCE

The physical characteristics of the mother which affect her
efficiency as a reproducer are not restricted to height and physical
grade. As early as 1933, Mellanby, while recognizing that "direct
and accurate knowledge of this subject in human beings is
meagre," asserted that nutrition was undoubtedly "the most important of all environmental factors in childbearing, whether the
problem be considered from the point of view of the mother or
that of the offspring." It was his conviction that the reduction of a
high perinatal mortality rate as well as of the incidence of maternal ill health accompanying pregnancy could effectively be
achieved by improving the quality of the diet. Acting upon these
views, he attempted to supplement the diets of women attending

London antenatal clinics and reported a significant reduction in morbidity rates during the puerperium.

Although Mellanby's own study is difficult to interpret for a number of methodologic reasons, indirect evidence rapidly came into being in support of his views. Perhaps the most important of these was the classical inquiry directed by Sir John Boyd-Orr and reported in *Food, Health and Income* (1936). This study demonstrated conclusively that the long recognized social differential in perinatal death rate was correlated with a dietary differential, and that in all respects the average diet of the lower income groups in Britain was inadequate for good health. Two years later McCance et al. (1938) confirmed the Boyd-Orr findings in a meticulous study of the individual diets of 120 pregnant women representing a range of economic groups ranging from the wives of unemployed miners in South Wales and Tyneside to the wives of professionals. The diet survey technique which they used and which has, unfortunately, been rarely imitated since, was designed to minimize misreport. The results showed that there was wide individual variation in the intake of all foods which related consistently neither to income nor to intake per kilogram of body weight. But when the women were divided into six groups according to the income available for each person per week, the poorer women proved to be shorter and heavier and to have lower hemoglobin counts. Moreover, though economic status had little effect on the total intake of calories, fats, and carbohydrates, "intake of protein, animal protein, phosphorus, iron, and Vitamin B_1 rose convincingly with income." The authors of the study offered no conclusions about the possible outcome of the pregnancies involved, but the poorer reproductive performance of the lower class women was clearly at issue. For as they stated, "optimum nutrition in an adult implies and postulates optimum nutrition of that person as a child, that child as a fetus, and that fetus of its mother."

A second body of indirect data supporting Mellanby's hypothesis derived from animal studies on the relation of diet to reproduction. Warkany (1944), for example, demonstrated that pregnant animals maintained on diets deficient in certain dietary ingredients produced offspring suffering from malformation. A diet which was adequate to maintain maternal life and reproductive capacity could be inadequate for normal fetal development. The fetus was not a perfect parasite and at least for some features of growth and differentiation could have requirements different from those of the maternal host.

It would divert us from the main line of our inquiry to consider the many subsequent studies in detail. However, Duncan et al. (1952), in surveying these studies, as well as the wartime experiences in Britain, have argued convincingly that the fall in stillbirth and neonatal death rate could only be attributed to a reduction in poverty accompanied by a scientific food-rationing policy. Certainly there was no real improvement in prenatal care during the war when so many medical personnel were siphoned off to the armed forces. Furthermore, the improvement took place chiefly among those deaths attributed to "ill defined or unknown" causes—that is, among those cases when low fetal vitality seems to be a major factor in influencing survival—and these types of death "are among the most difficult to influence by routine antenatal practice." Of all the possible factors then, nutrition was the only one which improved during the war years (Garry and Wood, 1945). Thomson (1959) commented that the result was "as a nutritional effect" all the more convincing "because it was achieved in the context of a society where most of the conditions of living other than the nutritional were deteriorating."

While this National "feeding experiment" was going on in the British Isles, a more controlled experiment was being carried out on the continent of Europe (Toverud, 1950). In 1939 Dr. Toverud set up a health station in the Sagene district of Oslo to serve pregnant and nursing mothers and their babies. Though war broke out shortly after the station was opened, and it became progressively more difficult to get certain protective foods, an attempt was made to insure that every woman being supervised had the recommended amounts of every essential nutrient, through the utilization of supplementary or synthetic sources when necessary. In spite of food restrictions which became increasingly severe, the prematurity rate among the 728 women who were supervised at the station never went above the 1943 high of 3.4 percent, averaging 2.2 percent for the period 1939–1944. Among the unsupervised mothers the 1943 rate was 6.3 percent and the average for the period 4.6 percent. In addition, the stillbirth rate of 14.2/1,000 for all women attending the health station was half that of the women in the surrounding districts.

Meanwhile, even as the British and Norwegian feeding experiments were in progress, there were some hopefully never-to-be-repeated starvation "experiments" going on elsewhere. When they were reported after the war, the childbearing experiences of various populations of women under conditions of severe nutritional restriction were to provide evidence of the ways in which deprivation could negatively affect the product of conception, just as dietary improvement appeared able to affect it positively.

Smith (1947), for example, studying infants born in Rotterdam and the Hague during a delimited period of extreme hunger brought on by a transportation strike, found that the infants were shorter and lighter (by about 240 g.) than those born both before and after the period of deprivation. Significantly enough Smith also found that those babies who were five to six month fetuses when the hunger period began appeared to have been reduced in weight as much as those who had spent a full nine months in the uterus of a malnourished mother. He was led to conclude from this that reduced maternal caloric intake had its major effect on fetal weight beginning around the sixth month of gestation. Antonov's study of babies born during the siege of Leningrad (1947) confirmed the fact of weight reduction as well as Smith's observations that very severe deprivation was likely to prevent conception altogether rather than reduce the birthweight. Antonov found that during a six month period which began four months after the start of the siege, there was an enormous increase in prematurity as judged by birth length—41.2 percent of all the babies born during this period were less than 47 cm. long and fully 49.1 percent weighed under 2,500 g. The babies were also of very low vitality—30.8 percent of the prematures and 9 percent of the full-term babies died during the period. Abruptly, during the latter half of the year, the birthrate plummeted—along with the prematurity rate. Thus, while 161 prematures and 230 term babies were born between January and June, 1942, 5 prematures and 72 term babies were born between July and December. Where information was available, it suggested that the women who managed to conceive during the latter part of the year, when amenorrhea was widespread, were better fed than the majority, being employed in food industries or working in professional or manual occupations which had food priorities. Antonov concluded that while the fetus might behave for the most part like a parasite, "the condition of the host, the mother's body, is of great consequence to the fetus, and that severe quantitative and qualitative hunger of the mother decidedly affects the development of the fetus and the vitality of the newborn child."

Long after the war, Dean (1951) was able to confirm the Smith and Antonov results with a careful analysis of a series of 22,000 consecutive births at the Landesfrauenklinik, Wuppertal, Germany, during 1937–1948. It was apparent from this series that the small reduction in the average duration of gestation recorded was insufficient to account for the degree of weight reduction observed. The study demonstrated, even more clearly than before, that severe hunger did not merely reduce the mother's ability to maintain the pregnancy to term, but could act directly through the placenta to reduce the growth of the infant.

POST-WAR STUDIES

These wartime and post-war analyses leave little doubt of an association between maternal diet and the growth and development of the child *in utero*. Moreover, they suggest that the nature of the diet is significantly associated with pregnancy course and complications.

It is unfortunate that most of the more recent studies of the relation of maternal nutrition to pregnancy course and outcome have tended to obscure rather than to clarify the issue. Most of these studies, such as the excellently conducted Vanderbilt Cooperative Study of Maternal and Infant Nutrition (Darby et al., 1953*a* and *b*; McGanity, 1954) have produced confusing and equivocal findings because of patient selection. Since the women included for study have tended to be those who registered for obstetrical care early in pregnancy, the lowest class women were markedly unrepresentative of their social group. As a result, these studies have failed to include the very women who are most central to our concern. What is sorely needed is a detailed study of nutrition and pregnancy course in socially disadvantaged women who come to obstetrical notice far too late to be included in the usual dietary surveys in obstetrical services. The design of such a study and its conduct would not be easy. However, if conducted, it would have one virtue absent in most extant studies—pertinence.

. . .

POST-NATAL CONDITIONS FOR DEVELOPMENT

Densen and Haynes (1967) have indicated that many types of illness are excessively represented in the non-white segments of the population at all age levels. I have selected one, nutritional status, as the model variable for consideration. A considerable body of evidence from animal experimentation as well as field studies of populations at nutritional risk (Cravioto et al., 1966) have suggested a systematic relation between nutritional inadequacy and both neurologic maturation and competence in learning.

At birth the brain of a full-term infant has achieved about one quarter of its adult weight. The bulk of subsequent weight gain will derive from the laying down of lipids, particularly myelin, and cellular growth. Animal experiments on the rat (Davison and Dobbing, 1966); the pig (Dickerson et al., 1967; McCance, 1960) and the dog (Platt et al., 1964) have all demon-

strated a significant interference in brain growth and differentiation associated with severe dietary restriction, particularly of
protein, during the first months of life. In these animals the
behavioral effects have been dramatic with abnormalities in
some cases persisting after dietary rehabilitation.

The relation of these data to the human situation is made
difficult by the extreme severity of the dietary restrictions. More
modest restrictions have been imposed by Widdowson (1965)
and Barnes et al. (1966) and the latter experiments indicated
some tendency for poorer learning in the nutritionally deprived
animals. Cowley and Griesel's work (1963) suggests a cumulative
effect of malnutrition on adaptive behavior across generations.

The animal findings as a whole can be interpreted either as
suggesting a direct influence of malnutrition on brain growth and
development, or as resulting in interference with learning at
critical points in development. In either case the competence of
the organism as a learner appears to be influenced by his history
as an eater. These considerations add cogency to an already
strongly held belief that good nutrition is important for children
and links our general concerns on the relation of nutrition to
health to our concerns with education and the child's functioning
as a learner.

Incidents of severe malnutrition appear rarely in the United
States today, but there is evidence to suggest that the low income
segments of the population suffer from subtle, sub-clinical forms
of malnutrition which may be partially responsible for the higher
rates of morbidity and mortality of children in this group. Brock
(1961) suggests that "dietary sub-nutrition can be defined as any
impairment of functional efficiency or body systems which can be
corrected by better feeding." Since "constitution is determined
in part by habitual diet . . . diet must be considered in discussing the aetiology of a large group of diseases of uncertain and
multiple aetiology. . . ." The relationship between nutrition and
constitution is demonstrated by the fact that the populations of
developed nations are taller and heavier than those of technically
underdeveloped nations and that "within a given developed na-
tion children from economically favoured areas are taller and
heavier than children from economically underprivileged areas."

In comparison to the vast body of data available on the diets
of people in tropical countries, very little research has been done
in recent years on the nutritional status of various economic
groups in the United States. The effects of long term sub-clinical
malnutrition on the health of the individual are not yet known,
and little research has been directed at this problem since 1939.
However, it is instructive to review the studies comparing the

diets of low income people with the rest of the population since these lay the basis for hypothesizing that nutritional differences may have some effect on the overall differences in health and learning ability between groups.

The nutritional differences between lower and higher income individuals begin before birth and continue thereafter. In a study of maternal and child health care in upper New York State, Walter Boek et al., (1957) found that babies from low income families were breast fed less often and kept on only milk diets longer than upper income infants. In a study of breast feeding in Boston, Salber and Feinleib (1960) confirmed Boek's results, and "social class was found to be the most important variable affecting incidence of breast-feeding."

Social class differences in feeding patterns continue after weaning. Filer and Martinez (1964) studied 4,642 6-month-old infants from a nationally representative sample and found that "infants of mothers with least formal education and in families with lowest incomes are fed more milk formula . . ." and less solid foods at 6 months old than those from higher educational and economic groups. Class differences in the intake of most nutrients varied primarily according to the amount of milk formula consumed.

The researchers found that for "almost all nutrients studied, the mean intakes were well above recommended levels. The single exception was iron; more than half of infants do not get the lowest recommended provision—a finding that corroborates the results reported by a number of other investigators." Iron deficiency was most prevalent among infants of mothers with low educational and income levels. Infants whose mothers attained no more than a grade school education received a mean intake of only 6.7 mg. of iron a day, as compared to the 9.1 mg. mean intake of infants whose mothers had attended high school. Since "nutritional iron deficiency is widespread and most prevalent in infants in the low socio-economic group," and iron deficiency is the most common cause of anemia in infants during the first two years of life, malnutrition at least with respect to this nutrient is widely prevalent in lower-class infants.

A study of Negro low income infants in South Carolina (Jones and Schendel, 1966) uncovered more extensive areas of malnutrition in this group; the death rate for Negro infants in South Carolina was twice the national rate. Thirty-six Negro infants from low income families were tested when they visited a Well-Baby Clinic for routine examinations. The subjects ranged in age from 4 to 10 months. "The bodyweights of 66 percent of the infants were below the 50th percentile in the Harvard growth charts, 34 percent below the 10th percentile, and 9 percent below the 3rd percentile." Twenty-nine percent of the subjects had "serum albumin concentrations, which have been associated with marginal protein nutrition," and serum globin concentrations below normal range. Sixty-one percent had total protein concentrations below normal and 33 percent had "serum ascorbic acid concentrations which have been associated with a sub-optimal intake of vitamin C." One infant's albumin concentration showed severe protein deficiency and "eight . . . infants had concentrations of serum ascorbic acid reflecting a severely limited dietary intake of vitamin C." The researchers concluded that "it would appear possible that malnutrition may be one of the many underlying causes for the high rate of Negro infant mortality in South Carolina." Since Greenville County, where the study was conducted, has a relatively small number of infant deaths, "it is possible that malnutrition may be even more severe and/or prevalent in many other counties of the state."

Since the sample used in this study is small (36 infants), the results must be viewed as suggestive rather than conclusive. But taken together with the findings on iron intake, a New York study which shows that anemia is common among Negro and Puerto Rican infants (James, 1966) and the recent finding of Arneil (1965) that "some anemia was present in 59 percent of Glasgow slum children," the suggestion is strengthened that poor diet may be partly responsible for the poor health of lower socio-economic class children.

The studies so far reviewed have dealt with populations that are in some way representative of the nutritional status of large groups of children. Since these studies are few in number and limited in approach, they cannot give a complete picture of the nutritional status of lower class Americans. Hints about areas of malnutrition which have not been thoroughly investigated can be drawn from studies of special groups within the American population. In a survey of the "Dietary and Nutritional Problems of Crippled Children in Five Rural Counties of North Carolina," Bryan and Anderson (1965) found that the diets of 73 percent of the 164 subject sample were less than adequate. The cause for the malnourishment of nine out of ten of the poorly fed children was poor family diet and in only one of ten cases was the malnutrition related to the physical handicap of the child.

Although all the children were from families in the low income group, the researchers found certain significant differentiations between the Negro and white families studied. Seventy-one percent of the Negro children and 35 percent of the white children's diets were rated as probably or obviously inadequate. Only a limited number of food items were used and "in many of the families . . . only one food was cooked for a meal and this would be eaten with biscuits and water, tea or Kool-Aid. . . . For the most part, the diet of our low income families contained few foods that are not soft or that require much chewing." Suggestions of poor nutrition in infancy and childhood can also be drawn from studies of constitutional differences as well as from measurements of food intake.

A study of the nutritional status of junior high school children in Onondaga County, New York (Dibble et al., 1965) compared subjects from broadly different economic groups. School "M" was 94 percent Negro, while schools "L" and "J" were overwhelmingly white. The schools were also differentiated on the basis of the occupation of the students' fathers: ". . . of the 58 percent of the employed fathers from school M, 52 percent were laborers, whereas only 10 percent from school L and 38 percent from school J were in this category." When the heights and weights of the subjects were compared, a greater percentage of students from the lower socio-economic class school fell in the short stature and low weight zones. There was also a tendency for students from the predominantly Negro school to have less subcutaneous fat by ranking of skinfold than students from other schools.

Blood and urine samples were taken for all the subjects and the researchers set up criteria to determine the level of adequacy for the various nutrients. "Subjects from school M (the Negro school) had a slightly lower average hematocrit, largely due to the greater number of female subjects from that school in the low classification, [and] the average plasma ascorbic acid value for school M was about half as great as the average in school L. There was also a tendency for the Negro population to have low values for hexose and pentose when erythrocyte hemolysate transketolase activity was determined. Average urinary excretions of riboflavin and thiamine was above acceptable level in all groups, but data for folinic acid indicated lower levels of excretion for children from school M than for children in schools L and J." The question [of] whether this observation was related to the lower ascorbic acid levels of these children indicates a need for further study in this area. The authors conclude that the differences between the schools show a relationship between nutrition and socio-economic status. These differences are greater than the differences between male and female students, and are related to each other on the various parameters of the study. "There was a slight indication that the growth of the male subjects in . . . school [M] had not been as great as that of the subjects in the other schools with whom they were compared. This fact was supported by somewhat lower average levels in the other parameters. . . ."

Although the students at the predominantly Negro school in Onondaga County did not appear to suffer from gross nutritional deficiencies, their diets were significantly less adequate than the subjects from the white, middle-class schools. The investigators did not attempt to link dietary habits with health records, but the results of the study lead to speculations about the relationship between suboptimal diet, rates of infection, school absence and academic performance.

CONCLUSIONS

In this review I have examined certain selected conditions of health which may have consequences for education. Other factors such as acute and chronic illness, immunizations, dental care, the utilization of health services, and a host of other phenomena, perhaps equally pertinent to those selected for consideration, have been dealt with either in passing or not at all, but in fact studies of these factors that do exist reflect the same picture that emerges from those variables which have been discussed. In brief, though much of the information is incomplete, and certain aspects of the data are sparse, a serious consideration of available health information leaves little or no doubt that children who are economically and socially disadvantaged, and in an ethnic group exposed to discrimination, are exposed to massively excessive risks for maldevelopment.

Such risks have direct and indirect consequences for the functioning of the child as a learner. Conditions of ill health may directly affect the development of the nervous system and eventuate either in patterns of clinically definable malfunctioning in this system or in sub-clinical conditions. In either case the potentialities of the child as a learner cannot but be impaired. Such impairment, though it may in fact have reduced functional consequences under exceptionally optimal conditions for development and education, in any case represents a primary handicap which efforts at remediation may only partially correct.

The indirect effects of ill health or of conditions of suboptimal health care on the learning processes may take many forms. Only two can be considered at this point. Children who are ill nourished are reduced in their responsiveness to the environment, distracted by their visceral state, and reduced in their ability to progress and endure in learning conditions. Consequently, given the same objective conditions for learning, the state of the organism modifies the effective environment and results in a reduction in the profit which a child may derive from exposure to opportunities for experience. Consequently, the provision of equal opportunities for learning in an objective sense is never met when only the school situation is made identical for advantaged and disadvantaged children. Though such a step is indeed necessary, proper, and long overdue, a serious concern with the profitability of such improved objective opportunities for socially disadvantaged children demands a concern which goes beyond education and includes an intensive and directed consideration of the broader environment, the health and functional and physical well-being of the child.

Inadequacies in nutritional status as well as excessive amounts in intercurrent illness may interfere in indirect ways with the learning process. As Cravioto et al. (1966) have put it, at least

three possible indirect effects are readily apparent:

1. *Loss of learning time.* Since the child was less responsive to his environment when malnourished, at the very least he had less time in which to learn and had lost a certain number of months of experience. On the simplest basis, therefore, he would be expected to show some developmental lags.

2. *Interference with learning during critical periods of development.* Learning is by no means simply a cumulative process. A considerable body of evidence exists which indicates that interference with the learning process at specific times during its course may result in disturbances in function that are both profound and of long term significance. Such disturbance is not merely a function of the length of time the organism is deprived of the opportunities for learning. Rather, what appears to be important is the correlation of the experiential opportunity with a given stage of development—the so-called critical periods of learning. Critical periods in human learning have not been definitively established, but in looking at the consequences associated with malnutrition at different ages one can derive some potentially useful hypotheses. The earlier report by Cravioto and Robles (1965) may be relevant to the relationship between the age at which malnutrition develops and learning. They have shown that, as contrasted with older patients, infants under 6 months recovering from kwashiorkor did not recoup their mental age deficit during the recovery period. In older children, ranging from 15 to 41 months of age, too, the rate of recovery from the initial men-

tal deficit varied in direct relation to chronological age at time of admission. Similarly, the findings of Barrera-Moncada (1963) in children, and those of Keys et al. (1950) in adults, indicated a strong association between the persistence of later effects on mental performance and the age at onset of malnutrition and its duration.

3. *Motivation and personality changes.* It should be recognized that the mother's response to the infant is to a considerable degree a function of the child's own characteristics of reactivity. One of the first effects of malnutrition is a reduction in the child's responsiveness to stimulation and the emergence of various degrees of apathy. Apathetic behavior in its turn can function to reduce the value of the child as a stimulus and to diminish the adults' responsiveness to him. Thus, apathy can provoke apathy and so contribute to a cumulative pattern of reduced adult-child interaction. If this occurs it can have consequences for stimulation, for learning, for maturation, and for interpersonal relations, the end result being significant backwardness in performance on later more complex learning tasks.

However, independently of the path through which biosocial pathology interferes with educational progress, there is little doubt that ill health is a significant variable for defining differentiation in the learning potential of the child. To intervene effectively with the learning problems of disadvantaged children it would be disastrous if we were either to ignore or to relegate the physical condition and health status of the child with whose welfare we are concerned to a place of unimportance. To do so would be to divorce education from health; a divorce which can only have disorganizing consequences for the child. Unless health and education go hand in hand, we shall fail to break the twin curse of ignorance and poverty.

REFERENCES

Antonov, A. N. (1947) 'Children born during the siege of Leningrad in 1942.' *J. Pediat.*, **30**, 250.

Arneil, G. C., McKilligan, H. R., Lobo, E. (1965) 'Malnutrition in Glasgow children.' *Scot. med. J.*, **10**, 480.

Barnes, R. H., Cunnold, S. R., Zimmerman, R. R., Simmons, H., MacLeod, R., Krook, L. (1966) 'Influence of nutritional deprivations in early life on learning behaviour of rats as measured by performance in water maze.' *J. Nutr.*, **89**, 399.

Barrera-Moncada, G. (1963) Estudios sobre Alleraciones del Crecimiento y del Desarrollo Piscológico de Sindrome Pluricarencial Kwashiorkor. Caracas: Editoria Grafos.

Baumgartner, L. (1962) 'The public health significance of low birth weight in the U.S.A., with special reference to varying practices in providing special care to infants of low birth weights.' *Bull. Wld. Hlth. Org.*, **26**, 175.
——. (1965) 'Health and ethnic minorities in the sixties.' *Amer. J. publ. Hlth.*, **55**, 495.
Birch, H. G. (1954) 'Comparative psychology.' *In* Marcuse, F. A. (Ed.) Areas of Psychology. New York: Harper.
—— (Ed.) (1964) Brain Damage in Children: Biological, and Social Aspects. Baltimore: Williams & Wilkins.
Boek, W. E., Boek, J. K. (1956) Society and Health. New York: Putnam.
—— and co-worker (1957) Social Class, Maternal Health and Child Care. Albany, N.Y.: New York State Department of Health.
Brock, J. (1961) Recent Advances in Human Nutrition. London: Churchill.
Bryan, H., Anderson, E. L. (1965) 'Dietary and nutritional problems of crippled children in five rural counties of North Carolina.' *Amer. J. publ. Hlth.*, **55**, 1,545.
Corner, B. (1960) Prematurity. London: Cassell.
Cowley, J. J., Griesel, R. D. (1963) 'The development of second generation low-protein rats.' *J. genet. Psychol.*, **103**, 233.
Cravioto, J., DeLicardie, E. R., Birch, H. G. (1966) 'Nutrition, growth and neuro-integrative development: an experimental and ecologic study.' *Pediatrics*, **38**, 319.
——, Robles, B. (1965) 'Evolution of adaptive and motor behaviour during rehabilitation from Kwashiorkor.' *Amer. J. Orthopsychiat.*, **35**, 449.
Darby, W. J., Densen, P. M., Cannon, R. O., Bridgeforth, E., Martin, M. P., Kaser, M. M., Peterson, O., Christie, A., Frye, W. W., Justus, K., McClellan, G. S., Williams, C., Ogle, P. J., Hahn, P. F., Sheppard, C. W., Crothers, E. L., Newbill, J. A. (1953*a*) ''The Vanderbilt co-operative study of maternal and infant nutrition. I. Background. II. Methods. III. Description of the sample data.' *J. Nutr.*, **51**, 539.
——, McGanity, W. J., Martin, M. P., Bridgeforth, E., Densen, P. M., Kaser, M. M., Ogle, P. J., Newbill, J. A., Stockell, A., Ferguson, E., Touster, O., McClellan, G. S., Williams, C., Cannon, R. O. (1953*b*) 'The Vanderbilt co-operative study of maternal and infant nutrition. IV. Dietary, laboratory and physical findings in 2,129 delivered pregnancies.' *J. Nutr.*, **51**, 565.
Davison, A. N., Dobbing, J. (1966) 'Myelination as a vulnerable period in brain development.' *Brit. med. Bull.*, **22**, 40.
Dean, R. F. (1951) 'The size of the baby at birth and the yield of breast milk.' *In* Studies of Undernutrition, Wuppertall, 1946–49. M. C. R. Special Report Series, No. 275. London: H.M.S.O. Chap. 28.
Delgado, G., Brumback, C. L., Deaver, M. B. (1961) 'Eating patterns among migrant families.' *Publ. Hlth. Rep. (Wash.)*, **76**, 349.
Densen, P. M., Haynes, A. (1967) 'Research and the major health problems of Negro Americans.' Paper presented at the Howard University Centennial Celebration, Washington. (Unpublished.)
Dibble, M. F., Brin, M., McMullen, E., Peel, A., Chen, N. (1965) 'Some preliminary biochemical findings in junior high school children in Syracuse and Onondaga County, New York.' *Amer. J. clin. Nutr.*, **17**, 218.

Dickerson, J. W., Dobbing, J., McCance, R. A. (1967) 'The effect of under nutrition on the postnatal development of the brain and cord in pigs.' *Proc. roy. Soc. B.*, **166**, 396.

Donnelly, J. F., Flowers, C. E., Creadick, R. N., Wells, H. B., Greenberg, B. G., Surles, K. B. (1964) 'Maternal, fetal and environmental factors in prematurity.' *Amer. J. Obstet. Gynec.*, **88**, 918.

Drillien, C. M. (1964) The Growth and Development of Prematurely Born Children. Edinburgh: Livingstone, Baltimore: Williams & Wilkins.

Duncan, E. H. L., Baird, D., Thomson, A. M. (1952) 'The causes and prevention of stillbirths and first week deaths. I. The evidence of vital statistics.' *J. Obstet. Gyncea. Brit. Emp.*, **59**, 183.

Erhardt, C. L., Joshi, G. B., Nelson, F. G., Kron, B. H., Weiner, L. (1964) 'Influence of weight and gestation on perinatal and neonatal mortality of ethnic group.' *Amer. J. publ. Hlth.*, **54**, 1,841.

Filer, L. J., Martinez, G. A. (1964) 'Intake of selected nutrients by infants in the United States: an evaluation of 4,000 representative six-year-olds.' *Clin. Pediat.*, **3**, 633.

Galbraith, J. K., (1958) The affluent Society. Boston: Houghton Mifflin.

Garry, R. C., Wood, H. O. (1945–46) 'Dietary requirements in human pregnancy and lactation: a review of recent work.' *Nutr. Abstr. Rev.*, **15**, 591.

Gold, E. M. (1962) 'A broad view of maternity care.' *Children*, **9**, 52.

Hartman, E. E., Sayles, E. B. (1965) 'Some reflections on births and infant deaths among the low socioeconomic groups.' *Minn. Med.*, **48**, 1,711.

Hunt, E. E. (1966) 'Some new evidence on race and intelligence.' Paper read at the meeting of the New York Academy of Sciences—Anthropology Section, Oct. 24, 1966. (Unpublished.)

James, G. (1965) 'Poverty and public health—new outlooks. I. Poverty as an obstacle to health progress in our cities.' *Amer. J. publ. Hlth.*, **55**, 1,757.

—— (1966) 'New York City's Bureau of Nutrition.' *J. Amer. dietet. Ass.*, **48**, 301.

Jeans, P. C., Smith, M. B., Stearns, G. (1952) 'Dietary habits of pregnant women of low income in a rural state.' *J. Amer. dietet. Ass.*, **28**, 27.

Jones, R. E., Schendel, H. E. (1966) 'Nutritional status of selected Negro infants in Greenville County, South Carolina.' *Amer. J. clin. Nutr.*, **18**, 407.

Kass, E. H. (1960) 'Bacteriuria and the prevention of prematurity and perinatal death.' *In* Kowlessar, M. (Ed.) Transactions of the 5th Conference on the Physiology of Prematurity. Princeton, 1960.

Keys, A., Brožek, J., Henschel, A., Mikelsen, O., Taylor, H. (1950) The Biology of Starvation. Vol. 2. Minneapolis: University of Minnesota Press.

Lilienfeld, A. M., Pasamanik, B., Rogers, M. (1955) 'Relationship between pregnancy experience and the development of certain neuropsychiatric disorders in childhood.' *Amer. J. publ. Hlth.*, **45**, 637.

McCance, R. A. (1960) 'Severe undernutrition in growing and adult animals. I. Production and general effects.' *Brit. J. Nutr.*, **14**, 59.

——, Widdowson, E. M., Verdon-Roe, C. M. (1938) 'A study of English diets by the individual method. III. Pregnant women at different economic levels.' *J. Hyg. (Lond.)*, **38**, 596.

McGanity, W. J., Cannon, R. O., Bridgeforth, E. B., Martin, M. P., Densen, P. M., Newbill, J. A., McClellan, G. S., Christie, A., Peterson, J. O., Darby, W. J. (1954) 'The Vanderbilt co-operative study of maternal and infant nutrition. VI. Relationship of obstetric performance to nutrition.' *Amer. J. Obstet. Gynec.*, **67**, 501.

MacMahon, B., Sowa, J. M. (1961) 'Physical damage to the foetus.' *In* Causes of Mental Disorders: A Review of Epidemiological Knowledge, 1959. New York: Milbank Memorial Fund, p. 51.

Mayer, J. (1965) 'The nutritional status of American Negroes.' *Nutr. Rev.*, **23**, 161.

Mellanby, E. (1933) 'Nutrition and child bearing.' *Lancet* ii, 1, 131.

Orr, J. B. (1936) Food, Health and Income. London: Macmillan.

Pakter, J., Rosner, H. J., Jacobziner, H., Greenstein, F. (1961) 'Out-of-wedlock births in New York City. II. Medical aspects.' *Amer. J. publ. Hlth.*, **51**, 846.

Pasamanik, B., Lilienfeld, A. M. (1955) 'Association of maternal and fetal factors with development of mental deficiency. I. Abnormalities in the prenatal and perinatal periods.' *J. Amer. med. Ass.*, **159**, 155.

Platt, B. S., Heard, R. C., Stewart, R. J. (1964) 'Experimental protein-calorie deficiency.' *In* Munro, H. N., Allison, J. B. (Eds.) Mammalian Protein Metabolism. New York: Academic Press. p. 446.

Salber, E. J., Feinleib, M. (1966) 'Breast feeding in Boston.' *Pediatrics*, **37**, 299.

Shapiro, S., Jacobziner, H., Densen, P. M., Weiner, L. (1960) 'Further observations on prematurity and perinatal mortality in a general population and in the population of a prepaid group practice medical care plan.' *Amer. J. publ. Hlth.*, **50**, 1,304.

Smith, C. A. (1947) 'Effects of maternal undernutrition upon the new born infant in Holland.' *J. Pediat.*, **30**, 229.

Stewart, W. H. (1957) 'The unmet needs of children.' *Pediatrics*, **39**, 157.

Thomson, A. M. (1959) 'Maternal stature and reproductive efficiency.' *Eugen. Rev.*, **51**, 157.

———. (1959) 'Diet in pregnancy. III. Diet in relation to the course and outcome of pregnancy.' *Brit. J. Nutr.*, **13**, 509.

———. (1963) 'Prematurity: socio-economic and nutritional factors.' *Bibl. paediat. (Basel)*, **81**, 197.

———, Billewicz, W. Z. (1963) 'Nutritional status, physique and reproductive efficiency.' *Proc. nutr. Soc.*, **22**, 55.

Toverud, G. (1950) The influence of nutrition on the course of pregnancy.' *Milbank mem. Fd. Quart.*, **28**, 7.

U.S. Welfare Administration. Division of Research. (1966) Converging Social Trends—Emerging Social Problems. Welfare Administration Publication No. 6. Washington: U.S. Government.

Walker, J. (1954) 'Obstetrical complications, congenital malformations and social strata.' *In* Mechanisms of Congenital Malformations. New York: Association for the Aid of Crippled Children, p. 20.

Warkany, J. (1944) 'Congenital malformations induced by maternal nutritional deficiency.' *J. Pediat.*, **25**, 476.

Wegman, M. E. (1966) 'Annual summary of vital statistics, 1965.' *Pediatrics*, **39**, 1,067.

Widdowson, E. M. (1966) 'Nutritional deprivation in psychobiological development: studies in animals.' *In* Proceedings of the Special Session, 4th Meeting of the PAHO Advisory Committee on Medical Research, June, 1965. Washington: World Health Organization.

The myth of the deprived child

HERBERT GINSBURG

The following selections are taken from an entire book of the same name by Dr. Ginsburg. The book is excellent and worth your further study. In order to give some flavor of Ginsburg's arguments in the short space available, I have selected two short sections, one from fairly early in the book, in which he gives his view of the "traditional" deficit hypothesis about poor children's intellect, and one from later in the book, in which he explains the application of Piaget's theory to the study of poor children's thinking. [Ed.]

POOR CHILDREN'S INTELLECT

Many psychologists believe—mistakenly, I think—that the poor child's intellect is deficient, although they disagree to some extent on the precise nature of the deficiency.

The *nativists* have traditionally asserted that poor children are characterized by inadequate "intelligence" as measured by the IQ test. Intelligence refers to a basic mental capacity which is at the root of the child's learning, his thinking, and his problem solving. Intelligence is the fundamental intellectual ability, the basic power of the mind. Superior intelligence permits the child to cope with the environment and to profit from experience. Deficient intelligence hinders both adaptation and learning.

The *empiricists* generally place less emphasis on general intelligence and tend to stress the role of specific intellectual abilities. For example, many empiricists propose that poor children employ an impoverished mode of speech which in turn

Herbert Ginsburg, *The Myth of the Deprived Child: Poor Children's Intellect and Education*, © 1972, pp. 12–14, 127–139. Reprinted by permission of Prentice-Hall, Inc., Englewood Cliffs, New Jersey.

degrades thought. In this view, the poor child uses a "restricted code"—a language which is simple and terse, containing few abstractions. Lower-class speech is emotional, not intellectual; it is authoritarian, not reasonable; it is concrete, not abstract. Speech of this type is not a good vehicle for complex thinking, for logical reasoning, for considered judgments. Deficient speech produces deficient thought: the poor child's language produces an intellect which is overly concrete and illogical and which bases its judgments on emotion rather than reason. It should therefore come as no surprise that the poor child, burdened as he is with a restricted language and a deficient intellect, cannot succeed in academic endeavor.

At first the nativist and empiricist positions seem quite reasonable, either alone or in combination. Yet closer examination reveals serious flaws in each argument.

There is a great deal of confusion regarding the notion of intelligence as it is usually employed by the nativists. Try to define what "intelligence" is. When people do this, they generally succeed in producing two or three definitions which are at odds with one another or which at least seem to refer to different things. For example, is intelligence the ability to engage in abstract reasoning or to profit from experience? Is it the ability to adapt to the environment or to use verbal and symbolic skills? Confusion over the meaning of intelligence is not limited to the lay public. David Wechsler, a leading worker in the area of intelligence testing and the originator of the Wechsler Intelligence Scale, writes as follows:

> Some psychologists have come to doubt whether these laborious analyses have contributed anything fundamental to our understanding of intelligence while others have come to the equally disturbing conclusion that the term intelligence, as now employed, is so ambiguous that it ought to be discarded altogether. Psychology seems now to find itself in the paradoxical position of devising and advocating tests for measuring intelligence and then disclaiming responsibility for them by asserting "nobody knows what the word really means" [Quoted in Tuddenham, 1962, pp. 470–471].

This confusion is obviously quite damaging to the nativist position. How can intelligence be so fundamental, so basic, when after years of research "nobody knows what the word really means"? How can a presumably scientific psychology employ so ephemeral a concept as that of intelligence to explain poor children's academic failure? And if poor children's IQ is relatively low, what does that fact mean?

The empiricist view also suffers from serious deficiencies. For one thing, the research evidence is full of contradictions. Some studies seem to support the empiricist view. They show that poor children's intellectual performance on a variety of measures is inadequate to some degree. But other research efforts support a different conclusion. They show that poor children's language and thought are generally no different from middle-class children's abilities in these areas. Moreover, one can make the argument that the empiricist position suffers from the limits of a middle-class perspective. For example, some empiricists ask whether poor children are capable of the kind of speech that the middle class happens to consider congenial. The empiricists generally do not attempt to determine whether poor children use a language which is both distinctive and well suited to their own environment.

These considerations raise many questions. Chief among them is whether poor children's intellect is really deficient. If not deficient, is it at least different from that of middle-class children?

In Chapters 2, 3, and 4, I attempt to deal with many of these issues—with the nature of poor children's cognition, their intelligence, language, and thought. I try to probe the nativist and empiricist positions, to identify defects in their reasoning, and to evaluate both the evidence which supports their arguments and the evidence which contradicts them.

My conclusion, which I call the *developmental view*, is that in many fundamental ways poor children's cognition is quite similar to that of middle-class children. There are *cognitive universals*, modes of language and thought shared by all children (except the retarded and severely emotionally disturbed) regardless of culture or upbringing. At the same time, there do exist social-class differences in cognition. Yet the differences are relatively superficial, and one must not make the mistake of calling them deficiencies or considering them analogous to mental retardation.

. . .

THE IMPORTANCE OF PIAGET

As I mentioned earlier, we have reviewed only a minute portion of Piaget's voluminous work. He has produced some forty books on different aspects of cognitive development, so that you have seen only a smattering of his theory in the last several pages.

Here I want to discuss why it is so important for us to study Piaget's ideas as they relate to poor children. You will recall that

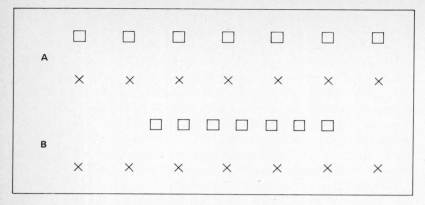

Figure 4-4.   Conservation of number.

earlier I described aspects of Palmer's and Lesser's work as superficial. I said that it was not particularly important to know that a child can attach the label "ball" to the proper object or that he can remember that two and two are four. I maintained that other aspects of thought are more fundamental. Now I must answer this question: Why is Piaget's work more basic than the others?

I will give two arguments. The first can be approached through a simple example concerning arithmetic. According to Lesser et al., the child shows a high degree of arithmetic ability when he can consistently solve problems such as finding the sum of three and four objects. What is the minimal set of skills needed to do something like this? First, the child must be able to count the objects properly so that he knows that there are three here and four there. Second, he must have some way of finding the sum. He can use a rote method, simply holding in memory the addition facts for small numbers. If the objects are all visible, he can use a counting procedure, simply combining the two sets and enumerating the elements.

Is all this fundamental? From one perspective, it is: The child cannot do arithmetic and succeed in school without being able to count and without remembering some basic number facts. So Lesser's work is important from this point of view. But from another perspective, counting and adding may be based on little understanding; arithmetic skills may function without the child's appreciating the underlying mathematical concepts which Piaget's work focuses on. For example, in one interview Piaget presented a child of 5 years with two sets of objects, arrayed as in A in Figure 4-4, and asked the child to count them. He did so and correctly maintained that each set had seven. Then, as the child watched, the examiner performed the classic conservation experiment, bunching up one of the sets. Again the child was asked to count the elements in the sets, and again he correctly reported the numbers: seven in each. Then the examiner asked whether the sets had the same number or whether one had more. The child maintained that the lower set had more because it was longer (Piaget, 1952, p. 45)!

The example shows what nearly everyone who has been through school knows quite well: you can correctly execute various calculations without understanding the ideas involved. In this case, the child could count, but the results were meaningless to him.

Piaget's work attempts to focus on the basic concepts of various areas of knowledge. In dealing with number, for example, Piaget examines the concepts of equivalence and of a series: he largely ignores counting and mastery of the addition or subtraction facts. This, then, is the first reason that Piaget's work is fundamental: it concentrates on the basic ideas of a discipline, not on the superficial aspects which schools often stress.

A second reason is that the mental operations which Piaget's theory describes underlie the child's thinking in a variety of areas. For example, Piaget has studied the "formal operations" which characterize adolescent and adult thought. Briefly, this kind of thinking involves the ability to imagine hypothetical possibilities, to consider in an exhaustive way the various combinations of events that may occur, to reason in a logical fashion, and so on. Piaget shows that the formal operations manifest themselves in several areas of endeavor. For example, when the adolescent acquires the formal operations, he can handle certain types of scientific problem solving (Inhelder and Piaget, 1958); he elaborates theories of society and of religion (1958), and he engages in advanced forms of moral judgment (Piaget, 1932). In brief, formal operations subsume many areas of content: they make possible scientific, social, religious, and moral thought. This, then, is the second reason for the importance of Piaget's theory: the mental activites it describes are central to many areas of intellectual endeavor.

Indeed, some of the mental activities which Piaget describes are almost essential for human survival. For example, some of Piaget's work deals with the development of basic categories of mind: concepts of space, time, causality. Without these, the child would have a difficult time surviving his first several years.

CROSS-CULTURAL STUDIES

Piaget's theory proposes, with a few minor qualifications, that the stages and order of cognitive development are universal. All children, regardless of culture, progress through the stages of the sensory motor period, as in the case of object permanence, and proceed from there to pre-operational thought, then concrete operational thought, and finally, in all but the most primitive societies, to the stage of formal operations.

The cultures may differ in the ages at which the various stages are attained, but not in the basic course of development. For example, in one culture children may acquire the conservation of number at age 6 whereas in another they cannot conserve until age 8. But in both cultures, all children eventually acquire the mental operations which make conservation possible. Also, in both cultures children first must progress through pre-operational thinking before the concrete operations will appear. What evidence is there to support these claims, and what bearing does it have on problems of poor children's intellect?

Goodnow (1962) attempted to determine whether children in a non-Western culture show cognitive abilities similar to those of Western children. The subjects were a large number of boys, from 10 to 13 years of age, all of whom lived in Hong Kong. One group consisted of 148 Europeans, mainly English and mainly middle class. A second group involved 151 Chinese boys of middle-class origin. They attended exclusive schools where instruction was in English. A third group involved 80 lower-class Chinese boys, whose parents had unskilled or semi-skilled jobs and who attended schools in which Chinese was the language of instruction. A fourth group consisted of 80 Chinese boys of lower-class background who had a minimum of schooling, education not being compulsory in Hong Kong. Each group had approximately equal numbers of subjects at ages 10, 11, 12, and 13. To summarize, Goodnow's four major groups of subjects were Europeans, Westernized middle-class Chinese, lower-class Chinese attending school, and lower-class Chinese with a minimum of education. Presumably the last two groups represent a non-Western culture, whereas the first two groups are Western or at least Western influenced.

Each boy was given four Piagetian tasks: conservation of weight, volume, and area, and a test of combinatorial reasoning. . . . the conservation of weight involves showing the child two identical clay balls which are of the same weight. When the child accepts this fact, one of the balls is transformed into a different shape, for example, a sausage, and he is asked whether the weight remains the same. The conservation of volume involves the same materials. The child is first shown that the two identical balls, placed in two identical beakers of liquid, displace the same volumes. Then both balls are removed from the water, one is transformed in shape, and the child must predict whether it will still displace the same amount of liquid. The conservation of area involves placing on two identical rectangular surfaces two identical arrays of objects (for example: houses arranged in the same way on two fields). After the child agrees that the objects cover up the same amount of surface, one set of objects is transformed so that it is arranged differently on the surface. The three conservation tasks are intended to assess the child's concrete operational thinking. The tasks are not of equal difficulty, however. Piaget has found that the conservation of area is mastered at about age 7 or 8, weight at about 10 years, and volume at about 12 years.

The fourth problem involved presenting each child with a collection of poker chips of six different colors. The task was to construct from the six colors all possible combinations of two colors at a time. There are 15 such combinations of elements. If we symbolize the six colors as A, B, C, D, E, and F, then the combinations are: AB, AC, AD, AE, AF, BC, BD, BE, BF, CD, CE, CF, DE, DF, EF. (Order does not count. Thus BA is not a legitimate combination since we already have AB.) Note that the sequence in which the combinations are listed is systematic. First, A was paired with each of the other, then B with each (except A), and so on. Without some system, it is easy to lose track of what has been paired with what. The test is intended to tap one aspect of formal operational thought, namely the ability to combine things in an exhaustive and systematic way. From the point of view of formal operations, the task is relatively simple, since it involves concrete objects. All four tasks were administered in a standard way, the questions being taken from published protocols of Piaget's clinical interviews.

The findings showed that on the conservation tasks there were only minor differences among the four groups. For example, in the conservation of weight, Europeans and Chinese children with a minimum of schooling received almost identical scores at all ages. Interestingly, the children who did most poorly, on the average, were not the Chinese children with a minimum of education, but the middle- and lower-class Chinese children who attended school: they tended to parrot "scientific" explanations referring to mysteries such as "center of gravity" which they did not understand and which were inappropriate. Further, the Chinese subjects' incorrect and correct answers generally took the form predicted by Piaget. A minor discrepancy with Piaget's results involved the sequence of mastery of the tasks. Piaget maintains that conservation of area is mastered first, then weight, then volume. Goodnow found, however, that area and weight were of about equal difficulty, and (in agreement with Piaget) that volume was hardest of all. Goodnow speculates, though, that the area task may have been presented in an especially difficult manner. In sum, the cultural and social-class differences on the three types of conservation are generally quite minor.

The results for the combinatorial task were much different. Europeans and Chinese boys of middle-class origin who attended Western type schools performed much better than did lower-class Chinese with or without schooling. Goodnow found, however, that lower-class Chinese, while doing poorly on the combinatorial task relative to the middle-class subjects, nevertheless improved with age. This suggests that in due course the lower-class Chinese acquire formal operations, too, albeit more slowly than the others. The lower-class boys lag behind but are not completely deficient in combinatorial thought.

To summarize, Goodnow finds that on the three conservation tasks, all cultural and social class groups perform at about the same level. On the combinations task, middle-class Chinese and European boys are superior to lower-class Chinese, although the latter show signs of improvement with age.

I wish to make several comments on these findings. First, while cultural and social-class factors have little effect on conservation, the meaning of the combinatorial reasoning results is not clear: several interpretations might account for them. One possibility is that success at the task depends on Westernization. The Europeans and the middle-class Chinese in Western type schools, both of which groups one might consider to be Westernized, performed at a higher level than the two non-Westernized groups, the lower-class Chinese. The difficulty with this interpretation is the postulate that the middle-class Chinese were Westernized. We do not know for a fact that they really were.

Another possibility is that social class is crucial. Those showing superior performance were middle class, and inferior performance, lower class. But is the middle class in Chinese culture really similar to the middle class in European culture? Does not cultural difference override class similarity?

A third possibility is that schooling is involved. Those doing well at the task attended English schools; those doing poorly either did not go to school or attended inadequate lower-class schools. But can schooling be a more important influence than either social class or culture?

Another interpretation still, which Goodnow originally offered, is that IQ is the important factor. She found that groups superior in the combinations task had higher IQs than the groups who did poorly on it. If the effect of IQ is eliminated by statistical means, then there are no major differences among the groups. But the IQ interpretation is ambiguous, too. What do IQ scores in foreign cultures mean? And are not the IQ findings confounded with social-class differences, the high IQ subjects being middle class and the low, lower class? As you can see, each interpretation is complex. Furthermore, there is the possibility that some combination of factors—not just a single one—is involved. Perhaps lack of schooling and social class and culture are all related to the observed differences.

My second comment is that it is hard to see why there were no group differences on the conservation tasks, while there were differences on the combinations test. Whatever the factor—culture, social class, schooling, or IQ—responsible for the group differences in the combination tasks, why should it not affect conservation tasks as well?

Further research clarifies some of these issues. Price-Williams (1961) found that West African children from 5 to 8 years of age showed roughly the same progression as European children in the development of conservation of continuous and discontinuous quantities.

These children were not in school, nor were they of European culture. The study indicates, then, that neither schooling nor Westernization is necessary for successful conservation in these cases.

Vernon (1965a) gave a battery of Piagetian tests, in a standardized fashion, to 100 British and 50 West Indian boys. All children attended school and were from 10½ to 11 years. The middle and lower classes were represented in each cultural group. First, consider overall cultural differences on the Piaget tasks. On several tests there were negligible or small differences between British and West Indian children: conservation of substance, conservation of volume, inclusion relations (classification), and imagery. The largest differences occurred in the case of conservation of continuous quantities, where 6 percent of the English children and 18 percent of the West Indian children were wrong on the standard problem; conservation of length, where 5 percent of the English and 40 percent of the West Indians were incorrect; conservation of area, where the error rates were 7 percent for the English and 18 for the West Indians. Of the three "large" differences, only conservation of length seems important. The Vernon results must be viewed with caution since the method of administration was extremely inflexible. Nevertheless, the findings suggest that on most of the tasks, with the possible exception of conservation of length, West Indian and British children perform at roughly equivalent levels. In a second paper

(1965*b*), Vernon reports that West Indian boys of different social classes did not differ on the Piagetian tasks. (He does not give social-class data for the English.)

Greenfield (1966) studied the conservation of liquid in West African children (Senegal). There were three groups: village children who did not attend school, village children who did, and urban children who attended school. In all groups there were three age levels: 6 to 7 years; 8 to 9; and 11 to 13. The results showed that the schooled children, both rural and urban, followed the typical course of development with regard to conservation: relative success at age 6 or 7 and almost perfect performance by the age of 11 to 13. By contrast, the unschooled rural Senegalese failed to improve after the age of 8 or 9; only about 50 percent succeeded at this age level and at ages 11 to 13. Thus culture does not affect the development of conservation; the urban-rural distinction is not important, either. What seems to matter is schooling.

Opper (1971) has performed what I think is the most thorough study in this area. Her aim was to examine Thai children's acquisition of the intellectual stages and types of reasoning described by Piaget. She studied two groups, one involving 142 children from the city of Bangkok, and the other involving 140 children from a small rural community engaged mainly in rice farming. The children in both samples ranged from 6 to 16 years of age. Opper administered to all children from 6 to 11 years of age a battery of 10 Piagetian tasks measuring concrete operational thought: class inclusion, conservation of length, conservation of liquid, one-to-one correspondence, and seriation. They also received tasks of mental imagery. In addition, she administered to children from 6 to 16 years of age two tests of formal operational thinking: conservation of volume and permutations. In testing the children, the examiners, who were native speakers of Thai, used Piaget's clinical method. This procedure produces data both on the children's stage of cognitive development (for example, whether or not they can conserve volume) and on the mental processes used to solve the problems. Too few studies of cross-cultural differences in cognition have employed the clinical method to examine the mental processes themselves.

Consider first the results concerning concrete operational tasks. On each task, both the urban and rural samples showed the same three-stage progression described by Piaget and displayed by Western children. Furthermore, at each stage of development, the Thai children used the same types of reasoning shown by Swiss children and often verbalized the reasoning in identical words.

In the tasks of mental imagery, there was a slight difference between the Thai and Swiss children. The Thai children do approximately as well on both static and dynamic problems, whereas Swiss children find the static tasks easier. Nevertheless, Thai children develop each type of imagery in the manner Piaget describes and in general make the same types of errors as do Swiss children.

In the case of formal operational tasks, Thai children again show the pattern of development described by Piaget.

In general, the similarities between Thai and Swiss children are remarkable when one considers the stages of development, and the similarities are especially striking when one considers the types of reasoning. Children from Geneva and children raised in rice paddies in central Thailand often justify their solution of a conservation problem in precisely the same manner!

At the same time, there were some differences between Thai and Swiss children. The rural Thai children develop at a slower rate than do either Genevan or urban Thai children. In general, the urban Thai and Swiss children acquired the various concepts at about the same age (although there were a few exceptions) whereas the rural Thai children acquired these concepts about 2 or 3 years later. Opper presents some evidence suggesting that the older the child, the less the lag between rural Thai children and the others. Thus, as the rural Thai child grows older, he becomes more similar to the urban Thai and Swiss child.

In brief, Opper's research shows overwhelming similarities in stages of development and types of reasoning between Thai and Swiss children (who are of course quite similar to American and other Western children). The major difference is in the age of acquisition of the various concepts: rural Thai children acquire them at a later age than do the others. Unfortunately there is no simple explanation for the Thai urban-rural difference in rate of cognitive development. Both groups go to school; both speak the same language. Presumably, some as yet unidentified differences in environment or experience can explain the results.

Table 1 summarizes the results from various studies. What do they show? First, consider the hypothesis that culture produces important differences in certain cognitive skills. The evidence does not support this hypothesis. Goodnow found minimal effects of culture; Price-Williams showed that conservation develops "normally" in West African children; Vernon found that culture had little effect on many tasks; and Greenfield's data indicate that schooled African children are similar to Europeans in performance on the conservation task. There were a few exceptions to the general rule: Goodnow found some differences, pos-

---

**TABLE 1   CROSS-CULTURAL
STUDIES OF COGNITIVE DEVELOPMENT**

I. Goodnow (1962), Hong Kong.
   Groups: Middle-class Europeans; middle-class Chinese attending English Language School; lower-class Chinese attending Chinese School; lower-class Chinese with a minimum of education.
   Tasks: Conservation of weight, area, volume, and combinatorial reasoning.
   Results: All groups were about the same on conservation tasks. On the combinatorial task, the middle-class European and Chinese were superior to the lower-class Chinese, schooled or unschooled.
II. Price-Williams (1961), West Africa.
   Groups: Unschooled African children of various ages.
   Tasks: Conservation of continuous and discontinuous quantities.
   Results: Performance is similar to what is found in Europeans.
III. Vernon (1965a, b), England and West Indies.
   Groups: Middle- and lower-class British and West Indian children.
   Tasks: A battery of conservation, classification, and imagery tasks.
   Results: There were negligible differences in the case of conservation of substance and volume, inclusion relations, and imagery. There were small differences in the case of conservation of continuous quantities and area. The West Indian children did poorly on the conservation of length. There were no social-class differences within the West Indian group.
IV. Greenfield (1966), Senegal.
   Groups: Urban schooled, rural schooled, rural unschooled.
   Tasks: Conservation of continuous quantity.
   Results: The schooled groups showed the normal pattern of development, and the unschooled group did poorly.
V. Opper (1971), Thailand.
   Groups: Urban schooled, rural schooled.
   Tasks: Concrete operational, imagery, formal operational.
   Results: Both groups were similar to the Swiss in developmental stages and types of reasoning. The rural group acquired the concepts at a later age than did the urban Thai or Swiss, both of which were similar.

---

sibly attributable to culture, in a combinatorial reasoning task; and Vernon found West Indians to be inferior in conservation of length. These results need to be replicated; all we can say now is that the bulk of evidence indicates little effect of cultural factors on the Piagetian tasks investigated.

Is social class a crucial factor? In general, the evidence seems to show that it is not. Goodnow found no such effects in the case of conservation, although social class might underlie some of the obtained differences in the combinatorial task. Vernon found no social-class differences on Piagetian tasks and neither did Greenfield (if one interprets the urban-rural factor as social class).

The only discrepant finding is Opper's. She found social-class differences in Thai children (if one interprets the urban-rural factor in this way). Of course, social-class differences in cognition may exist for tasks not yet studied or for groups within Western countries; not enough research has been done to rule out this possibility. Nevertheless, much of the evidence does not support the hypothesis.

Consider next the effects of schooling. Here the situation is ambiguous. Goodnow finds that schooling may make a difference for the combinatorial problem but not the conservation tasks. Price-Williams finds no effect of schooling in the case of conservation. Greenfield, however, shows that lack of schooling has marked effects on conservation. On the other hand, in Opper's study, both groups were schooled and yet there was a difference between urban and rural children. The picture seems confusing; schooling may or may not have an effect.

Finally, there is the hypothesis that IQ can account for observed cultural differences in cognitive development. Since the observed differences seem minor, this hypothesis has little work to do.

It should be pointed out that the cross-cultural studies, while in some respects illuminating, suffer from a major weakness. Much of the research does not obtain a clear measure of the reasoning process used in the solution of various problems. The conservation problem, for example, can be solved in a variety of ways, and Piaget is not interested so much in the fact that a child solved it, but in his method of doing so. He repeatedly points out that even complex problems, like Goodnow's combination task, can be solved by ontogenetically primitive modes of thought. To rule out this possibility, one must probe the child's thought by administering several problems in a flexible way. Only Opper's study does this. Such research is the only hope for clarifying some of the ambiguities posed by cross-cultural studies—for example, that West Indian children do well on conservation of substance but not length. If we had some idea of the reasoning process employed in both cases, we might be able to interpret the confusing results.

WESTERN STUDIES

What does Piagetian research tell us about social-class differences within Western culture? Several studies have compared the social classes on various Piagetian tasks. The results may be summarized as follows. Some studies find no social-class differences; some find minor ones; none of the research shows that lower-class children entirely lack the skills Piaget describes.

TABLE 2   PERCENTAGES OF
RESPONSES TO FOUR CONSERVATION PROBLEMS

Problems	Lower class		Middle class	
	2–5 to 3–4	3–5 to 4–4	2–5 to 3–4	3–5 to 4–4
1. CONS[a]	0.0	13.3	0.0	17.1
CNC	10.0	30.0	37.5	58.5
INC	90.0	56.7	62.5	24.4
2. CONS	3.3	10.0	6.3	31.7
CNC	10.0	23.3	12.5	24.4
INC	86.7	66.7	81.2	43.9
3. CONS	0.0	6.7	0.0	17.1
CNC	10.0	16.7	31.3	56.1
INC	90.0	73.3	68.7	24.4
4. CONS	0.0	3.3	0.0	12.2
CNC	6.7	26.7	37.5	56.1
INC	90.0	66.7	56.2	29.3

Source: Rothenberg and Courtney, 1969, p. 497.

[a] CONS means consistent conserving, CNC means consistent nonconserving, and INC means inconsistent.

Here are a few examples of research showing a social-class difference. Beilin, Kagan, and Rabinowitz (1966) studied visual imagery in 7-year-olds. . . . They found significant social-class and racial differences in the imagery problems. Unfortunately, the writers do not tell us how large the differences were or whether lower-class or black subjects are completely deficient in the skills under consideration.

Rothenberg and Courtney (1969) investigated social-class differences in the conservation of number. Table 2 shows the percentage of children passing four different conservation of number problems. The table shows that few young children (2–5 to 3–4) of either social class are consistent conservers and that at ages 3–5 to 4–4 a significantly greater percentage of middle-class children conserve consistently than do lower-class children. Of course, the study has nothing to say about what occurs after the age of 4–4. Do poor children eventually catch up?

Consider next a few studies showing no social-class differences. Beilin (1964) studied lower- and middle-class children's performance on a task analogous to Piaget's problem of the conservation of area. According to Beilin, "performance in the MC Kindergarten [about age 5] is not appreciably different from that of the LC Kindergarten groups on all measures" (p. 221).

What happens in the case of older children? Mermelstein and Schulman (1967) investigated the effect of lack of schooling on

TABLE 3 NUMBER OF SCHOOLED AND UNSCHOOLED CHILDREN SHOWING CONSERVATION OF ITS LACK ON FIVE CONSERVATION TASKS

Task		6-year-olds	
		Unschooled	Schooled
1	Nonconservers (NC)	17	23
	Conservers (C)	9	6
2	NC	25	28
	C	4	1
3	NC	27	29
	C	3	1
4	NC	24	26
	C	6	4
5	NC	24	29
	C	3	0
		9-year-olds	
1	NC	6	5
	C	24	25
2	NC	17	14
	C	9	13
3	NC	13	14
	C	14	14
4	NC	6	5
	C	21	20
5	NC	8	9
	C	21	18

Source: Mermelstein and Schulman, 1967, p. 47.

lower-class children's conservation performance. These writers studied 6- and 9-year-old Negro children. About half of the subjects at each age level were from a lower-class background in the American South and did not attend school. Another group (again both 6 and 9 years of age) was from a similar background in the North and did attend school. The question was whether the first group's lack of schooling affected its performance on the conservation of continuous quantity. The results showed that both groups performed at about the same level: by 9 years of age, children from both the North and South did well at the conservation problem. The data are given in Table 3. They plainly show that on the various forms of the conservation tasks, poor 6-year-olds, schooled or unschooled, do badly, whereas a high proportion of older children show evidence of an ability to conserve. The results are of interest in two ways. They show first that extremely deprived black children in the South eventually acquire conservation and, second, that attendance in school apparently makes no difference for this aspect of development.

CONCLUSIONS

In general, the available research supports Piaget's views. The cross-cultural studies show that the basics of cognitive functioning, at least as Piaget describes it, are quite similar in a variety of cultures throughout the world. The ages at which children master the Piagetian tasks may not be precisely the same in Geneva as in Hong Kong, but in both cases cognitive development seems to follow the same general course. In view of this, it seems unlikely that the minds of lower-class children within Western societies differ in remarkable ways from those of middle-class children. The available research supports this conjecture. Some studies show no social-class differences in intellect; other studies show minor differences.

The bulk of the evidence suggests that certain aspects of cognition are universal: all children acquire certain basic categories of thought. This is not to deny that there may be individual and social-class differences in other aspects of thought. Surely the *content* of poor children's thought must include unique features. Poor children in the ghetto often know about the numbers racket, whereas middle-class children may think of numbers in the context of adding lollipops.

Perhaps, too, poor children's *patterns* of thinking (not the content) are in some ways unique. The Lesser research suggests that this may be true of different ethnic groups. But as yet we know little about this possibility, however plausible it may be. As I pointed out earlier, the tests used in the Lesser research were rather superficial. To detect subtle differences in thought, we need subtle research—research which attempts to measure fine aspects of the reasoning process. It will benefit us little simply to tabulate the number of problems on which middle- and lower-class children are correct or incorrect. We should save wasted effort by attempting to measure instead the types of reasoning that both kinds of children employ.

So there must be social-class differences in the content of thought, and there may be some social-class differences to obscure the basic similarities—the cognitive universals. Taking this perspective we see that much current theory concerning poor children's intellect is often misleading and incorrect: poor children do not suffer from massive deficiencies of mind. If this is so, then a basic question remains. How do poor children develop powerful intellectual skills despite an apparently deprived environment?

The disadvantaged child and cognitive development in the early years

ROBERT J. SELTZER

We first see the culturally deprived child when he is three or four years old—in places such as Head Start programs. It seems unreasonable to believe that his problems at age three or four—what I shall call "The Cultural Deprivation Syndrome"—appear full blown at that time. Yet we simply do not know in any detail what happens to children in disadvantaged environments before they turn three. In fact, as Caldwell (1970) and White (1971) point out, we know next to nothing about what happens to children in adequate environments in those years.

To be sure, we have many plausible hypotheses concerning the antecedents of the cultural deprivation syndrome. There are hypotheses about protein deprivation, about undifferentiated noise, and about the adaptive consequences of poverty, to name just a few. However, most hypotheses have been derived from studies of animals or from the experiences and behaviors of the three- and four-year-old. No alternative has received the empirical support that would give us much confidence that it, alone or in combination with other hypotheses, is giving us a true picture of what has happened to bring on the cultural deprivation syndrome (Caldwell, 1970; Fowler, 1970; Schulz & Aurbach, 1971).

Some new perspectives may be needed; so, what I am going to do in the next few minutes is to discuss some ideas that have come from recent research in the origins of the cultural deprivation syndrome. The context will be cognitive development and

From *Merrill-Palmer Quarterly*, 1973, **19**. Reprinted by permission.
Read before The Society for Research in Child Development, Minneapolis, Minnesota, April 1971.

the time period will be the first three years of life. I want to treat the question from two sides—first with regard to what the mother brings to the situation, and then with regard to what the infant brings.

First, with regard to the mother, I think many of our colleagues are now no longer as willing as they once were to say that mothers of the lower socioeconomic group, which is the typical background of the disadvantaged child, uniformly deprive their children of sensory stimulation, or of contact with adults, or of meaning in spoken language. We now realize we must be more subtle in our environmental taxonomies, that we may learn more if we pay attention to individual characteristics in the disadvantaged population and deemphasize generalizations based on social class. Let me give you some examples. Bayley and Schaefer (1964) reported that in a middle-class group, demographic considerations showed only small correlations with intelligence in the first three years. A much more potent predictor was the affective-emotional aspect of the mother's behavior—a hostile mother promoted intellectual growth for boys while an affectionate mother promoted growth for girls. In a low-income group, Caldwell and Richmond (1967) found that the affective and achievement attitudes of the mother showed a strong relationship to scores on the Cattell scale as the child approached age two years.

We are far behind in devising adequate descriptions of the psychosocial environment, because we have assumed that widely different patterns of child rearing occur in different socioeconomic groups. When we look at the data, though, it is quickly apparent that mean differences between the groups are small and variability within the groups is large. The lower socioeconomic groups show the full range of caretaking practices and attitudes that are found in the middle socioeconomic groups. And while there are some variables that are related to socioeconomic status, there are few that are correlated perfectly with it. This means, to quote Caldwell and Richmond, that "One cannot legitimately infer the stimulation potential of the home from knowledge of social class alone" (1967, p. 459).

Because of this problem, some researchers have begun to investigate the behavior patterns of mothers from both adequate and potentially depriving environments. I believe this is a most important step, for at last we are going into the home to see if what happens in the mother-infant dyad can affect cognitive development. We have reports of scales, such as Caldwell's Inventory of Home Stimulation, which will clarify measurement of the psychosocial environment. Reports by Moss, Robson, and Pedersen (1969), Rubenstein (1967), and Yarrow (1963) have told us that the quality of maternal care is related to the infant's IQ, scanning activity, and exploratory activity in the first year of life. They have also told us that stable characteristics of the mother's personality which antedate the arrival of the infant are significant influences (Caldwell & Hersher, 1964; Moss, et al., 1969). This could mean that some infants are born to mothers who are, to some degree, incapable of responding to cues coming from the infant in the dyadic relationship.

As you may be aware, disadvantaged families have rarely been subjected to such careful analysis. We have case studies of the disadvantaged family; we are lacking, however, comparisons of different social groups to highlight whatever differences there may be among them along the lines I just mentioned; we are lacking studies of the effects of different caretaker arrange-ments—caretaking by older siblings, grandmother, neighbor, day care center—that are used by working mothers; we are also lack-ing studies of families with two or more children, because most empirical studies utilize firstborns from middle-class environ-ments. These would seem to be particularly important, as the style of mothering might be quite different the second, third, or fourth time around.

Substantial investigations of important psychological ele-ments in the environment of the disadvantaged are only now beginning to appear. Perhaps some of you heard the papers de-livered by Nechin, Jenkins, and Walsh (1971) or by Lewis (1971) at this conference. Lewis suggested that the important differ-ences between socioeconomic strata may not be in the quantity of mother-infant acts but may reside in the way the acts are distrib-uted, in what he called the "style" of the relation. Schoggen and Schoggen (1971) have applied ecological techniques to compare the behavior and experiences of three-year-old children in low- and middle-income urban and rural homes. As a final example, let me mention a doctoral thesis by Tulkin at Harvard. Tulkin (1970) compared the treatment of ten-month-old infants in work-ing and in middle-class homes. The main differences were in the realm of verbal exchange. Working-class mothers were much less likely to talk to their children. They felt foolish, or feared they would be the butt of jokes, or believed it did not matter since the babies would not understand what they heard.

So I think we are beginning to find out about the back-ground of the disadvantaged child and to relate it to his cognitive development. But we still stand to remain unsure of the ultimate relations between disadvantaged environments and the cognitive deficit we note at age three unless we can break away from the correlational approach, which was the format of almost all the studies I have mentioned, and move into prospective, experimental-manipulative work. One of the few options open to us is the enrichment paradigm in which we treat the child in an attempt to halt the onset of the deprivation syndrome. When we move into this area we are also starting to talk about the very new process of formalized "infant education." Skeels (1966) and Irwin (1960) gave us the prototypes and today we have reports of experimental programs in which mothers are trained as tutors for their two-year-old children. Reports by Painter (1969) and Karnes, Teska, Hodgins, and Badger (1970) are telling us that the deprivation syndrome does not appear in tutored children. Unfortunately, control groups that would pinpoint the source of the change in language, in mediation, or in sensory processes have not been included nor do we know if the deprivation syndrome is postponed forever. The only exception I know about is Levenstein and Sunley's (1968) demonstration that what we might call "intellectual play" rather than an increase in play per se was responsible for the absence of the deprivation syndrome.

What, now, about the infant? I want to consider with you the possibility that the infant has considerable resistance to the impact of a disadvantaged environment. In the early years it is very difficult to detect any effects of what will be identified later on at age three as a disadvantaged environment. As a matter of fact, sex differences are probably encountered more often than are differences due to environmental variation (Kate Millet take note).

As one example of this resistance, take the case of infant intelligence scores. Cultural deprivation effects on intelligence tests scores have rarely been reported for children under one year of age (Bayley, 1965; Ireton, Thwing, & Gravem, 1970). The few reports we have on the second year of life also report, in most cases, no differences between children in middle and low socioeconomic strata (Golden & Birns, 1968; Palmer, 1970). That is, the lower-class infants show no tendency to fall behind middle-class infants as they move through the second year of life. By the end of the third year of life, though, IQ test scores are different for the two groups (Golden, Birns, Bridger, & Moss, 1971).

Take an example from an institutionalized population that is often compared with the disadvantaged population because of some apparent similarities (Yarrow, 1970). Thérèse Gouin Décarie (1969) studied 22 deformed babies born to mothers who had taken the tranquilizer thalidomide. The youngest child was 17 months and the oldest was 44 months; each had spent one half or more of his life in a hospital. On the Griffiths Intelligence Scale, scores were only slightly below the norm. Gouin Décarie also

tested the infants with her object-concept scale which she derived from Piaget's observations. On the whole, the thalidomide
infants did not lag in development: 19 of the 22 infants went
through all levels.

A final example comes from my own research (Seltzer,
1971). I have been testing infants between the ages of three
months and two years in a two-choice preference task modeled
after a procedure used by Ricciuti (1965) a few years back. In my
design two colored geometric objects are put in front of the child
and he is permitted to pick one up. The pair is then removed and
two new objects are put in its place. Three stimulus dimensions
are varied simultaneously in each pair of objects—position (right
and left), color (yellow and pink), and form (triangle and circle).
The infants make twenty choices which are then evaluated for
consistency in choosing a particular color, form, or position. I like
this task, because it involves a spontaneous response of the infant
to the stimulus situation which is similar to categorizing behavior
of older children and adults. If the infant does choose with any
consistency, then we have the grounds for inferring the principles
he may be using to analyze his environment and to build his
picture of the world.

As it turns out, infants do show a considerable degree of
consistency in their choices—no mean feat since the criterion for
consistency, or categorizing, is selection of the same stimulus
seven times in a row. There is a shallow developmental-age function associated with this type of categorizing. About 40 percent of
infants between 3 and 7 months categorize while about 80 percent of 19- to 24-month-old infants categorize.

I used this paradigm to compare the categorizing and dimensional preferences of the children of university students with
that of the children of low-income, primarily rural households.
(Yes, I admit to using socioeconomic status as a cutting variable.)
The outcome was as I have been suggesting—no difference in the
frequency of categorizers and no difference in the selection of the
dimension along which they chose to categorize.

I found that the pattern of trial-by-trial choices in both
groups fit the mathematical model for concept identification proposed by Bower and Trabasso (1964). The parameter describing
the probability of the subject's moving into the state where a
stable preference would be shown indicated that a preference
emerged in the low-income sample much sooner in testing. But
while large, the difference between the parameters was not statistically reliable.

What can we make of the failure of many experiments to
find differences between potentially deprived and nondeprived

infants? One possibility is that the subject selection technique, which is usually, if not always, based on socioeconomic status, is not tapping the relevant environmental differences that lead to the cultural deprivation syndrome. This has already been discussed in relation to mother's behavior, and it may be necessary to resort to a careful analysis of the mother-child dyad before we can identify an infant as potentially culturally disadvantaged.

What I would rather point out is that the standardized tests we use are insensitive to the behavioral differences produced by a deprived environment. We have been so conscientious in eliminating the sex differences, emotional variations, and response style as sources of variability that we may have "thrown the baby out with the bathwater," to coin a phrase. It is necessary to test only a few infants with a standardized intelligence test to realize that we are ignoring a wonderful variety of behaviors that may be quite valuable. Are we missing examples of problem solving and other behavior traditionally treated as *intellectual?* Are we also missing infantile analogues of response style, achievement motivation, or response tempo? I think so.

A related problem is that of the norms we use. What do you say about lower- and middle-class groups which do not differ from each other but which both function at a level clearly below the age norm (Palmer, 1970)? Of course, it means that socioeconomic class as defined in the study is not an active variable, but notice how misleading it is to assume that by responding as did the middle-class children the lower socioeconomic group is not showing any deficiency.

We do have studies that use standardized tests other than the Bayley, Cattell, or Griffiths Scales. Palmer (1969) reports that he tested language facility and concept formation in two year-old Negro boys from two socioeconomic levels; he found there was no difference between the two groups. In another study involving children at the upper limit of the age range we are considering, at about three years, the Peabody Picture Vocabulary Test did reveal a socioeconomic influence, but it was the only test to do so from among sixteen tests administered (Palmer, 1970).

One approach to the problem of scale sensitivity has been the construction of scales based on Piaget's principles of cognitive development. The essential feature of these scales is their use of a sequence of behaviors that represent levels in the child's concept of objects, space, imitation, and causality (Uzgiris & Hunt, 1966). Some studies have reported that children from a deprived envirionment evolve object permanence and object-handling concepts at a slower rate than infants from middle-class environments (Uzgiris, 1967; Wachs, Uzgiris, & Hunt, 1971;

Gouin Décarie, 1965). But there are many studies that use these scales and find no difference between socioeconomic groups (Lewis, 1971; Golden & Birns, 1968).

The turn to Piagetian concepts implies that with our traditional standardized infant tests we may have been looking for the effects of disadvantaged environments in the wrong places. If we accept that premise, then we can consider still other ways to measure environmental impact. I think there have recently been some exciting methodological and conceptual developments that may help us to do just that.

These developments center on the discovery that an infant's response to a redundant stimulus can be related to his cognitive processing. For example, the rate at which infants stop looking at a repetitive stimulus can be analyzed in terms of "expectancies," according to Lewis and Goldberg (1969). An important difference among infants of various backgrounds, Lewis (1967) suggests, may be the manner in which these expectancies develop and function. Using a similar method, Jerome Kagan (1969) and Kagan and Tulkin (1971) recorded how infants behaved in the presence of different kinds of stimuli. They report that, relative to infants from a lower-middle socioeconomic group, infants from an upper-middle socioeconomic group were more responsive to schema discrepancy and possessed "richer nests of hypotheses" to use in evaluting stimulus input.

As you can see, this new methodology is relatively simple and brief and has already led to new ideas about the cognitive abilities of the young child. I am even further intrigued by the thought that the dependent variables it uses—smiling, vocalization, fixation, and heart rate—have traditionally been identified with the social and emotional side of the child. As I see it, the new methodology also represents a reawakening to the use of "social" and "emotional" behaviors in studies of cognition.

The idea of a tie among social, emotional, and cognitive behaviors is not new. In 1946, Hebb maintained that fear is the response to a discrepancy from familiar sights, and psychoanalytically oriented psychologists have always maintained that it is impossible to separate cognitive and social development. I think we get carried away by our labels too often and believe that if we can *think* about social behavior apart from cognitive behavior or write textbooks with seprate chapters titled "Cognition" and "Emotion" that in real life cognition and emotion are separate and unrelated.

Charlesworth (1968, 1969) and Ricciuti (1968) have called our attention to this newer integration of social, emotional, and cognitive disciplines. And Cohen (1968) and Flavell (1963) have both chided Piaget for his portrait of "cold blooded" cognition. Nevertheless, it still appears that students of cognition have ignored a good deal of the child's behavior because they mistakenly thought it to be part of his social and emotional life. Consider the phenomenon of social attachment in infancy. For some psychologists, attachment is an emotional foundation that is necessary for the appearance of adequate cognitive development (Bowlby, 1965; Goldfarb, 1955). But given the discrimination, recognition, storage, and retrieval processes that must underlie it, attachment may be just as much a cognitive act as it is a social act. One might even postulate a mechanism in which attachment depends on the prior development of some aspects of cognitive behavior (Schaffer, 1971).[1]

What I am suggesting is that as we increase the use of social and emotional behaviors in cognitive studies we may find dimensions useful for scaling. "Expectancy," "schema discrepancy," and perhaps "attachment" dimensions may turn out to be more reliable and more sensitive than our present measures of cognitive development. If disadvantaged environments do impair very young children, it may take special techniques to uncover the effect.

A third way to approach the problem of infant resistance to disadvantaged environments in the first two years is to consider the structure of intellect early in life. Some psychologists suggest that intelligence early in life is so structured that it is relatively immune to environmental deprivation. Bayley (1955) has argued this position as has Bloom (1964). More recently, psychologists have followed Piaget in maintaining that the infants will use, organize, and adapt his schemas under all circumstances. The motivation to form schemas and to use schemas is found in the cognitive apparatus itself; to have a schema is reason enough for its use (Piaget, 1952).

In fairness to Piaget, he does acknowledge that the environment has a significant role in the development of the sensorimotor schemas that characterize the first two or two and a half years of life. But because the schemas involve primarily the coordination of sensory inputs with motor outputs and with each other it has been suggested that the infant needs only some minimal amount of action and stimulation. Development proceeds

---

[1] Since this paper was presented, Littenberg, Tulkin, and Kagan (1971) have directly implicated cognitive factors in separation anxiety, a behavior frequently employed as a measure of attachment. They suggest that separation anxiety occurs when the manner in which a mother leaves her child is so discrepant from his established cognitive representations that the child cannot assimilate her action.

normally among the disadvantaged infants, because they receive
that minimum of stimulation, and display that minimum amount
of action.

The main problem with this conception is that Piaget may
have missed the mark in identifying action as the central component in schema formation during the early years. Both Charlesworth (1968) and Stechler and Carpenter (1967) propose that
action is not as important as are looking and emotionality. Furthermore, if one adheres to the Piagetian model, one has to con-
tend with the prediction that schemas in the disadvantaged will
not be as rich or robust as those in the middle-class child. But
from what we know of performance in the Piaget-type developmental scales there are few reliable differences.

What to do? There is one other alternative, the cumulative
deprivation hypothesis, that holds differences do not appear until
enough deprivation has occurred; *enough* means about three
years' worth. What accumulates? The effects of having missed a
critical period for intellectual growth; the effects of a neglectful
social environment; and the effects of a poor introduction to the
use of language. The problem with the cumulative deprivation
hypothesis is that, as Schulz and Aurbach (1971) point out, we do
not know whether there is a critical period for intellectual
growth; we do not know that the environment of most children
who develop the cultural deprivation syndrome really is neglectful of them—it probably is not; we are not really certain
what aspects of language are important for cognition and consequently we cannot be certain the disadvantaged child is deficient in those aspects.

Schulz and Aurbach favor an alternative I am not comfortable with but with which I will close this discussion. Schulz and
Aurbach propose, along the lines of the "production deficiency
hypothesis" of Flavell, Beech, and Chinsky (1966), that the
young child acquires the necessary cognitive mechanisms early
in life, but that he fails to acquire the necessary mechanisms that
will ensure he uses his cognitive abilities, especially when tested
for them. To use their formulation, we will have to learn more
about the action of achievement motivation, competence motivation, and the performance variables we use in discussing when
behaviors do and do not appear. We would particularly want to
know if during the third year of life the processes to which these
constructs refer are acquired or if in that period they begin to
influence behavior.

It would appear that our thoughts may be turning toward
the question of motivational variables in infancy. Last night and
this morning I heard three people—Jerome Bruner (1971),

Jerome Kagan (1971), and Dorothy Huntington (1971)—all argue that affective-motivational constructs such as "expectancy of success" and "hope" play a primary part in the development of competency in infancy. We already have data from older children that support the production deficiency hypothesis. For example, Jensen (1968) suggests that children from poor environments can use verbal mediation, but that they do not use it in all test situations. Similarly, Houston (1970) reported that the language of children from lower socioeconomic backgrounds is more complex on a playground than it is in a testing situation.[2]

There are two reasons for my discomfort with the production defiency formulation of the cultural deprivation syndrome as it may apply to infants and young children. The first reason is that we know very little about motivational variables in very young children. The second reason is that while we have recognized the problem of motivational deficits in older children for some time now, we are still far from an adequate remedial program to remove the deficiency. By recognizing the necessity to incorporate a motivational formulation in our theories of cognitive development, we add a whole new dimension to the problem of cognitive development in the first three years of life.

So here we stand, a phenomenon—the appearance of the cultural deprivation syndrome around the third year and not before—waiting to be explained. It pains me, as it must have pained many before, to close with the words "more research is needed," but, in truth, it is.

REFERENCES

Bayley, N. On the growth of intelligence. *American Psychologist,* 1955, Vol. 10, 805–818.

Bayley, N. Comparisons of mental and motor test scores for ages 1–15 months by sex, birth order, race, geographical location, and education of parents. *Child Development,* 1965, Vol. 36, 379–411.

Bayley, N. & Schaefer, E. S. Correlates of maternal and child behaviors with the development of mental abilities: Data from the Berkeley growth study. *Monographs of The Society for Research in Child Development,* 1964, Vol. 29, Serial No. 97.

Bloom, B. S. *Stability and change in human characteristics.* N.Y.: Wiley, 1964.

Bower, G. H., & Trabasso, T. R. Concept identification. In R. C. Atkinson

---

[2] Since this paper was presented, a monograph by H. Ginsburg (1972) has appeared in which the author denies that the intellect of the child from a disadvantaged background is deficient. Ginsburg attributes this child's poor performance on standard tests and serious learning difficulties to low motivation for test-taking, inadequate communication, and a school environment that aggravates his weaknesses rather than capitalizes upon his strengths.

(Ed.), *Studies in mathematical psychology*. Stanford; Stanford University Press, 1964.

Bowlby, J. *Child care and the growth of love*. Baltimore: Penguin, 1965.

Bruner, J. Competence of infants. Paper presented at the biennial meeting of The Society for Research in Child Development, Minneapolis, Minn., 1971.

Caldwell, B. M. The effects of psychosocial deprivation on human development in infancy. *Merrill-Palmer Quarterly*, 1970, Vol. 16, 260–277.

Caldwell, B. M., & Hersher, L. Mother-infant interaction in the first year of life. *Merrill-Palmer Quarterly*, 1964, Vol. 10, 119–128.

Caldwell, B. M., & Richmond, J. B. Social class level and stimulation potential of the home. In J. Hellmuth (Ed.), *Exceptional infant. Vol. I. The normal infant*. Seattle, Washington: Special Child Publications, 1967.

Charlesworth, W. R. Cognition in infancy: Where do we stand in the mid-sixties? *Merrill-Palmer Quarterly*, 1968, Vol. 14, 25–46.

Charlesworth, W. R. The role of surprise in cognitive development. In D. Elkind & J. H. Flavell (Eds.), *Studies in cognitive development*. New York: Oxford University Press, 1969.

Cohen, S. Piaget's children. Reprinted in J. L. Frost (Ed.), *Early childhood education rediscovered*. New York: Holt, Rinehart and Winston, 1968.

Flavell, J. H. *The developmental psychology of Jean Piaget*. Princeton, N.J.: Van Nostrand, 1963.

Flavell, J. H., Beech, D. H., and Chinsky, J. M. Spontaneous verbal rehearsal in a memory task as a function of age. *Child Development*, 1966, Vol. 37, 283–299.

Fowler, W. Problems of deprivation and developmental learning. *Merrill-Palmer Quarterly*, 1970, Vol. 16, 141–161.

Ginsburg, H. *The myth of the deprived child*. Englewood Cliffs, N.J.: Prentice-Hall, 1972.

Golden, M., & Birns, B. Social class and cognitive development in infancy. *Merrill-Palmer Quarterly*, 1968, Vol. 14, 139–149.

Golden, M., Birns, B., Bridger, W., & Moss, A. Social-class differentiation in cognitive development among black preschool children. *Child Development*, 1971, Vol. 42, 37–45.

Goldfarb, W. Emotional and intellectual consequences of psychologic deprivation in infancy: A reevaluation. In P. H. Hoch & J. Zubin (Eds.), *Childhood psychopathology*. New York: Grune and Stratton, 1955.

Gouin Décarie, T. *Intelligence and affectivity in early childhood*. New York: International Universities Press, 1965.

Gouin Décarie, T. A study of the mental and emotional development of the thalidomide child. In B. M. Foss (Ed.), *Determinants of infant behaviour IV*. London: Methuen, 1969.

Hebb, D. O. On the nature of fear. *Psychological Review*, 1946, Vol. 53, 259–276.

Houston, S. H. A reexamination of some assumptions about the language of the disadvantaged child. *Child Development*, 1970, Vol. 41, 947–963.

Huntington, D. Designs for infant mothering programs to develop a sense of self and competence in infancy. Paper presented at the biennial meeting of The Society for Research in Child Development, Minneapolis, Minn., 1971.

Ireton, H., Thwing, E., & Gravem, H. Infant mental development and neurological status, family socioeconomic status, and intelligence at age four. *Child Development,* 1970, Vol. 41, 937–945.

Irwin, O. C. Infant speech: the effect of systematic reading of stories. *Journal of Speech and Hearing Research,* 1960, Vol. 3, 187–190.

Jensen, A. R. Social class and verbal learning. In M. Deutsch, I. Katz, & A. R. Jensen (Eds.), *Social class, race, and psychological development.* New York: Holt, Rinehart and Winston, 1968.

Kagan, J. Some response measures that show relations between social class and the course of cognitive development in infancy. In A. Ambrose (Ed.), *Stimulation in early infancy.* London: Academic Press, 1969.

Kagan, J. Comments in a Symposium titled Developmental Research and Public Policy, biennial meeting of The Society for Research in Child Development, Minneapolis, Minn., 1971.

Kagan, J., & Tulkin, S. R. Social class differences in child rearing during the first year. In H. R. Schaffer (Ed.), *The origins of human social relations.* New York: Academic Press, 1971.

Karnes, M. B., Teska, J. A., Hodgins, A. S., & Badger, E. D. Educational intervention at home by mothers of disadvantaged infants. *Child Development,* 1970, Vol. 41, 925–935.

Levenstein, P., & Sunley, R. Stimulation of verbal interaction between disadvantaged mothers and children. *American Journal of Orthopsychiatry,* 1968, Vol. 38, 116–121.

Lewis, M. Infant attention: Response decrement as a measure of cognitive processes, or what's new, Baby Jane? Paper presented at the meeting of The Society for Research in Child Development, New York, March, 1967.

Lewis, M. Infant development in lower-class American families. Paper presented at the biennial meeting of The Society for Research in Child Development, Minneapolis, Minn., 1971.

Lewis, M., & Goldberg, S. Perceptual-cognitive development in infancy: A generalized expectancy model as a function of the mother-infant interaction. *Merrill-Palmer Quarterly,* 1969, Vol. 15, 81–100.

Littenberg, R., Tulkin, S. R., & Kagan, J. Cognitive components of separation anxiety. *Developmental Psychology,* 1971, Vol. 4, 387–388.

Moss, H. A., Robson, K. S., & Pedersen, F. Determinants of maternal stimulation in infants and consequences of treatment for later reaction to strangers. *Developmental Psychology,* 1969, Vol. 1, 239–246.

Nechin, H., Jenkins, D., & Walsh, B. Mother-infant behavior observed in the home. Paper presented at the biennial meeting of The Society for Research in Child Development, Minneapolis, Minn., 1971.

Painter, G. The effect of a structured tutorial program on the cognitive and language development of culturally disadvantaged infants. *Merrill-Palmer Quarterly,* 1969, Vol. 15, 279–294.

Palmer, F. H. Inferences to the socialization of the child from animal studies: A view from the bridge. In D. A. Goslin (Ed.), *Handbook of socialization theory and research.* Chicago: Rand McNally, 1969.

Palmer, F. H. Socioeconomic status and intellective performance among

Negro preschool boys. *Developmental Psychology*, 1970, Vol. 3, 1–9.

Piaget, J. *The origins of intelligence in children.* New York: International Universities Press, 1952.

Ricciuti, H. N. Object grouping and selective ordering behavior in infants 12 to 24 months old. *Merrill-Palmer Quarterly*, 1965, Vol. 11, 129–148.

Ricciuti, H. N. Social and emotional behavior in infancy: Some developmental issues and problems. *Merrill-Palmer Quarterly*, 1968, Vol. 14, 82–100.

Schaffer, H. R. Cognitive structure and early social behaviour. In H. R. Schaffer (Ed.), *The origins of human social relations.* New York: Academic Press, 1971.

Rubenstein, J. Maternal attentiveness and subsequent exploratory behavior in the infant. *Child Development*, 1967, Vol. 38, 1089–1100.

Schoggen, M., & Schoggen, P. Environmental forces in the home lives of three-year-old children in three population subgroups. *DARCEE Papers and Reports*, 1971, Vol. 5, No. 2.

Schulz, C. B., & Aurbach, H. A. The usefulness of cumulative deprivation as an explanation of educational deficiencies. *Merrill-Palmer Quarterly*, 1971, Vol. 17, 27–39.

Seltzer, R. J. Categorization processes in the first two years of life. Mimeograph, 1971.

Skeels, H. M. Adult status of children with contrasting early life experiences. *Monographs of the Society for Research in Child Development*, 1966. Vol. 31, Serial No. 105.

Stechler, G., & Carpenter, G. A viewpoint on early affective development. In J. Hellmuth (Ed.), *Exceptional infant. Vol. I. The normal infant.* Seattle, Washington: Special Child Publications, 1967.

Tulkin, S. R. Mother-infant interaction in the first year of life: An inquiry into the influence of social class. Unpublished doctoral dissertation, Harvard University, 1970.

Uzgiris, I. C. Ordinality in the development of schemas in relating to objects. In J. Hellmuth (Ed.), *Exceptional infant. Vol. I. The normal infant.* Seattle, Washington: Special Child Publications, 1967.

Uzgiris, I. C., & Hunt, J. McV. A scale of infant psychological development. Unpublished manuscript, 1966.

Wachs, T., Uzgiris, I., & Hunt, J. McV. Cognitive development in infants of different age levels and from different environmental backgrounds: An explanatory investigation. *Merrill-Palmer Quarterly*, 1971, Vol. 17, 283–317.

White, B. L. *Human infants: Experience and psychological development.* Englewood Cliffs, N.J.: Prentice-Hall, 1971.

Yarrow, L. J. Research in dimensions of early maternal care. *Merrill-Palmer Quarterly*, 1963, Vol. 9, 101–114.

Yarrow, L. J. The etiology of mental retardation: The deprivation model. In J. Hellmuth (Ed.), *Cognitive studies. Vol. I.* New York: Brunner/Mazel, 1970.

PART IV

COMPENSATORY EDUCATION

OVERVIEW

Compensatory Education

The compensatory education "movement" began in the early 1960s, first with a series of experimental, cognitively oriented preschools for poor or disadvantaged children, and then with the nationwide Head Start program in 1965. Both the originators of the early preschools and the creators of Head Start were concerned with the same phenomenon. Millions of children were entering school apparently without the skills to cope with the normal school environment. Such children, most often from poor or minority families, or both, did not do well in school and failed to acquire the basic skills that would presumably give them full and equal access to the economic system.

We have a long-standing tradition in this country of relying on our school systems to do all sorts of jobs other than basic education; in this case, we expect the schools to be the prime avenue of "equal opportunity" for all segments of society. As it became increasingly clear that the schools were not doing this job, psychologists, legislators, and many others were concerned and looked for some kind of solution.

But the kind of solution you look for depends heavily on your explanation of the phenomenon. As I have pointed out in Part III, there are at least three sorts of explanations possible. First, one can assume that some children because of lack of environmental stimulation, inadequate diet, or some other environmental factor simply do not acquire the needed intellectual skills during the first years of life. They do poorly in the school system because they do not possess the specific knowledge and the thinking tools that are required in the school setting. This is what is commonly referred to as the "deficit" hypothesis because it presumes that the explanation for the poor child's poor performance in school lies within the child or in his environment. A second explanation is that the observed deficits in knowledge and thinking tools come not from environmental deficits, but from the basic genetic differences. Poor children do not do well in school because inherently they are not as smart. Third, following Ginsburg's argument (1972) (which I discussed at length in Part III), one can assume that the typical school requires not only intellectual skill but also a particular kind of motivation and attitude. Many children with well-developed intellectual competencies may do poorly in school simply because the system of intellectual achievement emphasized there does not fit with their motivational system. This is often called the "cultural difference" hypothesis.

Obviously, the solution you seek depends on which of these three explanations (or combination of them) you favor. If you favor a genetic view, there is essentially no solution. If you favor Ginsburg's view, you may argue for new "open classrooms," in which each child has an opportunity to develop at his own pace and with his own motivations; or you may favor retraining of teachers so that they will be more sensitive to the attitudes and motivations of the poor children in their classrooms. A good deal of interest in the latter approach has appeared in the past several years (see, for example, Cole and Bruner, 1971; Cole and Hall, 1974). But the great majority of "compensatory" projects developed during the past decade and a half have been based on some variant of the deficit hypothesis.

In general, those who framed the early legislation and developed the programs were convinced that the child's cognitive deficits, presumably produced by environmental deficits, could be overcome—could be compensated for—by some kind of early educational intervention. If extra stimulation and specific educational instruction is provided *before* the child begins school, you might bring the child to the school setting "ready" for the tasks and demands he will face there.

But what kind of intervention would be best? Here there has been some divergence among those designing programs. There is disagreement both about the age at which the intervention should begin and about the proper target for the intervention. Interventions have begun with infants in the first year of life and some have been introduced after the child is already in school. Most commonly, the intervention has occurred when the child was 3 to 5, during the pre-kindergarten years. The target for the intervention has also varied. The most common approach has been to focus attention directly on the child, providing specific supplementary experiences. But some have argued that the family is a better target because the family shapes most of the child's experiences. If one can modify the family's behavior with the child, then long-term changes may occur. I will be discussing each of these options in more detail in the pages to follow; but first it is important, I think, to make some general comments about method and evaluation.

HOW DO YOU TELL IF THE PROGRAM "WORKED"?

For any program I have mentioned—preschools for children or interventions with the families—the researchers, the public policy planners, and the school system have a need to know whether the program has "succeeded." But what are the criteria by which you judge the success or failure of a particular program? In general, you look first at the goals set for the particular program and then compare the results with the goals. Since virtually every compensatory program in existence was designed to improve the poverty-level child's chances of achieving adequately in school, success in school is obviously one of the appropriate criteria by which to judge a program. If the children who have been in a program do better in school, then one could fairly conclude that the program was a "success." But to use this criteria clearly requires waiting for some years—six or seven years in the case of intervention programs begun when the children are infants, and two to four years for programs begun at preschool age. What do you do in the meantime? How do you know if you are on the right track? Normally, researchers have made interim judgments by testing the children on standard measures of intellectual performance, using infant tests such as the Bayley, a standardized IQ test, or a vocabulary test such as the Peabody Picture Vocabulary Test. Since we know that scores on these tests predict later school performance, an increase in the score suggests the possibility that there will be later improvement in school performance. The long-term follow-up is a better criterion, given the intent of the programs, but when the follow-up has not yet been done, we must be content with examinations of the child's current intellectual performance.

There are many people (including myself) who are made uncomfortable by the sort of evaluation strategy just described. This discomfort has two related facets. First, as Glick (1968) has so cogently pointed out, IQ tests or achievement tests inevitably are measures of *performance*. We ordinarily assume that such performances reflect the child's underlying cognitive competence, but that is merely an assumption (and an assumption that may be considerably less valid for a child from a poverty environment than for the middle-class child on whom the tests were largely standardized). When the IQ score changes, as it does in most children who have been in compensatory education programs, can we be sure that the changes result from changes in fundamental competence? Or have the children only learned "how to take tests"—that is, how to improve their performance without altering their competence? Improving performance is not a negligible thing, since it is the child's performance and not his underlying competence that the teacher sees and responds to. If, however, what we are aiming to do with a compensatory program is to improve the fundamental cognitive competencies of the children (which are assumed to be deficient), we need tests that more nearly assess changes in competence. In recent years there has been some movement toward including, as part of an assessment battery, tests based on Piagetian theory, such as the Hunt-Uzgiris scales or other measures more suitable to older children. This may be a step forward, but such tests are not the panacea that many of us had hoped. They do broaden our understanding of what changes, if any, occur in the child as a result of the compensatory program, but they will not give us all the answers.

A second, related discomfort about the customary evaluation procedure arises from the fact that the IQ test is too broad a measure of performance. It does not tell us enough about the specific areas in which the child may or may not have improved (White, 1968, 1975a). Even if we accept the fact that we are largely measuring changes in performance, it is still useful and important to have measures that give us a finer-grained analysis of the impact of the program. Lately there has been a commendable increase in the range of tests and behaviors assessed (see, for example, Miller and Dyer, 1975) and the exclusive reliance on IQ measures, so common in the early days of the compensatory education research, is giving way to a more detailed and sophisticated examination of the child's behavior.

Some researchers are attempting to assess the child's motivation as well, but this sort of research is hampered by the lack of adequate and well-tried measures of motivation, attitudes, or emotional state. It is agreed that it is important to know much more about this aspect of the child's functioning—particularly in view of the "cultural difference" model that is now more prevalent—but no one is sure how to measure any of these characteristics. So the tendency is to fall back on the cognitive measures because they are more familiar and more thoroughly tested and standardized.

Keep these problems of measurement and assessment in mind as I go through the several types of compensatory programs. Judgments about what type of programs "work" or "do not work" are necessarily based on imperfect measures and on imperfect understanding of the processes involved. But with that caveat out of the way, let me go on to review the evidence.

PROGRAMS FOR INFANTS
Compensatory programs focused on children under age 3 are comparatively more recent than are programs aimed at the nursery school age. In part, the emphasis on very early intervention came about because of the apparent failure of some of the early preschool programs. Some argued that the preschool compensatory efforts were having less success than had been hoped because they had not started early enough. There is a kind of "critical period" argument involved here. Those who begin interventions in infancy are convinced that there are basic patterns, habits, and skills established in the earliest months and years of life. If you can get the child on the "right path" at this age, it is thought, you will have made a permanent change in the way the child approaches and interacts with the environment. If you do not intervene until age 3 or 4, so the argument goes, you are working against all the already built-in patterns of response.

Interventions with the Infant
Following this argument, a number of researchers have undertaken major interventions with "high risk" infants beginning in the first months of life. Heber's program in Madison, Wisconsin, is probably the best known of these (Heber, Garber, Harrington, Hoffman, and Falender, 1972). Heber and his associates identified a group of 40 pregnant black women, all living in poverty circumstances and all with IQs of 75 or below. Half of the infants born to these women were then enrolled in a massive experimental program, beginning when the infant was 3 months of age. The remaining 20 infants and mothers served as the control group and experienced no intervention other than the standard periodic testing procedures used with both groups.

The experimental group infants spent most of each day in a center from 3 months of age on. Until the infants were 1 year old, there was a staff-to-child ratio of 1:1. For the 12- to 15-month-old children, there was a ratio of 1:2, and this ratio gradually increased as the children grew older. During the first two years, the focus of the intervention was on perceptual-motor, cognitive, linguistic, and social-emotional development. Beginning at age 2 and continuing until school age, the program included reading, mathematics, and problem solving—in addition to the continuing emphasis on language, social-emotional development, and basic cognitive skills.

The children were tested regularly, using infant development tests (the Gesell in this case), and later a more standard IQ test (in this case Cattell and then the Stanford-Binet). There were few differences on the cognitive measures between the intervention and control groups before about 22 months of age. (This is consistent with other research, as I mentioned in the discussion of the effects of poverty; typically there is little or no divergence of test scores between poor and middle-class children until about 2 to 3 years of age. See, for example, the Golden, Birns, Bridger, and Moss article in the selections in this volume.) Beyond 22 months, however, the experimental group showed steady gains and the disparity between the two groups widened. By age 5, the average IQ score of the children in the experimental group was 118 and that of the controls was 92. Six months later, at age 5½, the scores were 124 and 94, respectively. At this age, there was no overlap in the scores of the two groups—that is, the child in the experimental group with the lowest test score was higher than the best-scoring child in the control group.

On measures of language development there were similar disparities: by the time the children were 5 to 6, the control group was one to two years behind on all the measures of language skill used.

Heber grants that the ultimate test of his intervention program is going to be the functioning of the two groups of children in school; at the time of the latest published report, the children were entering first grade, and no data are yet available on their progress in school. But the kinds of performances observed in these children, and their general interest and curiosity, suggest strongly that they should outperform the controls in school.

Other long-term interventions begun in infancy show sharp gains in IQ. Robinson and Robinson (1971), whose paper appears in the Day Care section, found large differences between their center children (many of whom entered the center during the first year of life) and control children. Caldwell and Lally also report intellectual gains in children from poverty-level families enrolled in "enriched" day-care programs from earliest infancy (Caldwell, 1971; Lally, 1973).

Another group of infants who are "at risk" for later intellectual problems are low birth-weight infants. (The phrase *low birth weight* is currently being used to replace the term *premature*.) In particular, several researchers have designed compensatory intervention programs for low birth-weight infants from poor families. Scarr-Salapatek and Williams (1973) and Powell (1974) have combined extra stimulation to such infants while they are still hospitalized with interventions in the home with mother and child thereafter. Low birth-weight infants from poor families given such treatment show some gain on measures of infant functioning compared to controls.

It is clear from these few studies that both short-term and long-term compensatory interventions in infancy can have a marked impact on infants and toddlers' performance on standardized tests. The long-term outcome of such extensive (and expensive) interventions is still not known.

Interventions with the Families of Infants

The other compensatory education strategy used with children under age 3 has been intervention with the family, rather than, or in addition to, intervention directly with the child. A number of investigators have argued that particularly with the very young child it is more important to change the mother's behavior with the child than to attempt any extensive "education" with the infant.

The best project of this type is the Verbal Interaction Project run by Phyllis Levenstein (Levenstein and Sunley, 1968; Levenstein, 1970, 1975). A paper by Levenstein is included in the selections for this section, so I need not go into detail here except to emphasize that the intervention begins when the children are 2, and continues for one or two years. "Toy Demonstrators" go into the home once a week for the period of the intervention, bringing verbally stimulating toys with them. They show the mother, through modeling, how to play with the child and the toy, and encourage the mother to use the toys in playing with the child. Unlike many of the other programs of this type, Levenstein has followed the children who have been through her program; the oldest group is now in elementary school. She finds that the short-term IQ gains shown by infants whose families have participated in the program have held up remarkably well over the years. In particular, those families who participated in the program for two years, as opposed to only one, have children whose test scores remain high (above 100, ordinarily). These children also do better in school. For example, only about 25 to 30 percent of the children in the program for two years were having academic problems in school seven years later; among control children from the same type of background, about 60 to 70 percent were having academic difficulties in school. Nonacademic school problems were also substantially more prevalent among the control children than among those whose families had participated in the compensatory project.

Others who have begun interventions in the homes with infants or their families (Lambie, Bond, and Weikart, 1973; Gordon, 1972; Schaefer, 1969; Painter, 1969) have regularly found short-term gains in IQ for those children whose families have participated in the program, although in no other instance are there good follow-up data on the school performance of the children.

PROGRAMS FOR PRESCHOOLERS

Compensatory preschool programs for children aged 4 to 5 are far and away the most common form of compensatory education; Head Start programs are almost universally aimed at children of this age, and nearly all of the major early experimental intervention programs for disadvantaged children were directed at the preschool-age child.

Of course it is not accidental that this age group has received the bulk of attention. There had been efforts in the 1930s to use preschools for cognitive enrichment (see, for example, Skeels, Updegraff, Wellman, and Williams, 1938). The early experimental programs in the 1960s, such as Deutsch's program in New York, and Weikart's program in Ypsilanti, Michigan, were in some sense "reruns" of this earlier work. The logic that had led to the early efforts to improve the cognitive functioning of institutionalized children through enriched preschool experience still seemed persuasive—or at least possible—as an approach to the problem of cognitive functioning in poverty-level children. Then, too, there were already many preschools in existence in the 1960s. The majority of these preschools were designed for middle-class children and focused primarily on social and emotional development, but these "traditional" preschools at least provided an operating model, and there were many people who knew something about the mechanics of running a nursery school. What was needed, some thought, was to add academic content to the curriculum of the traditional nursery school in order to use the preschool format to reach the poverty-level child.

Head Start was molded along these lines, as were a number of experimental programs begun in the early 1960s. (Deutsch, 1963, 1969; Weikart, 1967, 1969, 1970; Klaus and Gray, 1968; Gray and Klaus, 1965, 1970; Bereiter and Engelmann, 1966.) I do not want to suggest with this description that all the experimental programs were alike or even that all Head Start programs were or are alike. They were not. The several experimental programs have varied along a number of lines, as Carl Bereiter mentions in his review paper included in the selections. Some programs, such as the Bereiter-Engelmann and the Gray and Klaus programs, were highly structured with a "strong instructional emphasis" (to borrow Bereiter's phrase). In these, children were generally taught in small groups with the teacher leading the group in a relatively fast-paced instructional sequence. Other programs were structured along Piagetian lines (such as Weikart's, or Deutsch's) with emphasis on the importance of the sequence of activities, but with less small-group activity and a slower pace. Still other programs followed a more "traditional" line, modeling themselves after the old-style nursery schools, with emphasis on social and emotional development and on the child's freedom to choose activities. Such programs did have greater cognitive emphasis than was commonly true in the "middle-class nursery school," but the instructional emphasis was certainly weaker than in Bereiter's or Weikart's or in Gray and Klaus's programs.

So what were the results? Are programs of this kind successful in ameliorating or eliminating the cognitive "deficit" of the poor child? Short-term gains—that is, gains made during the year or months that the child actually attends the preschool—vary from about 8 to 10 points of IQ gain, which is common in Head Start programs, to as high as 30 points in some experimental programs (for example, Weikart, 1969). However, the equally common finding is that these short-term gains do not last. The results from the Darcee program of Gray and Klaus are typical (Gray and Klaus, 1970). Their experimental group with the longest and most intensive intervention—including home visits as well as three summers of special preschool—showed a mean IQ gain of 15.6 points after the first summer of intervention compared to a gain of 2.8 for a control group in the same community (Nashville, Tennessee). However, this initial large gain was not maintained. After a second summer of preschool, when the children were 4, the experimental group had an average IQ of 96.4, whereas the control group was 89.6. The two groups continued to come closer together in test performance so that by the time the children were in fourth grade (about age 9), the experimental group had an average IQ of 86.7 and the control group, 84.9. Thus the children in the compensatory program showed a sharp initial rise, followed by a fairly steady decline, and the control children, from the same environment but without the compensatory experience, showed a steady decline in measured IQ.

Similar results may be found in a long-term study by Weikart (see Table 1). He reports the same magnitude of initial gain for the experimental groups as did Gray and Klaus, 16.1 points, compared to a gain of only 4.3 points for the controls. The two groups differed significantly in IQ through the first grade, after which there was no difference. In this instance, however, although the two groups were not different in IQ test scores by third grade, they did continue to differ on school achievement scores and on teachers' ratings of the children's academic, emotional, and social development (Weikart, 1972). The experimental group children achieved significantly higher scores on standard achievement tests as late as third grade.

Deutsch, too, has found small differences between the group of children who received compensatory preschool and the control subjects, and the differences persist five to seven years later (Deutsch, 1969). So there is *some* indication that the original goal of improving school performance has been achieved in a modest way in some programs. For most of the "ordinary" Head Start programs, however, there is no such long-term gain made by those in Head Start compared to those children who have not had this experience.

Thus the answer to whether compensatory preschools have worked is yes and no. They have not had the massive effect that was hoped for them; but some of the better experimental programs have shown that short-term intervention before school can have a small effect that lasts well into elementary school. The next, and much more interesting question is the one Bereiter deals with extensively in his paper, and the one more researchers are asking currently. Which *kinds* of programs work? What pieces or parts of programs seem to have been particularly helpful? Of course, it would be nice if there were some simple answer to this question, some simple

TABLE 1 RESULTS FROM WEIKART'S LONG-TERM FOLLOW-UP OF COMPENSATORY EDUCATION SUBJECTS: STANFORD-BINET IQ RESULTS, EXPERIMENTAL VERSUS CONTROL

			Time of
	Fall entering Yr, age 3	Spring entering Yr, age 3½	Spring 2nd Year, age 4½
Group size[a]			
Experimental	58	58	44
Control	65	65	49
Group IQ means			
Experimental	79.7	95.8	94.7
Control	79.1	83.4	82.7
F Ratio	<1	39.78	25.36
Significance	n.s.	<0.01	<0.01

[a] The group size declines over ages because the subjects who began the
Source: Weikart (1972), p. 58.

ingredient, like a special vitamin pill, which could be added to preschool programs and make them instantly effective. Not surprisingly, it does not work that way.

Bereiter's review suggests that the dimension that appears to differentiate the most successful from the less successful programs is one of structure or of intensiveness of educational experience offered to the child. The programs with greatest success appear to be the ones with the clearest goals and the most carefully planned and implemented programs. Generally these are also programs in which there is a strong "instructional emphasis," although the theoretical bias of the program originators varies considerably. But an excellent recent comparison of long-term outcomes of programs of different types (Miller and Dyer, 1975) calls even this general conclusion into question.

Miller and Dyer began in 1968 with models of preschool compensatory education and introduced these models into regular Head Start centers in Louisville, Kentucky. The four models compared were a Bereiter-Engelmann program, the Darcee program of Klaus and Gray, a Montessori model, and the "traditional" model as occurred in Head Start centers all over the country. Both the Bereiter-Engelmann and Darcee models emphasized cognitive tasks performed by small groups of children with a teacher's guidance and direction. Both emphasized the use of reinforcement in the shaping of behavior. Both are highly structured programs and relatively

data collection

Spring kindergarten	Spring 1st Grade	Spring 2nd Grade	Spring 3rd Grade
45	33	21	13
52	37	24	15
90.5	91.2	88.8	89.6
85.4	83.3	86.5	88.1
4.58	8.26	<1	<1
<0.05	<0.01	n.s.	n.s.

program in the later years have not yet reached elementary school.

teacher-oriented in that the pacing and planning of activities is largely under the control of the teacher. The Darcee program also included home visits and placed greater emphasis on involvement of parents. The Montessori program model used is focused more on the development of inner motivations than on specific cognitive skills. Activities in these centers were child-oriented. The Montessori system also emphasized a child-centered approach in which children selected their own activities. The "traditional" model, based largely on materials prepared for Head Start teachers, was also child-centered, with large portions of the day used for "free play." Emphasis was on social-emotional skills as well as on cognitive skills.

Four classrooms each of the Bereiter-Engelmann, Darcee, and traditional models, and two Montessori classrooms were established and the teachers of each sent for special training with the originators of each model. Consultants skilled in each approach also visited each classroom during the year, both to evaluate the accuracy with which the model had been exemplified, and to help the teachers improve their skills in using that particular approach.

Miller and Dyer have now followed the children who experienced these varying pre-kindergarten programs through second grade, and compared them to a control group of children from the same community who had not had the preschool experience. This study has several important methodological virtues that set it apart from other research of this type. First, except for some minor restrictions, the children were assigned randomly to the various programs or to the control group. Second, the battery of tests used to assess the impact of the different programs goes beyond the usual IQ or achievement tests and includes some measures of motivation and attitude. Third, observations were made of the preschools in operation to determine the *actual* content and structure of the different models. Fourth, some effort was made to assess the type of later school experiences of the children, including some classroom observations in the schools.

Obviously this is an enormously complex study, and I cannot begin to give you the richness of it here. However, let me emphasize a few points. First, short-term gains on standard IQ measures and other assessments of cognitive functioning show that the two most structured programs—the Bereiter-Engelmann and Darcee programs—generally produced the largest gains, although the magnitude of gains shown here is not as large as the originators of either model have obtained elsewhere. Miller and Dyer summarize this part of the study as follows:

> In general, if both overall levels and changes from fall to spring are considered, experimental programs were superior to no program at all on both cognitive and non-cognitive measures, and the immediate impact of each program was consistent with program emphasis. Effects of the BE program were largely confined to cognitive and academic areas and related test behavior. Effects of the DAR[cee] program were more diffuse and most efficient in the areas of motivation and attitudes. Darcee was consistently effective, as predicted, on motivational measures including tested inventiveness, Face Sheet ratings by testers, ambition, and verbal-social-participation ratings by teachers and aides. There were no differences between children in this program who had a Home Visitor and those who did not. Traditional was high on curiosity and verbal-social-participation, as would be expected, and the goals of MONT[essori] were reached in two areas, inventiveness and curiosity. (Miller and Dyer, 1975, pp. 86–87.)

But the effects of this pre-kindergarten experience did not, on the whole, last over the subsequent three years. All the experimental groups showed a fairly steady decline in IQ from kindergarten through second grade so that by the end of second grade, the control group was actually somewhat higher on this measure. The children who had been in the Bereiter-Engelmann program showed the largest drop in IQ, although it is not clear why this happened. There is some indication that the children in the compensatory programs did have an advantage in reading in the first grade. All the experimental groups were higher than the control on reading achievement in first grade, and the experimental groups were on the average at or above national norms on reading. But this effect had disappeared by second grade, and all the groups—experimental and control—were below norms in reading by the end of second grade.

The only effects of the early compensatory programs that lasted at all consistently into second grade were some measures of noncognitive behavior. Darcee and Montessori children were still somewhat higher on inventiveness and curiosity at the end of second grade, whereas Bereiter-Engelmann children and those in the traditional programs were lower on these measures at the end of second grade than were the control children.

I have described this study in some detail because it is so good methodologically and because it begins to answer some of the questions raised about the effect of the different types of programs. Of course, these data do not answer all the questions, and they raise new questions as well. It certainly does appear that the long-run effect of preschool compensatory programs is weak, at best, but these results suggest that the lasting effects may be more in the noncognitive than in the cognitive domains. And here the several different programs *may* have different effects. The effect of the Bereiter-Engelmann program appears to have been to depress the child's curiosity and inventiveness, whereas the Darcee and Montessori programs enhanced this quality to some small extent. But these changes are not reflected in different performances in school or on standardized tests.

Clearly there is no simple answer to the question of what program is best. Best for whom and for what purpose? Equally clearly, a few hours a day of "enriched experience" at age 4 for poverty children does not act as an innoculation against the special demands of later schooling. At best, such experience appears to be more like a vitamin pill; it has some positive immediate effect, but probably needs to be readministered regularly if it is to have any continuing effect.

Programs with Parents of Preschoolers

As was true with intervention programs with infants, there is a parallel set of intervention projects with preschool-age children that focuses attention on the parents rather than on the child. Most such intervention efforts with infants and toddlers involve home visits. At the preschool age, the most interesting parent program is one in which the mothers meet in groups and are given training in child development. They are helped to learn more effective ways of interacting with their children. Karnes in several studies (Karnes, Teska, Hodgins and Badger, 1970; Karnes, Studley, Wright, and Hodgins, 1968) has found IQ increases on the order of 15 points in children whose mothers have participated in such programs. Unfortunately, no one has done a long-term follow-up of these families, so it is difficult to tell whether these differences will hold up. But Levenstein's home-visit program, which also emphasizes maternal behavior, does show long-term gains for those who have been in the program. This suggests that programs aimed at parents may well be an effective strategy.

PROGRAMS FOR SCHOOL-AGE CHILDREN

In part because some of the early results from evaluations of Head Start programs showed that the early gains did not persist, a number of educators and policy makers argued that it was essential to maintain the compensatory effort into the regular school years. The initial gains in performance during Head Start might somehow be consolidated or supported if such children were given continuing compensatory programs in elementary school. So in 1968 Project Follow Through was born. From the beginning, no single model of elementary school compensatory program was urged. Rather there were a series of "planned variations," involving models of intervention developed by several researchers—similar to the different models explored in the Miller and Dyer study. Schools interested in participating in Follow Through could elect one of the models and receive training in that model from the model developers. The models varied in the expectable ways, with some emphasizing behavior modification techniques (similar to the Bereiter-Engelmann model described earlier), others emphasizing "open classrooms," and still others involving extensive parent involvement.

Early comparisons of the results of these different models showed that the children in the various behavior-modification programs showed sharp gains in reading and arithmetic and other school achievement areas; children in the open-classroom models often showed declines in performance in academic areas. A good many "Ahas!" were pronounced in various places and quite a few school districts dropped their less-structured models. Some longer-term follow-ups of children in different Follow Through programs have now been completed, however, and the results are intriguing. Larson (1975), for example, has compared the results of open-classroom models, behaviorally structured models, a "parent-implemented approach," and a bilingual language curriculum, all implemented in different schools in a single city. The children studied had all had four full years of exposure to the different models: kindergarten through third grade. The most interesting comparison is between the open classroom and the behaviorally structured model.

The children in the open-classroom Follow Through program showed an initial decline in math achievement-test scores and a more modest decline in reading. But by the end of third grade, these children had reached a level in mathematics achievement above the national norms, while the reading performance was still slightly low. The children in the behaviorally structured model showed initial sharp gains in math computations and reading, but these gains leveled off or dropped off over the next several years, so that by the end of third grade the children were above norms in math computations, below in math problems, and just about at the norm in reading. One of the morals of these findings is that short-term results can be very misleading. The early findings that seemed to show that behaviorally structured models were so much better than open-classroom models led to many policies and practical decisions. But Larson's data appear to show that over the four-year period, the open-classroom model is just as good or better in mathematics and only slightly poorer in reading.

Compensatory programs in the school system have had some modest success in helping poverty-level children achieve grade-level performance in several achievement areas; but like the Head Start program, the Follow Through program has not proven to be the major breakthrough that policy makers and educators had hoped it would be.

Where Do We Go from Here?

I suspect that after reading everything I have said and after you have looked over the material in the readings, you will agree with Harry Beilin's statement: "The most disappointing fact to face about preschool compensatory education is its inability to live up to the high expectations set for it" (1972, p. 165). Bereiter has expressed similar sentiments in his review.

How are we to interpret such modest results of such massive, expensive projects? First of all, it was incredibly naïve of us to expect that a two-hour-a-day intervention at age 4 could make a lasting difference despite all the other things going on in the child's environment during the intervention period and despite all that would occur later in his educational experience. In retrospect, now that we have a better understanding of the vast number of other factors influencing the child's intellectual performance, it seems amazing that any effect from compensatory preschool experience lasts as long as five to seven years.

But more importantly, I think we need to reexamine some of our assumptions about the processes involved. We thought that we knew enough about the characteristics of the children (for example, the nature of the "deficit") and about the processes of intellectual development in general so that we could design programs to cure what we perceived to be the problem. But we may have been wrong on both counts. There is now a good deal of argument about the "deficit hypothesis" itself. Are children reared in poverty environments really *deficient* in cognitive skills? Or do they merely approach cognitive tasks and educational settings in a different way? Many researchers and theorists, perhaps most consistently and eloquently Michael Cole (see, for example, Cole and Hall, 1974; and Cole and Bruner, 1971), have argued that the problem in school for most poverty and minority children is not that they do not have the basic cognitive competencies needed for academic work, but that there is a poor match between the motivation and style the child brings to school and what he encounters there. If this is a reasonable analysis, then the solution lies less in changing the child than in modifying the schools and the behavior of teachers. Positions taken on this issue, understandably, become tinged with political and moral colors, so it is often difficult to assess the evidence objectively. Clearly, there is a need for research on what does happen to children in real-life classrooms and on changes in children's performance when the "match" is improved.

At the same time, most researchers in this area are acquiring a heightened respect for the vast complexities of cognitive development during the preschool and early school period (or during any period for that matter). The prevailing view of cognitive growth during the years covered by most compensatory programs has been that the child acquired skills or competencies in some sequence. Thus enrichment involved providing the materials and opportunities for the child to progress through that sequence at a more rapid pace than he would have done otherwise. But this is a vastly oversimplified notion of what is going on, so our interventions too have probably been off the mark and oversimplified. Sheldon White for example, has said recently, "I believe that sooner or later we will have to abandon the theory that preschools can or should be the agents of generalized cognitive development in children" (1975*b*, p. 169). As our understandings of the complexities of cognitive development during this period become greater, we will need to come back for another look at the whole question of compensatory education.

Lest I leave you after this rather discouraging summary with the feeling that no early intervention program of any kind has had success, I should emphasize again that the *very* intensive infant programs, such as Heber's, may make large and lasting differences in the lives of the children involved. The home-visit program developed by Levenstein has also apparently produced robust effects over quite long periods of time. These projects have demonstrated that it is *possible* to design early interventions for poor children that have the effects the designers of Head Start and other compensatory projects had hoped for. What we do not know is *why* certain programs have this effect and others do not. Horowitz and Paden, in their recent review of intervention studies point out that it is often the most *expensive* programs that have lasting effects: "If the data are to be taken seriously in formulating national policy, economic feasibility is inevitably an issue" (1973, p. 392). The expensive programs are obviously able to offer more intensive kinds of interventions and services to the families involved. But the critical factor is to understand, if we can, the ingredients of the more successful programs. What is the *experience* of children in the more successful programs? And how does that experience interact with, build upon, or promote their intellectual growth? The Miller and Dyer study comes closest to asking this sort of question. If as a society we are going to continue to utilize compensatory programs as part of our educational system, then we need much more research of this kind.

QUESTIONS FOR POSSIBLE DEBATE AND DISCUSSION
1. In light of the evidence presented, should the federal or local government continue to subsidize compensatory programs such as Head Start? If not, why not? If yes, what kind?

2. What has been the impact of theories of cognitive development on the design of compensatory education projects?

ADDITIONAL REFERENCES USEFUL
IN PREPARATION FOR DEBATE OR DISCUSSION

Horowitz, F. D., and Paden, L. Y. The effectiveness of environmental intervention programs. In P. M. Caldwell and H. N. Ricciuti (Eds.), *Review of child development research.* Vol. 3.
Chicago: University of Chicago Press, 1973, pp. 331–502.

>An absolutely first-rate review of the literature on inter-
>vention programs of various kinds. The social and policy
>issues in intervention research are dealt with at some
>length. The Head Start program is also discussed quite
>extensively.

Bereiter, C., and Engelmann, S. *Teaching disadvantaged children in the preschool.* Englewood Cliffs, N.J.: Prentice Hall,
1966.

>A description of one controversial and highly effective
>compensatory program.

Ginsburg, H. *The myth of the deprived child.* Englewood Cliffs,
N.J.: Prentice Hall, 1972.

>See particularly pages 190–195 in which Ginsburg de-
>scribes the usual assumptions underlying compensatory
>education projects and gives his own views about the
>validity of those assumptions.

Kohlberg, L. Early education: A cognitive developmental view.
Child Development, 1968, **39,** 1013–1062.

>A really good and well-reasoned presentation of the
>Piagetian view of compensatory education. A very good
>theoretical overview of the role of theory in the design of
>educational programs.

Stanley, J. C. (Ed.) *Preschool programs for the disadvantaged.*
Baltimore: Johns Hopkins University Press, 1972.

>An excellent collection of papers, including the Bereiter
>paper that is in the selections.

Stanley, J. C. (Ed.) *Compensatory education for children, ages 2
to 8.* Baltimore: Johns Hopkins University Press, 1973.

>The sequel to the Stanley volume above, it includes a
>series of new papers on compensatory education, among
>them a paper by Bissell on the Planned Variations in Fol-
>low Through.

REFERENCES

Beilin, H. The status and future of preschool compensatory education.
In J. C. Stanley (Ed.), *Preschool programs for the disadvantaged.*
Baltimore: Johns Hopkins University Press, 1972, pp. 165–181.

Bereiter, C., and Engelmann, S. *Teaching disadvantaged children in the preschool.* Englewood Cliffs, N.J.: Prentice Hall, 1966.

Caldwell, B. M. Impact of interest in early cognitive stimulation. In H. E. Bie (Ed.), *Perspectives in child psychopathology.* New York: Aldine-Atherton, 1971.

Cole, M., and Bruner, J. S. Cultural differences and inferences about psychological processes. *American Psychologist,* 1971, **26,** 867–876.

Cole, M., and Hall, W. S. The social context of psychoeducational research. Paper presented at Lecture V, Series on Public Policy, Center for Urban Studies, Harvard University, May 1974.

Deutsch, M. The disadvantaged child and the learning process. In A. H. Passow (Ed.), *Education in depressed areas.* New York: Teachers College Press, 1963, pp. 163–179.

Deutsch, M. Happenings on the way back to the forum: Social science, IQ and race differences revisited. *Harvard Educational Review,* 1969, **39,** 523–557.

Ginsburg, H. *The myth of the deprived child.* Englewood Cliffs, N.J.: Prentice-Hall, 1972.

Glick, J. Some problems in the evaluation of preschool intervention programs. In R. D. Hess and R. M. Bear (Eds.), *Early education.* Chicago: Aldine, 1968, pp. 215–221.

Gordon, I. J. A home learning center approach to early stimulation. Research Reports, Institute for Development of Human resources, College of Education, University of Flroida, Gainesville, Florida, 1972.

Gray, S. W., and Klaus, R. A. An experimental preschool program for culturally deprived children. *Child Development,* 1965, **36,** 887–898.

Gray, S. W., and Klaus, R. A. The early training project: A seventh-year report. *Child Development,* 1970, **41,** 909–924.

Heber, R., Garber, H., Harrington, S., Hoffman, C., and Falender, C. Rehabilitation of families at risk for mental retardation. Progress report submitted to the Social and Rehabilitation Service, U.S. Department of Health, Education and Welfare, December 1972.

Horowitz, F. D., and Paden, L. Y. The effectiveness of environmental intervention programs. In P. M. Caldwell and H. N. Ricciuti (Eds.), *Review of child development research,* Vol. 3. Chicago: University of Chicago Press, 1973, pp. 331–402.

Karnes, M. B., Studley, W. M., Wright, W. R., and Hodgins, A. S. An approach for working with mothers of disadvantaged preschool children. *Merrill-Palmer Quarterly,* 1968, **15,** 174–184.

Karnes, M. B., Teska, J. A., Hodgins, A. S., and Badger, E. D. Educational intervention at home by mothers of disadvantaged infants. *Child Development,* 1970, **41,** 925–935.

Klaus, R. A., and Gray, S. W. The early training project for disadvantaged children: A report after five years. *Monographs of the Society for Research in Child Development,* 1968, **33** (Whole No. 120).

Lally, J. R. The family development research program: A program for prenatal infant and early childhood enrichment. Progress report submitted to the Office of Child Development, U.S. Department of Health, Education, and Welfare; February 1973.

Lambie, D. Z., Bond, J. T., and Weikart, D. P. Infants, mothers and teachering: A study of infant education and home visits. Summary of the final report of the Ypsilanti Carnegie Infant Education Project, High/Scope Educational Research Foundation, Ypsilanti, Michigan, 1973.

Larson, J. C. Comparative longitudinal trends in early education. Paper presented at the biennial meetings of The Society for Research in Child Development, Denver, 1975.

Levenstein, P. Cognitive growth in preschoolers through verbal interaction with mothers. *American Journal of Orthopsychiatry,* 1970, **40,** 426–432.

Levenstein, P. VIP children reach school: Latest chapter. Paper presented at the biennial meetings of The Society of Research in Child Development, Denver, 1975.

Levenstein, P., and Sunley, R. Stimulation of verbal interaction between disadvantaged mothers and children. *American Journal of Orthopsychiatry,* 1968, **38,** 116–121.

Miller, L. B., and Dyer, J. L. Four preschool programs: Their dimensions and effects. *Monographs of the Society for Research in Child Development.* 1975, **40** (5–6, Whole No. 162.)

Painter, G. The effect of a structured tutorial program on the cognitive and language development of culturally disadvantaged infants. *Merrill-Palmer Quarterly,* 1969, **15,** 279–294.

Powell, L. F. The effect of extra stimulation and maternal involvement on the development of low-birth-weight infants and on maternal behavior. *Child Development,* 1974, **45,** 106–113.

Scarr-Salapatek, S., and Williams, M. The effects of early stimulation on low-birth-weight infants. *Child Development,* 1973, **44,** 94–101.

Schaefer, E. Home tutoring, maternal behavior and infant intellectual development. Paper presented at the annual meeting of the American Psychological Association, Washington, D.C., 1969.

Skeels, H. M., Updegraff, R., Wellman, B. L., and Williams, H. M. A study of environmental stimulation: An orphanage preschool project. *University of Iowa Studies in Child Welfare,* 1938, **15,** 7–191.

Weikart, D. P. Preschool programs, Preliminary findings. *Journal of Special Education,* 1967, **1,** 163–181.

Weikart, D. P. A comparative study of three preschool curricula. Paper presented at the biennial meetings of The Society for Research in Child Development, Santa Monica, California, March 1969.

Weikart, D. P. Relationship of curriculum, teaching, and learning in preschool education. In J. C. Stanley (Ed.), *Preschool programs for the disadvantaged.* Baltimore: Johns Hopkins University Press, 1972, pp. 22–66.

White, S. H. Some educated guesses about cognitive development in the preschool years. In R. D. Hess and R. M. Bear (Eds.), *Early Education.* Chicago: Aldine, 1968, pp. 203–214.

White, S. H. Social implications of IQ. *National Elementary Principal,* March-April 1975a.

White, S. H. Commentary on Miller and Dyer, "Four preschool programs: Their dimensions and effects." Monographs of The Society for Research in Child Development, 1975b, **40** (5–6, Whole No. 162), pp. 168–170.

Educational intervention at home by mothers of disadvantaged infants

MERLE B. KARNES
JAMES A. TESKA
AUDREY S. HODGINS
EARLADEEN D. BADGER

Operation Head Start has, of course, generated widespread concern with compensatory education for disadvantaged preschool children, but it has also created an interest of a somewhat different sort: an interest in preventive programs of very early intervention which might forestall the developmental deficiencies characteristic of disadvantaged children by the age of 3 or 4 (Karnes, Hodgins, and Teska, 1969; Karnes, Studley, Wright, and Hodgins, 1968; Kirk, 1969; Radin and Weikart, 1967; Schaefer, 1969; Weikart, 1969). This investigation is based on similar assumptions of preventive programming through early intervention together with the notion that the mother might well serve as the primary agent of that intervention. During weekly meetings, mothers in disadvantaged families were provided a sequential educational program to use at home in stimulating the cognitive and verbal development of their children and were instructed in principles of teaching which emphasized positive reinforcement.

From *Child Development*, 1970, **41**. Copyright © 1970 by The Society for Research in Child Development, Inc. Reprinted by permission.

This study was part of a larger research project at the University of Illinois supported by the U.S. Office of Education, Bureau of Research, grant 5-1181, contract OE6-10-235, and by the Office of Economic Opportunity, grants CG 8884 and CG 8889.

In addition to these child-centered activities, a portion of each meeting was devoted to mother-centered goals related to fostering a sense of dignity and worth as the mother demonstrated self-help capabilities within the family-setting and the community at large.

METHOD
Recruitment

Twenty mothers (including two grandmothers responsible for the care of the child) with infants between the ages of 12 and 24 months were recruited from the economically depressed neighborhoods of Champaign-Urbana, a community of 100,000 in central Illinois. Staff workers at the offices of Aid to Dependent Children (ADC) and the Public Health Department were primary referral sources. In addition, an interviewer convassed acutely disadvantaged sections of the city to locate families new to the community or otherwise unknown to the referring agencies. Sixteen of the 20 mothers who comprised the original training group were ADC recipients. The families of the remaining four children met the OEO poverty definition acceptable for Head Start admission.

During these initial contacts, the mother was asked if she was willing to attend a 2-hour meeting each week where she would be instructed in teaching techniques to use with her infant at home. In order to make appropriate baby-sitting arrangements for her children, she would be paid $1.50 an hour to attend these meetings. Transportation would also be provided. She was asked, further, to agree to apply these teaching techniques with her infant each day. She would not be paid for this work at home, but the toys used to implement the instructional program would be given to her baby. Finally, it was explained that the infant would be tested to determine how successful the mother had been as a teacher. Although the mothers readily acknowledged the importance of education to their children, they did not recognize their contribution to that enterprise. The suggestion that they could learn ways to stimulate the cognitive and language development of their babies at home was received with skepticism, and many mothers agreed to participate with only a limited commitment.

Characteristics of the Mother

Fourteen Negro and one Caucasian mother completed the 15-month training program. Five of these mothers had been born in the North (Illinois), and the others had migrated from the South, principally from Mississippi but also from Arkansas. The ages of these mothers ranged from 22 to 55 years, with a median of 26 years. Their educational levels ranged from 5 to 13 years, with a mean of 9.5 years. These mothers had from one to 12 children, with a mean of 4.9 children. Only two mothers were employed on a full-time basis outside the home. With one exception (a family in which the mother worked a 16-hour day at a factory assembly-line job and an evening food-service job), the annual income of these families did not exceed $4,000.

The average attendance of the 15 mothers who continued in the program was more than 80 percent. The five mothers who left the program had an average attendance of less than 60 percent during the first 7 months.

Initial Characteristics of the Children

The initial mean chronological age of the 15 infants who completed the intervention was 20 months, with a range of 13 to 27 months. Five of these subjects were female and 10 were male. No child attended a day-care center or was enrolled in a preschool prior to or during this 2-year study.

A control (no intervention) group could not be maintained over the 2-year period, and the effectiveness of the mother training program is evaluated through comparisons between the scores on standardized instruments of the 15 children in the experimental group and 15 children of similar age with similar background characteristics chosen from a group of over 50 disadvantaged children who had been tested prior to intervention in the larger research project. The age range (31 to 44 months) within the experimental group at the conclusion of the program was divided into approximate thirds, and each third was comparably represented in the control group so that the ages of the control subjects would closely match those of the experimental children in range as well as mean. Within these age groupings, each experimental child was matched by a control child of the same race and sex. Further, the control child closely approximated his experimental match in the following family background characteristics: number of children in the family, working mother, birthplace of mother, educational level of mother, presence of father or father surrogate, and welfare aid (ADC) to the family. Since the effect of the interactions of these factors on the development of the child is unknown, background characteristics were matched on an individual rather than a group basis. A summary of these characteristics for both groups appears in Table 1.

In spite of the careful effort to establish a comparable control group, a conspicuous variable remains uncontrolled. The

TABLE 1   BACKGROUND CHARACTERISTICS

Variable	Experimental group	Control group
Mean Binet CA (months)	37.9	38.3
Race:		
Negro	14	14
Caucasian	1	1
Sex:	10	10
Male		
Female	5	5
Mean number of children	4.9	4.7
Working mother	2	2
Mother's birthplace:		
Illinois	5	4
Mississippi	7	6
Other South	3	5
Mean educational level of mother (years)	9.5	9.1
Father (or surrogate) present	11	7
ADC	10	9

mothers of the experimental children demonstrated a concern for the educational development of their children by participating in the training program over a 2-year period. A parallel level of motivation cannot be established for the mothers of the control children. This variable is, however, controlled in a second comparison. Six children in the experimental group had older siblings for whom test scores were available at similar chronological ages (within 12 months) and prior to the mothers' enrollment in the training program. The experimental child and his sibling control were not necessarily the same sex, but there were four males and two females in each group. Further, *all* data—the scores for the six experimental children and their sibling controls as well as the scores for the 15 experimental children and their matched controls—were obtained within a 3-year period; thus, family dynamics and community milieu remained relatively constant.

Evaluation Procedure

At the conclusion of the program, the 15 children in the experimental group received the Stanford-Binet Intelligence Scale, form L-M, and the experimental edition of the Illinois Test of Psycholinguistic Abilities (ITPA). The matched control and the sibling control children had been tested with these instruments in connection with recruitment for the larger research project. All tests were administered by qualified psychological examiners at a school site.

THE INTERVENTION
First Year

To encourage discussion, the 20 mothers met in two groups of 10 throughout the 7-month intervention of the first year. The weekly meetings were divided between child- and mother-centered activities. The first category, the presentation of educational toys and materials with an appropriate teaching model, required strong staff leadership. The mother-centered activities involved group discussion with the intention that the group would provide its own vehicle for attitude change through interactions among the members. Two staff members conducted these weekly 2-hour meetings; one functioned as a group leader while the other served as a recorder. After the meeting, both staff members made a written evaluation of the content presented and the interactions within the group. Staff members made monthly (more often when necessary) home visits to reinforce the teaching principles introduced at the meetings and to help each mother establish a positive working relationship with her baby. They observed the appropriateness of the infant curriculum as well as the mother's effectiveness in communicating teaching strategies. Certain principles of teaching were repeated often at the weekly meetings and were encouraged during home visits:

1. If you have a good working relationship with your child, you can become an effective teacher. A good relationship is based on mutual respect.
2. Be positive in your approach. Acknowledge the child's success in each new task, even when the child simply tries to do as he is instructed. Minimize mistakes, show the right way immediately, have the child attempt the task again, and praise him.
3. Break a task into separate steps. Teach one step at a time, starting with the simplest. Do not proceed to the next step until the child is successful with the first.
4. If the child does not attend or try to do as instructed (and you are absolutely sure he can do what is asked), put the toys away until later. Do not scold, beg, or bribe. This time together should be fun for both of you.

Toys were the instructional media for the intellectual and language stimulation of the infant but were, of course, equally important as the media in which a positive interaction between mother and child occurred; they included nested cans and boxes, snap and string beads, graduated rings, a form box, and masonite shapes in various colors and sizes. The materials used in the Kirk tutorial study served as an initial guide and are described in Painter (1968). In addition, art materials (crayons, scissors, play dough, and chalk and slate), inexpensive books, a lending library of wooden inlay puzzles (3 to 12 pieces), simple lotto games, toys for unstructured play (pounding bench, busy box, and musical ball), and toys to demonstrate transfer of learning (a stack tower and interlocking cubes) were provided. A home project which proved very successful in stimulating verbal responses was a picture scrapbook. The mother or older children in the family cut pictures from magazines which the infant was able to identify by naming or pointing and pasted these pictures in the scrapbook. "Reading" this book together fostered a sense of accomplishment shared by mother and child. A child's table and chair and a laundry basket for toy storage were supplied to encourage organization and good work habits. While the books were intended to foster language interactions between mother and child, all program toys created opportunities for verbal development. As the leader demonstrated teaching techniques with each new toy, she used key words which the mothers were to use and which they were to encourage their children to say. Initial work periods for mother and child were 10 minutes but lengthened as the child's attention span grew and the selection of toys increased.

The choice of discussion topics for the mother-centered portion of the meetings was guided by response to previous material. Child discipline, birth control, and the generation gap were among the topics which stimulated discussion. On occasion, pamphlets or magazine excerpts were distributed for reading prior to discussion sessions. Several films (*Guess Who's Coming to Dinner?* and *Palmour Street*) and speakers (a black-power advocate and a family-planning counselor) were included as were a trip to the public library to obtain library cards and to explore the resources of the children's library and a visit to a demonstration nursery school.

A more detailed description of the instructional program implemented by the mothers during the first year and a discussion of certain critical variables in mother participation and child performance can be found in Karnes and Badger (1969).

Second Year

The structure of the program the second year was patterned after that of the first year, and 15 of the original 20 mothers continued to attend weekly 2-hour meetings over an 8-month period. They were again paid to attend these sessions and transportation was provided. The group met as a single unit with only one staff member, with the exception of a group-leader trainee who participated during the last 2 months. Program responsibilities (note-taking during meetings, group leadership, program planning, and home visits) were shared by the mothers to develop their leadership capabilities.

Many of the child-centered activites of the second year extended those initiated the first year. Form perception, introduced the first year with the form box and the masonite shapes, was reinforced the second year with masonite templates. Most children were able to recognize and name three shapes and to distinguish big, little, and middle-sized. Matching skills acquired in the first year in object lotto games were incorporated into classification activities the second year. All children regularly used the art materials and pasted their own projects (snowmen, geometric shapes, collages) into a scrapbook. The lending library of wooden inlay puzzles was enlarged to include puzzles of 20 pieces.

New concepts and activities expanded the instructional goals of the first year. Each mother and child received a set of three books from which regular assignments were given, and mothers were encouraged to model the presentations offered by the teacher. A sequence of visual-motor activities from the Frostig Program for the Development of Visual Perception (Frostig and Horne, 1964) was used to emphasize lef-to-right progression and visual-motor coordination. Children learned to sort objects or pictures into two categories, and older children were able to sort by six categories at the same time. The ability to distinguish among the alphabet letters A through F was also developed in this manner. Rubber counting units and felt cutouts of familiar figures were used in patterning experiences. All children learned to sequence colored rods of five lengths and were exposed to seriational and dimensional vocabulary. Mothers encouraged the children to match concrete objects with pictured objects in inexpensive word books. Color and number concepts were emphasized with all program materials. In addition, a lending library of toys and materials which included picture files, puppets, beaded numeral cards, pegboards, blocks, and children's books was available for shared used.

The mother-centered aspect of the meetings during the second year emphasized topics related to programs of community involvement. Interactions during meetings were consistently lively. Mothers volunteered suggestions during the instructional demonstrations and offered comment on the teaching principles presented by the staff leader. Such spontaneous contributions had not been evident the first year and indicated improved self-confidence. Compared with their first-year reactions to guest speakers, the mothers seemed more receptive. Leadership capabilities emerged within the group during the year. Five mothers presented talks and moderated the discussion that followed. One mother served as notetaker at meetings for the year. Four mothers were trained to carry out home visits and performed ably. The group planned and presented a demonstration meeting for visitors from an out-of-state teachers college. Four mothers presented a taped panel discussion on family planning, and one mother arranged for a speaker on black history.

The confidence and capabilities demonstrated by the mothers within the program were reflected in increased community involvement. Four mothers assumed responsibility in the summer recruitment of Head Start children, and one was hired as an assistant teacher and promoted later to the position of head teacher. Two mothers spoke of their experiences in the mother training program at a Head Start parent meeting. Finally, total group involvement was demonstrated at a local Economic Opportunity Council meeting called to discuss the possibility of establishing a parent-child center in the community. Twelve of the 15 mothers attended this meeting and were, in fact, the only persons indigenous to the neighborhood in attendance.

RESULTS
The Matched Control Comparison

On both standardized measures, the performances of the experimental group were significantly superior to those of the control group (Table 2). The mean Binet IQ of the children whose mothers had worked with them at home was 16 points above that of the children who had received no intervention. The ITPA performance of the experimental group closely approximated its mean chronological age, and that of the control group was nearly 6 months below its chronological age. Since seven of the 15 control subjects scored below the normative range of the ITPA total and were arbitrarily assigned the lowest normative age score, the mean of this group is artificially inflated.

The Sibling Control Comparison

Greater differences in intellectual functioning and language development were found between the experimental subjects and their siblings than between the matched groups. The 28-point difference in Binet IQ between the six experimental children and their sibling controls was, in spite of the small sample, significant (Table 3). Virtually no overlap in the range of IQ scores was found between the two groups. In the experimental group, scores

TABLE 2 EXPERIMENTAL ($N = 15$) AND
MATCHED CONTROL ($N = 15$) GROUPS, STANFORD-BINET AND ITPA

Variable	Binet CA (months)		Binet MA (months)		Binet IQ		ITPA total language-age difference score (months)[a]	
	Exp.	Control	Exp.	Control	Exp.	Control	Exp.	Control
Mean	37.9	38.3	41.8	35.5	106.3	90.6	−0.8	−5.9
Standard deviation	3.92	3.45	6.84	5.43	12.46	9.87	6.59	5.42
Difference	0.4		6.3		15.7		5.1	
t[b]	0.24		2.72		3.70		2.25	
Level of significance	N.S.		0.01[b]		0.0005[b]		0.025[b]	

[a] To relate ITPA language age and chronological age and to compensate for slight differences in mean chronological ages between groups, a language-age *difference score* was computed by subtracting each child's chronological age at the time of testing from his language-age score. For example, a child who was 36 months old with a total language-age score of 32 months received a difference score of −4 months. All ITPA data are presented in this form. Children who scored below the norms provided for the ITPA total were arbitrarily assigned the lowest total language-age score (30 months). This scoring convention was required in three instances in the experimental group and in seven instances in the matched control.

[b] One-tailed test.

TABLE 3 EXPERIMENTAL ($N = 6$) AND
SIBLING CONTROL ($N = 6$) GROUPS, STANFORD-BINET AND ITPA

Variable	Binet CA (months)		Binet MA (months)		Binet IQ		ITPA total language-age difference score (months)[a]	
	Exp.	Control	Exp.	Control	Exp.	Control	Exp.	Control
Mean	38.2	40.3	46.5	36.7	116.7	89.0	3.0	−3.8
Standard deviation	3.33	3.20	6.95	5.76	12.43	10.28	7.68	7.73
Difference	2.1		9.8		27.7		6.8	
t[b]	0.86		3.00		5.90		2.54	
Level of significance	N.S.		0.05		0.01		0.10	

[a] Children who scored below the norms provided for the ITPA total were arbitrarily assigned the lowest total language-age score (30 months). This scoring convention was not employed for any of the six experimental children used in the sibling comparison but was applied to one of the six sibling controls.

[b] For correlated pairs of means.

ranged from 99 to 134, and in the sibling control group, from 71 to 102. Three of the six experimental subjects obtained scores of 124 or above. The experimental group achieved a mean acceleration in language development (ITPA) of 3 months, while the sibling control group scored nearly 4 months below its mean chronological age. The t for this difference approaches significance at the .05 level.

DISCUSSION

The comparability of a control group established after the intervention interval may be open to serious question. In this study, family background and mother motivation variables were of particular concern. Mother motivation, demonstrated to be high in the experimental group, may well have been lower in the matched control group, and differences in performance between these groups might, therefore, have been magnified. On the basis of this assumption, smaller differences would have been found between sibling groups than between matched groups. Such was not the case. In the sibling comparison, where mother motivation and family background characteristics were controlled, differences between experimental and control subjects were larger than those between matched groups and suggest that the comparison with the matched control group was legitimate.

The results of this study endorse the effectiveness of the mother training program in altering in positive ways the development of disadvantaged children before the age of 3. The 16-point Binet IQ difference between the infants whose mothers worked with them at home and the control infants nearly equals the 17-point Binet IQ difference between the experimental and control subjects in the Schaefer study, where the educational intervention was carried out by college graduates who served as tutors, visiting the child at home for 1 hour a day, 5 days a week, over a 21-month period. In the Kirk study, where professional tutors were used in a similar way over a 1-year period, the mean Binet IQ of the experimental group was seven points higher than that of the control. Since at-home intervention by mothers can be budgeted at a fraction of the cost of tutorial intervention, the direction for further research in preventive programs of very early intervention seems clear. Further, programs which train the mother to serve as the agent for intervention hold potential for developing her self-help capabilities and sense of personal worth, pivotal factors in effecting broader changes within the disadvantaged family. Not only may the mother represent the ideal agent for fostering an improved school prognosis for the young disadvantaged child, but through group interaction she may extend this sense of responsibility for infant, self, and family to the wider community in which they live.

The encouraging implications of this study must be interpreted with caution. Three-year-old disadvantaged children have been found to make gains in a structured preschool setting (Karnes, Hodgins, Stoneburner, Studley, and Teska, 1968) comparable to the difference between the experimental and control subjects in this study. The superiority of intervention before the age of 3 is not demonstrated unless earlier gains are more stable than the disappointingly transitory gains attained in preschools for the disadvantaged. It may be that gains obtained by intervention through the mother that affects the child's total environment on a sustained basis will prove more stable and will be reflected in later school competency. Conclusions based on the performance of 3-year-old children are obviously premature, but the results of this study suggest that a program of mother training can do much to prevent the inadequate cognitive and linguisitc development characteristic of the disadvantaged child.

REFERENCES

Frostig, M., and Horne, D. *The Frostig program for the development of visual perception.* Chicago: Follett, 1964.

Karnes, M. B., and Badger, E. Training mothers to instruct their infants at home. In M. B. Karnes, Research and development program on preschool disadvantaged children, Vol. 1. Final Report, May 1969, Project No. 5-1181, Contract No. OE6-10-235, Bureau of Research, Office of Education, U.S. Department of Health, Education and Welfare, pp. 245–263.

Karnes, M. B., Hodgins, A. S., Stoneburner, R. L., Studley, W. M., and Teska, J. A. Effects of a highly structured program of language development on intellectual functioning and psycholinguistic development of culturally disadvantaged three-year-olds. *Journal of Special Education,* 1968, **2**, 405–412.

Karnes, M. B., Hodgins, A. S., and Teska, J. A. The impact of at-home instruction by mothers on performance in the ameliorative preschool. In M. B. Karnes, Research and development program on preschool disadvantaged children. Vol. 1. Final Report, May 1969, Project No. 5-1181, Contract No. OE6-10-235, Bureau of Research, Office of Education, U.S. Department of Health, Education and Welfare, pp. 205–212.

Karnes, M. B., Studley, W. M., Wright, W. R., and Hodgins, A. S. An approach for working with mothers of disadvantaged preschool children. *Merrill-Palmer Quarterly,* 1968, **14**, 174–183.

Kirk, S. A. The effects of early education with disadvantaged infants. In M. B. Karnes, Research and development program on preschool disadvantaged children. Vol. 1. Final Report, May 1969, Project No. 5-1181, Contract No. OE6-10-235, Bureau of Research, Office of Education, U.S. Department of Health, Education and Welfare, pp. 233–248.

Painter, G. *Infant education.* San Rafael, Calif.: Dimensions, 1968.

Radin, N., and Weikart, D. P. A home teaching program for disadvantaged preschool children. In D. P. Weikart (Ed.), *Preschool intervention: a preliminary report of the Perry Preschool Project.* Ann Arbor, Mich.: Campus, 1967, pp. 105–116.

Schaefer, E. S. A home tutoring program. *Children,* 1969, **16,** 59–61.

Weikart, D. P. Ypsilanti Carnegie Infant Education Project. Progress Report, Ypsilanti, Michigan, Ypsilanti Public Schools, Department of Research and Development, 1969.

An academic preschool for disadvantaged children: conclusions from evaluation studies

CARL BEREITER

I shall set forth here some generalizations about preschool education, based on evaluative research that has been done on the academic preschool for disadvantaged children, more familiarly known as the Bereiter-Engelmann program. To base general conclusions on what is essentially product-testing research is, of course, a highly speculative if not fanciful undertaking. There is not true separation of variables in product-testing research, only the single variable of product entity, and so it is difficult to defend any generalization beyond the products tested. Nevertheless, I think the effort is worth making for two reasons. The first is that there is not much else besides product-testing research to base inferences on when it comes to questions of what leads to what in preschool education. There are the careful studies of Carolyn Stern and Evan Keislar that investigate, for instance, the conditions under which verbalization does or does not facilitate learning in young children; but these studies stand largely alone. For the rest, we have either program evaluations that do not separate variables or laboratory experiments that are remote enough

C. Bereiter, "An academic preschool for disadvantaged children: conclusions from evaluation studies." In J. C. Stanley (Ed.), *Preschool Programs for the Disadvantaged*. Copyright © 1972 by Johns Hopkins University Press. Reprinted by permission.

from real-life learning so that inferences from them are equally speculative.

Another reason for trying to draw inferences from product-testing research is that unless such general inferences can be drawn, the research will have been largely in vain, since the products themselves change from one study to another and tend to be obsolete by the time the testing is completed—certainly by the time that long-term effects have been evaluated. Thus, in the case of the Bereiter-Engelmann program, the target of evaluation studies has never actually been the program as set forth in the 1966 book, *Teaching Disadvantaged Children in the Preschool*, but rather local modifications or subsequent revisions of it. And also the original program has since been superseded by the DIS-TAR program of Engelmann and others, the Conceptual Skills Program of Bereiter and others, and, most recently, the Open Court Kindergarten Program of Bereiter and Hughes, all of which differ from one another and from the original program on practically any dimension one might name. Thus even a simple statement of product evaluation requires judgments about what factors in a given program are central and about the extent to which these factors have been controlled.

Unfortunately, evaluation studies of preschool programs have with few exceptions compared a single program with a control condition, the control condition usually involving no treatment. Such studies, even when adequately designed to test treatment effects, allow only the most tenuous comparisons between one program and another, because each program is evaluated by a different experiment conducted in a different location with a different population, different testers, and so on.

There have, however, been several studies in which the Bereiter-Engelmann program has been compared with other programs or types of preschool education, using experimental procedures designed to maximize comparability of results for the various treatments. These studies, on which the remainder of this discussion will be based, are described here briefly.

1. *The Illinois study* (Karnes et al., 1969) was primarily concerned with comparison of the Ameliorative program originated by Karnes, the Bereiter-Englemann program (called "Direct Verbal" in that study), and a Traditional program. However, related experiments evaluated a Montessori program and a treatment which merely involved placing disadvantaged children in various private nursery schools. Subjects for all the comparison groups were drawn by stratified random sampling from a common pool of children in Urbana-Champaign, Illinois, meeting Head Start eligibility criteria. Stratification was by three

levels of Binet IQ, and the children were between four and five years of age as of December 1 of the school year. All groups were tested by the same testers, although a blind procedure was not employed. It should be noted that this study, like most other preschool evaluation studies but unlike the studies to be described below, was a "home ball park" evaluation. That is to say, the Ameliorative and Direct Verbal treatments were carried out by the staffs that developed them.

2. *The Kalamazoo study* (Erickson et al., 1969) compared Bereiter-Engelmann, Traditional (called "Enrichment" in that study), and no-treatment control groups drawn from a common pool of Head Start-eligible four-year-olds by stratified random sampling according to geographical area. A novel feature of the evaluation was the employment of a cross-over design whereby the samples of children who had been in the two experimental preschool programs were each divided into two groups, one of which continued with the same treatment in kindergarten and one crossed over to the other treatment. Testing on the Stanford-Binet, the main dependent variable of the study, was blind.

3. *Ypsilanti Preschool Demonstration Project* (Weikart, 1972) compares the Cognitively Oriented curriculum developed at Ypsilanti, the Bereiter-Engelmann program (called "Language Training" in that study), and a Traditional program (called "Unit-Based curriculum"). Subjects were randomly assigned to treatment from among three-year-old black children identified as functionally mentally retarded (low IQ but no discoverable organic impairment).

4. *The Louisville study* (Miller and Dyer, 1970) compared Bereiter-Engelmann; the DARCEE program, developed at the George Peabody College for Teachers by Gray and Klaus (1968); Montessori; and Traditional. Over two hundred four-year-olds, almost all blacks, were involved in these experimental treatments. The design was not completely randomized, there being ten schools involved, with enough children for at most two different experimental treatments. This study included an extensive investigation of process variables as well as effect variables. Testing was carried out blind and with balancing to control effects of tester differences.

5. *The New York State study* (Di Lorenzo et al., 1969). Eight different preschool programs, each conducted in a different community, were included in this study. In effect there were eight separate experiments of the single treatment-versus-control group design, but the standardization of evaluation procedures and the centralized monitoring of program characteristics allows for somewhat more comparability than would be obtained from

unrelated experiments. The most clearly identifiable treatments were the Bereiter-Engelmann, adaptations of which were used in two communities, and the Montessori, which was used in one. One other community used a structured approach with cognitive emphasis, and the rest could be classed as traditional.

In describing the above studies, I have not indicated sample sizes, since they are a rather complex matter in every case. However, the size of the several studies can be approximated from the number of children in the Bereiter-Engelmann treatments of each study for whom end-of-preschool IQ scores were reported. The numbers are 29 for the Illinois study, 136 for the Kalamazoo study, 25 for the Ypsilanti study, 64 for the Louisville study, and 69 for the New York State study. The other experimental groups used in these studies were generally of similar size.

The fact that a number of independent researchers have chosen to deal with the Bereiter-Engelmann program in their investigations is easy to explain plausibly. It is not, I think, that they have found the program intrinsically interesting or appealing, but that they have seen it as representing an extreme on a dimension that they wished to study. As Erickson et al. (1969) put it, the program is "at the heart of one of the most burning issues in nursery school education today, namely, open-ended enrichment programs versus highly structured, detailed methods of instruction" (p. 3). If the issue is drawn as Erickson has stated it, then I think there would be little disagreement that the Bereiter-Engelmann program stands as the most extreme and clear-cut version of a "highly structured, detailed method of instruction."

I would, however, call special attention the term "instruction." There are other highly structured programs and there are other detailed methods, but in no other preschool program, to my knowledge, are the instructional goals quite so clear-cut nor the procedures so exclusively devoted to achieving those goals in the most efficient manner. Although certain features of the program, such as pattern drill and the rapid pace of teaching, attract notice, I would assert that the program is not bound or distinguished by any particular methods, but is at bottom distinguished entirely by the degree to which content and method are combined into a fully engineered instructional program.

Accordingly, the kind of general inferences that can be drawn from evaluations of the Bereiter-Engelmann program are likely to be inferences about the value of deliberate instruction at the preschool level. The remainder of this paper is devoted to the discussions of three general conclusions related to this issue.

1. *The Bereiter-Engelmann program has clearly had more impact on IQ and achievement than the traditional, child-centered approach, but not necessarily more impact than other programs with a strong instructional emphasis.* This conclusion has been borne out consistently by all the studies mentioned above. This is also the conclusion arrived at by Bissell (1970) in her reanalysis of data from the Illinois, Ypsilanti, and New York State studies. The results have been replicated widely enough and with a great enough variety of cognitive and achievement measures so that there is no serious problem in generalizing the conclusion to diverse populations of disadvantaged children or to diverse measures. The problem rather is to decide to what kinds of treatments the conclusions can be generalized: what are the limits of the categories *traditional, child-centered approach, and programs with a strong instructional emphasis?*

I have elsewhere (Bereiter, 1970) discussed the common body of cognitive content that seems to be found in preschool programs of all types: identification of colors, shapes, numbers, letters, materials, parts of objects, uses, and actions, and the use of prepositions, comparisons, categories, and logical operations. This content has been dealt with in traditional preschool materials and activities and figures prominently in intelligence tests for young children. By programs with a strong instructional emphasis I mean ones in which the teacher's activities are specifically geared toward seeing to it that every child masters this content. In the traditional or child-centered approach the teacher's activities may be intended to promote learning of this content, but the teacher is not held responsible for seeing that the learning actually occurs.

Among the programs that emphasize instruction, there are conspicuous differences in method and less conspicuous ones in content. Some investigators have also tried to distinguish them on the basis of broad goals, but in the absence of observational evidence to the contrary, I regard such distinctions as purely rhetorical. Bissell (1970), for instance, distinguishes a structured-cognitive approach, exemplified by the Ameliorative program of Karnes, and a structured-informational program, exemplified by the Bereiter-Engelmann program—the former emphasizing cognitive processes and the latter supposedly ignoring these and concentrating upon "correct" responses. I observed these two programs operating side by side for two years and, while I could detect many differences in method and organization, I did not observe anything to support the distinction Bissell has made. Such distinctions derive, apparently, entirely from the kinds of theoretical ornamentation that program originators use to raise the tone of their reports.

This is not to say that the instructional programs are identical in effect. In comparison with other instructional programs, the Bereiter-Engelmann program has tended to show higher immediate IQ gains on the Stanford-Binet (Miller and Dyer, 1970; Karnes et al., 1969; Weikart, 1972). The Karnes program has shown higher gains in reading readiness, the DARCEE program on Peabody Picture Vocabulary. These differences can be plausibly explained by differences in content emphasis. The Bereiter-Engelmann program contains relatively little work on vocabulary development or paper-and-pencil exercises of the kind used in readiness testing, but does entail more verbal reasoning and problem solving.

Having noted that different instructional programs appear to teach somewhat different things, we need not analyze the differences any further, as if to tease out all the differences and then weigh them up to decide which program offers the most of what. Such comparisons may be worthwhile if one is shopping for a program to install, but they are not instructive because there is very little evidence that learning one thing does more good than learning another. Gains on predictor variables are not necessarily predictive of gains on the criterion, as shown in studies of alphabet learning. Among preschool children, knowledge of the alphabet is a good predictor of future reading success, yet training in letter names did not transfer to subsequent reading achievement, although training in letter sounds did (Johnson, 1970; Samuels, 1970).

It would be helpful to have similar evidence on the relative value of vocabulary building versus training in the more precise and flexible use of words already known—on the transfer value, that is, of such learning to worthwhile tasks like reading. Merely to know that one kind of teaching yields better scores on a vocabulary test and the other on the Basic Concept Inventory is not much help. It is not known whether gains on these tests or on general intelligence or readiness tests are of any value.

From the data available on transfer of preschool treatment to later school learning, we have no grounds for distinguishing between programs with strong instructional emphasis. Again, they do better than the traditional, child-centered programs (Bissell, 1970), but they do not differ noticeably from one another. Comparative data on transfer effects are much more scanty than on immediate effects, however. The only strictly comparable follow-up data are those for the Karnes and Bereiter-Engelmann programs (Karnes et al., 1969), where no differences in subsequent achievement appear, although both show achievement in first and second grades superior to that obtained with children in a traditional program.

One seemingly implausible conclusion that may be drawn from the studies to date is that all programs that have set out in a deliberate fashion to teach the core content of preschool education have succeeded, no matter how they have gone about it. The conclusion is probably not true, in that the programs under consideration here are ones that had enough success to have enjoyed continued funding for long enough to carry out extended evaluations and to have been investigated by researchers interested in comparative evaluation. On the other hand, I think it is reasonable to say that the core content mentioned earlier, consisting largely of everyday concepts, is not very hard to teach. It is not like phonics or fractions where, if the teacher is not careful, she can muddle the children's minds so that they not only don't learn it but they are rendered to some extent incapable of learning it thereafter. From this standpoint it may be said that the differences in *method* represented in the various instructional programs have not been put to adequate test. They would need to be applied to the teaching of something difficult. Reading and arithmetic have been taught in the Bereiter-Engelmann program. These are hard to teach, and they were taught with success: children at the end of kindergarten were averaging second-grade level in word recognition and in arithmetic computation (Bereiter, 1968). Since the other programs have not tried to teach anything this difficult to children so young, there is no evidence to say they couldn't do it. I have only my own experience to go on in saying that I do not think that the more casual, unprogrammed kinds of instruction that characterize programs other than Bereiter-Engelmann are equal to the task of teaching anything difficult.

Special note must be taken of the showing made by Montessori classes. Three of the studies mentioned thus far included Montessori classes among the treatments compared (Di Lorenzo, 1969; Karnes, 1969; Miller and Dyer, 1971). In all of these the Montessori classes produced results similar to those of traditional classes and thus inferior to those that I have been calling instructional approaches. In a study involving middle-class children (Bereiter, 1966), Montessori-trained four-year-olds lagged far behind Bereiter-Engelmann-trained four-year-olds in reading, arithmetic, and spelling, although not in psycholinguistic skills. The Montessori method is so unusual, of course, that it is going to make a strange bedfellow no matter what category of program it is put into. Bissell (1970) labels it a "structured-environment" approach and puts it into a category with the "New Nursery School" of Nimnicht and Meier. Such a designation is reasonable, but doesn't take account of the very elaborate and systematic pedagogy of sense training and concept teaching which the Montessori method prescribes.

One source of difficulty in describing the Montessori program is that it is sequential, the infant program containing activities appropriate for children from three to five years or older. It is the higher-level activities, involving work with letters, numbers, and science concepts, that have drawn attention to the Montessori method as a possible vehicle for cognitive enrichment and acceleration, but it is entirely possible that disadvantaged preschool children, brought in for one year of Montessori schooling, never work their way up to these activities. The lower-level activities, which center upon housekeeping skills and sense training, are not ones that would be expected to produce noteworthy cognitive gains. As for the higher-level activities, they differ from those in most instructional programs in being strictly tied to a few concrete representations of concepts. As Mussen, Conger, and Kagan (1969, pp. 432–33) point out, such a method tends to produce failure to abstract in young children.

2. *The "traditional" nursery-school and kindergarten program is not a serious contender as an educational program.* Not only has the "traditional" approach failed to achieve as good results in cognitive learning as the more instructional approaches, it has failed to demonstrate any redeeming advantages. In the Kalamazoo and Louisville studies a variety of motivation and adjustment measures were taken; in the Kalamazoo study, teacher ratings of adjustment, observer tabulations of deviancies, and records of attendance; in the Louisville study, ratings by teachers, ratings by testers, and scores on the Cincinnati Autonomy Battery. On none of these indicators did the traditionally taught children show themselves to be better off than those in the more instructional programs. In the Kalamazoo study they were significantly lower, although superior to controls.

One of the cleanest sets of results is from the Kalamazoo study's analysis of kindergarten attendance records. Here children who had been in a Bereiter-Engelmann preschool showed higher kindergarten attendance than those who had been in a traditional preschool, who in turn showed higher attendance than those who had not been to any preschool. But within each of these three groups, those who attended a Bereiter-Engelmann kindergarten showed higher attendance than those who attended a regular kindergarten. Now it is not at all clear what child characteristics attendance is an indicator of; but the same may be said of any other available measure of childhood personality and adjustment, impressive test labels notwithstanding. One thing that can be said of attendance that cannot be said confidently of test variables is that it must indicate something important and not some trivial instrument factor. School attendance would seem to be a social indicator, a very gross index of how well things are going with a child in relation to school. Its very lack of specificity guards it from the complaint that can be made against other variables in the evaluation of preschool effects—that they do not do justice to the broad socio-emotional goals of a child-centered program. I do not know any way to interpret a difference in school attendance in favor of children in the Bereiter-Engelmann program that is not damaging to the claims made for the traditional child-centered program.

Experimenters who have used a traditional program as one kind of treatment have all evidenced difficulty in defining what such a program is. The name itself, of course, isn't descriptive of what goes on and is regarded by many early childhood educators as pejorative. Yet even to find a name that distinguishes it from competing programs is difficult. Early childhood educators have also complained to me that there is no such thing as a traditional program or a "regular" Head Start approach, that they differ widely. Such differences, however, have always escaped my observation and apparently they also escape detection by systematic classroom observation. (Lois-ellin Datta [private communication] reports that efforts to study the effects of natural variations among Head Start programs have had little success because there simply was not enough variation to work with.)

Miller and Dyer, in the Louisville study, offered a systematic point-by-point comparison of the four types of programs they studied. The traditional approach, interestingly enough, is largely distinguished from the rest on the basis of things that are not done. The video-tape monitoring of teacher behavior in the same study provides striking support for the ideological distinction. Teachers in the traditional program are not so much distinguished by differences in the relative frequency of different kinds of teaching acts (as are teachers in the other three programs) as by the generally low frequency of teaching acts of any kind. The mean frequency of teaching acts of any kind among the traditional teachers is less than half that of teachers in the Bereiter-Engelmann classes (Miller and Dyer, 1970, p. 53).

Furthermore, the only categories of behavior in which traditional teachers showed up as noticeably more active than teachers in the other programs were Contingent Negative Verbal Reinforcement, Conduct Modification, and Academic-Verbal Giving (lecturing).

The picture that emerges from these results is one that accords with my own observations. It is that the traditional approach does not represent a *different* way of teaching from those represented in newer programs but simply represents a lower order of program, one that is more custodial and less purposefully educational. The lesser overall amount of teaching behavior and the greater emphasis on behavior management suggest the custodial function. The greater use of straight verbal presentation as a way of giving information is entirely out of keeping with traditional doctrine if it is taken to indicate deliberate pedagogical method. It is quite understandable, however, on the assumption that instruction occurs only incidentally in traditional classrooms, without prior planning, so that the teacher is not prepared to communicate information in any other way than through just talking. To demonstrate or model a concept, to ask leading questions, to develop a concept through sequenced tasks—any of these require more preparation and a more deliberate intent to teach than is found in the traditional class.

It seems to me somewhat misleading to go on treating the traditional approach as one among a host of alternative approaches to teaching young children. It is better seen, not as a distinctive approach to teaching, but as a system of custodial child care that may incorporate to a greater or lesser extent various educational components similar to those found in instructional programs for young children, but that is primarily distinguished by its minimization of teaching. The true issue between the traditional approach and the various instructional approaches is not *how* young children should be taught but *whether*. This is still a live issue, far from having been settled by research. It is to this issue that I now turn.

3. *The long-term effects of preschool instruction are about as good as can be expected.* However impressive the immediate results of preschool compensatory instruction may be, and however much encouragement may be drawn from follow-up achievement data, the fact remains that no preschool program shows any promise of making, by itself, any *permanent* difference in the scholastic success of poor children.

The standard against which long-term results of preschool intervention are judged seems to be that of the Skeels (1966) experiment, where thirty years later the experimental subjects were leading successful lives and the control subjects were in miserable shape. This is a very unfair standard, however, for the

Skeels intervention (taking children out of an institution and putting them in foster homes) was not only much more extreme, but it was an intervention that continued lifelong. Would anyone expect that putting children into foster homes at age five for one year and then sending them back to the institution would show such effects thirty years later?

To me it is quite remarkable that some preschool interventions are showing statistically significant effects for three years or more after the cessation of treatment. It is also noteworthy that these programs are the same kinds of instructional programs that produce the greatest immediate results.

To treat the eventual vanishing of preschool effects as failure is to imply either that preschool compensatory education is futile or that the effective method has yet to be discovered. Either of these conclusions *could* be true, but those who think they follow from current evidence are applying criteria of success to preschool education that are not applied in any other realm of human effort. They are asking the doctor for a pill they can take when they are ten that will prevent them from getting fat when they are fifty.

Reason would have it that if we have designed a preschool program that produces benefits lasting for three years, then instead of agonizing that they didn't last for five or ten, we should be concerned with what can be done in the years after preschool to produce further benefits. This, of course, is a popular notion, one that lies behind the entire Follow-Through program. It raises, however, some troubling questions concerning preschool education.

a. If it is granted that education for poor children must be improved over the whole span of school years, then is it any longer necessary or practical to invest heavily in preschool education for such children? In other words, is preschool education anything more than the stone in the stone soup?

b. Is there justification for heavy investment in a continued search for more effective methods of preschool education, or have the limits of effectiveness largely been reached?

Both of these are policy questions that have to be acted upon whether there is any pertinent evidence or not, and so whatever faintly valid evidence may be dredged out of evaluation studies is that much to the good.

The cross-over data from the Kalamazoo study afford some evidence that is directly pertinent to the first question. Put more crudely, the first question reads: If you are going to follow up anyway, does it make any difference what you follow up on? The Kalamazoo study found that children in regular kindergarten classes did better if they had been in a Bereiter-Engelmann preschool than if they had been in a traditional one, or had had no preschool at all. On the other hand, children from these three preschool conditions who went into a Bereiter-Engelmann kindergarten all ended up at about the same level of performance. If the Bereiter-Engelmann kindergarten is taken to represent follow-up—that is, the continuation of special treatment—then it would appear that it does not make much difference what one follows up on: the preschool treatments could have been eliminated without loss. On the other hand, when there was no follow-up—that is, when children were put into a regular kindergarten program—performance was highly dependent on the nature of preschool experiences.

This finding is pregnant with implications. Consider, for instance, how the results might have been interpreted if all the children from the three preschool conditions had gone into a Bereiter-Engelmann kindergarten, and if this kindergarten program had somehow gotten itself established as normal, so that no mention was made of what kind of kindergarten program it was. Then the data would have shown that preschool effects "washed out" when the children got to kindergarten. One might even have been tempted to blame the kindergarten for washing out those grand effects. Under the actual circumstances, however, with traditional kindergarten classes for comparison, it appears that the washing out of effects was a good thing, since it consisted of bringing those children with the less favorable preschool experience up to the level of those with the more favorable experience.

A rather more complex set of results from recent phases of the Louisville study (Miller and Dyer, 1971; Miller et al., 1971) appears to support the same interpretation of "wash out." After completing the preschool treatments described previously, children were branched into either a regular kindergarten or into a Follow-Through kindergarten program described as "a highly academic, individualized program structured as a token-economy" (Miller and Dyer, 1971, p. 4). Children who received the Follow-Through treatment did significantly better than those who went to regular kindergarten, regardless of their preschool experience. There was also a clear wash out of differences in the Follow-Through treatment, with children who had received no preschool education and those who had received a traditional one scoring as well as those who had received the more effective experimental treatments. On the other hand, in the regular kindergarten there were significant differences due to preschool experience. However, in contrast to the Kalamazoo findings, the differences were by no means a simple carry-over of differences observed at the end of preschool. On one of the main measures, the Metropolitan Readiness Test, the lowest scores were obtained by regular kindergarten children who had had Bereiter-Engelmann preschool. A number of other shifts in relative standing are puzzling as to what kinds of interactions with preschool experience actually took place in the regular kindergarten classrooms of this study; but the overall result, that an effective instructional program in kindergarten can wash out preschool differences in a favorable way while a conventional kindergarten does not do so, remains consistent with the Kalamazoo findings.

Extrapolated, these results would suggest that a highly effective program at any level of schooling will overcome the effects of variations in educational experience up to that level. The suggestion is probably not true, of course. If it were we could concentrate all our efforts on making a bang-up success of the last year of schooling and not worry about whether children learned anything in the years preceding. But so long as it appears true that an effective kindergarten program will overcome differences in preschool experience, we must question the wisdom of concentrating compensatory education on the preschool period.

The wise strategy for the present would seem to be to look for elementary school programs that are more successful than the present ones at washing out the effects of differences in earlier school experience. This strategy does not, however, preclude the continued search for more effective methods of preschool education. On this matter we have to ask ourselves what increased effects we would want or have any reason to expect were possible.

Such a question invites visionary responses à la George Leonard (1966). Generalizing from what we have been able to teach in our experimental programs, however, I am inclined toward the more pedestrian position that existing technology already enables us to teach young children far more than they can benefit from. What we need to do is not discover ways to teach them more but rather construct articulated educational programs that permit us to teach in the preschool what will be of use later and to teach later what builds upon what was learned in the preschool.

Thus I do not believe we need to be devoting resources to developing a better preschool program because we are in no position to say what a preschool program ought to accomplish that present ones do not. As we noted previously, the various effective instructional programs do not accomplish precisely the same things, but there is no basis for saying that the accomplishment of one is more valuable than that of another. I think, therefore, that we are at a point where development of preschool programs, if it is to proceed any further, has to be joined to elementary school curriculum design. The two questions: "What does a child need to know in order to be ready for first grade?" and "What does a child need to know in order to get the most out of being four years old?" have about yielded their all. The first has yielded the core content of preschool education mentioned previously and the second has yielded such things as handling a paint brush and putting on a coat (to mention only objectives that can be acted on; the second question also gives rise to an abundance of fine sentiments). Only by joining preschool education with elementary school curriculum can we begin plausibly asking the potentially much more productive question: "What things can we teach a child of four and five that can then be built upon in the first grade and after?"

My attitude toward the failure of preschool programs to produce lasting gains is perhaps cavalier. I realize that the more accepted behavior, which I have on occasions engaged in myself, is to express sincere regrets that things haven't turned out better and then offer an explanation which, while vague and speculative, makes it clear that I am not at fault. It is also possible to find cause for optimism in follow-up results. Verbal reports from Karnes and Erickson indicate that Bereiter-Engelmann children continue to show achievement advantages over control and traditionally taught children as far as the third grade. Weikart children, from his original experimental treatment, show achievement advantages as late as sixth grade. To me, however, the most parsimonious hypothesis to account for these persisting advantages is that there was a degree of continuing differential treatment given to experimental group children—by virtue of their being assigned to different streams on entry into regular school. I know this to have been the case in the Illinois study, where the schools used IQ and other scores from the research testing to place children in first grade streams. Differential treatment in the Ypsilanti study may have been even more marked, judging from Weikart's verbal report of a substantially larger proportion of control group children being assigned to special classes for the mentally retarded.

The data on long-term effects of preschool intervention are disillusioning but not, to me at least, discouraging. The illusion that they serve to dispel is that there is some magic in the early years of intellectual development, such that a little difference there will make a lot of difference later. What we seem to be finding instead is that a lot of difference there may just possibly make a little difference later. Weakening of the "magic years" illusion will, I hope, render more credible the position that Engelmann and I have argued from the beginning, that learning in young children is just learning: some things can be taught to young children and some cannot; some of the things that can be taught will prove useful later and some will not; what will prove useful later is not determined by some innate chain of development but by the actual course of real-life events. The corollary that I have argued in this section is that one way to make pre-school learning more useful is to alter the actual course of subsequent school events so as to make use of it.

IMPLICATIONS FOR DAY CARE AND FOR EARLY CHILDHOOD EDUCATION RESEARCH

Because of the twin concerns of the Hyman Blumberg Memorial Symposium with the providing of day care services for children of working parents and with research in early childhood education, it seems appropriate to comment specifically on the implications that the foregoing conclusions have for these two concerns.

With respect to day care I am an outsider, and I make the following observations without pretending to know the complexities of the enterprise. It appears that the main thing wrong with day care is that there is not enough of it, and the main reason there is not enough of it is that it costs too much. At the same time, those who are professionally dedicated to advancing day care seem to be pressing continually to make it more costly by setting certification requirements for day care workers and by insisting that day care should be educational and not just high-quality institutionalized baby-sitting.

What the previous discussion should suggest is that producing a measurable educational effect in young children is far from easy, that it requires as serious a commitment to curriculum and teaching as does education in older children. I cannot imagine day care centers on a mass basis carrying out educational programs of the kind needed to produce measurable effect. If they cannot do so, then it will prove in the long run a tactical blunder to keep insisting that day care must be educational. Sooner or later those who pay for it will begin demanding to see evidence that educational benefits are being produced, and there will be no evidence.

It would seem to me much wiser to seek no more from day care than the sort of high-quality custodial care that a child would receive in a well-run home, and to seek ways to achieve this level of care at a cost that would make it reasonable to provide for all those who need it. One should not have to justify day care on the grounds that it will make children do better in school, any more than one should seek such justification for a hot lunch program. A child has a right to a square meal regardless of whether or not it helps him read better.

A well-run and well-equipped day care center resembles very closely a traditional preschool—which I have argued is also primarily custodial in its function. The traditional preschool has managed to flourish, with its clientele of upper-middle-class families willing to pay, without having to promise educational benefits. It has earned a place for itself simply by providing a wholesome experience for children in pleasant surroundings and in the company of other children. I do not see why day care centers should have to promise more in order to justify their existence.

Early childhood education has been a thriving area of research and development during the past five years. High expectations and availability of money combined to draw talented investigators into the area. Both the expectations and the money are likely to diminish and with them, no doubt, the special attractiveness of the field. The likely result, however, is that early childhood education research will merge more with educational research in general. There is much to be done in the early childhood field, for instance in the discovery of the critical variables in instructional treatment and in the closer analysis of particular learning problems; but there is no reason why such research should stand apart from the main body of research into classroom learning. Abandonment of the "magic years" illusion should have, in the long run, beneficial effects on research as well as on educational practice.

REFERENCES

Bereiter, C. 1966. *Acceleration of intellectual development in early childhood.* Washington, D.C.: U.S. Office of Education.

——. 1968. A nonpsychological approach to early compensatory education. Pp. 337–46 in M. Deutsch et al. (Eds.), *Social class, race, and psychological development.* New York: Holt, Rinehart and Winston.

——. 1970. Designing programs for classroom use. Pp. 204–7 in F. F. Korten et al. (Eds.), *Psychology and the problems of society.* Washington, D.C.: American Psychological Association.

Bereiter, C., and Engelmann, S. 1966. *Teaching disadvantaged children in the preschool.* Englewood Cliffs, N.J.: Prentice-Hall.

Bissell, J. S. 1970. *The cognitive effects of pre-school programs for disadvantaged children.* Bethesda, Maryland: National Institute of Child Health and Human Development, June 1970 (mimeographed).

Di Lorenzo, L., Salter, R., and Brady, J. J. 1969. *Prekindergarten programs for educationally disadvantaged children.* Washington, D.C.: U.S. Office of Education.

Erickson, E. L., McMillan, J., Bennell, J., Hoffman, L., and Callahan, O. D. 1969. *Experiments in Head Start and early education: Curriculum structures and teacher attitudes.* Washington, D.C.: Office of Economic Opportunity, Project Head Start.

Gray, S. W., and Klaus, R. A. 1968. The Early Training Project and its general rationale. Pp. 63–70, in R. D. Hess and R. M. Bear (Eds.), *Early Education.* Chicago: Aldine.

Johnson, R. J. 1970. The effect of training in letter names on success in beginning reading for children of differing abilities. Paper presented at annual meeting of the American Educational Research Association, Minneapolis, Minnesota, March 1970.

Karnes, M. B., Hodgins, A. S., Teska, J. A., and Kirk, S. A. 1969. *Research and development program on preschool disadvantaged children.* Vol. I. Washington, D.C.: U.S. Office of Education.

Leonard, G. B. 1968. *Education and ecstasy.* New York: Delacorte Press.

Miller, L. B., and Dyer, J. L. 1970. Experimental variation of Head Start curricula: A comparison of current approaches. Annual progress report, June 1, 1969–May 31, 1970. Louisville, Kentucky: University of Louisville, Department of Psychology.

———. 1971. Two kinds of kindergarten after four types of Head Start, Lousiville, Kentucky: University of Louisville, Department of Psychology.

Miller, L. B., et al. 1971. Experimental variation of Head Start curricula: A comparison of current approaches. Progress Report No. 9, March 1, 1971–May 31, 1971. Louisville, Kentucky: University of Louisville, Department of Psychology.

Mussen, P. H., Conger, J. J., and Kagan, J. 1969. *Child development and personality* (3rd ed.). New York: Harper & Row.

Samuels, S. J. 1970. Letter-name versus letter-sound knowledge as factors influencing learning to read. Paper presented at annual meeting of the American Educational Research Association, Minneapolis, Minnesota, March 1970.

Skeels, H. M. 1966. Adult status of children with contrasting early experiences. *Monograph of the Society for Research in Child Development,* **51,** no. 3.

Weikart, D. P. 1972. Relationship of curriculum, teaching, and learning in preschool education. Pp. 22–66, in [J. C. Stanley (Ed.), *Preschool programs for the disadvantaged.* Baltimore: Johns Hopkins University Press].

Longitudinal IQ outcomes of the mother-child home program: verbal interaction project

JOHN MADDEN
PHYLLIS LEVENSTEIN
SIDNEY LEVENSTEIN

The Mother-Child Home Program (MCHP) has combined child's play with mother-child dialogue to foster the cognitive and socioemotional development of low-income 2- to 4-year-olds to prevent educational disadvantage in their later years. This paper summarizes one cognitive outcome, IQ scores on standardized tests for children who entered this early childhood intervention program in 1967, 1968, and 1969, and for untreated groups compared with them, and also contains an initial report of recent experimental results for children who entered in 1973.

The MCHP was first developed by the Verbal Interaction Project as a pilot project in 1965 (Levenstein and Sunley, 1968). The program's major assumption was that the principal cognitive element missing from the early experience of many children vulnerable to educational disadvantage was a sufficient amount of verbal interaction in the family, centered on perceptually rich

From *Child Development*, 1976, **47**, 1015–1025. Copyright © 1976 by The Society for Research in Child Development, Inc. Reprinted by permission.

The research described in this report was sponsored by Family Service Association of Nassau County, Inc., and State University of New York at Stony Brook, and was supported by the U.S. Department of HEW: Children's Bureau, National Institute of Mental Health, and Office of Education; and by the Carnegie Corporation of New York; and the Rockefeller Brothers Fund.

and ordered stimuli, and embedded in the affective matrix of the child's most enduring relationships, especially that with his mother.

The program essentially consisted of home visits by "Toy Demonstrators" to model for mother-child dyads the verbal interaction features of books and toys permanently assigned to the child. The MCHP was developed by the Verbal Interaction Project from a pilot project in 1965–1966 (Levenstein and Sunley, 1968). Its rationale, method, and short-term results have been described in detail elsewhere (Levenstein, 1970; Levenstein, 1975; Levenstein, 1977).

Preliminary results suggested that the program had a substantial short-term effect on IQ scores (Levenstein, 1970), and stimulated several questions about this effect:

1. Will program "graduates" retain a satisfactory level of IQ scores into the school years?
2. Will subsequent cohorts of the program perform as well with Toy Demonstrators of lower educational and work skills than those of the social workers with Masters' degrees who pioneered this role in 1967–1968?
3. What will be the long-term effects of varying the length of the program?
4. Which background variables relate to IQ score, and can posttreatment differences be plausibly attributed to pre-existing group differences?

The primary focus of this report will be IQ comparisons between differently treated groups at one posttest period referred to hereafter as follow-up. A brief report of recently obtained short-term experimental results will also be included.

The purpose of the program is not to modify IQ scores. However, if the rationale and conduct of the program are valid, the program should have at least an indirect effect on IQ.

METHOD
Design
The research followed a "quasi-experimental" design (Campbell and Stanley, 1963). The basic plan consisted of pretesting intact groups with repeated measures following pretest. There was also one "after-only" comparison group which was not pretested. The specific intervention and testing schedules for each group are provided below in the group descriptions. In 1967, when five groups were started, randomization was by location of three suburban housing projects, from which dyads were recruited. In 1968 and 1969 there was no random assignment of

groups to varying treatments as treatments did not vary. Group and family differences were controlled by their shared residence in low-income housing.

Subjects

The long-term data were gathered on 151 children (80 boys and 71 girls) 4 to 6 years old at follow-up. All lived in three suburbs (A, B, and C) of New York City and were from low-income families financially eligible for low-income housing. Almost all were American-born, English-speaking, and socially defined as black.

The 96 treated dyads were recruited at ages 2 and 3 years, by letter followed by door-to-door canvassing, from low-income housing projects in Towns A and B in 1967 and 1968. In 1969, about half came from these sources and half were referred by social agencies and lived outside of the projects.

Of the 55 comparison dyads, 25 were similarly recruited from the Town A and C Housing Projects in 1967. The remaining 30 comparison families (all found post hoc to be black) were recruited as an out-of-project, English-speaking, American-born "after-only" group on four low SES criteria from the first grade of the Town A school system in 1972. The criteria were eligibility for low-income housing, residence in rented housing, occupation less than skilled, and neither parent with an education above high school.

Procedure: Mother-Child Home Program (MCHP)

In 1967 the basic MCHP consisted of 52 semiweekly visits to the dyad over a seven-month period during which 28 toys and books were assigned to the family (Levenstein, 1970). Toy Demonstrators (TDs) were Master's degree social workers. Several variations of this basic program that were carried out in 1967 and 1968 are included in the group descriptions provided below.

In 1968 the MCHP was changed to its present format. The program consisted of 46 semiweekly visits to the dyad each year following the local ten-month school calendar. The visits began at age 2 (Program I) and continued throughout the following year (Program II). During these visits, the TDs demonstrated verbal interaction with the child and encouraged the mother to participate in the interaction. The interaction centered on permanently assigned play materials which the TD brought weekly, a total of 12 books and 11 toys each year. These Verbal Interaction Stimulus Materials (VISM) were selected on explicit criteria, foremost of which was their capacity to stimulate verbal interaction (Levenstein, 1975).

After 1967 the TDs were unpaid women volunteers (usually with four years of college) and paid former mother-participants (of no more than high school education). All were trained together in an initial eight-session training workshop, in weekly group conferences, and by individual supervision throughout the program year, learning the rationale, the structured cognitive curriculum, and the less formal "affective curriculum," built around the increasingly complex sequence of books and toys presented to the child. They were taught to model for the mother (rather than teach) verbal interaction techniques focused on the toys and books and spelled out in guide sheets contained in a "Toy Demonstrator's VISIT Handbook." The TD involved the mother early in the home session with the aim of fading into the background while the mother took over the main responsibility for the verbal interaction, utilizing as much of the modeled behavior as she wished.

The aim of the cognitive curriculum contained in the "Toy Demonstrator's VISIT Handbook" was to help the mother to assist the child in building concepts through "instrumental conceptualism," Bruner's phrase applied to the child's conceptual development through his interchange of language with his mother around meaningful experiences in his envirionment (Bruner et al., 1966). The general goal of the affective curriculum was to promote, without counseling or teaching, the socioemotional development of the child, and to promote child-rearing behavior functional to the child's learning and the well-being of both. The two curricula have been described in detail elsewhere (Levenstein, 1977). The cost of the program, without research components, was estimated to be about $400 per year for each dyad.

Treated Groups: Variations of the MCHP

The 96 treated dyads were scheduled to receive one of six one- or two-year variations of the MCHP, and were pretested and enrolled in the program in September of 1967, 1968, and 1969. Group membership in this report is based on intended treatment, rather than on the treatment actually received, and families who received much less than the amount of treatment intended are included here. The ages of the children as they are specified below were defined at the time of pretest as the range from four months less to six months greater than the stated age.

Treated Groups: One-Year Variations

T67-I + Short II. This group, from the Town A Housing Project, entered in September 1967 at age 2 and received Program I plus one of two shortened versions of Program II during the following year. In the second year the mothers were offered nine additional home sessions and seven VISM. Of the group, eight accepted the full short Program II, seven accepted only the VISM, and two declined any further intervention. TDs for this group were social workers. The group was posttested six times (5/68, 5/69, 12/69, 12/71, 1/73, and 1/74).

T67-I. This group, from the Town A Housing Project, entered in September 1967 at age 3, received only Program I, with social workers as TDs, and was posttested five times (5/68, 12/69, 12/70, 1/73, and 1/74).

T67-C_1 + I. This group, age 2 and 3, from the Town B Housing Project, entered and was pretested in September 1967. The group received one year of placebo treatment (home visits plus non-VISM gifts) to serve as a comparison group to control for the Hawthorne effect. In the following year the MCHP was offered to all eligible families in this group's housing project. For ethical and human relations reasons, this group was also offered, and accepted, Program I with non-social worker TDs, following its year of placebo treatment with a social worker. Group T67-C_1 + I was posttested six times (5/68, 5/69, 11/69, 12/71, 1/73, and 1/74).

Treated Groups: Two-Year Variations

T68-I + II. This group, from the Town A and Town B Housing Projects, entered in September 1968 at age 2 and received Program I and Program II (the first group to receive the full MCHP) with non-social worker TDs. The group was posttested seven times (5/69, 5/70, 12/70, 12/71, 1/73, 1/74, and 1/75).

T69-I + II. This group, from the Town A and Town B Housing Projects and from non-project residence, entered in September 1969 at age 2 and received Programs I and II, with non-social worker TDs, the same treatment received by the T68-I + II Group. The group was posttested four times (5/70, 5/71, 1/73, and 1/74).

T69-VISM only. This group, from Town A non-project residence, entered and was pretested in September 1969 at age 2 and received only the VISM, delivered weekly, for Programs I and II. The group was posttested four times (5/70, 5/71, 1/73, and 1/74).

Untreated Comparison Groups

The 55 comparison (test only) dyads entered the research project in three different groups in two years, 1967 and 1972.

C_2-**67.** This group, from the Town C Housing Project, entered in September 1967 at age 2 and 3. The group was pretested in September 1967 and posttested together five times (5/68, 12/69, 1/73, 1/74, and 1/75). The group was also tested as two subgroups, the subgroup of children age 2 at entry in 12/71, and the subgroup age 3 at entry in 12/70, making a total of six posttests for each subgroup.

C_4-**67.** This group, from the Town A Housing Project, entered in September 1967 at age 4 and was pretested in 1967 (having been recruited for a version of the program for 4-year-olds which was canceled when it was discovered that these children were going into the then new Head Start program). This group was posttested three times (12/71, 1/73, and 1/74).

C_5-**72.** This group, from Town A nonhousing-project residence, entered at age 6 and was tested three times (1/73, 1/74, and 1/75), having been recruited on low-income criteria previously described. Group C_5-72 entered the 1972–73 follow-up study as an "after-only" group with no previous project contact.

IQ Tests and Test Schedules

IQ measures were the Cattell Developmental and Intelligence Scale (Cattell) for children age 2 or younger, the Stanford-Binet Intelligence Scale (S-B) for children from age 3 through kindergarten, and the Wechsler Intelligence Scale for Children (WISC) for children in and beyond first grade. A verbal IQ score was obtained from the Peabody Picture Vocabulary Test (PPVT).

The group comparison of most interest is at follow-up. For each of the seven groups in this comparison, follow-up was defined as that test period when the mean group age was nearest to 5 and when nearly all children in the group were tested on the S-B. WISC scores are also reported at one later test period for those groups who have reached third grade.

Although all children but one were pretested, no clear adjustment can be made for pretest IQ's because pretest IQ's were composed of both Cattell and S-B scores mixed within and between groups. The Cattell was intended as a downward extension in age of the 1937 S-B, but the standardization data do not provide a basis for conversion of Cattell to S-B scores (Cattell, 1940).

Since the bulk of these data was gathered, the S-B (1960) and the WISC (1949) have been revised. Because the S-B test items have not essentially changed in the new standardizations, it is possible to convert old into new scores. To give a rough idea of the effect of such a conversion on the data reported here, at age 61 months the score of a child who received the same score as the mean of the untreated C_2-67 Group would be reduced from 97.8 points to 89, and the score of a child who received the same score as the mean score of the treated T68-I + II Group at age 65 months would be reduced from 106.2 to 99 (Terman and Merrill, 1973). No such conversion can be made from WISC to WISC-R scores at this time.

Demographic Data

The demographic data reported here were systematically collected in two interviews. The first occurred just before pre-testing in a home interview with the child's mother, conducted by the program supervisor responsible for supervising the dyad's Toy Demonstrator throughout the program. The second was conducted at follow-up.

RESULTS
Demographic Characteristics of Sample

Table 1 presents demographic data for the nine treated and control groups in areas usually considered associated with low-income status of the family, education of both parents, occupation of father, frequency of the father's presence in the home, family size, and proportion of mothers receiving welfare aid.

Most of the group means and proportions of Table 1 items are as expected for a low-income sample. The average level of father's education was below high school graduation, from mid-ninth to mid-eleventh grades, but higher than that sometimes reported for poverty groups (e.g., Klaus and Gray, 1968). Most fathers in the sample were in low status occupations: unemployed, unskilled, or semiskilled. This was the pattern for all groups; but it was less true for the T68-I + II and T69-I + II Groups than for the others, raising a question of group equivalence on this variable. Two-thirds of the fathers in the total sample were living in the home, but here there was wide variation among the groups, with two comparison groups showing the greatest extremes, from 20 percent present for the C_4-67 Group to 93 percent present for the C_2-67 Group.

TABLE 1   DEMOGRAPHIC CHARACTERISTICS OF TREATED AND COMPARISON GROUPS AT ENTRY

Entry year	Program designation[a]	Child N	Child Age	Child % Male	Father Years of school	Father % Occ. 6 or 7[b]	Father % Always present	Mother Years of school	Mother % Rec. welfare	Family Size	Family Residence[c] proj.	Family Residence[c] Non-proj.
							Treated					
1967	T67-I	14	3	35.7	9.6	85.7	57.1	10.7	28.6	4.9	x	
1967	T67-I + Short II	17	2	58.8	10.1	100.0	76.5	11.2	17.6	6.2	x	
1967	T67-C$_1$ + I	8	2 & 3	75.0	9.8	85.7	62.5	10.2	12.5	6.1	x	
1968	T68-I + II	24	2	41.7	10.5	71.4	60.9	10.5	37.5	5.5	x	
1969	T69-I + II	27	2	55.6	11.3	59.1	65.4	10.6	38.5	5.0	x	
1969	T69-VISM-only	6	2	50.0	10.5	100.0	33.3	10.5	66.7	4.7	x	x
							Comparison					
1967	C$_2$-67	15	2 & 3	73.3	10.5	80.0	93.3	11.3	6.7	5.3	x	
1967	C$_4$-67	10	4	50.0	10.3	71.5	20.0	10.6	60.0	5.9	x	
1972	C$_5$-72[d]	30	6	50.0	9.6	100.0	23.3	9.8	82.1	5.8		x

[a] Subjects defined by inclusion in follow-up test.
[b] Hollingshead Scales 6 or 7 (unemployed, unskilled, semiskilled).
[c] Proj.: Residence in low-income housing project. Non-proj.: residence out of low-income project.
[d] Entry in 1972–1973 as after-only group.

TABLE 2   PERCENTAGES OF SUBJECTS
COMPLETING ASSIGNED PROGRAMS AND
PERCENTAGES AVAILABLE AT FOLLOW-UP

| | | Time Period | | |
| | | | | |
Subject group	N at entry	% Completing first program year	% Completing second program year	% Available for testing at follow-up
T67-I	16	100	—	88
T67-I + Short II	17	100	88	100
T67-C_1 + I	10	90	—	80
T68-I + II	29	90	70	86
T69-I + II	33	94	76	85
T69-VISM-only	12	100	75	50
C_2-67	19	—	—	84
C_4-67	10	—	—	100
C_5-72	30	—	—	—

The average level of mother's education was a little higher than that of fathers and ranged from ninth to eleventh grade. About one-third of the mothers in the total sample were receiving welfare aid; but there was great variation among the groups, from 6.7 percent mothers on welfare for the C_2-67 Group to 82 percent on welfare for the C_5-72 Group. The proportion of mothers receiving welfare in every group was roughly similar to the proportion of fathers absent from home.

Family size (total number of home residents) varied among the groups, from means of 4.7 (T69-VISM-only) to 6.2 (T67-I + Short II), with an average of 5.5 for the total sample.

Apart from the C_5-72 Group, which was consistently lower than the other groups on SES indicators, SES variations did not clearly favor one level of treatment over another.

Retention Rates

The number of children in each group at program entry, completing designated programs, and available for testing are reported in Table 2.

These rates are of concern not only as they affect the data but as an indicator of the feasibility of the program.

In follow-up, 84 percent of the children originally enrolled were available for testing, excluding the C_4-67 and C_5-72 Groups, which had no opportunity for attrition. This number includes those who did not complete their assigned program but who were tested at follow-up. Maternal acceptance of the programs appeared to be high. Of all treated dyads, 95 percent completed the first year, and 80 percent completed the second year of intended treatment. The T68-I + II and T69-I + II dyads completed about 85 percent of the planned number of home sessions, and anonymous evaulations mailed by program mothers nearly all reported a highly favorable opinion of the program. The rate of return of the anonymous questionnaires was 46 percent. In untreated groups, acceptance of the testing seemed equally high. All mothers appeared to view it as a service from which they received information about impending developmental disabilities, and they gave good cooperation. Of course, such evaluations by "happy consumers" must be treated with caution.

IQ Status

IQ test scores are summarized in Tables 3 and 4 for all nine groups. Pretest Cattell and S-B scores are reported to give an indication of pretest group equivalence even though it may not be assumed that the two tests are equivalent. The follow-up test period was defined separately for each group as the period when (a) nearly all subjects were tested on the S-B, and (b) the group mean age was nearest to 5. Third-grade WISC scores are also reported for groups entering in 1967 and 1968. Test scores obtained at the other time intervals indicated in the group descriptions are not reported here because they do not permit clear comparisons between groups.

IQ status of treated groups. The mean WISC score for the T68-I + II Group is well above the national norm of 97.7 for 6- to 11-year-old children with fathers completing 9 to 11 years of schooling (Roberts, 1971, p. 55). The S-B scores of the other group receiving two full years of treatment predict similar WISC scores for that group as well.

The other treated groups present a more variable picture. There is relatively little difference between the larger two groups (T67-I and T67-I + Short II), both obtaining WISC scores below the 97.7 norm. The performances of the T67-C_1 + I and the T69-VISM-only Groups were better than those of the larger one-year treated groups, but the small size of these groups and the 50 percent attrition of the T69-VISM-only Group limit confidence in their mean performance as an estimate of treatment effect.

IQ status of comparison groups. Table 4 presents a consistent picture of IQ scores for the comparison groups. All three

TABLE 3 IQ SCORES FOR TREATED GROUPS

Subject Group	Variable	Pretest Cattell	Pretest S-B	Follow-up S-B	Third grade WISC
T67-I	N[a]	—	14	14	12
	IQ	—	89.5	102.8	94.6
	SD	—	11.9	13.9	10.6
	Age (grade)[b]	—	3	5½(K)	8½(3)
	Months after pretest	—	—	28	64
T67-I + short II	N	17	—	17	14
	IQ	83.2	—	100.8	97.4
	SD	6.7	—	9.9	10.5
	Age (grade)	2	—	4½	8½(3)
	Months after pretest	—	—	28	76
T67-C_1 + I	N	3	4	8	7
	IQ	86.7	94.2	106.6	108.0
	SD	15.0	6.1	9.4	11.2
	Age (grade)	2	3	4½, 5½(−, K)	8½, 9½(3, 4)
	Months after pretest	—	—	28	76
T68-I + II	N	13	11	24[c]	24[c]
	IQ	88.4	91.3	106.2	103.9
	SD	12.2	3.7	11.2	10.9
	Age (grade)	2	2	5½(K)	8½(3)
	Months after pretest	—	—	40	76
T69-I + II	N	25	2	27[d]	—
	IQ	86.4	117.0	111.8	—
	SD	10.1	21.2	15.2	—
	Age (grade)	2	2	5½(K)	—
	Months after pretest	—	—	40	—
T69-VISM-VISM-only	N	6	—	6	—
	IQ	87.0	—	103.2	—
	SD	7.4	—	10.1	—
	Age (grade)	2	—	5½(K)	—
	Months after pretest	—	—	40	—

[a] Subjects tested on S-B at follow-up.
[b] For 50% + of group.
[c] Excludes one subject who scored 109 on the WISC at follow-up.
[d] Excludes one subject who scored 107 on the WISC at follow-up.

TABLE 4 IQ SCORES FOR COMPARISON GROUPS

Subject Group	Variable	Pretest Cattell	Pretest S-B	Follow-up S-B	Third grade WISC
C_2-67	N	10[b]	5	15[b]	14[b]
	IQ	94.1	88.0	97.8	96.1
	SD	7.8	10.3	12.8	15.0
	Age (grade)[a]	—	2, 3	4½, 5½(−K)	8½, 9½(3, 4)
Months after pretest		—	—	28	76
C_4-67	N	—	—	10	10
	IQ	—	—	91.0	96.3
	SD	—	—	8.2	10.3
	Age (grade)	—	—	4	8½(3)
Months after pretest		—	—	0	56
C_5-72	N	—	—	—	27
	IQ	—	—	—	93.9
	SD	—	—	—	8.6
	Age (grade)	—	—	—	8½(3)
Months after pretest		—	—	—	24

[a] For 50% + of group.
[b] Excludes one who scored 40 on the Cattell in follow-up and 36 on the S-B at third grade.

groups obtained WISC scores below the 97.7 norm, and the available S-B scores were below those of the treated subjects.

These group summaries provide a preliminary set of answers to the first three questions raised above. The two-year treated groups with TDs who had no formal social work training retained satisfactory levels of IQ scores into the school years. With the exception of the T67-C_1 + I and T69-VISM-only Groups, groups receiving less than two years of treatment obtained somewhat lower scores at follow-up. The comparison groups consistently obtained scores at or below their expected level based on norms for children with fathers of 9 to 11 years of education.

Treatment Comparisons
The long-term effects of varying intensities of the program were examined at follow-up for seven of the nine groups. The T69-VISM-only Group was excluded from these analyses because the treatment received by this group is not qualitatively

comparable to other treatments, and the C_5-72 Group because it was not tested at follow-up as defined above.

To test the relation between length of program treatment and follow-up IQ, the remaining groups were classified into three levels of treatment. The two-year treated level contained the T68-I + II and T69-I + II Groups; the one-year treated level contained the T67-I, T67-I + Short II, and the T67-C_1 + I Groups; and the untreated level was composed of the C_2-67 and the C_4-67 Groups. As above, children originally assigned to a group and available for testing were included in the analysis, regardless of treatment actually received. Distributed throughout the groups were 26 younger siblings of treated or comparison children who were removed from the analysis to reduce violations of the analysis of variance assumption of independence of observations.

Differences between levels of treatment for the remaining subjects were tested by a hierarchical analysis of variance (Kirk, 1968, p. 232). An approximate method suggested by Snedecor (1956, p. 271) was used to correct for the unequal number of subjects per group. Differences between groups receiving the same kind of treatment were not significant, F (4,82) < 1, allowing pooling of variance. After pooling, the difference between the three levels of treatment was significant, F (2,86) = 4.23, p < .05. The mean IQ difference between two-year treated and untreated groups after removing siblings was 12.9 points.

These results indicate, first, that there were significant differences in follow-up IQ scores between differently treated groups and, second, that these differences were not due to group differences which occurred within treatment categories. The results are consistent with the hypothesis of a linear relation between amount of intervention and follow-up IQ scores.

Although this analysis was somewhat conservative in classifying subjects according to assigned treatment rather than treatment received, the IQ differences cannot be unequivocally attributed to the MCHP because most groups were not randomly assigned to treatments, and dyads were not randomly assigned to groups. Even though no major systematic differences between the groups in this analysis were evident at pretest, it is possible that there were relevant pretest differences that were not evident because they were imperfectly measured.

Sibling IQ Differences

One possible source of the IQ differences reported above could be differences between the kinds of families recruited for the different groups. The presence of siblings in the data allows at least a partial test of this alternative hypothesis.

From 1967 through 1974, 52 sibling pairs entered the program in which the older child was the first family member to enter the program, in which the older entered at least a year before the younger, and in which both siblings were pretested on the Cattell. The mean pretest IQ score for the older siblings was 87.1, and for the younger siblings it was 95.4. The mean "pretest differential" (Phillips, 1973) was 8.3 points (t (51) = 4.19, $p < .001$).

It appears that the pretest differential does not extend to posttest. Of the 52 sibling pairs, both members of 28 pairs were tested immediately after receiving the full program. The mean posttest difference on the S-B was 2.4 points, which was not significant. The pretest differential is consistent with the hypothesis that there is some effect of the program on IQ that occurs within the home. The failure to find posttest differences between siblings indicates that the effect of the program (or other effective agents) is not to add some number of points to pretest IQ.

Of more interest here are IQ scores after completion of the program. Seven of the ten C_4-67 children had younger siblings who completed the program and who were posttested at approximately 4 years of age. The C_4-67 children had themselves been pretested at age 4. The mean difference in S-B scores favoring program children over their older comparison siblings was 16.1 points (t (6) = 3.70, $p < .01$), contradicting the hypothesis that IQ differences between treated and comparison children are due to preexisting differences between families rather than the program.

In all of these comparisons, younger siblings scored higher than had their older siblings at about the same age. However, it does not appear likely that this systematic age order of differences caused the IQ differences. The birth-order literature would not predict such an effect, and our data do not indicate a general increase in local IQ scores that would account for the effects. The major weaknesses of these findings are the small number of comparisons of treated and comparison children after the program and the possibility that these families, being to some extent self-selected, are atypical.

Subject to these qualifications, the available data for siblings suggest that effects of different treatments are evident within families and thus may not be completely accounted for by preexisting differences between families.

Correlation Between IQ and Other Variables

The remaining question concerned the relation of follow-up IQ to other background and outcome variables. Follow-up IQs were correlated with 50 background and outcome variables, a full list of which is available from the authors. The 50 background variables included demographic attributes of parents, grandparents, and family (e.g., education, occupation, health, family size), other characteristics of parents (e.g., father's employment and mother's style of dealing with home physical environment), other characteristics of index children (e.g., psychosocial problems).

Table 5 lists only those Pearson r's and point-biserial coefficients, significant at $p < .05$ for the combined two-year treated groups (T68-I + II and T69-I + II), one-year treated groups (T67-I, T67-I + Short II and T67-C_1 + I), comparison groups (C_2-67 abd C_4-67), or for all of these groups combined. The T69-VISM-only and C_5-72 Groups are not represented for the same reasons they were not considered in the treatment comparisons above.

Eighteen of the 200 correlations with follow-up IQ were significant at or beyond the .05 level. Some chance-large correlations are to be expected, but most relations are as expected. The correlation between S-B and PPVT is high, and there were several low and moderate correlations between IQ and SES indicators.

Of the SES and demographic variables in Table 5, data were available for all dyads only for mother's education which correlated positively with IQ. As Table 1 indicates, the groups scoring highest in IQ are not highest in mother's education. Correlations with father's father's [paternal grandfather, *Ed.*] education and occupation were both in the expected direction and were largest in the two-year treated group, but these data were missing for many families. There was a small positive correlation between IQ and the project-developed physical environment description. This score is composed of 10 Likert-scale items rating interview room features (e.g., spatial arrangement of furniture), and is intended to reflect styles of physical home management.

Correlations between entry age and IQ and between follow-up age and IQ reflect in part the fact that the comparison and one-year treated groups were slightly older at entry and younger at follow-up than were the two-year treated groups.

Several correlations may have resulted from artifacts or from small numbers of observations. The correlation of S-B with moving after the MCHP may have resulted from the residential stability of project dwellers who were most heavily represented in the groups receiving less than two years of treatments. Two correlations are based on small numbers of observations. For 11 control children, having a mother who worked part- instead of full-time was associated with a higher S-B score. Mothers' reports that their children had psychosocial problems were associated with higher IQs, but there were only five such reports.

TABLE 5 CORRELATIONS OF BACKGROUND AND FOLLOW-UP VARIABLES WITH STANFORD-BINET IQ AT FOLLOW-UP FOR ONE- AND TWO-YEAR TREATED, UNTREATED, AND ALL GROUPS COMBINED (PEARSON'S AND POINT-BISERIAL r)

	Total two-year treated group		Total one-year treated group		Total untreated group		All groups combined	
	r	N	r	N	r	N	r	N
Background variables								
Entry age	-.21	51	.25	39	-.22	25	-.25*	115
Mother's education	.23	51	.35*	39	.46*	25	.24*	115
Hollingshead 2-factor ISP score	-.36	49	-.21	36	-.15	25	-.28**	110
Father's education	.63**	27	.31	21	-.07	15	.25*	63
Father's father's occupation	.60	24	.06	24	-.06	14	.24	62
Follow-up variables								
Age at follow-up	-.06	51	.16	39	.23	25	.28**	115
PPVT	.57**	51	.77**	39	.75**	25	.64**	115
Home "physical environment description"	.09	46	.33*	37	.38	15	.13	98
C's psychological-social problems	.36*	46	—	—	—	—	.36*	46
Post MCHP contact	.09	46	.19	37	—	—	.21*	98
Mother's follow-up work hours	-.02	23	.04	21	-.60**	11	-.17	55
Moved post MCHP	.15	46	.33	35	-.06	14	.22*	95

* p < .05; ** p < .01

One variable not included in Table 5 is preschool attendance. No correlation was possible for any groups except the C_5-72 Group (where the correlation was $-.07$) because virtually all other children had some form of preschool experience in addition to the MCHP. Thus, if the program is found to be effective, it must be added that the program plus some form of center-based preschool attendance was effective. That preschool attendance was not of itself effective is indicated by the performances of the C_2-67 and C_4-67 Groups who attended preschool but did not receive the program.

In general, the correlations between IQ and background and demographic variables that are based on enough cases to be stable go in the expected directions. Across all such variables, there appears little evidence that the IQ scores of one group are more influenced by such variables than those of others, or that follow-up IQ differences between treatments were caused by differences in background or concomitant variables.

Feasibility of MCHP Variations

The data suggested that the full two-year variations of the MCHP, conducted by paid or volunteer interveners with a wide range of education and prior skills, were more effective than the one-year versions. The 1968 changes from a shortened second year to a full two-year program were less costly than the 1967 MCHP, and, contrary to expectation, the full two-year program was easier to administer. The shortened two-year variations (T67-I + Short II) took as much staff time and effort and caused more staff frustration than did the full program. When dyads were seen less often in home sessions in the second year, the mothers tended to forget appointments and withdraw from their involvement, requiring an unusual expenditure of effort by the TDs and their supervisors. Since personnel and administrative time absorbed the main cost of the program, the full two-year MCHP (T68-I + II and T69-I + II) seemed the most feasible of all the two-year variations, with the possible exception of the T69-VISM-only treatment.

Short-Term Experimental Results

In 1973 it became possible to begin a true field experiment, randomly assigning 51 dyads to treated and control conditions after the mothers had agreed to accept the outcome of such a lottery. The design was $2 \times 2 \times 2$ factorial with factors of treatment, sex and high versus low number in family. At the end of the usual two-year program, conducted as described above, there remained 19 treated and 16 untreated dyads. The treated children obtained a mean S-B score of 104.8, and the control children, 100.9.

An analysis of covariance was performed on posttest S-B scores with a covariate of pretest Cattell. A least-squares correction was made for unequal numbers of scores per cell following Overall and Spiegel's (1969) experimental method. No effects in the analysis were significant except a correlation of .68 between pretest and posttest IQ. From an estimate of the power of the analysis, we can be somewhat better than 60 percent certain that there was not a true ten-point difference between treatments. Further, the initial data do not suggest that a substantial program effect on IQ is being masked by selective attrition or by chance difference between groups.

There are few other outcome variables on which both experimental treated and comparison groups may be compared. As these groups are followed up in long-term studies, more outcomes will be accumulated, but, for the present, there is no definitive explanation for the apparent contradiction between these short-term experimental results and the long-term quasi-experimental results.

DISCUSSION AND CONCLUSIONS

This report of findings from a longitudinal study of 151 dyads began with four questions about the long-term cognitive effects of the Mother-Child Home Program after the one-year program had been followed by large short-term effects in 1967–1968, when conducted with social workers as interveners. The questions concerned IQ stability, the feasibility and effectiveness of utilizing volunteer and nonprofessional interveners, the amount of intervention necessary for maximum effect, the relation of these effects to other outcomes or events in the child's life, and whether the program did indeed have a significant effect on the IQ's of treated children as compared with untreated subjects.

The long-term data support the first year's promise of the MCHP's effectiveness. Satisfactory IQ scores were retained by program graduates at least into first grade when the program was expanded to two full years instead of the original one year. The results for the full two-year program have thus been demonstrated to be stable over time.

At the same time that the program was expanded to its present two-year format, non-social worker TDs were introduced as interveners. Because the most stable results were obtained under these conditions, we concluded as a practical matter that interveners with a range of education from less than high school completion through college were at least as effective as graduate social workers in producing long-term effects. This finding greatly increased the feasibility of the program for application in other settings outside of the research project, a feasibility supported by the estimated annual unit cost of $400 in the model program and an average of $550 in 11 replications away from the model program.

The MCHP graduates appeared to benefit along a continuum of amount of exposure to the program, with groups in the full two-year version superior to other treated groups and to untreated groups, an observation first made by Bronfenbrenner (1974). The full two-year program was also found to be more feasible than abbreviated versions with the exception of the VISM-only variation. Since results for the latter treatment could not be clearly interpreted, this treatment is being repeated, with a larger, randomized sample, which began in September 1974.

The long-term results have thus far been encouraging, and, insofar as IQ scores may be taken as an index of level of cognitive functioning, the children who have received two full years of the MCHP do not appear to be laboring under the cognitive disadvantage usually associated with the demographic attributes which determined their acceptance into the program.

Confidence in the results of these original studies is limited due to their quasi-experimental design. The available data have generally indicated that no easily identifiable factor other than the program is likely to have been responsible for the effect. To use a legal model, the effectiveness of the program appeared to be supported by a preponderance of evidence but not beyond a reasonable doubt.

Our original plan was to validate these long-term studies with experimental data rather than to study the quasi-experiment in more detail. It now appears that both must be done. The results for cohorts entering from 1967 through 1972 are promising enough to mandate continued experimental research. The short-term experimental findings require a suspension of judgment concerning the effectiveness of the program and increased care in the conduct of the program and of its evaluation.

REFERENCES

Bronfenbrenner, U. *Is early intervention effective? A report on longitudinal evaluations of preschool programs* (Vol. 2). Washington, D.C.: DHEW Publication No. (OHD) 74–25, 1974.

Bruner, J. S., Olver, R. R., Greenfield, P. M., et al. *Studies in cognitive growth.* New York: Wiley, 1966.

Campbell, D. T., and Stanley, J. C. *Experimental and quasi-experimental designs for research.* New York: Rand McNally, 1963.

Cattell, P. *The measurement of intelligence of infants and young children.* New York: The Psychological Corporation, 1940.

Kirk, R. E. *Experimental design: Procedures for the behavioral sciences.* Belmont, Calif.: Brooks/Cole, 1968.

Klaus, R. A., and Gray, S. W. The early training project for disadvantaged children: A report after five years. *Monographs of The Society for Research in Child Development*, 1968, 33 (Serial No. 120, No. 4).

Levenstein, P. Cognitive growth in preschoolers through verbal interaction with mothers. *American Journal of Orthopsychiatry*, 1970, **40**, 426–432.

Levenstein, P. A message from home: findings from a program for nonretarded low-income preschoolers. In M. J. Begab and S. A. Richardon (Eds.), *The mentally retarded and society.* Baltimore: University Park Press, 1975.

Levenstein, P. The Mother-Child Home Program. In M. C. Day and R. K. Parker (Eds.), *The preschool in action*, (2nd ed.). Boston: Allyn and Bacon, 1977.

Levenstein, P., and Sunley, R. Stimulation of verbal interaction between disadvantaged mothers and children. *American Journal of Orthopsychiatry*, 1968, **38**, 116–121.

Overall, J. E., and Spiegel, D. E. Concerning least squares analysis of experimental data. *Psychological Bulletin*, 1969, **72**, 311–322.

Phillips, J. R. Family cognitive profile study. Final report to the Foundation for Child Development, October, 1973.

Roberts, J. *Intellectual development of children by demographic and socioeconomic factors.* Vital and health statistics data from the national health survey, series 11, No. 10. U.S. Department of Health, Education and Welfare, 1971, DHEW Publication No. (HSM) 72–1012.

Snedecor, G. W. *Statistical methods applied to experiments in agriculture and biology.* Ames, Iowa: Iowa State University Press, 1956.

Terman, L. M., and Merrill, M. A. *Stanford-Binet Intelligence Scale 1972 norms edition.* Boston: Houghton Mifflin, 1973.

PART

V

FATHERS

OVERVIEW

On the Importance of Fathers

I am sure you have already discovered that there is a strong "maternal" bias in most psychological research and writing. Ordinarily psychologists do not speak of parental behavior or "parenting," rather, of maternal behavior and "mothering." Most studies of *parents* are really studies of mothers, because mothers are usually a lot easier to observe with their children for purely practical reasons and because we assume that mothers spend more time with young children than do fathers, and are therefore the more important parent to study.

But this attitude is changing. There are important social forces at work that are bringing about changes in fathers' roles within families, and there has been a parallel increase in research on the fathering role. At least two major social forces are involved. On the one hand, there is pressure from women, and from men who share an egalitarian view of sex roles, for fathers to share more in the care and nurture of children. It is *not* yet clear how widely this "liberated" view of family life has actually influenced the behavior of fathers and mothers with children, but there is pressure at least at an ideological level. On the other hand, there is a high (and rising) divorce rate in this country and the number of children raised without a father is increasing.

In 1970, 10 percent of the children under age 18 were living in families headed by a female, but only four years later this had risen to 13.6 percent. In 1974, 11.4 percent of all children under age 6 were living in father-absent families and nearly 15 percent of children aged 6 to 18 were without a father (U.S. Department of Labor, 1975). Precisely why the number of female-headed households is on the increase is open to debate. Lynn (1974), who has written the most comprehensive book on fathers and their role in child development, suggests that some of the forces pushing toward more egalitarian sex roles have also contributed to the rising divorce rate. Because women increasingly think that their needs for personal fulfillment are critical, they are more likely to look to divorce as a reasonable option if they do not find satisfaction in a marriage. Regardless of the origin of the trend, the *fact* is that over 8 million children in 1974 were living in families headed by women. Under these conditions, it becomes even more critical to understand the implications of such family arrangements for children's growth and development. What is the role of the father in intact families? What is the effect of the father's absence on the child? And what do we know about the potential impact of more egalitarian life-styles on the roles of fathers and mothers?

The limited research data on fathers and their role do not permit me to answer all these questions completely or clearly; but we can begin to explore some of the issues and see where more information is needed.

FATHERS AS NURTURERS

Let me begin with what is perhaps the most fundamental question. Is there some basic difference between the "maternal" and "paternal" roles? Or is there a "nurturing" role that both men and women can occupy? I have touched on these questions in the overview on sex differences, so you are already aware of the fuzziness of the information. We know that among various primates males sometimes nurture the young, but in many species they do not and may in fact be quite aggressive toward infants. Other research (with rats and mice) suggests that mothers may be hormonally "ready" to become attached to and care for their infants just after birth, but if the mothers are separated from the young for a period of time, their caregiving behaviors diminish. But it is also true that virgin females and males will show nurturant caregiving behavior toward the young, although it takes them longer to respond. Limited research with primates also points to the possiblity that the male monkey will care for an infant if no one else does so, but in many species the male's initial reaction toward the young seems to be aggression rather than nurturance. If this aggressive response can be inhibited or waited out, then nurturance may be shown.

Does any of this apply to the behavior of human beings? Maccoby and Jacklin (1974) review a series of cross-cultural studies of nurturance toward infants on the part of young boys and girls. In a wide variety of cultures, girls spend more time in nurturant interaction with younger siblings or other infants.

Further, boys who do show such caregiving are usually less aggressive than are boys in societies in which boys do little nurturing. These findings are thus in general agreement with the studies of primates: Aggression and nurturance may be incompatible behaviors and nurturance toward the young on the part of males may emerge only when aggression has been inhibited in some way.

There is also some evidence, which I discussed in the overview on sex difference, that some contact between the mother and the infant immediately after birth tends to accentuate or augment the attachment and nurturance of the mother toward the infant (see, for example, Leifer, Leiderman, Barnett, and Williams, 1972). So here too there is some correspondence between the studies of human and animal subjects.

Obviously the most direct way to explore fathers' nurturance toward their children would be to observe them directly caring for or relating to their infants. There is almost no research of this kind that I know of. Maccoby and Jacklin (1974) cite a single such study by Parke and O'Leary [published in 1974]. In this study observers noted the amount and type of nurturant interaction between fathers and their newborn infants and between mothers and the newborns. A nurse brought the infant to the mother and father when the two were together and at different times to each parent separately. In general, fathers were observed to spend as much *or more* time in nurturant interaction with the infant than did mothers in this setting, and this was as true of working-class as of middle-class fathers.

A study by Bem (cited in Maccoby and Jacklin, 1974) provides indirect confirmation of the Parke and O'Leary finding. Bem studied a group of college males and females. Each subject was given an opportunity to play with a kitten and observers noted the amount of time the subject spent in any kind of nurturant interaction (for example, touching or stroking) with the kitten. There were no sex differences in the amount of such nurturant overtures. Obviously kittens are not quite the same thing as human infants, but the Bem findings suggest that nurturant responses are in the repertoire of both sexes, and the Parke and O'Leary study suggests that the newborn infant elicits such responses about equally in men and women. Whether this means that men could take on the primary caregiving role as easily as could women, or whether the man's nurturance would be of the same quality or quantity as that of a woman over a period of months or years, we simply cannot tell from these data. But the findings are at least consistent with the notion that nurturance toward infants is present among males in our society. Extrapolating from the animal research, we might expect that fathers who have extensive contact with their children during early infancy would become more strongly attached to the child and show more nurturant behavior.

Time Spent by Fathers with Their Children

One way to get at the question of fathers' involvement with, or nurturance toward, their children would be to ask how much time fathers spend with their infants or young children. Again the data are very sparse. Rebelsky and Hanks (1971), whose paper appears in the selections in this section, found that fathers spent *very* little time interacting verbally with their infants—as little as a few mintues each day. These fathers may have spent other caregiving time without vocalizing, but the data do not suggest that there is any large involvement on the part of fathers in this sample. What about older infants? Pederson and Robson (1969) provide about the only data. They asked mothers of 9-month-old infants to describe the fathers' caregiving activities. According to these mothers, the fathers were present at home while the infant was awake for an average of 26 hours per week, but the fathers varied enormously in the amount of time they actually spent with the infant, either playing or caregiving. The most involved fathers spent about an hour a day with the child, but many fathers spent a great deal less time than this. The fathers also differed in their patience with the child's fussiness or irritability. Ten of the fathers were described by the mothers as very irritated with the infant's crying or fussiness. (Of course, the mothers may have been just as irritated, so we do not know whether this is a higher rate of irritation among the fathers.) Bear in mind that in this study all the information about fathers comes from an interview with the mother. It is entirely possible that many mothers exaggerate the amount of time the father spends with the child, so even these levels of involvement may be inflated somewhat.

Information about the time spent by fathers with preschool or older children is virtually nonexistent, although there are several authors who have speculated about it. Bronfenbrenner (1970) concludes from his observations that both fathers and mothers in the United States spend very little time with their children and that the amount of time is decreasing over the years. Lynn (1974) has also suggested that particularly among the middle class, fathers may be unavailable to the child a preponderance of the time because they tend to work long hours or have long commutes, or work on weekends at home, or travel as part of their jobs. It seems likely that working-class fathers may also be frequently unavailable to their children because of over-time, work-related travel, and non-family recreational activities. Unfortunately, we have no good data about the time parents spend with children of various ages, so this is largely speculative.

It does seem likely in the case of preschool children whose mothers do not work that the mother spends considerably more time with the child than does the father. But an increasing percentage of women with preschool children *do* work (see the review on working women) and a still greater percentage of women of school-age children are employed, so for many children there may not be a great deal of difference in the accessibility of the father and mother. (In fact, in families in which both father and mother are employed, one could argue that the mother is *less* accessible to the child in a number of ways since in such families the woman frequently continues to have the major responsibility for house cleaning, cooking, and other homemaking chores.)

Clearly, this is an area in which we need to have a great deal more information. What little we have suggests that fathers spend very little time with their infants. Probably the same pattern continues through the school years, the mothers being the dominant figures. By school age, however, *neither* parent may be spending much time in individual interaction with the child, and we do not know whether fathers are spending more or less time than are mothers with children of this age.

Attachment of Young Children to Fathers and Mothers

How attached are infants or young children to fathers? The findings are mixed. If it is true that infants spend more time with mothers than with fathers, then it would be entirely reasonable to expect them to show stronger attachment to the mother than to the father, particularly during the period of strongest single attachment, which for most children occurs between about 8 months and perhaps 14 or 16 months. There is *some* evidence to support this, but it is not overwhelming. Ban and Lewis, in the study in the selections, found that 1-year-olds—both boys and girls—spent more time touching, being near, and vocalizing to the mother. But boys spent more time looking at the father. These findings suggest a somewhat stronger attachment to the mother than to the father at 1 year. But among 2-year-olds there appears to be no equivalent preference for the mother over the father. Weinraub and Lewis (1973, abstracted in Maccoby and Jacklin, 1974), using a procedure similar to that of Ban and Lewis, found no differences in the amount of time spent looking at or being near the mother versus the father.

We should not leap too readily to conclusions about attachment to fathers based only on these two studies, particularly since both used a single methodology. But the findings are at least consistent with what is known about the sequence of development of attachment. Ordinarily the child forms a single strong attachment at about 8 months, which continues to be dominant until perhaps the middle of the second year. After that time, there is usually a "spread" of attachment to one or more of the figures. So the apparent preference for the mother at age 1, but not at age 2, is consistent with this. It is important to note, however, that the attachment to the mother, although probably stronger than to the father at age 1, does not appear to involve any *rejection* of the father. Whether there would be equal preference or equal attachment to the father in a family in which the father was a major caregiver from earliest infancy, we simply cannot say from these data.

Overall, it looks as if fathers are probably more capable of a major nurturing role with infants and young children than they are usually given credit for, but the data base is still extremely weak.

EFFECTS OF FATHERS ON SEX-ROLE DEVELOPMENT

What impact does a father have on his children's adoption of sex roles? Do fathers press for "traditional" sex roles for their sons or daughters? And what are the characteristics of fathers whose sons and daughters adopt traditional sex roles? Note that I am asking empirical questions here, not questions of value. Let us set aside, if we can, the question of whether traditional sex roles *ought* to be encouraged or fostered. Regardless of one's views on this issue, it is still legitimate to ask the factual question about the relationships between paternal behavior and the child's sex-role adoption.

It is clear from a number of sources that many fathers are concerned that their children adopt traditional sex roles; in particular they worry that their sons may adopt feminine characteristics and press fairly hard for traditional "masculine" choices in toys and activities for their sons. Mothers appear to share these concerns, but their reactions seem to be less polarized than those of fathers.

For example, Lansky (1967) asked parents of preschool children a series of hypothetical questions, such as, "If a boy had a choice between playing with a toy shaving kit and playing with a toy cosmetic kit, how would his father feel if his son wanted to play with the toy shaving kit?" In each case the father indicated whether he felt "generally happy and pleased," "neutral," or "generally unhappy and displeased" about the possibility described. Mothers were asked parallel questions. In this study both fathers and mothers were more concerned about "inappropriate" sex-role choices on the part of sons than they were about cross-sex choices of daughters. Most parents were neutral about cross-sex choices in girls but negative about such choices in boys. This difference was stronger for fathers than for mothers.

Fling and Manosevitz (1972) asked parents a similar set of questions about activities they thought appropriate, encouraged, or discouraged for their son or daughter. They found that both mothers and fathers were more concerned about cross-sex choices for their sons than for their daughters. Fathers also were more likely to encourage "appropriate" sex-role choices in their sons, whereas mothers were more likely to encourage appropriate sex-role choices in daughters. Thus each parent seemed to be primarily concerned with the appropriate sex-role adoption of the same-sex child, and *both* parents were concerned about *in*appropriate choices in the son.

Despite this concern about a son's or daughter's sex-role adoption on the part of fathers, it is not at all obvious that the pressure to adopt "appropriate" roles is successful. Fling and Manosevitz did not find that the child's own sex-role preferences were related to the father's or mother's concerns. And Mussen and Rutherford (1963) found that encouragement of appropriate sex-role adoption on the part of parents "succeeded" only in the case of fathers and daughters. Fathers who expressly encouraged traditional masculine roles for their sons did *not* have more masculine sons, but fathers who encouraged traditional feminine roles for their daughters did have somewhat more traditionally feminine daughters.

If explicit encouragement of traditional sex-role adoption does not always have the desired effect, is there anything fathers do that is predictive of traditional versus unconventional role adoption in sons? Lynn's review (1974) of this evidence suggests that two characteristics of fathers are most highly predictive of the son's sex-role adoption. First, fathers high in nurturance have sons who are more traditionally masculine than are sons of less nurturant fathers. Second, families in which the father is dominant are also likely to have more traditionally masculine sons. On the surface these seem to be a fairly puzzling set of findings. Dominance *and* nurturance? Dominance is certainly part of the traditional masculine stereotype, so it makes sense that dominant fathers would have more traditionally masculine sons, if only because the father is providing a role model of that type. But why nurturance? The finding makes sense if you think about the availability of the father to the son. The highly nurturant father Lynn describes is one who spends quite a lot of time with his son in a warm interaction. Not only is the father thus available more often as a role model, but there may be stronger identification with or imitation of the father because of the nurturant relationship. If this father also occupies a more traditional masculine role in the family, then it is this traditional role the son emulates.

Note here both that fathers' direct efforts to enhance sons' masculinity do *not* appear to produce more masculine sons and that very traditionally masculine fathers do *not* have the most traditionally masculine sons. It is the father who combines some features of stereotypic masculinity with some of the expressive features associated with the feminine stereotype who appears to rear the most masculine boy. Although the evidence is weaker, Lynn also concludes that such a father is likely to have more traditionally feminine daughters as well; however, for girls the mother's adoption of a traditional versus a more unconventional role is also important.

In sum, then, fathers appear to be slightly more concerned than mothers about the "correct" role adoption of their children, particularly their sons. At the same time, such direct pressure has less effect on the child's developing masculine or feminine choices than do several aspects of the father's personality, such as his nurturance and his dominance in the family.

Effects of Fathers on Intellectual Development of Their Children

Not surprisingly, a father's level of education or his measured intelligence is somewhat predictive of his child's school success or IQ score. Part of this similarity is clearly the result of genetic influences, but there also may be specific environmental influences from the father.

A number of recent studies by Norma Radin and her associates are relevant to this point (Radin, 1972, 1973; Epstein and Radin, 1975; Jordan, Radin, and Epstein, 1975). Radin initially found, in several studies, that there was a correlation between paternal nurturance and intellectual performance in sons. More nurturant fathers had sons who performed better on a variety of tests, although this relationship was stronger for middle-class father-son pairs than for working-class pairs. Epstein and Radin (1975) have suggested that the relationship between paternal nurturance and the child's intellectual accomplishments is quite indirect. They suggest that "paternal nurturance provides positive experiences for the child, leading to a desire to explore the environment and also to feel comfortable with adults, and that this factor in turn gets expressed as a motivation to achieve in a testing situation" (Epstein and Radin, 1975, p. 837).

Other evidence reviewed by Lynn (1974) suggests that nurturance or support from fathers for their sons is predictive particularly of greater skill on "analytic" tasks, such as the Embedded Figures Test—tasks on which males often do better. (See the Overview in Part I for a fuller discussion of such a sex difference.) Evidence from studies of boys whose fathers have been absent during part or all of their childhood is consistent with the general conclusion that a nurturant, supportive father enhances the more "masculine" aspects of intellectual functioning. Boys raised without a father tend to show a more "feminine" pattern of intellectual abilities.

If we can take the father's nurturance toward the son as some kind of gross index of the father's interest and involvement in the son's upbringing, then these results and those on sex-role adoption are telling us that fathers who are more involved have a greater impact on the son's developing skills and preferences.

THE ABSENT FATHER

There is quite an extensive literature about the effect of father absence on children's development, and much of our early knowledge about the impact of fathers emerged from this literature. This may seem a backward way to go about it, but presumably one can get some estimate of the effect of the father's presence by looking at what happens to a child when the father is absent during various periods in the child's early years. Fatherless children are also of interest in their own right, as I pointed out at the beginning of this chapter, since they make up an increasingly large percentage of children in this country.

As was true for sex differences, we again find that a number of the apparently tried-and-true generalizations about the effect of father absence are not holding up well to close scrutiny. Herzog and Sudia (1973) offer the most cautious interpretation of the findings. They emphasize that the effect of the father's absence is not massive and direct but, rather, may be fairly modest and come about indirectly through changes in the mother's behavior brought about by her sole-parenting role. The effects may also vary as a function of the child's age at the time of separation from the father or the social-class level of the family.

For example, one of the frequently reported conclusions about father-absent children (particularly boys) is that they have higher rates of juvenile delinquency. After analyzing the findings in this area, Herzog and Sudia conclude that the father's absence from the home may be involved but appears to be far less critical in predicting delinquency than such factors as the family's economic level or the mother's ability to supervise the child. Herzog and Sudia make the important point that fatherless families are different from father-present families in a variety of ways in addition to the father's status in the home. Perhaps most importantly, fatherless families are *far* more likely to live in poverty than are father-present families. According to recent data from the U.S. Department of Labor (1975), the median family income for female-headed families with children under 18 was $4,729, and nearly 27 percent of such families had yearly incomes below $3,000. Intact families in which the mother does not work had a median family income of $11,867, and only about 2½ percent had incomes below $3,000 annually. For families with children below 6 years of age, the discrepancy between those headed by a female and intact families is even greater. These financial disparities occur among minority group as well as among white families.

In addition to the economic pressures accompanying the father's absence, as Hetherington and Deur point out in their review (1972), the loss of the father is nearly always associated with other kinds of heightened stress in the family—tensions surrounding divorce or separation or grief following the death of the father—and such increased tension may continue as the mother struggles to cope with the myriad problems of being head of household as well as single parent.

The presence of stress in the father-absent family is nicely documented in an extremely interesting study of recently divorced families by Hetherington, Cox, and Cox (1975). They have studied 48 divorced families, beginning their observations shortly after the divorce and following the families for two years. An equivalent sample of intact families was studied for comparison. Hetherington and her associates found that the households of divorced families were much more disorganized than those of intact families. Meals were likely to be pick-up and the children were less likely to eat with the parent. Bedtimes were more erratic and children were read to less at bedtime. The divorced parents also made fewer maturity demands on and communicated less well with their children. They did not solicit the child's opinion as often and used reasoning and explanation less often. The discipline meted out by the divorced parents was also less consistent than was discipline in intact families. All of these effects were more marked during the first year after the divorce; during the second year a new equilibrium between mother and children seemed to develop (and between the divorced father and the children when he was with them) and greater family stability resulted.

The findings from this study certainly point to the need to be careful not to attribute things to the father's absence per se that may be more related to the changes in the mother's behavior resulting from a divorce or desertion or death of the father.

With these cautions in mind, however, there are a few conclusions about the impact of father absence that still seem reasonably valid.

1. The impact of an absent father appears to be greater on boys than on girls. It is hard to tell whether this conclusion arises because in the majority of studies of father absence *only* boys have been studied or whether there is really less effect on girls. But tentatively it seems to be a fair generalization. An exception, however, is the finding Hetherington reports in her study in the selections. In this study, girls with absent fathers were found to have some disturbance in heterosexual relationships during adolescence.

2. The impact of father absence on the boy seems, very generally, to be one of "feminization" both in behavior and in cognitive skills. Not all of the research is consistent with this conclusion, as Herzog and Sudia point out, but there is a fair amount of research suggesting either a reduced aggressiveness in father-absent boys (Hetherington, 1966) or a kind of compensatory masculinity characterized by heightened aggressiveness (Lynn and Sawrey, 1959). In the cognitive area there are a number of studies, of which the Carlsmith paper in the selections is the earliest, that show father-absent boys to have lowered math test scores or a change in the ratio of math to verbal skills in the direction of proportionately greater verbal skills (see also Sutton-Smith, Rosenberg, and Landy, 1968; Nelson and Maccoby, 1966). Since the pattern of relatively higher verbal than math scores is more often found in girls, the effect of father absence on the boy seems generally to move him toward a more "feminine" pattern of intellectual skill. This need not, and probably does not, imply that boys from father-absent homes have any generalized lowering of academic performance or tested intellectual ability. The results here are equivocal and heavily confounded by social-class and income differences. Some researchers have found that boys from father-absent homes are lower in school performance, but controls for social-class differences in the father-absent versus the father-present families have not been entirely possible, so this question must remain open.

3. The age at which the separation occurs is probably important. Generally the results show that father absence during the early years of life has a greater impact on the child than later separation. But again this conclusion may not be invariably drawn because some studies show that the impact is greater for older children.

4. The presence of alternative male figures probably has considerable mitigating effect. The alternative male figure need not even be an adult. Sutton-Smith, Rosenberg, and Landy (1968) found that the presence of a brother seemed to modify the effects of the father's absence considerably.

These general conclusions are consistent with what one would suppose might be the effect of father absence. Boys without fathers lack a male role model in the home, and we would expect them to be less "masculine" as a result. But it is important to realize that this is a *greatly* oversimplified view of what goes on in families. The effects of the father's absence are confounded with changes in the mother's behavior after the separation. And families in which separation results from divorce were different and stressful *before* the father's departure. So while there may be some important implications of the father's absence, particularly for boys, it is important to understand that the process is very complex, and social policies designed to "solve" the problem need to be attuned to those complexities.

SOME UNANSWERED QUESTIONS AND SOCIAL ISSUES
Although the amount of literature now devoted to the role of the father has expanded considerably in the past years, there are still gaping holes in our knowledge about the role and effect of fathers. We know almost nothing about the amount of involvement fathers have in the caregiving role with infants or even with older children. And we know equally little about attachment between children and fathers (or fathers and children), or about the effect varying levels of contact may have on the father's feeling toward the child or the child's relationship with the father. Since these are aspects of the fathering role now receiving a good deal of attention from those concerned with sex roles, it seems vital that we know more about these questions. What *is* the result of the father's taking the primary caregiving role? Is a father in this role qualitatively different from a mother? Does he nurture in a different way? And what is the effect on the child, both in the short run and in the long run? What happens in mother-absent families? The number of cases of such families is rather small, and there have been no systematic studies of them that I know of. (Although George and Wilding, 1972, have done a

study of the effect of mother absence on *fathers,* they did not study the impact on the child.) But the question is not just a research issue. There are important practical reasons for needing to know more about father-reared children, partly because the courts are increasingly granting custody of children to fathers in divorce cases.

While we know a fair amount about the impact of fathers on traditional sex-role adoption in sons (and in daughters), we have no information about the ways in which one might foster egalitarian sex-roles among children. Does nurturance in a father invariably lead to traditional sex roles? Or would nurturance when combined with egalitarian roles within the family lead to equivalently egalitarian role adoption on the part of the sons and daughters?

It is also important that we know more about the impact of father absence, and of other family factors that interact with father absence, to produce effects on the child. With increasing numbers of children being raised in households headed by women, it is again of practical as well as of theoretical importance that we know the nature of possible effects. The assumption has been that it is the absence of the father per se that is critical, and such an assumption leads logically to programs like Big Brothers. But if the problems experienced by fatherless families are largely the result of economic and other stresses experienced by the mother, then, as Herzog and Sudia point out, the greatest benefit to the child might be achieved by providing services and support to the mother.

I am sure you can think of other relevant questions that should be asked about the role of the father in the family. Among other things, it is obviously important that we continue to look at the impact of fathering on behaviors other than sex-role adoption. With our increased sensitization to the importance of fathers and to their potentially increased role in child rearing, I suspect (and hope) that this whole area will continue to be a fruitful area for research exploration and social policy analysis.

QUESTIONS FOR DEBATE AND DISCUSSION
1. If you were a judge charged with deciding whether children in a divorce case should live with the father or the mother, what factors would enter into your decision? What information would you need or like to have?
2. What might be the effects of maternal absence on the child? Can you generate any hypotheses about the potential effects of such rearing conditions?

ADDITIONAL REFERENCES USEFUL
IN PREPARATION FOR DEBATE OR DISCUSSION

Herzog, E., and Sudia, C. E. Children in fatherless families. In B. M. Caldwell and H. N. Ricciuti (Eds.), *Review of child development research.* Vol. 3. Chicago: University of Chicago Press, 1973, pp. 141–232.

> An absolutely first-rate analysis of the literature on father absence. Their interpretation is cautious and their discussion of the social issues involved is excellent.

Hetherington, M., and Deur, J. The effects of father absence on child development. In W. W. Hartup (Ed.), *The young child: Reviews of research.* Vol. 2. Washington, D.C.: National Association for the Education of Young Children, 1972, pp. 303–319.

> A much shorter and much easier to read review of the father absence literature. I suggest that you try this one first and then look at Herzog and Sudia.

Lynn, D. B. *The father: His role in child development.* Belmont, Calif.: Wadsworth, 1974.

> By far the most complete review now in existence of literature on fathers. Lynn covers the history of the role of fathers in several cultures and also analyzes the current literature on fathers' role and impact in the family. If you are looking for a single good source, this is your best bet.

Nash, J. The father in contemporary culture and current psychological literature. *Child Development,* 1965, **36,** 261–297.

> This review predates Lynn's and thus covers a smaller segment of the literature. I think it is very good, however, and worthwhile if you are interested in this area.

REFERENCES

Bronfenbrenner, U. *Two worlds of childhood.* New York: Russell Sage Foundation, 1970.

Epstein, A. S., and Radin, N. Motivational components related to father behavior and cognitive functioning in preschoolers. *Child Development,* 1975, **46,** 831–839.

Fling, S., and Manosevitz, M. Sex typing in nursery school children's play interests. *Developmental Psychology,* 1972, **7,** 146–152.

George, V., and Wilding, P. *Motherless families.* London: Routeledge and Kegan Paul, 1972.

Herzog, E., and Sudia, C. E. Children in fatherless families. In B. M. Caldwell and H. N. Ricciuti (Eds.), *Review of child development research.* Vol. 3. Chicago: University of Chicago Press, 1973, pp. 141–232.

Hetherington, E. M. Effects of paternal absence on sex-typed behaviors in Negro and white preadolescent males. *Journal of Personality and Social Psychology,* 1966, **4,** 87–91.

Hetherington, E. M., Cox, M., and Cox, R. Beyond father absence: Conceptualization of effects of divorce. Paper presented at the biennial meetings of The Society for Research in Child Development, Denver, 1975.

Hetherington, M., and Deur, J. The effects of father absence on child development. In W. W. Hartup (Ed.), *The young child: Reviews of research.* Vol. 2. Washington, D.C.: National Association for the Education of Young Children, 1972, pp. 303–319.

Jordan, B. E., Radin, N., and Epstein, A. Paternal behavior and intellectual functioning in preschool boys and girls. *Developmental Psychology,* 1975, **11,** 407–408.

Lansky, L. M. The family structure also affects the model: Sex-role attitudes in parents of preschool children. *Merrill-Palmer Quarterly,* 1967, **13,** 139–150.

Leifer, A., Leiderman, P. H., Barnett, C. R., and Williams, J. A. Effects of mother-infant separation on maternal attachment behavior. *Child Development,* 1972, **43,** 1203–1218.

Lynn, D. B. *The father: His role in child development.* Belmont, Calif.: Wadsworth, 1974.

Lynn, D. B., and Sawrey, W. L. The effects of father-absence on Norwegian boys and girls. *Journal of Abnormal and Social Psychology, 1959,* **59,** 258–262.

Maccoby, E. E., and Jacklin, C. N. *The psychology of sex differences.* Stanford, Calif.: Stanford University Press, 1974.

Mussen, P. H., and Rutherford, E. Parent-child relations and parental personality in relation to young children's sex-role preferences. *Child Development,* 1963, **34,** 589–607.

Nash, J. The father in contemporary culture and current psychological literature. *Child Development,* 1965, **36,** 261–297.

Nelson, E. A., and Maccoby, E. E. The relationship between social development and differential abilities on the scholastic aptitude test. *Merrill-Palmer Quarterly,* 1966, **12,** 269–284.

Pederson, F. A., and Robson, K. S. Father participation in infancy. *American Journal of Orthopsychiatry,* 1969, **39,** 466–472.

Radin, N. Father-child interaction and the intellectual functioning of 4-year-old boys. *Developmental Psychology,* 1972, **6,** 363–361.

Radin, N. Observed paternal behaviors as antecedents of intellectual functioning in young boys. *Developmental Psychology,* 1973, **8,** 369–376.

Sutton-Smith, B., Rosenberg, B. G., and Landy, F. Father-absence effects in families of different sibling compositions. *Child Development,* 1968, **39,** 1213–1221.

U.S. Department of Labor, Bureau of Labor Statistics. *Children of Working Mothers,* March 1974. Special Labor Force Report **174,** 1975.

Effect of early father absence on scholastic aptitude

LYN CARLSMITH

Theories of identification, whatever their form, usually agree on two points: for the boy to identify successfully with the father, the father must be present during at least some portion of the boy's childhood; development of an appropriate masculine identity or self-concept is predicated upon the success of this early identification with the father. One of the most direct methods of investigating these general propositions is to study boys whose fathers were absent during their childhood. The present study, by considering a sample of boys whose home life was presumably normal in every respect except for the temporary absence of the father in World War II, seeks to answer two questions. First, are there lasting measurable effects due to the absence of the father at an early age? Second, is the age of the child during the father's absence an important variable in determining these effects?

Previous studies on the effect of father absence during the first years of life represent three different approaches: (1) studies

Lyn Carlsmith, "Effect of early father absence on scholastic aptitude," *Harvard Educational Review*, 34, Winter 1964, 3–21. Copyright © 1964 by President and Fellows of Harvard College.

The research for this paper was done at the Laboratory of Human Development at Harvard University. It is a part of a larger project on sex identity being carried on at the Laboratory under the direction of John W. M. Whiting. A more extensive report of this study appears in a Ph.D. thesis of the same title under the author's former name, Karolyn Gai Kuckenberg, which was accepted by the Department of Social Relations in June 1963. The author is grateful to John W. M. Whiting, Beatrice B. Whiting, and J. Merrill Carlsmith for their generous assistance in the planning and execution of this research.

of the fantasy and behavior of children (Bach, 1946; Sears, Pintler, and Sears, 1946; Stolz, 1954; Lynn and Sawry, 1959; Tiller, 1957; D'Andrade, 1962); (2) restrospective accounts from the case histories of delinquents (Zucker, 1943; Glueck and Glueck, 1950; Rohrer and Edmonson, 1960); (3) studies of other cultures (Burton and Whiting, 1961). Each of these sources suggests that absence of the father significantly affects personality development and behavior in certain ways. The results of all these studies are generally consistent: father-absent boys show more underlying feminine traits and, at least in lower or working class families, they attempt to compensate by demonstrating extreme masculinity. However, the effect of the early experience of father absence on later development under normal circumstances has not been studied in this culture.

The study to be reported in this paper stems from an early and serendipitous finding that aroused considerable interest at the outset of this research on the effects of father absence. The finding was this: boys who experienced early separation from their fathers had a different pattern of aptitude scores on the College Board tests than boys who were not separated. Since the finding concerned the differential development of Mathematical and Verbal ability, it dovetailed into the current interest and research on the learning of mathematical or analytical modes of thought. It seemed possible that we had hit upon an unexpected antecedent variable—the presence or absence of the father in early childhood. Although the finding was initially based on a very small sample of Harvard students, it seemed sufficiently intriguing to explore further with a much larger group of students.

Whiting's (1960) theory of cross-sex identification provided the framework from which this study developed. This theory provides a set of explicit hypotheses concerning the development of cross-sex identification. However, it should be pointed out that the present study was not designed to discriminate between theories of identification; rather, it provides evidence relevant to any general theory of identification by showing certain strong effects of father absence at various ages.

Let us now consider the relevance of aptitude scores to sex-role identification. Accumulated evidence from a large number of studies on Math and Verbal aptitudes clearly demonstrates that females are generally superior to males in Verbal areas, while males are superior to females in quantitative pursuits, particularly numerical reasoning (e.g., McCarthy, 1954; Samuels, 1943; Heilman, 1933). These differences are well replicated and seem to hold over a broad age range, increasing from the elementary school years. Preferences for school subjects follow the same pattern. A particularly relevant study by Milton (1957) indicates a striking correlation between the problem-solving ability of adolescents and their scores on masculinity-femininity scales (MMPI and Terman-Miles). That is, both boys and girls who obtain a high masculinity score show superior problem-solving ability. In a retrospective study of the autobiographies of professional mathematicians, Plank and Plank (1954) report that female mathematicians have a "strong identification with a masculine figure in their lives. Parallel with it, seems to go a lack of feminine identification . . ." (p. 268). The lives of male mathematicians are characterized by a "loss of relationship to the mother."

These findings suggest that superior ability in mathematics reflects a typically masculine way of thinking or "conceptual approach." For the purposes of this study, the pattern of Math and Verbal aptitude scores from the College Entrance Examination Board seemed to provide a clear, objective measure of this sex-typed ability. That is, students who score relatively higher on Math aptitude than on Verbal aptitude tests have an aptitude pattern that is typical of a masculine conceptual approach; students who score relatively higher on Verbal aptitude tests have a more feminine conceptual approach.

Finally, there is considerable evidence that aptitude is a fairly stable characteristic, showing little variation with time (*College Board Score Reports*, 1960). A special mathematics teaching program which followed schoolchildren from fourth to seventh grade (Alpert, 1963) indicates that aptitude for mathematics is fairly well established by fourth grade and is highly resistant to change during subsequent school training. These data suggest that aptitude patterns are a useful index for the measurement of primary sex-role identity since they are apparently little influenced by the external pressures or expectations that occur in the subject's later experience. That is, while we would expect many indices of personality and behavior to be strongly influenced by our cultural norms for males and females, it is likely that aptitude patterns are both relatively free from and impervious to such expectations and that they are therefore a good indicator of the primary or underlying identity.

Children who were born during the war years (1941 to 1945) and whose fathers were away during their first years of life are now [in the 1960s, *Ed.*] finishing school or attending college. This group offers a number of advantages for a study of the effects of early father absence on subsequent development. It is possible to locate students from stable families who have shared this common experience, the reason for father absence was socially acceptable and even desirable, the exact periods of father ab-

TABLE 1 LENGTH OF FATHER ABSENCE

Length of time father was absent after child's birth	Harvard class of 1963	Harvard class of 1964
Over 3 years	38	3
2–3 years	53	36
Less than 2 years	124	44
Not absent	666	224
	High school boys	High school girls
1–5 years	19	14
Less than 1 year	19	12
Not absent	99	109

sence may usually be ascertained, and all other background factors (except the wartime separation) can be matched in the two groups studied. The present study includes only boys from intact families (both parents living and not divorced) of middle or upper-middle class background. The majority of students were sophomores at Harvard College; one small sample includes high school seniors who planned to attend college the next year. Thus all students have achieved a relatively high level of academic success and have also made a reasonably satisfactory adjustment in terms of our social and cultural norms.

SAMPLES

Both college and high school students were subjects in this study. The college population consists of 881 Harvard freshmen in the class of 1963 and 307 Harvard freshmen in the class of 1964. The high school sample includes 137 boys and 135 girls from the 1961 senior classes at Concord, Lexington, and Newton South Public High Schools. All students in both college and high school samples are American-born and are from intact families (i.e., natural parents are not separated, divorced, or deceased). The high school sample is limited to those students on whom aptitude scores from the College Entrance Examination Board were available.

All students in the study were born during the war years, 1941 to 1945. Approximately one-third of their fathers served overseas and were separated from their wives and young children for varying lengths of time. Table 1 presents this distribution.

METHODOLOGY

In March 1961, I administered a simple questionnaire on father absence to 450 Harvard freshmen (class of '64) who were voluntarily taking a series of interest-aptitude tests through

AVERAGE SAT SCORES		
	Math	Verbal
Boys	527	479
Girls	467	486

facilities of the Harvard Testing Service. On this form, three questions were asked: was your father in the service during World War II; was he overseas during this time; if so, estimate the dates that he was overseas. Verbal and Math aptitude scores from the College Entrance Examination Board tests were then obtained on all students whose fathers had served overseas. Students whose fathers were in the service but did not go overseas were eliminated from the study because I felt it would be too difficult to ascertain the periods of father-separation for this group. Foreign-born students and those from broken homes (due to death, separation, or divorce) were also excepted. Finally, the median College Board aptitude scores for the entire freshman class were obtained.

A similar procedure was used with the high school students, except that the father-absence questionnaire was addressed to the parents to increase accuracy of the dates of the father's military service. Math and Verbal aptitude scores were then obtained for all students who had taken the College Entrance Examination Board tests. Since no other aptitude test had been uniformly administered in the high schools, the majority of high school students could not be included in this survey.

To further test the relationship between father absence and aptitude, I studied a second group of Harvard freshmen (class of '63). Questions on the father's military service had been included in the medical history record filled out by all entering students. Data on these students were provided by Dr. Stanley King from material collected in the Harvard Student Study.

SCHOLASTIC APTITUDE TEST (SAT)

This test is administered to high school juniors and seniors by the College Entrance Examination Board. The test yields two scores: a Verbal score and a Mathematical score. Norms for the test were established nationally over a period of years, and it is possible to make direct comparisons between students taking the test in different years. The reported reliability coefficient for the tests is .91. In *College Board Score Reports* (1961), the average aptitude scores achieved by all high school seniors taking the test in a recent year are reported. The booklet also states: "In

TABLE 2 A. BACKGROUND VARIABLES ON
WHICH TWO GROUPS OF STUDENTS WERE MATCHED

Fathers' occupations	Fathers' education	Subjects' education
8 physicians	14 advanced degrees	5 prep school—boarded at
2 architects	5 attended college	school
1 lawyer	1–4 years	5 prep school—lived at home
1 minister	1 high school only	10 public school—lived at home
1 professor		
4 business, managerial		
3 business, sales		

B. OTHER BACKGROUND VARIABLES:
SUBJECTS' AGE, ORDINAL POSITION, AND PARENTS' AGE

	Father absent	Father present
Mean age of subjects	19.3	19.4
Only child	4	4
Oldest child	11	8
Second or third child	5	8
Mean age of fathers	53	55
Mean age of mothers	49	51
Age range of fathers	40–70	45–68
Age range of mothers	39–62	43–57

general girls do less well than boys on the Mathematical parts of the test and should not be surprised if their Mathematical scores are noticeably lower than their Verbal" (p. 8).

DATA ANALYSIS

In addition to mean Math and Verbal aptitude scores, a single Math-minus-Verbal score was computed for each subject. In this paper, the Math-minus-Verbal difference score will be represented by the term M-V. This single difference score is preferred for all comparisons between groups since it controls to some extent for general level of ability. That is, by considering only the relative superiority of Math to Verbal aptitude for each individual, differences in absolute level of ability between individuals are not weighted. For this reason, the single M-V difference score is used for all statistical comparisons between the Father-absent and Father-present groups. Several methods were used to test the significance of the difference between groups; these will be described with the presentation of results.

RESULTS

The independent variables considered here are: (1) length of the father's absence and (2) age of the child when the father left. Since each of the three samples included in this survey represents a different class year in school and different age group (by year of birth), there is considerable variation in the periods of father absence between groups. In addition, data on both independent variables were not available for one of the samples. Because of these limitations, it is not possible to combine groups or to present uniform tables on the dates of father absence for all groups. In the data analysis, father-absent categories for each sample are determined by the distribution of dates of father absence, sample size, and the information available for that group. All Math and Verbal scores presented in these tables are from the Scholastic Aptitude Test (SAT) of the College Entrance Examination Board.

Harvard Class of 1964

For the entire Harvard class of 1964 ($n = 1180$), the median Math aptitude score was 695; the median Verbal score was 677. Clearly the students in this class scored higher on the Math aptitude test than on the Verbal aptitude test. The first evidence to be presented on the effects of father absence comes from an attempt to compare as extreme groups as possible. Twenty students whose fathers went overseas before they were 6 months old and were away for at least two years were chosen as the father-absent group. A matched sample of twenty students whose fathers were not in the service at all were selected as the control group. The two groups were matched on the basis of father's occupation, education, marital status (both parents living and not divorced), and on the student's previous academic experience (public or private school). Table 2A shows the breakdown on these background variables which are identical in both groups. Table 2B

TABLE 3 RELATIONSHIP OF MATH
TO VERBAL APTITUDE FOR A SELECTED GROUP OF 20
MATCHED PAIRS OF SUBJECTS, HARVARD CLASS OF 1964

	Aptitude scores	
	Verbal higher than math	Math higher than verbal
Father absent	13	7
Father not absent	2	18

TABLE 4 RELATIONSHIP OF MATH
TO VERBAL APTITUDE FOR 9 MATCHED
PAIRS OF DOCTOR'S SONS, HARVARD CLASS OF 1964

	Aptitude scores	
	Verbal higher than math	Math higher than verbal
Father absent	8	1
Father not absent	2	7

gives the mean age and ordinal position of subjects as well as the
age of parents in the father-absent and father-present groups.[1]
Except for the wartime separation of the father-absent group,
none of the students in either group had been separated from his
father for more than two months during his childhood or adolescence. Five students in each group attended boarding prep
schools; all other students lived at home with both parents until
college. During the wartime period, no other adults lived as permanent members in any of the family households of either group.

Table 3 compares these two matched groups, indicating the
number of cases in which Verbal aptitude is superior to Math
aptitude.

As Table 2 suggests, many doctors were sent overseas early
in the war, and it is interesting to look at the findings for this
single occupational group. A total of 18 doctors' sons were found
to be included in the original sample of 450 students; 9 of these
boys were separated from their fathers during the war years and 9
were not separated. Table 4 compares these groups of doctors'
sons, again showing the number of cases in which Verbal aptitude
is superior to Math aptitude.

In these matched samples, the performance of the control
group is representative of the relative aptitude scores typically
obtained by males, both nationally and at Harvard (i.e., Math
superior to Verbal). However, the performance of the father-
absent group is similar to the pattern typically achieved by girls
(Verbal superior to Math).

To further explore the relationship between father absence
and aptitude, the scores for the 83 students in the father-absent
sample were analyzed. In Figure 1 the relationships between
length of father absence, age of son when father left, and relative
superiority of Math or Verbal aptitude are presented graphically.

---

[1] Additional background information was obtained on this sample of students as part of a more intensive interview study reported in Kuckenberg, Karolyn
G., Effect of Early Father Absence on Scholastic Aptitude.

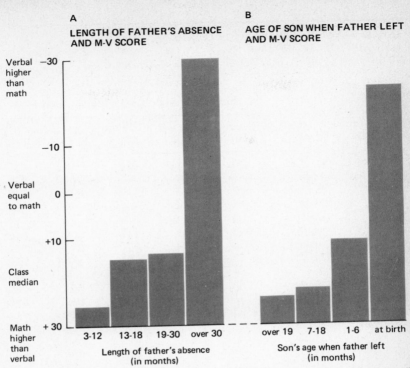

A
**LENGTH OF FATHER'S ABSENCE
AND M-V SCORE**

B
**AGE OF SON WHEN FATHER LEFT
AND M-V SCORE**

Figure 1. Father-absent students, Harvard class of 1964. Relationship of Math to Verbal aptitude (SAT) ($n = 83$).

These drawings clearly show that both independent variables are systematically related to aptitude: the relative superiority of Verbal to Math aptitude increases steadily the longer the father is absent and the younger the child is when the father left. This effect is strongest for students whose fathers were absent at birth and/or were away for over 30 months.

The interaction of the two independent variables with aptitude is presented in Table 5, which shows the mean Math and Verbal scores and the mean M-V difference scores for these students. The table employs a two-way break: age of the child when his father left (horizontal axis); total length of time the father was away after his son's birth (vertical axis). A minus sign preceding any of the M-V scores indicates that the mean Verbal score is higher than the mean Math score for that group.

To test the significance of the relationships shown here, a regression analysis was performed. This analysis showed that each variable was significantly related to the M-V aptitude scores ($p < .05$ for each). That is, in Table 5 each variable considered alone shows a significant effect on the M-V score. Because of the high correlation between age at absence and length of absence

TABLE 5 FATHER-ABSENT STUDENTS,
HARVARD CLASS OF 1964 MEAN MATH,
VERBAL, AND M-V APTITUDE SCORES (SAT) (n = 83)

Length of father's absence (in months)		Over 19	7–18	1–6	At birth	Total
			Son's age when father left (in months)			
3–12	n	10	1	—	4	15
	Math	687	601	—	702	685
	Verbal	643	685	—	694	660
	M-V	44	−84	—	8	25
13–18	n	3	3	4	1	11
	Math	595	761	691	609	677
	Verbal	623	704	670	615	661
	M-V	−28	57	21	−6	16
19–30	n	1	22	8	9	40
	Math	708	696	697	665	689
	Verbal	731	668	669	693	675
	M-V	−23	28	28	−28	14
over 30	n	—	4	3	10	17
	Math	—	680	653	656	661
	Verbal	—	685	696	690	690
	M-V	—	−5	−43	−34	−29
Total	n	14	30	15	24	—
	Math	669	697	687	665	—
	Verbal	645	674	674	689	—
	M-V	24	23	13	−24	—

($r = -.59$), neither variable added significantly to prediction of the M-V score when the other had already been taken into account.

High School Class of 1961

A similar method of analysis was used for the sample of high school boys. Table 6 again shows a two-way break for length of father absence and age of son when father left.

There are two striking differences to be seen in this table. If the father left when his son was very young (0–12 months) and was away for a long time (1–5 years), the relative superiority of Math to Verbal aptitude shows a sharp decrease. This is consistent with the finding for the Harvard sample. However, if the father left late in the boy's childhood and was gone for only a brief time, a reverse effect apparently takes place. The other two conditions show no strong effect. An analysis of variance shows the differences between the groups (on the M-V score) to be significant beyond the .001 level.

TABLE 6 CONCORD, LEXINGTON, NEWTON
HIGH SCHOOL BOYS, CLASS OF 1961 MEAN MATH,
VERBAL AND M-V APTITUDE SCORES (SAT) (n = 137)

Length of father's absence	Son's age when father left	n	Mean aptitude scores		
			Math	Verbal	M-V
	1–5 years	12	633	536	97
3–12 months	0–12 months	7	568	517	51
	1–5 years	7	555	499	56
1–5 years	0–12 months	12	517	505	12
Not absent		99	576	529	47

While this sample is too small and unstable to draw any firm conclusions, the second finding of a sharp increase in Math aptitude, relative to Verbal aptitude, for one of the father-absent groups is intriguing. Returning to Table 5, there are ten cases in a somewhat comparable cell in the upper left corner: again the father left relatively late in the boy's childhood (after he was 18 months old) and was gone for only a brief time (3–12 months). These ten cases show a noticeable superiority in Math ability and are the chief contributors to the mean total scores for their column. The mean M-V difference score for these 10 cases is 44; the comparable score for the entire class is 18. Although many more cases in this experimental condition are needed, these two findings suggest that there may be a reverse effect operating if the child first knows his father and then is briefly separated from him.

To summarize these findings in comparable form for both the high school and college samples, a simple breakdown on each of the independent variables is shown in Tables 7 and 8. These tables are a condensation of the data already presented for the two groups.

Despite the sizeable difference between the groups in range of aptitude scores, the effect of father absence is similar for both groups. Comparing the father-absent students with the control groups, these data indicate that if the father leaves early (before his son is 12 months old) and if he is gone for more than a year, the son's Verbal aptitude is relatively superior to his Math aptitude. However, both late and brief separation from the father are associated with a relative increase in Math ability.

Although the independent variables are presented separately in these tables, it should be noted that for both samples of students there is a high negative correlation between length of

TABLE 7 RELATIONSHIP BETWEEN LENGTH
OF FATHER'S ABSENCE AND APTITUDE FOR BOTH THE
COLLEGE AND HIGH SCHOOL SAMPLES

Length of father's absence	Harvard class of 1964				High school classes of 1961			
		Mean aptitude scores				Mean aptitude scores		
	n	Math	Verbal	M-V	n	Math	Verbal	M-V
3–12 months	15	685	660	25	19	609	529	80
More than 12 months	68	680	677	3	19	532	503	29
Control[a] group	1180	695	677	18	99	576	529	47

father's absence and son's age when father left. Thus the findings
presented here should be considered as resulting from an interaction of the two variables, rather than as the result of either variable taken alone.

In addition to the high school boys, a small sample of girls
from Lexington, Concord, and Newton High Schools (class of
1961) were also included in this survey. In general, the effect of
father absence on aptitude appears to be the same for girls as for
boys, with both early and long separation from the father being
positively related to a relatively higher Verbal aptitude.

Harvard Class of 1963

As a further replication, available data on the Harvard class
of 1963 were analyzed. This sample includes the entire freshman
class with the exception of (1) foreign students, (2) students from
broken homes, and (3) students whose fathers were in the service
but did not go overseas. For this class, since it was not possible to
determine the age of the child when the father left, only the
duration of the father's absence will be considered here.

Table 9 compares the mean aptitude scores obtained by the
father-absent and father-present groups; it also shows the relative
superiority of Math to Verbal aptitude (M-V) for each group. As
for the previous sample, the M-V difference score shows an orderly progression with length of time father was absent, indicating that father absence is related to relatively lower Math ability.[2]

[2] Since only the distribution of Math and Verbal aptitude scores were available for this sample, it was not possible to determine the M-V score for each
individual subject, and thus an analysis of variance test could not be performed
on these data.

TABLE 8 RELATIONSHIP BETWEEN SON'S
AGE WHEN FATHER LEFT AND APTITUDE FOR BOTH THE
COLLEGE AND HIGH SCHOOL SAMPLES

| Son's age when father left | Harvard class of 1964 | | | | High school classes of 1961 | | | |
| | | Mean aptitude scores | | | | Mean aptitude scores | | |
	n	Math	Verbal	M-V	n	Math	Verbal	M-V
More than 12 months	21	683	658	25	19	604	522	82
0–12 months	62	682	679	3	19	536	509	27
Control[a] group	1180	695	677	18	99	576	529	47

[a] For the Harvard class of 1964, the scores for the control group are the median aptitude scores obtained by the *entire* class, and therefore include both father-absent and father-present students. For the high school classes, the control group includes only students who were not separated from their fathers at any time.

Throughout this paper, emphasis has been placed on the M-V difference scores rather than on the independent Math or Verbal scores. Although it is interesting to speculate whether a decrease in Math or an increase in Verbal ability is the chief contributor to the observed differences in the M-V scores of the father-absent students, it is impossible to tell from these data. In Table 9 the main effect of father absence seems to be a progressive depression of the Math score. However, for the first Harvard sample presented in Table 5, the principal effect of father absence appears to be an increase in Verbal ability. A careful study of these two tables strongly suggests that this discrepancy is an artifact resulting from different levels of ability between groups rather than a contradictory statement about the effects of father absence. For example, in Table 9 the group that was father-absent for over three years is considerably lower in both Math and Verbal aptitude than any of the other groups, which suggests a generally lower level of ability for this group. If we attempt to compensate for the lower ability of this group by adding 20 points to *both* their Math and Verbal aptitude scores, the M-V difference score remains unchanged, and the discrepancy between Tables 5 and 9 disappears.

This discrepancy between the two Harvard groups points up the danger of comparing Math or Verbal aptitude scores between groups, unless the absolute level of ability is partialed out. From the data at hand, there is no reason to argue that father

TABLE 9 HARVARD CLASS OF 1963 MEAN
MATH, VERBAL AND M-V APTITUDE SCORES (SAT) ($n = 881$)

Length of father's absence	n	Math	Verbal	M-V
Less than 2 years	124	669	660	9
2–3 years	53	671	663	8
Over 3 years	38	649	646	3
Not absent	666	680	656	24

absence is consistently related to a lower level of intelligence.[3] The results do indicate however that father absence is consistently related to a discrepancy between Math and Verbal abilities and that the father-absent boys have a lower Math aptitude, relative to their Verbal aptitude, than do their father-present peers.

DISCUSSION

Two major questions were asked at the outset of this paper. First, are there lasting measurable effects due to the absence of the father at an early age? Second, is the age of the child during the father's absence an important variable in determining these effects? The evidence presented provides clearly affirmative answers to both questions.

Stated concisely, the results of the aptitude survey of father-absent and father-present students indicate: (1) early and long separation from the father results in relatively greater ability in Verbal areas than in Mathematics; (2) no separation produces relatively greater ability in Mathematics; and (3) late brief separation may produce an extreme elevation in Mathematical ability (relative to Verbal ability).

The first two findings are consistent with predictions derived from any general theory of sex-role identification. Although the third finding has intriguing theoretical implications, it is based on a small sample and therefore must be considered less reliable than the other two findings. Since we have no additional information on this latter group, further pursuit seems unprofitable until more stable findings are obtained on a larger sample.

While the findings reported here are provocative, they leave several questions unanswered. For example, is the principal ef-

---

[3] Data from a recent study at Dartmouth College (Landauer and King, personal communication, 1963) indicate that the father-absent students (early wartime separation) scored *higher* than the class average on both the Math and Verbal aptitude tests of the College Entrance Examination Board. In the Dartmouth study, the M-V discrepancy between matched groups of father-absent and father-present control students is consistent with the findings reported here.

fect of early separation from the father an acceleration of Verbal ability or a depression of Math ability? This question cannot be answered from the data presented here. However, the studies of problem-solving techniques used by children (e.g., Seder, 1955; Milton, 1957; Bieri, 1960) suggest that this may be an inappropriate question. More specifically, these studies suggest that Math and Verbal aptitude scores may simply reflect two aspects of a single, more general characteristic: conceptual style or approach to problem solving. In these studies, two styles of conceptualization are usually differentiated: an "analytic approach" which is characterized by clear discrimination between stimuli, a direct pursuit of solutions, and a disregard for extraneous material; a "global approach," characterized by less clear discrimination of stimuli and a greater influence from extraneous material. The first approach is more typically used by boys while the second is more typical of girls. It seems reasonable to assume that boys using the analytic approach to problem solving would score relatively higher on Math aptitude than on Verbal aptitude tests; boys using the global approach would show relatively greater ability on Verbal comprehension tests. Thus the relative superiority of Math or Verbal aptitude is, in effect, a single measure of the boy's conceptual style or approach to problem solving. It follows that any antecedent variable, such as presence or absence of the father, may directly influence conceptual approach (i.e., aptitude pattern), but only indirectly influences performance on a particular test.

A second query that is sometimes raised in response to the data reported here concerns the possible influence of anxiety on the Math aptitude of father-absent boys. It is argued that the early experience of father absence produces high anxiety and that anxiety has a more debilitating effect on proficiency in Mathematics than on Verbal skills. Data in support of this argument are drawn largely from studies of emotionally disturbed individuals which indicate that some aspects of Verbal ability are less vulnerable to stress and are therefore used as indicators of the "premorbid" level of intellectual functioning (e.g., Mayman et al., 1951). Contrary to this position is a directly relevant study by Alpert (1957) which relates a number of anxiety scales[4] with the Math and Verbal aptitude scores obtained on the College Board tests by a large sample of Stanford males. While most of the anxiety scales correlate negatively with both aptitude scores, the author states that "in *every* instance in which the data were significant, the correlations with mathematical aptitude were in the same direc-

[4] Taylor Manifest Anxiety Scale; Welsh Anxiety Index; Freeman Anxiety Scale; Mandler-Sarason Test Anxiety Scale; Achievement Anxiety Scale.

tion as those with verbal aptitude but in no instance were they of as large magnitude" (p. 46). Several of the correlations between anxiety and Verbal aptitude are fairly high, but not one of the correlations with Math aptitude reaches an acceptable level of significance. Since none of the father-absent students in this study can be considered severely emotionally disturbed, there is no reason to suspect that extreme stress or anxiety is responsible for the observed differences in their aptitude scores. If anxiety had any effect at all, the Alpert study indicates that Verbal aptitude, rather than Math aptitude, would be expected to show the greater decrement. This is clearly contrary to the data reported here.

What other variables or conditions might be considered possible contributors to the aptitude differences between the father-absent and father-present groups? In the large high school and college samples, no attempt was made to match subjects on background variables (except, of course, that all subjects were from intact homes, academically successful, and from a reasonably homogenous population). In the small matched samples, however, such variables as age, occupation and education of parents, number and age of siblings, and high school experience of subject were considered and controlled for (cf. Table 2). Whether there may be some further variable correlated with father absence in World War II and capable of producing such large effects on Mathematical and Verbal aptitude cannot be answered from these data. It should be borne in mind, however, that any such variable would have to account not only for differences between father absence and father presence but also for the effects due to the age of the child at the time the father departed, as reported in this paper. Thus, such an explanatory variable would have to be correlated with the exact age of the child when the father was called into active duty as well as with the gross fact that the father was called overseas.

A final puzzling question is why conceptual approach or pattern of aptitudes should be so clearly sex-typed in our culture. An adequate explanation of this recurrent finding is not available, but several studies suggest that the masculine analytical approach is acquired through close and harmonious association with the father. Seder (1955) found that boys who used the global approach to problems had fathers who spent little time with them or who were very passive in their interaction with their sons. Bieri (1960) reports that boys who willingly accept authority and describe themselves as more similar to their mothers are poor performers on differentiation-analytic tasks. Levy (1943) reports the same finding for "maternally over-protected" boys. Finally,

Witkin (1960) reports that boys who perform poorly on analytic problems perceive their fathers as dominating and tyrannical.

A study of male college students at Stanford University relates College Board aptitude scores with certain childhood experiences reported by the students (Maccoby, 1961). Boys who achieve a more feminine pattern of aptitudes (i.e., Math aptitude relatively lower than Verbal aptitude) than their peers report that in their childhood: (1) their fathers were away from home for one to five years; (2) they almost never talked about personal problems with their fathers; (3) they were often fearful of their fathers; and (4) they were punished exclusively by their mothers.

All of these studies consistently point to close, positive relationships between father and son as a prerequisite for development of a masculine conceptual approach. However, they still do not explain why the relationship exists or how this approach develops. Milton (1957), who reports a striking correlation between problem-solving skill and sex-role identification in both boys and girls, suggests simply that girls typically won't learn the necessary skills since problem solving is inappropriate to the female sex-role. This reasoning suggests that a conceptual approach is developed fairly consciously and probably not until after the child enters school. The accumulated evidence on learning of sex-role identity suggests that this occurs quite early in childhood through a largely unconscious process of imitation or identification with one of the parents. Whether the conceptual approach develops later as a result of sex-role identity (as Milton suggests) or early along with sex-role identity (through a similar process of identification) cannot be ascertained from the information available. However, studies of the problem-solving behavior of very young children may be designed to answer this part of the question. Studies of the interaction of mothers and fathers with their young children may also give us some ideas about the direct roles parents play in the development of a conceptual approach. At the present time, we can only say that aptitude patterns or conceptual approaches are related to both sex-role identity and to father-son relationships and that absence of the father during certain early periods of the child's life has an important effect on later cognitive development.

REFERENCES

Alpert, R. School mathematics study group: a psychological evaluation. 1963, in press.

Alpert, R. Anxiety in academic achievement situations: its measurement and relation to aptitude. Unpublished Ph.D. thesis, Stanford University, 1957.

Bach, G. R. Father-fantasies and father-typing in father-separated children. *Child Developm.*, 1946, **17**, 63–80.

Bieri, J. Parental identification, acceptance of authority, and within-sex differences in cognitive behavior. *J. abnorm. soc. Psychol.*, 1960, **60**, 76–79.

Burton, R. V., and Whiting, J. W. M. The absent father and cross-sex identity. *Merrill-Palmer Quarterly*, 1961, **7**, 85–95.

College board score reports. Princeton: Educational Testing Service, College Entrance Examination Board, 1960.

D'Andrade, R. G. Father-absence and cross-sex identification. Unpublished Ph.D. thesis, Harvard University, 1962.

Dember, W. N., Nairne, F., and Miller, F. J. Further validation of the Alpert-Haber achievement anxiety test. *J. abnorm. soc. Psychol.*, 1962, **65**, 427–428.

Glueck, S., and Glueck, E. *Unravelling juvenile delinquency.* N.Y.: The Commonwealth Fund, 1950.

Heilman, J. D. Sex differences in intellectual abilities. *J. educ. Psychol.*, 1933, **24**, 47–62.

Hill, J. P. Sex-typing and mathematics achievement. Unpublished thesis prospectus, Harvard University, 1962.

Landauer, T. K., and King, F. W. Personal communication, 1963.

Lynn, D. B., and Sawrey, W. L. The effects of father-absence on Norwegian girls and boys. *J. abnorm. soc. Psychol.*, 1959, **59**, 258–262.

Maccoby, Eleanor E., and Rau, Lucy. *Differential cognitive abilities.* Final report, U.S. Office of Education, Cooperative Research Project No. 1040, 1962.

Mayman, M., Schafer, R., and Rapaport, D. Interpretation of the Wechsler-Bellevue Intelligence Scale in personality appraisal. In H. H. Anderson and G. L. Anderson (Eds.), *An introduction to projective techniques.* New York: Prentice-Hall, 1951.

McCarthy, Dorothea. Language development in children. In L. Carmichael (Ed.), *Manual of child psychology.* New York: Wiley, 1954, pp. 492–630.

Milton, G. A. The effects of sex-role identification upon problem-solving skill. *J. abnorm. soc. Psychol.*, 1957, **55**, 208–212.

Milton, G. A. Five studies of the relation between sex-role identification and achievement in problem-solving. Technical Report, Office of Naval Research, Contract Nonr 609(20) (NR150-166). New Haven: Yale University, 1958.

Munroe, Ruth. The role of the father in the development of the child: a survey of the literature. Unpublished report, Harvard University, 1961.

Plank, Emma N., and Plank, R. Emotional components in arithmetical learning as seen through autobiographies. *The psychoanalytic study of the child.* Vol. IX, N.Y.: International Universities Press, 1954.

Rohrer, J. H., and Edmonson, M. S. *The eighth generation.* New York: Harper, 1960.

Samuels, F. Sex differences in reading achievement. *J. educ. Res.*, 1943, **36**, 594–603.

Sears, Pauline S. Doll play aggression in normal young children: influence of sex, age, sibling status, father's absence. *Psychol. Monogr.*, 1951, **65**, 1–43.

Sears, R. R., Pintler, M. H., and Sears, Pauline S. Effect of father separation on preschool children's doll play aggression. *Child Developm.* 1946, **17**, 219–243.

Seder, Joan A. The origin of difference in the extent of independence in children: developmental factors in perceptual field dependence. Senior Honors Thesis, Social Relations, Radcliffe College, 1955. (As reported by Witkin, H. A., The problem of individuality in development. *loc. cit.*)

Stolz, Lois M. *Father relations of war-born children.* Stanford, Calif.: Stanford University Press, 1954.

Tiller, P. O. Father absence and personality development of children in sailor families: a preliminary research report. Part II. In N. Anderson (Ed.), *Studies of the family.* Vol. 2. Gottingen: Vandenhoeck and Ruprecht, 1957, pp. 115–137.

Tukey, J. W. The future of data analysis. *Annals Math Stat.*, 1962, **33**, 1–67.

Whiting, J. W. M. Social structure and child rearing: a theory of identification. Unpublished lectures presented at Tulane University as part of the Mona Bronsman Scheckman Lectures in Social Psychiatry, March, 1960.

Witkin, H. A. The problem of individuality in development. In Kaplan, B., and Wapner, S. (Eds.), *Perspectives in psychological theory.* New York: International Universities Press, 1960.

Zucker, H. J. Affectional identification and delinquency. *Arch. Psychol.*, 1943, **40**, No. 286.

Mothers and fathers, girls and boys: attachment behavior in the one-year-old

PEGGY L. BAN
MICHAEL LEWIS

Studies of attachment in the past have focused almost exclusively on the mother-infant relationship. Certainly in most naturalistic conditions the mother is the first object of infant attachment, but it is also recognized that the infant continues on to form other attachments during early childhood.

Attachment studies vary in terms of the situations used to measure them: separation from the mother (Ainsworth & Bell, 1970; Rheingold & Eckerman, 1970; Schaffer & Emerson, 1964); reunion with her (Maccoby & Feldman, 1972); and during a free-play, low-stress situation (Brooks & Lewis, 1973a; Coates, Anderson, & Hartup, 1972a; Goldberg & Lewis, 1969; Maccoby & Jacklin, 1973). Unfortunately the results across situations demonstrate little generalizability (Masters & Wellman, 1973).

Measurement differences also appear in the study of attachment. Obviously the measures will depend in part on the situational context. For example, protest such as crying will be studied if the situation is one of separation, although decrease in the toy play of the child has also been used (Spelke, Zelazo,

From *Merrill-Palmer Quarterly*, 1974, **20.** Reprinted by permission.

This research was supported by a grant from the Early Childhood Research Council. An earlier version of this paper was presented at the Eastern Psychological Association meetings, New York, April 1971.

Kagan, & Kotelchuck, 1973). Proximity seeking has been defined in several ways, from moving toward (Rheingold & Eckerman, 1970) to looking at the mother (Lewis & Ban, 1971) and can be measured in a variety of situations. The consistency and stability of the various measures of attachment, although studied extensively (for example, Coates et al., 1972b; Lewis & Ban, 1971; Maccoby & Feldman, 1972; Masters & Wellman, 1973), also have failed to show clear patterns. Brooks and Lewis (1973a) have argued that part of the instability of results across studies has been the failure to take into account such variables as time in situation, sequence order, size and shape of room, etc. Until these variables are controlled the different results are difficult to interpret.

The present study is concerned with the study of attachment of the infant to its father as well as its mother. Attachment in this study was observed in a free-play, low-stress situation similar to that reported previously in this laboratory (Brooks & Lewis, 1973a, b; Goldberg & Lewis, 1969; Lewis & Ban, 1971; Messer & Lewis, 1972).

The father has been traditionally considered a part of the nuclear family, yet little has been known to date of the role he plays in the infant's life and of the attachment behavior which the infant directs toward him. There is little information in the literature to help answer this question. Rebelsky and Hanks (1971) observed the interaction of fathers with their infants 2 weeks to 3 months of age. By continuous recording—six 24-hour records per child—it was possible to determine how much time the father spent interacting with his infant. While it is possible that the father could play silently with his infant, it was possible to hear and record all interaction and especially all vocalizations. The results reveal that at this age fathers interact a minimum amount of time: 37.7 seconds per day. Moreover, seven of the ten fathers decreased their vocalization time during the second half of the study as compared to the first half. While no comparable data for the mothers is available, a comparison of similar data from Moss (1967) and Lewis (1972) reveals this to be quite low!

The other reported study of father interaction is that of Spelke et al. (1973). Infants' protest following separation from both the mother and father was studied in a group of one-year-old infants. No differences in the infants' protest behavior was observed when either the mother or father left. Other than this study and an unpublished dissertation of Kotelchuck (1972), there has been little work on the infant's response to the father.

In the present study we investigated the attachment behavior of a sample of one-year-old infants toward mothers and fathers. The questions posed were: For a selected number of behaviors, is the attachment behavior directed toward the mother different from that directed toward the father? Are there any differences in the expression of this attachment behavior as a function of the sex of the child? Finally, we wished to know how much time the father spends with the child as a function of sex of the child and whether this has any relationship to the expression of attachment from the child.

PROCEDURE

Ten male and ten female one-year-old infants (±2 weeks) made two visits, a week apart, to our laboratory. On one visit, the mother accompanied the child; and on the other, the father. The sample was split, such that for half the subjects, the mother accompanied on the first visit; and for the other half, the father accompanied on the first visit.

During each visit, the infant was placed in a room, 12' × 12'. The room was divided into a series of squares so that the infant's positioning could be observed and recorded. Toys were placed within a number of squares. A chair in one corner of the room was provided for the parent. The parent was instructed to hold the child on his lap and on an arranged signal to place the child in a designated square. They were told to respond in kind to the child's advances, but not to initiate any interaction with the child. The child was free to roam about the room at will. Parent and child remained in the room for about 15 minutes.

Observation of the subjects took place from behind a one-way mirror. An observer operated an event recorder which recorded the four specific behaviors. (a) Looking at the parent; that is, the amount of time the infant's eyes and head were turned in the direction of the parent. (b) Touching the parent; the amount of time any part of the infant's body made contact with the parent's body. This would include holding on or leaning against behavior. (c) Proximity to the parent; this was defined as the infant staying in the three squares immediately surrounding the parent's chair. In this case the distance was approximately 2 feet ± 6 inches. (d) Vocalization to the parent; this included all vocalizations which were not frets, cries, sneezing or coughs, etc. It is nearly impossible to differentiate between vocalizations directed toward the parent and those that are not. Because of this all vocalizations were scored.

Interobserver reliability was obtained by having a second observer record these same variables. Each subject's scores were then compared for each measure. The reliabilities as determined by Pearson Product Moment Correlations were .91, .97, .96, and .87, respectively.

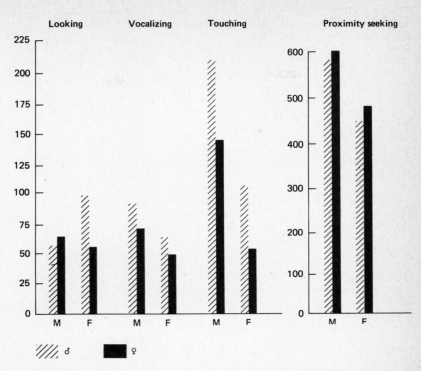

Figure 1. The mean number of seconds of looking, vocalizing, touching and proximity seeking of infants toward their mothers and fathers.

RESULTS
Mean Data

Figure 1 presents the means of the four attachment behaviors, and observations of the data reveal interesting differences as a function of the sex of the parent and sex of the child. These behaviors have been characterized in the past (Lewis & Ban, 1971) and will be treated here as "proximal" (including touching and proximity seeking) and "distal" (including looking and vocalizing).

For the proximal mode, touching and proximity seeking, there are no infant sex differences or interactions. In general, there is almost twice as much touching and proximity seeking for mothers as for fathers ($F = 8.53$, $df = 1/16$, $p < .01$; $F = 24.32$, $df = 1/16$, $p < .001$, respectively).[1] For the distal behaviors the differences between mothers and fathers are minimal, reaching significance for vocalizing ($F = 5.57$, $df = 1/16$, $p < .05$), but not

---

[1] All data were treated with a log $(X + 1)$ transformation. Separate analyses of variance were performed for each of the four measures.

TABLE 1 PEARSON PRODUCT CORRELATION MATRICES FOR THE FOUR ATTACHMENT BEHAVIORS AS DIRECTED BY ONE-YEAR-OLD BOYS TO THEIR MOTHERS AND FATHERS

(a) Mother-directed behaviors

	Proximity	Look	Vocalize
Touch	+.78**	+.50	+.64*
Proximity	—	+.65*a	+.21a
Look	—	—	+.23

(b) Father-directed behaviors

	Proximity	Look	Vocalize
Touch	+.66*	+.63*	+.64*a
Proximity	—	+.85**a	+.81**a
Look	—	—	+.80**a

(c) Mother-directed behaviors with father-directed behaviors

	Touch F	Proximity F	Look F	Vocalize F
Touch M	+.69*a	+.75*a	+.66*	+.42a
Proximity M	+.48	+.85**	+.78**a	+.57
Look M	+.30	+.24	+.26	−.00
Vocalize M	+.32	+.22a	+.11	+.00

* $p < .05$.
** $p < .01$.
[a] Correlations which showed significant sex differences.

for looking. For looking there is a significant sex of child-sex of parent interaction. While girls look equally at both parents, boys look at fathers significantly more than at mothers ($F = 9.93$, $df = 1/16$, $p < .01$).

In general, then, infants respond more toward their mothers in terms of their proximal behaviors. Their looking behavior reflects a sex of parent × sex of infant interaction.

Intercorrelation Matrix

In order to determine the interrelationships of each of the four attachment behaviors, Pearson Product Correlation Matrices

TABLE 2 PEARSON PRODUCT CORRELATION MATRICES FOR THE FOUR ATTACHMENT BEHAVIORS AS DIRECTED BY ONE-YEAR-OLD GIRLS TO THEIR MOTHERS AND FATHERS

(a) Mother-directed behaviors

	Proximity	Look	Vocalize
Touch	+.28	−.16	−.12
Proximity	—	−.35[a]	−.75*[a]
Look	—	—	+.25

(b) Father-directed behaviors

	Proximity	Look	Vocalize
Touch	+.10	+.69*	−.32[a]
Proximity	—	−.29[a]	−.17[a]
Look	—	—	−.29[a]

(c) Mother-directed behaviors with father-directed behaviors

	Touch F	Proximity F	Look F	Vocalize F
Touch M	−.10[a]	−.12[a]	+.19	−.59[a]
Proximity M	−.28	+.72*	−.25[a]	−.19
Look M	+.11	−.35	+.62	−.03
Vocalize M	+.14	−.68*[a]	+.17	−.02

* $p < .05$.
** $p < .01$.
[a] Correlations which showed significant sex differences.

were prepared (see Tables 1 and 2). The first matrix in each table deals with the interrelationship of those behaviors directed to the mother; the second, of those directed to the father; and the third, the interrelationship of those directed to mother with those directed to father.

Mother. The intercorrelation of the four behaviors to mother indicate interesting sex of infant differences. For infant girls there were few significant correlations. However, both proximal behaviors correlate positively, and these correlate negatively with the distal behaviors, which correlate positively themselves. On the other hand, boys' correlations indicate a high level of integration. All the correlations for boys are positive and although some are weak, they suggest that, generally, high touchers are also high in proximity seeking, looking, and vocalizing. Touching itself correlates strongly with the other behaviors. The correlation differences between the sexes for proximity-look and proximity-vocalization are significant ($Z = 2.12$, 2.02, $p < .05$). The differences between touch and look and touch and vocalization approach significance ($Z = 1.31$, 1.63, respectively).

Father.   Tables 1b and 2b present the correlations of the behaviors directed to the father. Again, a similar pattern emerges. The boys show a highly integrated pattern, all behaviors correlating positively and significantly. On the other hand, the girls again show little significant relationship among the behaviors. Sex differences between the correlations were significant for all correlations except touch-proximity and touch-look (Z scores greater than 2.02, $p < .05$).

Mother-Father.   Tables 1c and 2c present the four behaviors directed to mother as compared with the four behaviors directed to father. Again, an interesting pattern emerges. The boys' correlations are nearly all positive, touching, proximity seeking, and looking exhibiting very strong interrelationships. That is, the boys directing these behaviors strongly to one parent are likely to do so with the other parent as well. Thus, boys exhibit consistency in expression of attachment behavior across parents, such that those strongly attached to one parent are strongly attached to the other, and employing the same attachment behaviors in both cases. Girls show little relationship between the parents. In fact, while the boys show a total of 14 out of 16 positive correlations between behavior directed at each parent, girls show only 6 out of 16. Sex differences between the correlations were most significant for the touch variable where most of the correlations were positive for boys and negative for girls.

DISCUSSION
In a free-play, low-stress situation lasting at least 15 minutes, girls and boys show differential attachment behavior toward their mothers and fathers. Toward mothers, both girls and boys spend approximately twice as much time in proximity seeking and in touching behaviors than toward their fathers. This finding does not agree with the results of the Spelke et al. (1973) study; however, there are a variety of reasons for these differences. Brooks and Lewis (1973a) have suggested that the context of the

observations is terribly important in producing differential effects. For example, we have shown that time in the playroom affects the display of attachment behavior such that individual differences which were not obvious after only 3 minutes of interaction became so after 15 minutes. The ecology of the room, for example, the number and nature of the toys, should also affect the child's attachment behavior. However, the most marked difference between the present study and that of Spelke et al. is that their measure of attachment took place in a stressful situation while ours was designed not to be stressful. Data from another study by Brooks and Lewis (1973b) has shown that when you produce a stressful situation you tend to reduce sex differences. If one can generalize this finding to the present studies, we might suggest that stressful situations minimize the infant's differential behavior toward its parents.

The distal behaviors, especially looking, show a somewhat different pattern. Boys look more at their fathers than mothers. While girls look more at their mothers than fathers, this difference is not significant. Thus, looking behavior indicates that while mothers receive more proximal contact, fathers are receivers of as much and more looking behavior. The infants differ in terms of the mode of expression of their contact behavior toward parents; mothers receive proximal contact while fathers receive distal contact.

We were interested in obtaining some idea of the amount of contact fathers had with their children. Recall that this sample was made up of upper-middle and professional class families almost exclusively, and that this would likely reduce the variability of such estimates. Further, since it is "socially desirable" to appear to spend a reasonable amount of time with one's infant, we anticipated a certain amount of bias in the estimates. Keeping these qualifications in mind, the reports averaged 15 to 20 minutes of contact a day, with a low of "no minutes" (child asleep when father returns home from work) to a high of two hours. Thus, like Rebelsky's and Hanks' (1971) data, fathers as compared to mothers spend little time with their infants one year of age and younger. In order to determine whether there was any relationship between the amount of contact with the father (as reported by the fathers) and the infant's behavior, four Pearson Product Moment Correlations were computed. Low positive, nonsignificant correlations were obtained. Thus there was no relationship between parent report and behavior in the play situation. Spelke et al. (1973), on the other hand, report significant correlations between protest at separation and father interaction such that low father-interaction children showed the most crying.

In the present study the amount of father contact was obtained from self report whereas in the Spelke et al. study this variable was determined by an interview with the parent himself. The failure to find a relationship between father contact and infant interaction may be a function of the measure of father interaction. Alternatively, the relationship of the father's home contact and the infant's attachment behavior may only appear during a stressful situation. Finally, it may be the case that amount of contact of a parent with its child is not the important variable. Instead the quality of the relationship may be the important variable independent of amount (see Suomi, Eisele, Grady, & Tripp's 1973 work with rhesus monkeys).

While sex differences in the behavior of infants toward their mothers have been reported elsewhere (Brooks & Lewis, 1973a, b; Goldberg & Lewis, 1969; Messer & Lewis, 1972), relatively few mean differences, especially in proximity, are apparent here. This may be a function of the biased SES level of this sample. The professional and upper middle class perhaps engages in less sex-related socialization than the middle SES. This is an interesting possibility which only further research can consider.

Sex of child differences are apparent from the correlation matrices presented in Tables 1 and 2. Foremost is the fact that boys direct a highly integrated set of attachment behaviors to both mother and father. That is, boys high in the expression of one behavior tend to be high in the expression of the others as well. Interestingly, the boys' integration is strongest in the father-directed behaviors. In contrast, the girls exhibit a lower order of integration and, when the mother is the object, the behaviors dichotomize into proximal and distal forms. Many of the boy-girl correlation differences attain significance. Thus, the sexes operate differently in their use of these four behaviors toward their parents.

When the behaviors toward the father are intercorrelated with those toward the mother, the same patterns emerge for boy and girl infants. Boys exhibit a high level of integration—that is, boys attached to one parent tend to be attached to the other. One might say that the attachment motive for boys is more generalized. For girls, on the other hand, the poor correlations in attachment behaviors from one parent to the other (except for proximity) suggest that girls are more likely to favor one parent over the other, and be not as consistent in the expression of the attachment motive across parents. Thus, girls are more differentially attached to their parents than boys.

In summary, the following important aspects of attachment have been observed; during a free-play, low-stress situation children generally are more proximally attached to their mothers than to their fathers. For looking behavior, fathers receive as much if not more than mothers. When the behavior patterns of the four attachment measures are examined, it appears that boys are highly integrated in the expression of their attachment. That is, highly attached boys, particularly when the father is the object, tend to employ the full repertoire of behaviors under investigation. Girls exhibit little overall behavior integration. Finally, boys show consistency in the expression of attachment across parents, whereas girls do not. Boys highly attached to mother tend to be highly attached to father as well, whereas girls show no such consistency.

REFERENCES

Ainsworth, M. D. S. *Infancy in Uganda: Infant care and the growth of love.* Baltimore: Johns Hopkins University Press, 1967.

Ainsworth, M. D. S. Attachment and dependency: A comparison. Unpublished manuscript, 1971.

Ainsworth, M. D. S., & Bell, S. M. V. Attachment, exploration, and separation: Illustrated by the behavior of one-year-olds in a strange situation. *Child Development,* 1970, Vol. **41**, 49–67.

Brooks, J., & Lewis, M. The effect of time on attachment as measured in a free play situation. *Child Development,* 1974a, 45, 311–316.

Brooks, J., & Lewis, M. Attachment behavior in thirteen-month-old, opposite sex twins. *Child Development,* 1974b, 45, 243–247.

Coates, B., Anderson, E. P., & Hartup, W. W. Interrelations in the attachment behavior of human infants. *Developmental Psychology,* 1972a, Vol. **6**, 218–230.

Coates, B., Anderson, E., & Hartup, W. W. The stability of attachment behaviors in the human infant. *Developmental Psychology,* 1972b, Vol. **6**, 231–237.

Goldberg, S., & Lewis, M. Play behavior in the year-old infant: Early sex differences. *Child Development,* 1969, Vol. **40**, 21–31.

Kotelchuck, M. The nature of the child's tie to his father. Unpublished doctoral dissertation, Harvard University, 1972.

Lewis, M. State as an infant-environment interaction: An analysis of mother-infant interaction as a function of sex. *Merrill-Palmer Quarterly,* 1972, Vol. **18**, 95–122.

Lewis, M., & Ban, P. Stability of attachment behavior: A transformational analysis. Paper presented at The Society for Research in Child Development Meetings, Minneapolis, April, 1971.

Lewis, M., & Wilson, C. Infant development in lower class American families. *Human Development,* 1972, Vol. **15**, 112–127.

Maccoby, E. E., & Feldman, S. S. Mother-attachment and stranger-reactions in the third year of life. *Monographs of the Society for Research in Child Development,* 1972, Vol. 37 (1, Whole no. 146).

Maccoby, E. E., & Jacklin, C. N. Stress, activity, and proximity seeking: Sex differences in the year-old child. *Child Development,* 1973, Vol. 44, 34–42.

Masters, J. C., & Wellman, H. N. Human infant attachment: A procedural critique. Paper presented at the Society for Research in Child Development, Philadelphia, March, 1973.

Messer, S., & Lewis, M. Social class and sex differences in the attachment and play behavior of the year-old infant. *Merrill-Palmer Quarterly*, 1972, Vol. **18**, 295–306.

Moss, H. A. Sex, age, and state as determinants of mother-infant interaction. *Merrill-Palmer Quarterly*, 1967, Vol. **13**, 19–37.

Rebelsky, F., & Hanks, C. Fathers' verbal interaction with infants in the first three months of life. *Child Development*, 1971, Vol. **42**, 63–68.

Rheingold, H., & Eckerman, C. The infant separates himself from his mother. *Science*, 1970, Vol. **168**, 78–83.

Schaffer, H. R., & Emerson, R. E. The development of social attachments in infancy. *Monographs of The Society for Research in Child Development*, 1964. Vol. **29**.

Spelke, E., Zelazo, P., Kagan, J., & Kotelchuck, M. Father interaction and separation protest. *Developmental Psychology*, 1973, Vol. **9**, 83–90.

Suomi, S. J., Eisele, C. D., Grady, S. A., & Tripp, R. L. Social preferences of monkeys reared in an enriched laboratory social environment. *Child Development*, 1973, Vol. **44**, 451–460.

Effects of father absence on personality development in adolescent daughters

E. MAVIS HETHERINGTON

Although the absence of a father in the preschool years has been demonstrated to affect the sex-role typing of preadolescent sons (Bach, 1946; Biller & Bahm, 1971; Hetherington, 1966; Lynn & Sawrey, 1959; Sears, 1951), few effects have been found with daughters. There has been some indication of greater dependency on the mother by girls who have limited access to their fathers (Lynn & Sawrey, 1959); however, this finding has not been reliable. For example, it is reported in a recent study by Santrock (1970) that there were no differences in preschool black girls in dependency, aggression, and femininity as a function of father absence. This lack of disruption of feminine sex-role typing is surprising in view of the evidence of the salience of the father in the sex-role typing of daughters in intact families (Hetherington, 1967; Mussen & Rutherford, 1963).

All major developmental theories of sex-role typing attribute importance to the father's role in this process. Psychoanalytic theorists emphasize the daughter's competition with the mother for the father's love as a critical factor in identification. Role

E. Mavis Hetherington, "Effects of father absence on personality development in adolescent daughters." In *Developmental Psychology*, 1972, 7. Copyright © 1972 by the American Psychological Association. Reprinted by permission.

The author wishes to extend her appreciation to Jan L. Deur for his assistance in the data analysis of this study.

theorists have suggested that because of his differential treatment of sons and daughters, the father is the most important figure in the reciprocal sex-role learning of offspring of either sex (Johnson, 1963). Social learning theorists have assumed that the daughter's acquisition of feminine behavior and of the specific skills involved in interacting with males is at least partly based on learning experiences and reinforcements received in interactions with the father (Hetherington, 1967; Mussen & Rutherford, 1963). This is reflected in the subsequent development of security and culturally appropriate responses in later heterosexual relations (Biller & Weiss, 1970). Since few effects of paternal absence on the development of daughters have been found in the preschool or elementary school years, it may be that such effects only appear at puberty when interactions with males become more frequent.

Studies of delinquent girls suggest that paternal absence may result in disruptions in heterosexual behavior. Although girls are less frequently arrested on delinquency charges than are boys (Glaser, 1965), girls who do become delinquent are more likely than delinquent boys to be the product of a broken home (Monahan, 1957; Toby, 1957), and their delinquency is more often due to sexual misconduct (Cohen, 1955; Glaser, 1965).

It has been found that time of separation and reason for separation are important factors in determining the effects of father absence on boys. Separation before age 5 is more disruptive than later separation (Biller & Bahm, 1971; Hetherington, 1966), and a higher incidence of clinic problems (Tuckman & Regan, 1966), delinquency (Burt, 1929), and recidivism (Nye, 1957) is associated with separation due to divorce than with separation due to death of the father.

The present study was designed to explore the effects of time of and reason for paternal separation on the behavior of father-absent adolescent girls.

METHOD
Subjects
The subjects were three groups of 24 lower- and lower-middle-class, firstborn, adolescent, white girls who regularly attended a community recreation center. They ranged in age from 13 to 17 years. None of the subjects had male siblings. The first group came from intact families with both parents living in the home, the second group from families in which the father was absent due to divorce and in which the child had had minimal contact with the father following the divorce, and the third group

from families in which the father was absent due to death. None of the father-absent families had any males living in the home since separation from the father occurred. There were no differences between groups on mean age or education of the subjects, occupation, education, or age of the mothers or fathers, maternal employment, religious affiliation, or number of siblings. Six daughters of divorcees, five daughters of widows, and six daughters from the intact families were only children.

Procedure

The study was comprised of five sets of measures: (a) observational measures of each girl's behavior in the recreation center; (b) measures of each girl's nonverbal behavior in interacting with a male or female interviewer; (c) ratings based on an interview with the daughter; (d) ratings based on interviews with the mother; (e) scores on the California Personality Inventory Femininity Scale (Gough, 1957), the Internal-External Control Scale (Rotter, 1966), the short form of the Manifest Anxiety Scale (Bendig, 1956), and the Draw-a-Person Tests for mothers and daughters (Machover, 1957).

Observational procedures in the recreation centers. The frequency with which subjects exhibited 21 behaviors during 10 randomly sampled, 3-minute observations was recorded by two female observers. Observations were made in 1-minute units, yielding a total of 30 units. Two of the 3-minute observations were done at a recreation center dance. Interjudge agreement ranged from 84 percent to 100 percent across the various scales. The 21 behaviors recorded were prosocial aggression; verbal aggression toward males and females separately; separate measures for male peers, female peers, male adults, and female adults of instrumental dependence; seeking praise, encouragement, and attention; and subject-initiated physical contact and nearness. In addition, presence in male, female, or neutral areas in the center and participation in masculine, feminine, or neutral activities were obtained.

Measures of masculine, feminine, and neutral areas and activities were originally standardized on 20 girls and 20 boys. The frequency with which these adolescents participated in activities or were present in a given area of the center during 20 randomly sampled, 3-minute periods was recorded. Activities and locations were classified as masculine if boys obtained significantly higher scores than girls, feminine if girls' scores were higher than boys', and neutral if there was no sex difference in frequency.

Procedure for the assessment of nonverbal behavior.
When the subjects were first brought into the laboratory, they
participated in a 15-minute interview involving neutral content about such things as movies, school, television, etc. Half of
the subjects were interviewed by male and half by female interviewers. Three interviewers of each sex were used in the study.
Two observers, seated behind a one-way vision screen, recorded
the frequency of nonverbal behaviors occurring in 30-second
units. Thus there were thirty, 30-second observation units in the
15-minute period. The interview was tape-recorded and the
number of seconds of subject and experimenter speaking time
and silence was calculated. Since it was necessary to control the
amount of interviewer looking behavior and since a fixed gaze
was awkward, the interviewer was permitted to look down six
times, for 5 seconds each, during the interview.

When the subject was initially ushered into the room by a
female experimenter, the interviewer was seated behind a desk
with three empty chairs positioned with varying proximity to the
interviewers. One chair was at the end of the desk adjacent to the
interviewer, one was directly across the desk facing the interviewer, and one was across and about 3 feet down the desk from
the interviewer. The subject was instructed to sit down and was
permitted to select her own seat.

During the course of the interview the observers recorded
eye contact when the subject was speaking, when the interviewer
was speaking, and when there was silence by depressing tele-
graph keys which activated the pens of an Esterline-Angus mul-
tipen recorder. These procedures are described in greater detail
by Exline, Gray, and Schuette (1965). The two observers agreed
96 percent of the time in their judgments of the subjects' visual
fixations. Since eye contact is related to who is speaking, these
measures were converted into proportions of eye contact relative
to the amount of silence and speaking time by the interviewer
and subject.

Five postural measures, adapted from those of Mehrabian
(1968), were obtained: (a) shoulder orientation, in terms of 10-
degree orientations away from the interviewer; (b) arm openness,
as rated on a 7-point scale from 1 (arms crossed in front) to 7
(hands touching in the back); (c) leg openness on a 4-point scale
from 1 (legs crossed) to 4 (legs and feet apart); (d) backward lean
on a 5-point scale from 1 (more than 20 degrees forward) to 5
(leaning backward more than 20 degrees); and (e) sideways lean
in 10-degree units. Interjudge reliabilities were .90 for shoulder
orientation, .98 for arm openness, .94 for leg openness, .96 for
backward lean, and .95 for sideways lean.

Finally, five expressive measures were recorded (Rosen-feld, 1966): smiles, positive head nods, negative head nods, ges-ticulations, and self-manipulations. Interrater agreement varied from 89 percent to 100 percent across these measures. These postural and expressive measures were scored only once per 30-second interval.

Daughter-interview measures. When the neutral 15-minute interview was concluded, a female interviewer entered the room, the previous interviewer left, and a structured inter-view proceeded. These interviews were tape-recorded and later rated by two judges on a series on 7-point scales. The interjudge reliabilities for these scale scores ranged from .73 to .96 with an average reliability of .82. The scales were concerned with feminine interests; female friendships; positive attitude to the feminine role; security around female peers, female adults, male peers, and male adults; perceived warmth of mother; perceived restrictiveness-permissiveness of mother; conflict with mother; closeness to mother; similarity to mother; similarity to father; positive attitude to father; warmth of father; competence of father; masculinity of father; control in family decision making of father; conflict with father before separation; disturbance at sep-aration; close relation with any available adult male substitutes; and self-esteem. The scale for disturbance at separation was omit-ted in the interviews of girls from intact families. Eight of the father-absent girls, mainly those early separated, could offer no information on conflict with father before separation and six could offer no information about disturbance at separation.

Mother-interview measures. Mothers were brought into the laboratory and given a structured interview by a female inter-viewer about child-rearing practices and attitudes toward her daughter, herself, and her spouse. Interviews were tape-recorded and rated on a series of 7-point scales by two raters. Interjudge reliabilities ranged from .70 to .96 with a mean of .85. Some attempt to assess shifts in parent-child interaction over time was made by having separate ratings on 11 scales developed to assess maternal behavior before and after adolescence. This was done with the following scales: intrusiveness, overprotection, permis-siveness for sexual curiosity and activity, permissiveness for aggression, punishment for sexual activity, punishment for ag-gression, warmth, ambivalence, psychological and physical pun-ishment, consistency in discipline, and conflict with daughter. The interview was also rated for reinforcement of daughter for sex-appropriate behaviors, attitude toward spouse, attitude toward men, acceptance of feminine role, anxiety about female adequacy, anxiety about adequacy as a mother, happiness and fulfillment in life, happiness in marriage, frequency of contact with male adults, conflict with father preceding separation, intensity of disturbance following separation, length of disturbance following separation, support from friends and family following separation, resentment at being a single woman with a child, negative shift in self-concept following separation, child's preseparation closeness to father, and child's disturbance at separation. The last 8 scales were given only to the divorced and widowed mothers.

Personality measures. Following their interviews both the mother and daughter were administered the Draw-a-Person Test, the California Personality Inventory Femininity Scale, the Internal-External Control Scale, and the Bendig Short Form of the Manifest Anxiety Scale. The Femininity Scale measures femininity of interests, activities, and preferences, whereas the sex of the first figure drawn on the Draw-a-Person Test is often used as a measure of unconscious sex-role identification or orientation. The Internal-External Control Scale measures the extent to which an individual feels she has control over the reinforcements that occur in association with her behavior. The Manifest Anxiety Scale is frequently assumed to measure generalized anxiety.

RESULTS
Observational Measures in Recreation Centers

Separate one-way analyses of variance for the three groups (father absence due to divorce, father absence due to death, and father present) were performed on the 21 observational measures. The means of variables for which significant F ratios ($p < .05$) were obtained are presented in Table 1. For significant factors in these and all subsequent analyses of variance, comparisons between means were made with two-tailed t tests, and, unless otherwise noted, the discussed results of these comparisons were significant at less than the .05 level.

Both father-absent groups showed more instrumental dependency on female adults than did the father-present group. Daughters of divorcees sought more attention from male adults and initiated more proximity seeking and physical contact with male peers than did the other girls. This seeking of contact with male peers also was supported by their greater time spent in male areas of the recreation center. In contrast, an avoidance of male areas and preference for female areas by daughters of

TABLE 1 GROUP MEANS FOR
OBSERVATIONAL VARIABLES IN THE RECREATIONAL CENTER

	Group				
	Father absent		Father present	F	p
Observational variable	Divorce	Death			
Instrumental dependency on female adults	3.17_a	3.17_a	1.62_b	4.00	.02
Seeking praise, encouragement, & attention from male adults	2.50_b	1.17_a	1.12_a	4.83	.01
S-initiated physical contact and nearness with male peers	3.08_b	1.71_a	1.79_a	3.03	.05
Male areas	7.75_a	2.25_b	4.71_c	7.91	.001
Female areas	11.67_a	17.42_b	14.42_a	5.37	.007

Note: All row means which do not share a common subscript differ at least at $p < .05$ with two-tailed t tests.

widows was found. The groups did not differ with respect to any of the other 16 measures.

The father-absent groups were divided into girls who had lost their fathers before age 5 and those who lost them later (divorced early, $N = 14$; divorced late, $N = 10$; widowed early, $N = 13$; widowed late, $N = 11$). Two-way analyses of variance for unequal Ns, with type of father absence and age of separation as the factors, were performed on each of the observational measures of the father-absent girls. All significant findings are reported below. In addition to the previous differences reported between daughters of widows and divorcees, the results of these analyses suggest that early separation from the father has a greater effect on daughters' behavior than later separation. Means for variables associated with significant F ratios are presented in Table 2. The only significant interaction occurred on prosocial aggression where girls from divorced early families exhibited more prosocial aggression than girls from divorced late or widowed early families. Early, in contrast to late, separation is associated with greater attention seeking from both male and female adults, greater subject-initiated physical contact with male adults and female peers, more time spent in male areas and less in feminine activities.

TABLE 2 MEANS FOR OBSERVATIONAL
VARIABLES IN THE RECREATION CENTER FOR
EARLY AND LATE SEPARATED FATHER-ABSENT GIRLS

	Father absent			
Observational variable	Divorced early	Divorced late	Death early	Death late
Prosocial aggression	5.14	2.60	2.15	3.54
Seeking praise, encouragement, & attention from male adults	3.14	1.60	1.46	.82
Seeking praise, encouragement, & attention from female adults	2.14	.80	2.31	1.27
S-initiated physical contact & nearness with male adults	2.28	1.50	2.69	.91
S-initiated physical contact & nearness with male peers	2.93	3.30	2.31	1.00
S-initiated physical contact & nearness with female peers	3.21	1.50	3.38	1.73
Male areas	9.14	5.80	3.23	1.09
Female areas	11.64	11.70	16.54	18.45
Female activities	12.78	18.00	15.38	16.91

Nonverbal Behavior in the Daughter's Interview

Presented in Table 3 is the frequency with which daughters from the three groups of subjects seated themselves with varying gradations of proximity from male and female interviewers. Position 1 is the seat immediately adjacent but at right angles to the interviewer, Position 2 directly across from the interviewer, and Position 3 across and further removed from the interviewer. There were no significant differences as measured through the index of predictive association (Hays, 1963, pp. 606–609) when the interviewer was a female; however, with a male interviewer the daughters of divorcees tended to choose the most proximate seat, the girls from intact families the seat directly across the table, and the daughters of widows the most distant seat.

The means of the summed scores in 30 observational units for the remaining nonverbal measures, plus amount of silence, and subject and interviewer speaking time for the three groups with male and female interviewers are presented in Table 4. A 3 (Father Status) × 2 (Sex of Interviewer) analysis of variance was performed on each of these measures. The analyses yielded

TABLE 3 POSITION OF CHAIR
SELECTED WITH MALE AND FEMALE INTERVIEWERS

| | Male interviewer | | | Female interviewer | | |
| | Father absent | | Father present | Father absent | | Father present |
Position	Divorced	Death		Divorced	Death	
1	8	0	1	1	2	1
2	3	2	8	8	7	9
3	1	10	3	3	3	2

either a significant main effect or interaction on all variables with the exception of gesticulations. There was a significant main effect for father status on all variables except for interviewer speaking time and positive head nods. Sex of interviewer had a significant main effect on subject speaking time, interviewer speaking time, eye contact when the subject was speaking, positive head nods, and manipulations. Interpretation of some of these main effects must be qualified by the significant interactions associated with subject speaking time, silence, shoulder orientation, arm openness, leg openness, backward lean, sideways lean, smiles, proportion of eye contact when the interviewer was speaking, and proportion of eye contact during silence. In general, few differences were found between father status groups with a female interviewer. Most differences were obtained with male interviewers and the means tended to be ordered with the divorced and widowed groups at the extremes and the intact family group in an intermediate position.

In spite of the fact that interviewers had been trained in a structured interview method, male interviewers talked more than female interviewers. This may have been because subjects talked less with male interviewers. Daughters of widows with a male interviewer spoke significantly less and were more silent than any other group of subjects. There was also a trend ($p < .06$) for daughters of divorcees to be less silent with a male than female interviewer.

Subjects in the divorced group with male interviewers tended to assume a rather sprawling open posture, often leaning slightly forward with one or both arms hooked over the back of the chair. In contrast, subjects in the widowed group sat stiffly upright or leaned backward with their back often slightly turned to the male interviewer, their hands folded or lying in their laps and their legs together. Compared to girls in any other group,

TABLE 4　MEAN NONVERBAL MEASURES
FOR SUBJECTS WITH MALE AND FEMALE INTERVIEWERS

| Nonverbal variable | Male interviewer | | | Female interviewer | | |
| | Father absent | | | Father absent | | |
	Di-vorced	Death	Father present	Di-vorced	Death	Father present
S speaks	619.17	463.92	601.58	614.50	632.67	624.25
Interviewer speaks	156.00	201.58	143.50	123.00	111.08	121.33
Silence	116.50	234.50	154.92	161.83	156.25	154.42
Shoulder orientation	496.67	1318.33	802.50	817.50	804.17	804.17
Arm openness	159.50	109.33	125.33	131.58	129.58	134.67
Leg openness	68.33	49.50	48.42	50.08	55.00	51.83
Backward lean	72.58	96.42	80.67	80.25	77.00	83.50
Sideways lean	434.17	300.83	399.17	406.67	400.00	402.50
Smiles	13.58	8.50	10.17	11.75	11.92	10.83
Positive head nod	7.25	4.75	6.00	7.83	8.00	6.83
Gesticulations	9.75	5.00	5.25	6.58	6.58	6.50
Manipulations	12.67	13.83	8.00	8.25	8.58	7.58
Negative head nods	2.17	2.50	2.42	2.08	2.08	2.33
Eye contact when interviewer speaking	.59	.31	.41	.44	.44	.43
Eye contact when S speaking	.68	.47	.66	.73	.67	.69
Eye contact during silence	.84	.29	.34	.34	.34	.37

daughters of widows with a male interviewer showed more
shoulder orientation away from the interviewer, more backward
lean, less arm openness, less sideways lean, and less eye contact
during silence or when the interviewer was speaking. In contrast,
daughters of divorcees with a male interviewer showed more
forward lean, more arm and leg openness, more eye contact when
the interviewer was speaking and during silence than did any
other group of subjects. They also smiled more than did the other
two groups with a male interviewer. Daughters of widows smiled
less with a male than a female interviewer. It should be noted
that there were no differences between means on these variables
with a female interviewer.

There were more manipulations with a male interviewer
than female interviewer, and manipulations were more frequent
in both the father-separated groups than the intact group. There
were more positive head nods and more eye contact when the

TABLE 5 MEANS OF THE NONVERBAL MEASURES FOR EARLY AND LATE SEPARATED FATHER-ABSENT GIRLS WITH MALE AND FEMALE INTERVIEWERS

Nonverbal variable	Father absent early				Father absent late			
	Male interviewer		Female interviewer		Male interviewer		Female interviewer	
	Divorced (N=7)	Death (N=7)	Divorced (N=7)	Death (N=6)	Divorced (N=5)	Death (N=5)	Divorced (N=5)	Death (N=6)
S speaks	652.57	401.86	601.00	629.50	572.40	550.80	633.40	635.83
Interviewer speaks	158.00	259.57	137.71	118.33	153.20	120.40	102.40	103.83
Silence	89.43	238.57	106.14	152.17	154.40	228.80	164.20	160.33
Shoulder orientation	432.86	1340.00	864.28	801.67	586.00	1288.00	752.00	806.67
Arm openness	164.28	100.57	132.28	133.33	152.80	121.60	130.60	125.83
Leg openness	75.14	46.86	50.43	58.83	58.80	53.20	49.60	51.17
Backward lean	67.86	104.14	83.86	80.17	79.20	85.60	75.20	73.83
Sideway lean	508.57	270.00	392.87	406.66	330.00	344.00	426.00	393.33
Smiles	14.71	7.00	12.43	12.83	12.00	10.60	10.80	11.00
Positive head nod	8.43	4.14	8.00	8.33	5.60	5.60	7.60	7.67
Gesticulations	13.28	4.00	7.57	7.17	4.80	6.40	5.20	6.00
Manipulations	13.14	13.28	9.00	9.00	12.00	14.60	7.20	8.17
Negative head nods	2.28	1.71	1.71	2.17	2.00	3.60	2.60	2.00
Eye contact when interviewer speaking	.65	.26	.45	.44	.51	.39	.42	.44
Eye contact when S speaking	.77	.39	.67	.65	.55	.58	.83	.69
Eye contact during silence	.67	.28	.36	.36	.38	.31	.32	.33

subject was speaking and the interviewer was a female. Also, when the subject was speaking, there was less eye contact for daughters of widows than the other father-status groups. Although the interaction associated with this variable was not significant, an inspection of the means suggests that this finding was largely attributable to the small amount of eye contact when subjects in the widowed group were speaking to male interviewers.

Three-way analyses of variance with unequal Ns involving type and time of separation and sex of interviewer were performed on each of these same nonverbal variables for father-separated girls only. The means for this anslysis are presented in Table 5. The results associated with type of separation and sex of interviewer paralleled those of the previous analyses and are not discussed again. In addition, significant main effects for time of separation were obtained on interviewer speaking time, gesticulations, and eye contact during silence. Significant interactions between type and time of separation were obtained on backward lean, gesticulations, eye contact when the interviewer was speaking, and eye contact during silence. Triple-order interactions were obtained on subject speaking time, backward lean, sideways lean, smiles, gesticulations, eye contact when the subject was speaking, and eye contact during silence.

Interviewers spoke more with early than late separated girls Daughters whose fathers died early talked less to a male interviewer than did any other group of girls. When the interviewer was speaking, there was less eye contact in the widowed early group than in either the divorced early or divorced late groups. The late separated daughters of widows showed less eye contact when the interviewer was speaking than did the divorced early girls. When they were speaking to a male interviewer, the girls in the early widowed group showed a smaller proportion of eye contact than did girls in any other group. Girls whose parents were divorced late looked directly when speaking to a female interviewer more often than girls whose parents were divorced early, or than did either group of late separated girls with a male interviewer. However, in talking to a male interviewer, the divorced late girls showed less eye contact than the divorced early girls. During silence with a male interviewer, these divorced late girls showed more eye contact than did any other group of girls with either a male or female interviewer.

The openness and approach of the divorced early girls and inhibition of widowed early girls with a male interviewer was reflected in the differences between means in the significant triple interactions on some of the postural and gestural measures. The widowed early girls showed more backward lean with a

TABLE 6 MEANS FOR DAUGHTER-INTERVIEW MEASURES

Interview variable	Father absent		Father present	F	p
	Divorced	Death			
Security around male peers	2.71_a	2.62_a	3.79_b	4.79	.01
Security around male adults	2.12_a	2.12_a	3.66_b	11.25	.001
Heterosexual activity	4.83_a	2.62_b	3.83_c	12.96	.001
Conflict with mothers	5.08_a	3.62_b	4.08_b	5.64	.005
Positive attitude toward father	3.08_a	4.66_b	4.21_b	7.57	.001
Father's warmth	3.33_a	4.50_b	$3.87_{a\,b}$	2.82	.06
Father's competence	3.16_a	4.75_b	4.12_b	6.65	.002
Conflict with father	4.43_a	2.25_b	3.46_c	7.03	.002
Relations with other adult males	3.29_a	3.12_a	4.54_b	5.08	.009
Self-esteem	2.87_a	$3.58_{a\,b}$	4.04_b	3.34	.04

Note. All row means which do not share a common subscript differ at least at $p < .05$ with two-tailed t tests.

male interviewer than did any other group of girls. In contrast, divorced early girls showed less backward lean with a male than a female interviewer.

Congruently, divorced early girls with a male interviewer showed more sideways lean than did the other three groups with a male interviewer or the divorced early group with a female interviewer. In addition, with a male interviewer, widowed early girls showed less sideways lean than did any group of subjects with a female interviewer.

The widowed early girls with a male interviewer smiled less than any other group of girls. The divorced early girls with a male interviewer not only smiled more than the widowed early girls, but also more than any late separated group except divorced with a male interviewer. In addition, they made more gesticulations than any other group.

Daughter-Interview Measures

Separate one-way analyses of variance with father status as the factor were performed on the 22 daughter-interview variables. Significant results were obtained for the 10 variables presented in Table 6 along with the group means. Deviations of the daughters with absent fathers appeared most often in relation to feelings and interactions with males. It is interesting to note that there were no differences on variables such as feminine interests, attitudes to the feminine role, or similarity to mother and father, each of which might have been related to sex typing or identification. There also were no differences with respect to relationships with other females including the mother. All groups reported themselves as equally secure around female adults and peers, equally close to their mothers, and their mothers as equally warm and permissive. The exception to this was that daughters with divorced parents reported more conflict with their mothers.

Both daughters of widows and divorcees felt insecure around male peers and adults; however, this was manifested in different ways. The daughters of divorcees reported more, while the daughters of widows reported less, heterosexual activity than any other groups. There was some evidence of more negative feelings toward the father by daughters of divorcees than by daughters of widows. Girls of divorcees reported more negative attitudes toward the father, more conflict with the father, and regarded the father as less competent than either of the other two groups of girls. Girls of widows reported having less conflict with their fathers than did either of the other groups of girls and described their fathers as warmer and more competent than did daughters of divorcees. It is interesting that both groups of father-absent daughters reported less contact with other adult males than did children from intact families. Girls from intact families frequently reported being attached to their parents' male friends. Girls from father-present homes and from widowed families showed higher self-esteem than girls from divorced families.

Separate two-way analyses involving type and time of separation were performed on the father-absent daughters' interview data. These analyses yielded little additional information except that daughters of widows reported more disturbance at loss of the father than did daughters of divorcees. The effects for type of separation paralleled those in the previous discussion and no significant age effects or interactions were obtained.

Mother-Interview Measures

Separate one-way analyses of variance for the father-status groups were performed on each rating measure of the maternal interview. The means for groups on the variables for which significant F ratios were obtained are presented in Table 7.

Divorced mothers appear to have had a negative attitude toward their ex-spouses, themselves, and life in general. Their

TABLE 7 GROUP MEANS FOR
MATERNAL INTERVIEW RATING SCALES

	Father absent				
Variable	Divorced	Death	Father present	F	p
Overprotection before adolescence	3.62_a	3.71_a	2.67_b	3.39	.04
Punishment for sexual curiosity & activity after adolescence	3.87_a	2.79_b	3.00_b	4.32	.02
Consistency after adolescence	3.54_a	4.67_b	4.67_b	4.46	.02
Conflict before adolescence	4.25_a	2.92_b	3.71_a	4.06	.02
Conflict after adolescence	4.75_a	3.46_b	3.75_b	5.55	.006
Negative attitude toward spouse	4.67_a	3.30_b	3.33_b	5.46	.006
Anxiety about adequacy as mother	4.50_a	3.83_b	3.54_b	3.30	.04
Happiness & fullfillment in life	2.75_a	3.58_b	3.75_b	2.31	.05
Happiness in marriage	2.79_a	4.75_b	4.12_b	9.36	.001
Conflict with father	4.71_a	2.67_b	3.33_b	11.84	.001

Note: All row means which do not share a common subscript differ at least at $p < .05$ with two-tailed t tests.

lives and marriages had not been gratifying, and they were concerned about their adequacy as mothers. However, these mothers reported positive relationships with their daughters, and exhibited similar patterns of affection and discipline to that of the widowed and still married mothers in the preadolescent period. Most deviations followed and may have been a reaction to the daughters' adolescent behaviors. Both groups of mothers without husbands were overprotective and solicitous of their preadolescent daughters. High conflict with spouse before separation and with daughter after adolescence was found in divorced women. The lowest preadolescent conflict with the daughter was reported by the widowed group; however, there were no differences in preadolescent conflict between the divorced and intact groups. Divorcees reported themselves as being more punitive toward their daughters for sexual activity and as being inconsistent in discipline only after adolescence. This similarity in affection for their daughters, but difference in response to adolescent behavior, by widows and divorcees is reflected in the following portions of representative interviews by two mothers, the first from the widowed group, the second from the divorced group.

[Daughter's name] is almost too good. She has lots of girl friends but doesn't date much. When she's with the girls she's gay and bouncy—quite a clown but she clams up when a man comes in. Even around my brother she never says much. When boys do phone she often puts them off even though she has nothing else to do. She says she has lots of time for that later, but she's sixteen now and very pretty, and all her friends have boy friends.

That kid is going to drive me over the hill. I'm at my wits end. She was so good until the last few years then Pow! at eleven she really turned on. She went boy crazy. When she was only twelve I came home early from a movie and found her in bed with a young hood and she's been bouncing from bed to bed ever since. She doesn't seem to care who it is, she can't keep her hands off men. It isn't just boys her own age, when I have men friends here she kisses them when they come in the door and sits on their knees all in a very playful fashion but it happens to them all. Her uncle is a sixty-year-old priest and she even made a "ha ha" type pass at him. It almost scared him to death! I sometimes get so frantic I think I should turn her into the cops but I remember what a good kid she used to be and I do love her. We still have a good time together when we're alone and I'm not nagging about her being a tramp. We both like to cook and we get a lot of good laughs when we're puttering around in the kitchen. She's smart and good-looking—she should know she doesn't have to act like that.

Again, separate 2 (Type of Separation) × 2 (Age of Separation) analyses of variance were performed on ratings of separated mothers. In addition to the previously obtained differences for type of separation, early separation was found to result in greater overprotection preceding and following adolescence than does later separation. The only significant interaction was on intrusiveness, following adolescence, which indicated that early divorced mothers were more intrusive than late divorced or early widowed mothers.

On the analyses of scales only rated for separated mothers, widowed mothers, in contrast to divorced mothers, reported greater intensity of disturbance following loss of husband, more emotional support from friends and family, and less resentment at being a woman bringing up a child alone. Many widowed mothers described having the child as "a blessing" or as "giving them something to live for."

Personality Measures for Mothers and Daughters

No differences were found among groups for mothers or daughters on the number of subjects drawing a female figure first on the Draw-a-Person Test (daughters: divorced, 18; death, 19; present, 16. Mothers: divorcees, 17; widows, 19; intact, 17). One-way analyses of variance for the three father-status groups were done separately for mothers', and daughters', scores on the California Personality Inventory Femininity scale, Rotter's Internal-External Control Scale, and the Bendig Short Form of the Manifest Anxiety Scale.

Mother groups and daughter groups did not differ in their responses to the Femininity Scale. On the analyses for mothers, both divorced and widowed mothers were found to feel more externally controlled than mothers from intact families. No differences on the total Internal-External Control Scale scores were found for daughters. However, Mirels (1970) has recently factor-analyzed this scale and has concluded that it is not unidimensional but includes two factors. The first factor is comprised of items involving a felt mastery over the course of one's life, the second concerns the extent to which an individual is capable of influencing political institutions. Five items which loaded heavily on each of the factors were selected, and separate analyses of variance were performed on scores on the five personal and political control items. There were no differences between groups for either mothers or daughters on the scores on political control, but both groups of separated mothers and daughters scored lower on internalization on the personal control items than did mothers and daughters from intact families. Both groups of daughters without fathers also reported themselves as more anxious on the Manifest Anxiety Scale than daughters with the father living in the home. Divorcees were more anxious than the other two groups of mothers. No time of separation effects were found on any of the scale scores when subsequent analyses of time and type of separation were performed.

DISCUSSION

The results of this study suggest that there are different patterns of effects of father absence on the development of girls and boys. Past research indicates that in boys, separation results in disruptions in sex-role typing during the preschool years, but with increasing age and extrafamilial interaction these effects are attenuated or transformed into compensatory masculinity. In contrast, previous studies with young girls have demonstrated no effects of father separation except an occasional finding of greater dependency.

These studies in combination with the present one suggest that the effects of father absence on daughters appear during adolescence and are manifested mainly as an inability to interact appropriately with males, rather than in other deviations from approprite sex typing or in interactions with females. There was little apparent disturbance in sex-typed behaviors or preference for the female role as assessed by observational or interview measures or the California Personality Inventory Masculinity-Femininity Scale. Father absence seems to increase dependency in girls, but this is viewed as an appropriately feminine attribute. It does not appear to be related to masculine behaviors such as aggression. Even when aggression appeared in the group of girls whose parents had been divorced early it took the form of prosocial aggression, which is a characteristically feminine form of aggressive behavior (Sears, 1961). Although these girls also scored low in female activities, this seemed to be largely attributable to their spending time in seeking proximity with male peers by hanging around the male areas of the recreation center. These girls spent so much time in the carpentry shop, basketball court, and other male areas that they had little opportunity to sew, do beadwork, or participate in female activities usually located elsewhere. During recreation center dances they spent much of their time at the boys' end of the hall around the "stag line," in contrast to the daughters of widows who stayed at the girls' end, often at the back of the group of girls. Two of the girls in the widowed group hid out in the ladies' room for the entire evening of one dance. This was not because of differences in popularity between the groups of girls. When they were present in the hall the two groups of father-absent girls were asked to dance equally often. It is interesting to note that in spite of their greater time spent in male areas, daughters of divorcees did not participate in masculine activities more than the other girls. There were also no differences between groups in sex-role orientation as measured by sex of the figure drawn first on the Draw-a-Person Test, although in father-absent boys disruptions in sex-role orientation tend to be more enduring than those in sex-role preference or sex-typed behaviors.

Except for greater dependency on female adults in the recreation center, girls with absent fathers showed few deviations in relations with females. The effects of father absence on relationships with males is particularly apparent in the nonverbal measures recorded during the girls' interviews with male and female interviewers. Few group differences were found with female interviewers; however, with male interviewers, clear group differences in nonverbal communication emerged. With male interviewers, daughters of widows demonstrated relatively infrequent speech and eye contact, avoidance of proximity with the interviewer in seat selection and body orientation, and rigid postural characteristics. In contrast, daughters of divorcees again showed proximity seeking and a smiling, open, receptive manner with the male interviewer. This greater receptiveness to males by the girls whose fathers are absent because of divorce also is supported by their interview reports of earlier and more dating and sexual intercourse, in contrast to daughters of widows who report starting to date late and being sexually inhibited.

When effects of time of father separation were found, the effects of early separation were usually greater than later separation. This is in agreement with studies of the effects of father absence on sons and suggests that the first 5 years of life represent a critical period for the impact of father absence on children. This effect was most apparent in some of the nonverbal measures of communication in the daughter interview where early separation tended to increase the disparity between the behavior of the daughters of widows and divorcees. However, on the observational measures in the recreation center, time of separation tended to affect the behavior of the two groups of father-separated girls in a similar direction. It is interesting that few time of separation effects were found on interview or test measures; they emerged most frequently in observational measures.

It might be proposed that for both groups of father-absent girls the lack of opportunity for constructive interaction with a loving, attentive father has resulted in apprehension and inadequate skills in relating to males. Their tension in relating to males was supported by their reports in the interview of feelings of insecurity in interacting with male peers and male adults, and in their high rate of manipulations such as nail-biting, hair, lip, and finger pulling, and plucking at clothes and other objects while being interviewed by a male. Their general feeling of anxiety and powerlessness was also reflected in relatively high scores on the Manifest Anxiety Scale and relatively low scores on the factor dealing with a sense of personal control over the course of one's life on the Internal-External Control Scale. This may be intensified in daughters of divorced parents by their low sense of self-esteem.

If it is argued that both groups of girls were manifesting deviant behaviors in attempting to cope with their anxiety and lack of skills in relating to males, the difficult question that remains is how they developed such disparate patterns of coping mechanisms to deal with this problem.

It seems likely that differences in the behavior of the divorced and widowed mothers may have mediated differences in their daughters' behaviors. However, in relationships with their daughters, widows, divorcees, and mothers from intact families were remarkably similar in many ways. In affection, control and discipline these mothers were similar. The differences between divorcees and the other two groups which appeared after adolescence in consistency, conflict, and punishment of the daughter for sexual activity could well have occurred as a reaction rather than a precursor to their daughter's disruptive adolescent behavior with males. However, there was less strife between widows and daughters than in any other family. All groups of mothers were equally feminine, reinforced daughters for sex-appropriate behaviors and, surprisingly, had equally positive attitudes toward men. Since these mothers were offering their daughters appropriately feminine models and rewarding them for their assumption of the feminine role, the finding that there were no disruptions in traditional measures of sex typing for the father-absent girls is compatible with expectations of social learning theorists.

The only measures on which both father-separated groups of mothers differed from those in intact families were on over-protection of the daughter before adolescence and in feeling more externally controlled. These too could be associated with loss of a husband.

It seems mainly in attitudes toward herself, her marriage, and her life that the divorcee differed from the widow. She is anxious and unhappy. Her attitude toward her spouse is hostile; her memories of her marriage and life are negative. These attitudes are reflected in the critical attitude of her daughter toward the divorced father. Although she loves her daughter, she feels she has had little support from other people during her divorce and times of stress and with her difficulties in rearing a child alone. This is in marked contrast to the positive attitudes of the widows toward marriage, their lost husbands, the emotional support of friends and family at the loss of a husband, and the gratifications of having children. These attitudes are reflected in the happy memories their daughters have of their fathers.

Any explanation of the relationship between these maternal behaviors and the daughters' behavior in interacting with males is highly speculative. It may be that daughters of divorcees view their mother's separated lives as unsatisfying and feel that for happiness it is essential to secure a man. Their lack of experience in interacting with a loving father and their hostile memories of their father may cause them to be particularly apprehensive and inept in their pursuit of this goal. It might be argued that rather than being inept these girls are precociously skillful and provocative in their relationship with men. However, such things as their reported anxiety around males and the fact that they were no more popular than the other groups of girls at the recreation center dances suggests that their coping mechanisms are not effective. It may also be that life with a dissatisfied, anxious mother is difficult, and these daughters are more eager to leave home than daughters of widows living with relatively happy, secure mothers with support from the extended family. Daughters of widows with their aggrandized image of their father may also feel that no other males can compare favorably with him, or alternately may regard all males as superior and as objects of deference and apprehension.

It should be noted that the mothers in the father-separated groups are not representative of all divorcees and widows since they have not remarried. This might be more difficult for the divorcee than the widow, who reports more support by her family and even frequent closeness with her dead husband's family. The widow may have less to gain by remarriage, although both groups report an equal number of male friends and dates.

There are many questions about the effects of father absence on the development of daughters that remain unanswered. It is apparent that reasons for and age of separation, as well as current age of the daughter are important factors which must be considered in future investigations of this problem.

REFERENCES

Bach, C. R. Father-fantasies and father-typing in father-separated children. *Child Development*, 1946, **17**, 63–80.

Bendig, A. W. The development of a short form of the Manifest Anxiety Scale. *Journal of Consulting Psychology*, 1956, **20**, 384.

Biller, H. B., & Bahm, R. M. Father-absence, perceived maternal behavior, and masculinity of self-concept among junior high school boys. *Developmental Psychology*, 1971, 4, 178–181.

Biller, H. B., & Weiss, S. D. The father-daughter relationship and the personality development of the female. *Journal of Genetic Psychology*, 1970, **116**, 79–93.

Burt, C. *The young delinquent.* New York: Appleton, 1929.

Cohen, A. K. *Delinquent boys: The culture of the gang.* Glencoe, Ill.: Free Press, 1955.

Exline, R., Gray, D., & Schuette, D. Visual behavior in a dyad as affected by interview content and sex of respondent. *Journal of Personality and Social Psychology*, 1965, 1, 201–209.

Glaser, D. Social disorganization and delinquent subcultures. In H. C. Quay (Ed.), *Juvenile delinquency.* New York: Van Nostrand, 1965.

Gough, H. G. *Manual for California Personality Inventory*. Palo Alto, Calif.: Consulting Psychologists Press, 1957.

Hays, W. L. *Statistics*. New York: Holt, Rinehart and Winston, 1963.

Hetherington, E. M. Effects of paternal absence on sex-typed behaviors in Negro and white preadolescent males. *Journal of Personality and Social Psychology*, 1966, **4**, 87–91.

Hetherington, E. M. The effects of familial variables on sex typing, on parent-child similarity, and on imitation in children. *Minnesota Symposium on Child Psychology*, 1967, **1**, 82–107.

Johnson, M. Sex role learning in the nuclear family. *Child Development*, 1963, **34**, 319–333.

Lynn, D. B., & Sawrey, W. L. The effects of father absence on Norwegian boys and girls. *Journal of Abnormal and Social Psychology*, 1959, **59**, 258–262.

Machover, K. *Personality projection in the drawing of the human figure*. Springfield, Ill.: Charles C Thomas, 1957.

Mehrabian, A. Inference of attitudes from the posture orientation and distance of a communicator. *Journal of Consulting and Clinical Psychology*, 1968, **32**, 296–308.

Mirels, H. L. Dimensions of internal versus external control. *Journal of Consulting and Clinical Psychology*, 1970, **34**, 226–228.

Monahan, T. P. Family status and the delinquent child: A reappraisal and some new findings. *Social Forces*, 1957, **35**, 250–258.

Mussen, P., and Rutherford, E. Parent-child relations and parental personality in relation to young children's sex-role preferences. *Child Development*, 1963, **34**, 489–607.

Nye, F. I. Child adjustment in broken and in unhappy unbroken homes. *Marriage and Family Living*, 1957, **19**, 356–361.

Rosenfeld, H. M. Instrumental affiliative functions of facial and gestural expressions. *Journal of Personality and Social Psychology*, 1966, **4**, 65–72.

Rotter, J. B. Generalized expectancies for internal versus external control of reinforcement. *Psychological Monographs*, 1966, **80**(1, Whole No. 609).

Santrock, J. W. Paternal absence, sex typing, and identification. *Developmental Psychology*, 1970, **2**, 264–272.

Sears, P. S. Doll play aggression in normal young children: Influence of sex, age, sibling status, father's absence. *Psychological Monographs*, 1951, **65**(6, Whole No. 323).

Sears, R. R. The relation of early socialization experiences to aggression in middle childhood. *Journal of Abnormal and Social Psychology*, 1961, **63**, 466–492.

Toby, J. The differential impact of family disorganization. *American Sociological Review*, 1957, **22**, 505–512.

Tuckman, J., and Regan, R. A. Intactness of the home and behavioral problems in children. *Journal of Child Psychology and Psychiatry*, 1966, **7**, 225–233.

Fathers' verbal interaction with infants in the first three months of life

FREDA REBELSKY
CHERYL HANKS

In his review of the psychological literature on the father, John Nash (1965) suggests that most American psychologists regard the United States as a matriocentric child-rearing society. In support of this statement, Nash cites numerous publications dealing with child-rearing practices and parent-child relations which make no mention of the father, thereby equating parent with mother, and child-rearing practices with mothers' child-rearing practices.

The dearth of studies that deal with fathers may be partially explained by the fact that fathers are not as available for study as mothers. It may also be due to the fact that psychologists consider fathers unimportant to child rearing and, therefore, make less of an effort to study them. In the light of recent studies of the effects of father absence, this assumption does not seem tenable: the absence (or presence) of a father does seem to have important effects, especially on the male child (Carlsmith, 1964; Lynn & Sawrey, 1959). Carlsmith's (1964) study of the relationship be-

From *Child Development*, 1971, **42**. Copyright © 1971 by The Society for Research in Child Development, Inc. Reprinted by permission.

The data were gathered under grants M-2921 and M-5268, National Institute of Mental Health, to Eric H. Lenneberg, while the first author was at Children's Hospital Medical Center in Boston. Data analyses were partially supported by a Boston University Graduate School Faculty Research Grant to the first author. We want to thank Marshall Taylor for his help with data analysis.

tween father absence and the aptitude patterns of male college students showed that the effects were greatest if a father left when his son was 0–6 months old. Thus it appears that, especially in infancy, the presence or absence of a father is important to the subsequent development of male children. It is difficult to explain many of the data that we do have because there have been no studies on fathers' interactions with infants. The present study, part of a larger study of infant vocalization (Lenneberg, Rebelsky, & Nichols, 1965), was designed to supply some basic descriptive data on fathers' verbal interactions with their infants.

METHOD
Subjects

The sample consisted of 10 normal, full-term, white, winter-born babies, seven males and three females. They were born into lower-middle- to upper-middle-class families who lived in Boston suburbs. Only two of the babies were firstborn. The sample was obtained through professional contacts with pediatricians. The research was presented to the parents as a general study of how infants live, what they do, etc., with the explanation that such basic data are not as yet known. The experimenter explained that she did not want to interfere in any way with the household schedule and that no changes in the babies' normal environment or routine should be made for *E*'s convenience.

Procedure

Beginning in the second week of life, 24-hour tape recordings were made approximately every 2 weeks for a 3-month period. Thus, there were six 24-hour observation periods for each infant. A microphone approximately the shape of a half-dollar, with a cord of about 27 feet, was attached to the infant's shirt such that the infant could be moved around without removing him from the sound field. The microphone picked up both the noises emitted by the infant and the noises to which he was exposed. In order to eliminate silent periods on the tapes, a recording instrument (described more fully in Chan, Lenneberg, & Rebelsky, 1964) was operated by a voice key which turned the recorder off if there was a silence of more than 20 seconds, and turned it on if there was noise in the sound field.

Coding the tape recordings. Two coders listened to the tapes for the 10 infants and recorded the duration, time of day, and activity occurring each time a father vocalized to his infant. Ten percent of the tapes were coded by both coders, with an

TABLE 1 MEANS AND RANGES OF
FATHERS' DAILY INTERACTIONS WITH THEIR INFANTS

	Number of seconds per day	Number of interactions per day	Length of interactions in seconds
Mean	37.7	2.7	13.9
Range	0–1,370	0–17	4–220

interjudge reliability of over .90 for each of the items scored. An interaction began with a father vocalizing to his infant and ended if there was an interval of silence longer than 30 seconds. The silent period was not included in the interaction time.

RESULTS

The data indicate that fathers spend relatively little time interacting with their infants. The mean number of interactions per day was 2.7, and the average number of seconds per day was 37.7. While there were large individual differences, even the father with the most interactions spent an average of only 10 minutes, 26 seconds interacting with his infant each day. This is low when compared with the Moss data on mothers' verbal interactions with their infants (Moss, 1967). Table 1 summarizes the group data on fathers' daily interactions with their infants. In addition, there was a Spearman rank correlation of $+.72$ between the number of interactions per father and the mean length of each father's interaction. This is significant at the .05 level ($p < .05$).

As might be expected, fathers talked to their babies most often in the morning hours before going to work (41 percent of all interactions) and in the evening hours after work (33 percent of all interactions).

The amount of fathers' interactions varied by the age and sex of their infants. Unlike mothers, who increase their vocalization time during the first 3 months of life (Moss, 1967; Rebelsky, 1967), seven out of 10 of the fathers spent less time vocalizing to their infants during the last half of the study (8–12 weeks) than in the first half (2–6 weeks). This decrease of vocalization over time is more marked among the fathers of female infants. While all three of the fathers of female infants decreased their number of vocalizations during the last 6 weeks, only four out of seven fathers of male infants decreased their number of vocalizations in the same time period. None of these interactions reached significance.

Of the 164 verbal interactions of these fathers with their

TABLE 2 SEX DIFFERENCES IN DEVELOPMENTAL TRENDS
IN THE NUMBER OF FATHERS' VERBAL INTERACTIONS
DURING CARETAKING AND NONCARETAKING ACTIVITIES

| | Weeks 2, 4, 6 | | | Weeks 8, 10, 12 | | |
	Male	Female	Total	Male	Female	Total
Vocaliza-tion during care-taking	24(52%)	34(64%)	58(59%)	13(34%)	17(62%)	30(46%)
Vocaliza-tion not during care-taking	22(48%)	19(36%)	41(41%)	25(66%)	10(38%)	35(54%)
Total	46(100%)	53(100%)	99(100%)	38(100%)	27(100%)	65(100%)

infants, about half (54 percent) were during caretaking activities
(e.g., diapering, feeding) and 46 percent were not during caretaking (see Table 2).

When the data are analyzed in terms of the kinds of activities that were occurring while the father was vocalizing to his
infant, the decrease of vocalization during caretaking activities is
largely responsible for the overall decrease in vocalization over
time. With only one exception, all fathers decreased their number
of vocalizations during caretaking activities during the second
three observations. On the other hand, the number of vocalizations during noncaretaking activities remained about the same for
the fathers of male infants, but decreased somewhat for the
fathers of female infants.

DISCUSSION

Fathers talk infrequently and for short periods of time to
their infants in the first 3 months of life. When compared with
similar data on mothers' verbalizations to infants (Moss, 1967;
Rebelsky, 1967), the data suggest that fathers do some things
differently from mothers. For example, whereas mothers increase
their vocalization time during their infants' first 3 months, seven
of the 10 fathers in this study spent less time verbalizing to their
infants during the last month and a half compared with the first
month and a half of life.

Like mothers, fathers seem to behave differently toward
male and female infants; however, the differential behavior of

fathers toward their infants is opposite from the differential behavior of mothers. While the fathers of female infants verbalized more than did the fathers of male infants at 2 weeks and 4 weeks of age, Moss's data show that mothers of male infants vocalized more than mothers of female infants at 3 weeks of age (Moss, 1967, p. 23). By the time infants reach 3 months of age, these patterns are reversed. Fathers of male infants vocalize somewhat more than do fathers of female infants at 12 weeks; by 12 weeks, mothers of female infants vocalize more than mothers of male infants (Moss, 1967). To account for his data, Moss suggests that mothers initially respond more to male infants because the infants are awake more and are generally more irritable than female infants. He suggests that the shift in behavior at 3 months is due to the more reinforcing nature of the mother's interactions with her less-irritable female infant (Moss, 1967).

While this explanation is reasonable, it cannot be extended to apply to the data which show a shift in the opposite direction on the part of fathers. However, it may easily be that mothers and fathers are responding to different things in their infants. For example, the mother may be responding to the sex-related behavior of her infant, whereas the father may be initially responding more to his role of father-of-daughter or father-of-son. That is, fathers may perceive the role of father-of-daughter as a more nurturant, verbal role than the role of father-of-son. This suggestion receives some support from our finding that fathers of female infants verbalize more during caretaking activities than do fathers of male infants. If this is true, it may be that father absence has greater effects on males than on females because fathers of female infants define their role as more similar to the maternal role (i.e., nurturant) than do fathers of male infants. This is at best a tentative hypothesis; moreover, it does not clarify the father's definition of his role as father-of-son.

This study has raised some interesting questions. We now know that the patterns of mothers' and fathers' vocalizations to infants differ, but we do not know about other than vocal interactions of the fathers. It may be that fathers are more physical than verbal with their infants; it may be that fathers interact more physically with sons and more verbally with daughters. We do know that the presence or absence of a father has effects on the subsequent development of his children. What we now need are more comprehensive observations of fathers' interactions with their children to determine how they do interact so that we can hypothesize more clearly about how the effects we have seen might occur.

REFERENCES

Carlsmith, L. Effect of early father absence on scholastic aptitude. *Harvard Educational Review*, 1964, **34**, 3–21.

Chan, C. H., Lenneberg, E. H., & Rebelsky, F. G. Apparatus for reducing play-back time of tape recorded, intermittent vocalization. In U. Bellugi & R. Brown (Eds.), The acquisition of language. *Monographs of The Society for Research in Child Development*, 1964, **29**, (1, Serial No. 92), 127–130.

Lenneberg, E. H., Rebelsky, F. G., & Nichols, I. A. The vocalizations of infants born to deaf and to hearing parents. *Human Development*, 1965, **8**, 23–37.

Lynn, D. B., & Sawrey, W. L. The effects of father absence on Norwegian boys and girls. *Journal of Abnormal and Social Psychology*, 1959, **59**, 258–262.

Moss, H. A. Sex, age and state as determinants of mother-infant interaction. *Merrill-Palmer Quarterly*, 1967, **13**, 19–36.

Nash, J. The father in contemporary culture and current psychological literature. *Child Development*, 1965, **36**, 261–297.

Rebelsky, F. G. Infancy in two cultures. *Nederlands Tijdschrift voor de Psychologie*, 1967, **22**, 379–385.

INDEX

77 78 79 80 9 8 7 6 5 4 3 2 1

7627